Agricultural Precedents
Handbook

Agricultural Precedents Handbook

Nigel Davis

Graham Smith

Angela Sydenham

JORDANS
2001

Published by
Jordan Publishing Limited
21 St Thomas Street
Bristol BS1 6JS

British Library Cataloguing-in-Publication Data
A catalogue record for this book is available from the British Library.

ISBN 0 85308 386 X

Typeset by Mendip Communications Ltd, Frome, Somerset
Printed by MPG Books Ltd, Bodmin, Cornwall

PREFACE

The idea to produce a collection of precedents came about as long ago as 1994. At that time, I was receiving an ever-increasing number of enquiries from non-specialist practitioners, requesting help with precedents they were unable to locate in the larger, more traditional volumes. The precedents included in this book consequently cover a wide range of topics and, we hope, provide the non-specialist with precedents he would wish to have at his elbow.

It is unfortunate that the gestation period for this project has been somewhat longer than any of us would have hoped. For that delay, I have to take the lion's share of the blame.

Angela Sydenham and Graham Smith have both brought their intellect to bear, and have been invaluable allies. Without their input there would be no Handbook.

As well as thanking my co-authors for their agreement to be involved in this particular project, I would also like to thank Martin West and Gary Hill at Jordans for their forbearance when deadlines were missed. A great debt of gratitude is also due to Joyce Watts and Chris Frances for their IT skills and assistance in drawing the precedents together.

The authors' spouses and families can now rest a little easier, with the task complete and the authors restored to something approaching normality!

NIGEL DAVIS
Turnditch, Derbyshire
March 2001

CONTENTS

TABLE OF CASES

References are to page numbers.

TABLE OF STATUTES

References are to page numbers.

TABLE OF STATUTORY INSTRUMENTS

References are to page numbers.

TABLE OF EU LEGISLATION

References are to page numbers.

TABLE OF ABBREVIATIONS

AHA 1986	Agricultural Holdings Act 1986
farm business tenant	a tenant under the terms of the 1995 Act
1995 Act/ATA 1995	Agricultural Tenancies Act 1995
IHTA 1984	Inheritance Tax Act 1984
LTA 1987	Landlord and Tenant Act 1987
MAFF	Ministry of Agriculture, Fisheries and Food
IACS	Integrated Administration and Control System

HOW TO USE THIS BOOK

Purpose

The purpose of this book is to provide in one volume a comprehensive collection of precedents which will be useful to the non-specialist adviser confronted with an agricultural case. It is hoped that the accompanying practical commentaries and notes will assist such advisers when presented with drafts prepared by a specialist firm and will highlight points of concern. There are many different bases for the occupation of land and these are considered in this book. For example:

(1) Sole trader owner and occupier (the simplest arrangement).
(2) Sole trader AHA 1986 tenant.
(3) Sole trader farm business tenant.
(4) Land subject to a contract farming arrangement.
(5) Land subject to a share farming arrangement.
(6) Land subject to a farm management agreement.
(7) Land farmed in partnership.
   (a) Owned as a partnership asset.
   (b) Owned by one or some of the partners and farmed without any tenancy subsisting.
   (c) Owned by one or some of the partners and let to the partners.
   (d) Owned by a third party and let to one or some of the partners.
   (e) Owned by a third party and let to the partners.
(8) Land farmed by a company, either limited or unlimited.
   (a) Owned by the company.
   (b) Owned by one or more of the shareholders and farmed by the company.
   (c) Owned by one or more of the shareholders and let to the company.
   (d) Owned by a third party, let to one or more of the shareholders and farmed by the company.
   (e) Owned by a third party and let to the company.

Contents

The book has been structured as follows.

Structure

At the front of each chapter is a detailed contents, listing out all the precedents in that chapter.

Each chapter then starts with an introductory commentary giving practical advice and guidance specific to the area covered. This is followed by checklists containing important points to consider before using and adapting the precedents.

The precedents are drafted to cover all the common clauses as well as some optional clauses. They can all be adapted to suit individual requirements by amending the text supplied on the accompanying free disk. Text in italics in square brackets gives instructions. Text in roman in square brackets gives suggestions. Ellipses are to be filled in.

In many instances, there are notes to the precedents which give additional guidance.

CHAPTER 1: AGRICULTURAL PARTNERSHIPS AND COMPANIES

INDEX

CHAPTER 1: AGRICULTURAL PARTNERSHIPS AND COMPANIES

INTRODUCTION

It is not intended to highlight here general items of partnership law which will be well known to the reader. There are, however, certain aspects of agricultural partnerships which are unique to the type of business or which crop up in a particularly extreme form. These can perhaps best be brought out by way of an annotated checklist (see below).

Many of the points which arise in respect of partnerships arise also in relation to companies. Various differences arise because the company is an independent entity in its own right and separate from its shareholders.

Particular points which arise in an agricultural context are as follows.

Companies

(1)   Where a tenant intends to farm through a company, it is very likely that the arrangement will be in breach of his tenancy agreement. Most tenancy agreements contain an obligation 'not to part with possession' and as the company is an independent entity the tenant will have to part with possession. A new arrangement of this nature will therefore be a breach of covenant, although that may be less disastrous than it was following *Pennell v Payne* (1995) 06 EG 152 where it was held by the Court of Appeal that an unlawful sub-letting did not give the landlord the right to serve notice to quit under Case E because his interest in the holding had not been prejudiced since the company's interest would terminate at the same time as the tenant's interest. The only exception to this was if the tenancy was surrendered and the landlord could not be compelled to accept a surrender. Many tenants have farmed for many years through the medium of a limited company and it is likely that the landlord will have acquiesced in this arrangement. However, in the case of a difficult landlord, the possibility of changing the arrangements should be considered. Where land is let to one or more shareholders and farmed by their company, consideration should be given as to whether or not the tenancy is a company asset and the position documented for the avoidance of doubt.

Many landowners make their land available for use by their family companies. Because the company has exclusive possession, arguably such letting will create a tenancy unless it can be shown that it was not intended to create legal relations. To date, there has not been too much difficulty over this with the Revenue authorities who are primarily likely to be interested. However, it is an aspect that should be borne in mind.

Many other landowners have let their land to their family company.

(2)   If succession to tenancy is in point, the applicant's income will have to be carefully looked at as to the extent to which it is derived from agricultural work on the holding or a unit of which it forms part. There may be more difficulties with this in respect of income from companies rather than partnership income.

As regards the commercial unit occupation test, occupation by a company which is not controlled by the applicant will not be imputed to the applicant.

Schedule 6 to the AHA 1986 refers only to 'a body corporate controlled by' the applicant.

(3)   If the company is a tenant under an AHA 1986 tenancy, then in ordinary circumstances the tenancy will continue for as long as the company remains in existence. Accordingly, this asset may well be valuable.

(4)   The rights attributable to the various shareholdings in the company must be considered carefully. For example, if the company has valuable assets including land and it is intended to protect a shareholder's investment by reference to full asset value, the articles of association would need to be altered or there would need to be a separate shareholders' agreement in this respect. Care must always be taken to ensure that the shareholders understand the implications, and in the absence of any other agreement, a minority shareholder's interest is likely to be discounted. This may be an advantage if it is sought to 'lose' value for Revenue purposes.

Often where there is an unwritten AHA 1986 tenancy or an assignable AHA 1986 tenancy, the possibility is explored of assigning that asset to a limited company. While this is highly desirable from a landlord and tenant point of view, so far as the tenant is concerned it may be less desirable from a fiscal point of view, as it may be preferable to keep the value of the tenancy in the hands of individuals rather than the company. If this is so, then an appropriate declaration of trust whereby the company confirms that it holds the tenancy on trust for the individuals or a partnership arrangement with the company may be more appropriate.

The partnership implications, some of which will also be relevant to companies, are explored in the following checklist.

CHECKLIST

CHECKLIST FOR FARMING PARTNERSHIPS

The following points may be regarded as a checklist.

1. **What is to happen at the end of the partnership?**

Strangely enough, at the commencement of a partnership, this is the first question a lawyer always tends to ask. This may be regarded as a negative way of looking at things, but it is absolutely essential that the parties know and appreciate what the procedure is for extricating themselves from the arrangement should it fail or simply cease to have a purpose. The possibilities are as follows.

1.1 *Dissolution of the partnership.*

The partnership will be dissolved and the assets realised under the Partnership Act 1890. If this route is to be followed, consideration should be given as to whether at the very least the former partners should be expressly entitled to bid for partnership assets at auction.

1.2 *Automatic accrual on the death or retirement of one partner to the other or others.*

This is sometimes appropriate and means that the share of the outgoing partner in the partnership automatically accrues to the others with or without payment.

If it accrues without payment, then it will be a transfer of value for inheritance tax purposes, although on current law, if it has been owned for two years, it will attract 100% relief. If it accrues with payment, then if a full price is paid no transfer of value will occur. If the price is less than open market value, then it is likely that a transfer of value will occur unless it can be argued that the transfer is for full consideration. See, for example, *Attorney-General v Boden* [1912] 1 KB 539; *Attorney-General v Ralli* (1936) 15 ATC 523. The Revenue tends to be unwilling to accept these arguments.

It is particularly important if there is to be an accrual with payment that the agreement should not be construed as an agreement for sale and purchase of the outgoing partner's share. If it is, this is a complete disaster from an inheritance tax point of view as business relief will be denied on the basis that the property is subject to a binding contract for sale (IHTA 1984, s 113).

If payment is to be made, then there may be a period during which the payment is due. While this payment is outstanding, it is likely to be an unsecured loan from the outgoing partner to the remaining partners with all the disadvantages that can follow from that.

1.3   *An option for the continuing partner or partners to purchase the share of the outgoing partner.*
        This should give a reasonable time for the exercise of the option and, for example, in the case of a death, it may be more appropriate to link the time for the exercise of the option not to the date of death but to the date of grant of probate. Similar comments apply to this as apply to the accrual.

1.4   In fixing payments which are to apply on a partner leaving, a balance always has to be drawn between the interest of the outgoing partner and the interest of the remaining partners. In general terms, it is intended that the outgoing partner should have sufficient money for his retirement but that the continuing partners should be able to afford to buy out a partner without the business being put at risk. Often, therefore, in farming partnerships the outgoing partner is not entitled to full value. For example, he is often entitled only to a payment calculated in accordance with the book value of his interest without any revaluation. Alternatively, often only certain items are valued, for example, land, milk quotas or tenancies.

1.5   Life assurance policies can be taken out to assist with the burden of financing a deceased partner's share. The policy can either be drawn on the life of a partner for the benefit of his remaining partners which will put them in funds to buy his share or, alternatively, taken out in trust for his own family but with the price of his share in the partnership reduced by the amount of the insurance policies. The tax implications of both these possibilities should be considered before they are entered into and the trust's wordings carefully checked.

2.   Is there to be a right to introduce further partners?
        Prima facie partners have no right to introduce additional partners without their partners' consent. Sometimes, however, partners wish to have a right to introduce their children, certainly if they are deemed to be suitable, the test often being borrowed from that applicable in the case of succession tenancies under the AHA 1986.

3.   Sometimes trustees and/or personal representatives are intended to be or to become partners. If they are, then particular clauses will be needed to deal with their share.

4.   What land will the partners be farming?
4.1   *Land owned by the partners.*
        If the partners own land, then the principal point of interest will be the basis of valuation on a partner's leaving.

4.2   *Land owned by one of the partners or a third party and let to the partners under an AHA 1986 tenancy.*

If the tenancy is to be a partnership asset, then this should be stated either in the partnership agreement or in a supplemental declaration of trust so that everybody knows where they stand. If the named tenants are only some of the partners, then they will be obliged to hold the tenancy upon the trusts of the partnership. The tenancy will be secure for the life of the survivor of the tenants in ordinary circumstances and succession rights may be applicable. Perhaps consideration should be given as to whether any documentation should be entered into between the families, if there is more than one, as to the ownership of any succession tenancy which may be granted.

In the 1970s and 1980s, partnership arrangements were entered into seeking to give the landlord a right to recover possession. The landlord would let the farm to a partnership including his nominee and the intended farmer. Since a counter-notice under s 26 of the AHA 1986 required the signatures of all the tenants, the landlord or his nominee would refuse to join in and therefore the tenancy would terminate. However, in *Featherstone v Staples* [1986] 2 All ER 461, this ruse was rejected by the Court of Appeal who said that the other tenants alone could serve the appropriate counter-notice. It is likely, therefore, that any such arrangement would be unsuccessful.

4.3   *Land owned by a partner and farmed by the partners.*

Where no rent is payable, it was held in *Harrison-Broadley v Smith* [1964] 1 All ER 876 that the non land-owning partner had a non-exclusive licence which would not constitute a tenancy. On this basis, no tenancy will subsist between the land owner and the partners and therefore, presumably, the land owner can recover possession on reasonable notice. Such notice may or may not be specified in the partnership agreement.

4.4   *Land owned by a third party and let to one or more of the partners.*

The terms of the tenancy agreement should always be checked when a partnership is proposed to ensure that there is not a clause in that agreement which would forbid the formation of a partnership. Some more modern agreements contain a covenant against 'sharing possession' which would be breached by the tenant entering into partnership.

If the tenancy is intended to be a partnership asset, even if in the names of one or more of the partners only, then this should be expressly agreed and, if there is to be a value placed upon it in any circumstance, this should be documented.

If the tenancy is one with succession rights, then care should always be taken to try and ensure that the requirements for succession are met as appropriately as possible. In particular, suitability and eligibility in respect of the occupation of other commercial units are usually of prime importance.

One problem on succession is that para 7 of Sch 6 to the AHA 1986 referring to joint occupation does not mention land expressly held as partners. The reference to joint licensees may suffice but, to be on the safe side, it may be worth expressly having the land held as tenants-in-common rather than a partnership asset.

Land held 'as a licensee' is disregarded under para 6(e) of Sch 6 to the AHA 1986. The difficulty with that is the case of *Brooks v Brown* (see *The Conveyancer and Property Lawyer* (1986) Vol 15 at p 327). The case is not satisfactory and was at divisional court level and therefore might not be upheld in the Court of Appeal if it arose again. In that case, it was suggested that the word 'only' caused difficulty because the land was not occupied only as a licensee but as a licensee coupled with an interest by virtue of the partnership.

If this is relevant, it may be safer to seek to bring oneself within para 6.1 of Sch 6 by letting under a farm business tenancy for less than five years.

5.   **Are capital profits and losses intended to be divided in the same way as income profits and losses?**
In the absence of contrary agreement, even if not stated in the tenancy agreement, capital profits and losses will be divided in the same way as income profits and losses. In particular, if there is land which is a partnership asset, this must be borne in mind by the partners and care should be taken that this is the intention. If certain assets are to be revalued, this should be stated. If no revaluation is to take place, this should also be stated.

6.   **Is there to be an expulsion clause and, if so, on what grounds is it to be exercisable?**
The draft in this book does not include an expulsion clause but it can be easily modified to include one if that is what is required.

7.   **Should there be any obligation on partners to reside at any particular place?**
In *Anderton v Lamb* (1981) STC 43, rollover relief was denied on houses occupied by the partners as they were considered not to be business assets for capital gains tax purposes. While it may be possible to shuffle the joint interests and then claim private residence relief if the values of the residences are the same, another possible way of improving the chances of obtaining rollover relief would be obliging the partners to live in certain property for the better performance of their duties.

8.   **In many farming businesses the *pater familias* will require the final say in management matters.**
If this is what is needed, an appropriate clause must be included.

9.   **Is the farm a dairy farm?**
If so, then the position regarding milk quota will have to be considered. In *Faulks v Faulks* (1992) 15 EG 82, the quota was registered in the name of the partners but it was held on the interpretation of that particular partnership agreement that both the tenancy of the land, which was in the surviving partner's name, and the quota passed to the surviving partner without payment on the determination of the partnership.

Similarly, in *Davies v H & R Ecroyd Limited* (1996) EGCS 77, where a freehold farm was made available for use by partners, the quota was held to belong to the freeholders.

The position is further complicated where the partners have paid for quota. It is best that the implications of ownership of quota be addressed at the commencement of the partnership and documentation completed to cover the situation.

There is the further complication that, under the Agriculture Act 1986, s 13, compensation for milk quota is payable to a tenant where it is 'registered as his'. So far, the question of milk quota registered not in the name of the tenant but in the name of a partnership of which the tenant is a member has not been litigated. There is a reasonable argument that, as the tenant is one of the partners, he falls within the Act, although the position is less clear where there is a company. If it is felt that there may be difficulty with the landlord and there is enough at stake, then it may be worth remodelling the arrangement to try and bring oneself firmly within the provisions of the Agriculture Act 1986.

10.   Sheep quota (Sheep Premium Quota Rights)
Sheep quota is complicated because, under the EC rules relating to sheep quota, quota is not registered in the name of the partners but in the name of each member of the partnership and the partnership is a producer group as defined in Commission Regulation 3493/90 (OJ 1990 L337/7) amended by Regulation 2070/92 (OJ 1992 L215/63) and Regulation 233/94 (OJ 1994 L30/9). Under Commission Regulation 2385/91 (OJ 1991 L219/15) amended by Regulation 3676/91 (OJ 1991 L349/14) and Regulation 826/94 (OJ 1994 L95/8), the formula for division of the quota and the sheep should correspond with the way the producer group's assets would be apportioned were the group to be disbanded. Accordingly, it is desirable to have a separate provision relating to the sheep and the quota so that this requirement can be met.

On any change of partnership arrangements, the siphon of quota may be a problem. Commission Regulation 2134/95 (OJ 1995 L214/13) partially deals with this but not fully. Moreover, retention periods and forage area requirements must also be borne in mind. Reference should be made to the appropriate textbook to minimise the risk of loss.

11.   Suckler cow quota (Suckler Cow Premium Quota Rights)
Suckler cow quota does not carry the difficulties which attach to sheep quota in respect of ownership. However, forage area and retention periods should be borne in mind in the same way as for sheep quota on a change of partnership arrangements.

PRECEDENTS

1 MEMORANDUM OF ASSOCIATION – EXTRACT FOR FARMING COMPANY

THE COMPANIES ACTS 1985 to 1989

PRIVATE COMPANY LIMITED BY SHARES

MEMORANDUM OF ASSOCIATION OF

1. The Company's name is [*name*].

2. The Company's registered office is to be situated in England and Wales.

3. The Company's objects are:

(a) (i) To carry on the business of farming in all its branches, and in connection therewith to acquire and deal in farm and other land and premises; to act as farm managers and experts, consultants and advisers in every branch of farming, stockbreeding, grazing and other agricultural enterprises; to carry on all or any of the businesses of graziers, millers and corn merchants, stock and poultry breeders, producers, raisers and growers of and dealers in agricultural, horticultural, farm, garden and orchard produce of all kinds, market gardeners, nurserymen, seedsmen and florists, dairymen, contractors for the supply and delivery of milk, wholesale and retail butchers, bakers, grocers and provision merchants, manufacturers and merchants of, agents for, and dealers in feeding stuffs, manurial products and fertilisers of every description, buyers, keepers, breeders, exporters and commission salesmen of, and dealers in cattle, horses, sheep, pigs, poultry and all kinds of live and dead stock, manufacturers, merchants, hirers and letters on hire of, and dealers in agricultural and dairy implements, machinery and utensils of all kinds, contractors for tractor work, ploughing and all operations connected with the cultivation of the soil, harvesting and storage of crops; haulage and cartage contractors, garage proprietors, builders and contractors, builders' merchants, coal, coke and timber merchants, proprietors of camping and caravan sites, and general merchants, agents and traders; to buy, sell, manufacture, repair, alter, hire, let on hire, export, import and deal in plant, machinery, appliances, apparatus, utensils, materials, produce, articles and things of every description capable of being used in connection with the foregoing businesses, or any of them, or likely to be required by any of the customers of, or persons having dealings with the Company.

(ii)   To carry on any other trade or business whatever which can in the opinion of the Board of Directors be advantageously carried on in connection with or ancillary to any of the businesses of the Company.

---

2   PARTNERSHIP AGREEMENT

Particulars

Date of agreement: ....

Parties: (1) ....

(2) ....

(3) ....

(4) ....

Name of firm: ....

Business: ....

Commencement date: ....

Place of business: ....

Bankers: ....

Cheque signing: ....

The profit and loss-sharing proportions:[1] ....

Account date: ....

Interest rate:[2] ....

Payment period:[3] ....

Partnership accountants: ....

1.   Definitions and Interpretations

1.1   The terms used in the Particulars shall unless the context otherwise requires have the same meaning throughout this Agreement.

1.2   'the Partners' means the parties hereto or such of them as remain for the time being Partners under the terms hereof.

1.3   'the Business' means the business referred to in the Particulars and carried on by the Partners pursuant to the terms hereof.

1.4   'the Account Date' means the account date specified in the Particulars or such other date as may be agreed by the Partners from time to time.

1.5   'the Accounting Period' means the period of twelve months ending on the Account Date or such other period as the Partners agree.

1.6   'an Outgoing Partner'[4] means a Partner who dies or gives notice under clause 15 hereof or is adjudicated bankrupt or enters into an arrangement or composition for the benefit of his creditors or applies for an interim order under the Insolvency Act 1986 or becomes a patient under the Mental Health Act 1983 and includes the personal representatives, trustee or receiver of such a Partner or his estate.

1.7   'determining event' means in relation to an Outging Partner his death or the expiry of such notice or such adjudication arrangement composition or application or becoming such a patient (as the case may be).

1.8   'the Remaining Partners' means the Partners other than the Outgoing Partner.

1.9   'the option' means the option contained in clause 16 of this Agreement.

1.10   'the Purchasing Partners' means such of the Remaining Partners as exercise the option.

1.11   'the option date' means:

in the case of a deceased Partner the date of the grant of representation to his estate;[5]

in the case of a Retiring Partner the date of the expiry of the notice given under clause 15 hereof;

in the case of a bankrupt Partner the date of appointment of a trustee of his estate;

in the case of a Partner entering into an arrangement or composition with his creditors the date of such arrangement or composition;

in the case of a Partner applying for an interim order under the Insolvency Act 1986 the date of such application; and

in the case of a Partner becoming a patient as aforesaid the date of appointment of a receiver of his estate.

1.12   'the relevant Accounting Period' means the Accounting Period during which the determining event occurs.

1.13   References to the singular include the plural and vice versa, references to one gender include the others and references to legislation include legislation by which it is amended or replaced.

1.14   The clause headings are for convenience only and do not form part of this Agreement.

2.   Commencement

The Partners shall carry on the Business and the Partnership shall commence on the Commencement Date.

3.   Determination

The Partnership shall continue until determined in manner hereinafter provided.

4.   Place of business

The Business shall be carried on at the Place of Business and/or at such other places as the Partners from time to time decide.

5.   Bankers

The bankers of the Partnership shall be the Bankers or such other bank as the Partners from time to time decide.

6.   Cheque signing

All cheques on the Partnership bank account shall be signed as set out in the Particulars.

7.   Capital

The capital for the time being of the Partnership shall belong to the Partners in the proportions in which it is deemed to have been contributed by them.

8.   Partners' salaries

The Partners or any of them may be paid such sum by way of salary as the Partners from time to time agree such salary to be deemed to accrue or to have accrued from day to day. Any such salary shall be treated as a working expense of the Partnership before the profits and losses thereof are ascertained.

9.   Profits and losses[6]

The profits and losses of the Partnership shall be divided among and borne by the Partners as set out in the Particulars.

[There shall be no revaluation of freehold land/tenancies/milk quota/herd unless all the Partners agree.]

10.   Accounts

As at the Account Date in each year an account shall be taken by the Partnership Accountants of all assets and liabilities of the Partnership and of its profits and losses for the Accounting Period ended on that date.

A copy of such account shall be furnished to and signed by each Partner who shall be bound thereby unless some error therein is discovered within three months from the signing thereof in which case such error shall be rectified and any appropriate adjustments made.

11.   Drawings

Each of the Partners may draw out of the Partnership banking account such sums on account of his share of the profits as the Partners from time to time agree but if when the account is taken in respect of any Accounting Period it appears therefrom that any of the Partners has drawn from the said banking account any amount in excess of his share of the profits of that Accounting Period he shall (if so requested by any of the other Partners) forthwith repay the amount of such excess to the said banking account.

12.   Time and attention

Each of the Partners shall devote such time and attention to the Business as is from time to time requisite.

13.   Partners' obligations

Each Partner shall at all times:

13.1   punctually pay and discharge his separate debts and engagements and indemnify the other Partners and the Partnership assets against the same and all proceedings costs claims and demands in respect thereof; and

13.2   be just and faithful to the other Partners in all matters relating to the Partnership and at all times give to the other Partners a true account of such transactions.

14.   Restrictions on Partners

No Partner shall without the consent of the others:

14.1   engage or be concerned or interested either directly or indirectly in any other business or occupation,

14.2   assign or charge the whole or any part of his interest in the Partnership.

15.   Retirement

A Partner may retire from the Partnership by giving to the other Partners not less than six months' written notice expiring at the end of any Accounting Period.

16.   Purchase option

16.1   When a determining event occurs, the Remaining Partners shall have the option to purchase the share of the Outgoing Partner in the capital assets and future profits of the Partnership as at the date of such determining event in accordance with the terms in this clause contained.

16.2   The option may be exercised by notice in writing to the Outgoing Partner not later than three months after the option date.

16.3   If the option is exercised the share of the Outgoing Partner in the capital and assets and future profits of the Partnership shall vest in the Purchasing Partners (if more than one in the proportions in which they were entitled to share *inter se* in the net profits of the Partnership immediately prior to the determining event or such other proportions as they agree) and the purchase price of the said share shall be paid by the Purchasing Partners (if more than one in the like proportions).

16.4.1   The purchase price to be paid by the Partners shall be a sum equal to the Outgoing Partner's capital in the books of the Partnership without any revaluation or addition as at the date of the determining event [subject to the next following sub-clause].[7]

16.4.2   Any freehold or leasehold property and suckler cow quota being a Partnership asset shall be valued on the application of the Purchasing Partners or the Outgoing Partner on the date of the determining event. Such valuation shall be agreed between the Purchasing Partners and the Outgoing Partner or in default of agreement determined on the application of any party by a valuer appointed by agreement between the parties to the dispute or in default of agreement within two months after the exercise of the option by a valuer appointed by the President of the Royal Institution of Chartered Surveyors on the application of any party. Such valuer shall act as an expert and not as an arbitrator and his decision shall be final and binding on the parties. Any profit or loss on such revaluation shall be credited or debited to the Partners' capital accounts in proportion to their respective shares in the [capital] profits of the Partnership immediately prior to the date of the determining event.

16.5   The purchase price shall be paid in accordance with the Payment Period specified in the Particulars.

16.6   So much of the purchase price as is for the time being unpaid shall carry interest at the interest rate calculated on a daily basis in accordance with the Particulars and payable with each instalment of the purchase price.

16.7   If any instalment of the purchase price or the interest thereon is in arrear for more than twenty-eight days the whole amount or the balance thereof then outstanding shall become immediately due and payable.

16.8   In the event of arrears interest shall be compounded at the interest rate on the instalment dates.

16.9   Any payment on account of the moneys payable under these provisions shall in default of agreement be apportioned rateably as between the purchase price and interest outstanding at the date of payment.

16.10   There shall also be paid to the Outgoing Partner by the Remaining Partners any undrawn balance of his share of the net profits of the Partnership for the relevant Accounting Period.

16.11   There shall be paid by the Outgoing Partner to the Remaining Partners:

16.11.1 any sum due from the Outgoing Partner in respect of losses of the Partnership for the relevant Accounting Period;

16.11.2 any amount drawn by the Outgoing Partner on account of his share of the profits of the Partnership for the relevant Accounting Period in excess of his share thereof;

16.11.3 any sum by which his capital account is overdrawn.

16.12   If the determining event does not fall on the last day of an Accounting Period the Outgoing Partner's share of profits or losses during the relevant Accounting Period shall be deemed to be a proportionate part calculated on a daily basis of the share of the net profits or losses of the Partnership for that Accounting Period to which the Outgoing Partner would have been entitled or which he would have borne if he had been a Partner throughout the relevant Accounting Period.[8]

16.13   Any sums payable under clauses 16.10 and 16.11 shall be payable as soon as ascertained and if not paid within fourteen days shall bear interest at the interest rate calculated on a daily basis.

16.14   There may be retained out of any sum payable hereunder to the Outgoing Partner such sum as the Partnership Accountants certify to be a reasonable retention on account of the tax to be borne by the Outgoing Partner the appropriate adjustments to be made when the amount of such tax is ascertained.

16.15   The Purchasing Partners shall indemnify the Outgoing Partner from and against all existing and future debts, liabilities and engagements of the Partnership.

16.16   All necessary and proper instruments shall be executed for vesting the share of the Outgoing Partner in the Purchasing Partners.

16.17   At the request of the Purchasing Partners the Outgoing Partner shall without delay execute all such documents as may be required to make any election available under the legislation relating to income tax for the time being in force. The Purchasing Partners shall indemnify the Outgoing Partner against the amount of any additional income tax payable by the Outgoing Partner in consequence of the making of such election.

17.   Dissolution[9]

17.1   If by the end of the period limited for its exercise an option referred to in Clause 16 hereof has not been duly exercised or if all the Remaining Partners agree in writing not to exercise such options the Partnership shall thereupon be dissolved and on such dissolution the affairs of the Partnership shall be wound up in accordance with the provisions of the Partnership Act 1890.

17.2   If on the winding up of the Partnership any Partnership asset is to be offered for sale by public auction any Partner shall be entitled to bid therefor.

18.   Partners' residences

Any Partner residing in any house on any holding occupied by the Partnership shall not be required to pay or reimburse any rent in respect of such residence.

19.   Voting

All matters relating to the management and conduct of the affairs of the Partnership shall be decided by a majority of the votes of the Partners each Partner being entitled to such number of votes as is directly proportionate to his share of the net profits of the Partnership for the time being.

20.   Property occupied by the Partners[10]

In the absence of contrary written agreement where any land is held by a Partner ('the land holder') (whether as owner tenant or licensee) but farmed by the Partnership:

20.1   such land shall remain vested in the land holder beneficially and the other Partners shall have no beneficial interest therein;

20.2   the other Partners shall occupy such land jointly with the land holder as licensees only and shall vacate the same forthwith on demand; or

The [freehold property] [tenancy of the tenanted land] shall continue to be held on behalf of the Partnership and the Partnership shall indemnify the Partner in whom the tenancy is vested against the rent reserved by and the liabilities of the tenant under the said tenancy; or

in respect of any period during which any land is held by a Partner as tenant but farmed by the Partnership the Partnership shall indemnify such Partner against the rent reserved by and the liabilities of the tenant under the tenancy of that land.

21. Sheep and Sheep Quota[11]

21.1 In this Clause 'the Flock' means the sheep owned by the Partners.

21.2 The Flock is owned by the Partners in the profit-sharing proportions and each Partner's share of the Flock constitutes part of the capital contributed by him to the Partnership.

21.3 Notwithstanding the provisions of clause 9 of this Agreement:

21.3.1 Any increase or decrease in the value of the Flock shall be credited to or borne by the Partners in the profit-sharing proportions.

21.3.2 The proceeds of any sale of sheep quota owned by the Partners shall be credited to the Partners in the profit-sharing proportions.

21.3.3 On dissolution of the Partnership each Partner shall be entitled to share in the Flock or the proceeds of sale thereof in the profit-sharing proportions.

21.4 If the option is exercised the Outgoing Partner may elect either:

21.4.1 to retain his share of the Flock and sheep quota so far as it relates to the Partnership; or

21.4.2 to sell his share of the Flock and such quota to the Purchasing Partners.

21.5 Such election shall be made by notice in writing to the Purchasing Partners within one month of the receipt by the Outgoing Partner of the notice exercising the option.

21.6 In the event of the Outgoing Partner electing to retain his share of the Flock and sheep quota the Remaining Partners shall sign all necessary documents to facilitate such retention.

21.7 In the event of the Outgoing Partner electing to sell his share of the Flock and sheep quota the following provisions shall apply:

21.7.1 The price shall be the value of the Outgoing Partner's share of the Flock and sheep quota on the open market on the date on which the option is exercised subject if applicable to the siphon.

21.7.2 Such value shall be agreed between the Outgoing Partner and the Purchasing Partners or in default of agreement determined by a surveyor appointed on the application of either party by the President of the Royal Institution of Chartered Surveyors. Such surveyor shall act as an expert and not as an arbitrator and his decision shall be final and binding on all persons interested.

21.7.3 The value of the Outgoing Partner's share of the Flock and sheep quota shall be added to the sum payable to the Outgoing Partner pursuant to clause 16 hereof.

21.8   The Outgoing Partner's share of any values attributable to the Flock and sheep quota in the books of the Partnership otherwise than in consequence of this clause shall be deducted in arriving at the sum payable to the Outgoing Partner in accordance with clause 16 hereof.

22.   Milk Quota[12]

22.1   The Milk Quota ('the Milk Quota') registered in the name of the Partners is an asset of the Partnership.

22.2   If the Partners wish to dispose of all or any part of the Milk Quota or on dissolution of the Partnership each Partner will facilitate such disposal so far as practicable.

22.3   If notwithstanding the terms hereof any part of the Milk Quota becomes vested in one or more of the Partners without payment such Partners shall pay to or reimburse the Partners the full value thereof.

22.4   If an option is exercised the Milk Quota shall be valued and its value credited to the capital accounts of the Partners immediately prior to the determining event in their [capital] profit-sharing proportions at that time. The Outgoing Partner's share thereof shall be added to the sum payable to him in accordance with clause 16.5 hereof together with interest in accordance with clause 16.4 hereof.

22.5   The Outgoing Partner's share of any value attributable to the Milk Quota in the books of the Partnership otherwise than in accordance with this clause shall be deducted in arriving at the sum payable to the Outgoing Partner in accordance with clause 16 hereof.

22.6   If any Milk Quota is to be valued pursuant to this Clause such value shall be agreed between the Outgoing Partner and the Purchasing Partners or in default of agreement determined by a surveyor appointed on the application of either party by the President of the Royal Institution of Chartered Surveyors. Such surveyor shall act as an expert and not as an arbitrator and his decision shall be final and binding on all persons interested.

OR

22.1   The Milk Quota registered in the name of the Partners in fact belongs to [name] as the Partners hereby admit.

22.2   The Partners will take such steps as may reasonably be requested by [name] to comply with his wishes in respect of such Milk Quota including the disposal and transfer thereof to any person.

AS WITNESS the hands of the parties hereto the day and year first before written.

SIGNED by the said [name]
in the presence of:

....

....

....

....

SIGNED by the said [*name*]
in the presence of: $\Big\}$

....

....

....

....

SIGNED by the said [*name*]
in the presence of: $\Big\}$

....

....

....

....

1 Consider whether there should be differential profit and loss sharing proportions for capital and income profits and losses.

2 This varies a lot depending on the philosophy of the partners between, say, 5% and 1% over base rate. The philosophy will need to be discussed.

3 This should be a fair compromise between the interests of the outgoing partners who will be making an unsecured loan to the continuing partners and the interests of the continuing partners who have to finance the purchase.

4 There is no provision in this Agreement for expulsion. If this were to be included, consequential amendments to this clause and others would have to be made.

5 It will be noted that the date of the grant of representation is shown as the option date. On the whole this is thought to be more satisfactory than having the date of death as the start of the option period. It also means that it will be clear on whom the notice should be served.

6 If there is to be no differential in respect of capital profits and losses, it would be well to include 'including capital profits and losses' after 'losses'.

7 It will be necessary to consider what, if any, revaluation is considered appropriate.

8 In general terms, it is felt inappropriate to require a set of accounts to be prepared up to the date of the determining event.

9 It is extremely unlikely that the partners will wish dissolution to occur and therefore essential that the notice is served within the appropriate time-scale or an agreement entered into for the continuation of the business.

10 It is essential to consider how the property is to be held and there may be further variants on this clause.

11 See note 10 in Checklist.

12 See note 9 in Checklist.

3   DECLARATION OF TRUST[1]

THIS DECLARATION OF TRUST is made the [*date*]

BY [*names*] ('the Trustees')

WHEREAS

1.   The Trustees are the Estate Owners in fee simple of the property described in the schedule ('the Property').[2]

2.   The Trustees together with [*names*] (together called 'the Partners') carry on in partnership the business of farmers under the firm name of [*name*] ('the Partnership').

NOW THIS DEED WITNESSES that:

The Trustees declare that henceforth they will hold the Property upon trust for the Partners as part of the property of the Partnership.[3]

IN WITNESS whereof this Deed has been executed by the parties hereto the day and year first before written.

SCHEDULE

SIGNED and delivered as a Deed by
the said [*name*] in the presence of: }

....

....

....

SIGNED and delivered as a Deed by
the said [*name*] in the presence of: }

....

....

....

----

1   Stamp duty of £5 on Declaration of Trust if no value passes. If there is a transfer of value, a certificate of value or certificate of exemption may be appropriate or *ad valorem* duty chargeable.

2   Similar declarations can be made in respect of other assets. It is important to ensure that any documentation relating to a tenancy of land owned by a third party cannot be construed as an assignment that would lead to a notice to quit.

3   The fiscal consequences of any change in partnership arrangements are complicated and, in particular, capital gains tax may be an issue, subject to hold-over relief if appropriate. See Revenue SP D12 and guidance in the Revenue Manual.

4   DEED OF GIFT

THIS DEED OF GIFT is made the [*date*]

BETWEEN: (1) [*name*]
                       (together referred to as 'the Donor')

AND   (2) [*name*]
                       ('the Donee')

WHEREAS:

1. The Donor and Donee (together referred to as 'the Partners') carry on in partnership the business of farmers under the firm name of [*name*] ('the Partnership').

2. The Donor has agreed to give to the Donee part of his capital in the partnership.[1]

NOW THIS DEED WITNESSES as follows:

1. The Donor assigns to the Donee by way of gift £ ... of the Donor's capital in the partnership TO HOLD unto the Donee absolutely.[2,3]

2. The Donor certifies this Deed falls within category L in the Schedule of the Stamp Duty (Exempt Instruments) Regulations 1987.

IN WITNESS whereof this Deed has been executed by the parties hereto the day and year first before written.

SIGNED and delivered as a Deed by
the said [*name*] in the presence of:

....

....

....

SIGNED and delivered as a Deed by
the said [*name*] in the presence of:

....

....

....

1 Reservation of benefit for inheritance tax purposes is perceived to be a problem in respect of gifts of partnership capital.

2 One partner could give another a cheque which he would then introduce to the partnership. While reservation of benefit would not be a problem, business relief would not be available on the gift and therefore this may be a serious problem.

   If the capital is to be assigned and the donor continues as a partner, then on the face of it reservation of benefit will apply. One way around this may be to impose a provision for the payment of interest on capital at a market rate. This will still be earned income for income tax purposes as it is regarded as a distribution of the profits of the partnership rather than unearned income and should avoid the reservation of benefit problem on the basis that the full price is being exacted for making the cash available. There does not, however, seem to be any authority specifically on this point.

   Alternatively, profit shares can be linked to capital investment in the business. On this basis, the Revenue will treat the property as jointly enjoyed in proportion to ownership and no reservation of benefit problem will arise. However, this is not always entirely satisfactory in practice or possible to monitor given that partners tend to leave in undrawn capital. If part of the capital left in is converted to loan account, then there is a risk that business relief on that will not be available.

3 If land farmed by the partners is gifted, then again a full market rent will be necessary in order to avoid reservation of benefit arising.

CHAPTER 2: MANAGEMENT CONTRACTING AND SHARE FARMING

INDEX

2 MANAGEMENT CONTRACTING AND SHARE FARMING

CHAPTER 2: MANAGEMENT CONTRACTING AND SHARE FARMING

INTRODUCTION

Where it is intended to share the farming rather than entering into a letting agreement, the most common arrangements used are farm management agreements, contract farming agreements and share farming agreements. Whichever one of these arrangements is entered into, the idea will be that exclusive possession is not granted to the third party. If a tenant is entering into one of these arrangements, the terms of the tenancy must first be checked to see whether it would constitute a breach. Unless 'sharing possession' or the arrangement is specifically forbidden, then it will be allowed. Under farm management agreements and contract farming agreements, the essence of the arrangement is that the manager or contractor is employed under a contract for service, usually on the basis of receiving a modest fixed fee or basic income and a share of the profits. Under a share farming agreement, the land owner and the share farmer both have independent businesses which work the land together. Both of those businesses occupy the land. Whatever arrangement is entered into, it is essential that the agreement records what is to happen in practice and that the parties stick to those arrangements. Otherwise, there is a risk that a partnership or a tenancy will in fact have been created.

In the current farming climate, joint venture arrangements have become much more common. The object here is that a number of farmers may decide to merge their machinery fleet in a new enterprise. They will therefore form either a partnership with each farmer as a partner, or a company with each farmer as a shareholder. The parties will need to consider whether or not they transfer labour and, if they do, the implications of any future redundancy payments.

The parties will need to look at the total machinery available and decide what machinery they wish to keep. That machinery will then be transferred at market value to the new enterprise. The remaining machinery will be sold and the proceeds received by the selling farmer. Any new machinery that may be required will be bought by the joint venture enterprise.

Whether a partnership or company is appropriate will depend on a number of factors. From a tax point of view, a company may be better having regard to the lower tax rate on retained profit which would be available for re-equipping. On the other hand, any capital subscribed as loan capital will not be available for inheritance tax business relief.

From a partnership point of view, there is the higher tax rate on partners (unless they themselves are companies) and the liability that each partner has for the acts of his partners. Any capital will be capital in the business and attract 100% relief for inheritance tax purposes. As with all legal arrangements, whichever basis is chosen, careful thought will need to be given to what happens if a party wishes to withdraw. There will need to be a valuation of assets and, presumably, an option to purchase that party's share would be appropriate.

It will be important to consider whether there should be a notice period with a fixed term within which any withdrawal would attract a penalty. It will also be important to consider the write-off period for equipment and depreciation. There is nowadays more opportunity to hire rather than buy equipment and this might be a better solution.

Consideration should also be given to whether the new enterprise will also be involved in marketing crops and purchasing inputs. If bigger quantities are marketed, then this should be an advantage.

Unless the acreages and the contributions of the parties are the same, careful consideration will need to be given to the arrangements between the new enterprise and each of the parties. Contracting arrangements and management agreements may be appropriate. It is likely to be important to ensure that each party remains farming its own property simply using the joint venture as a contractor.

PRECEDENTS

1   CONTRACTING AGREEMENT

Particulars

Date of agreement: ....

Parties:

      The Farmer: ....

      of: ....

      The Contractor: ....

      of: ....

Farm: ....

Acreage total: ....

Commencement date: ....

Accounting date: ....

Farm Accountants: ....

Annual fixed contracting charge[1] £ ....

Bonus percentage ....%

Base figure[2] £ ....

Payment dates ....

Service cottages[3] ....

Bankers ....

Farmer's agent ....

Description of Farm

Acreage Schedule

Parcel No.	Description	Acreage

1.   Definitions and interpretations

1.1   The terms used in the Particulars shall unless the context otherwise requires have the same meaning throughout this Agreement.

1.2   'the Farm' means the property described on pages [00] and [00] of this Agreement or such part or parts of it as are prior to the commencement of each Accounting Period notified in writing by the Farmer to the Contractor.[4]

1.3   'the Accounting Period' means the period of twelve months ending with an Accounting Date with the exception that the first Accounting Period shall end on the Accounting Date that shall first occur following the expiry of twelve months after the Commencement Date and the last Accounting Date shall fall on the date upon which this Agreement is terminated in the manner provided below.

1.4   'the Net Profits' means the profits of the Farming Business as determined in accordance with the provisions of the Schedule to this Agreement.

1.5   'the Quotas' means all quotas belonging either to the Farmer or the Farm.

1.6   'the Farming Business' means the business of farming carried on by the Farmer on the Farm.

1.7   'the Policy' means such works of cultivation and other works as may reasonably be required by the Farmer who will after consulting the Contractor establish the farming policy for the Farm.

1.8   The clause headings are for convenience only and do not form part of this Agreement.

1.9   Words importing the singular number shall where appropriate include the plural and words importing the masculine gender shall where appropriate include the feminine and neuter genders.

2.   Commencement

This Agreement shall take effect from the Commencement Date and shall continue until determined in the manner provided below.

3.   Engagement

The Farmer agrees to engage the Contractor and the Contractor agrees to be so engaged as Contractor for the duration and upon the terms of this Agreement to carry out the services hereinafter described.

4.   Contractor's responsibilities

4.1   The Contractor shall be responsible for carrying out the Policy having due regard to the Contractor's ability to carry out the Policy the nature of the Farm and any other financial or other constraints.

4.2 The Contractor shall provide all the manpower and machinery additional to any supplied by the Farmer required for the cultivation of the Farm and shall carry out such operations as shall reasonably be directed by the Farmer or the Farmer's Agent for the cultivation, planting, harvesting, drying, storage and preparation for sale of all crops to be grown on the Farm using all reasonable means to maintain improve and extend the Farming Business and to protect and further the reputation and interest of the Farmer and shall cultivate the Farm and carry out all other operations so that the full and efficient use of the Farm is made for agriculture according to the nature of farming practised in the neighbourhood and so as to preserve the fertility of the soil and to keep the land in good order.

4.3 The Contractor shall prepare and submit as agent for the Farmer all necessary forms under the Integrated Administration and Control System of the European Union and ensure that the requirements thereof for the payment of aid are met and shall ensure that all aid received is forthwith credited to the bank account of the Farming Business.

4.4 The Contractor shall comply with the requirements of any relevant Crop Assurance Schemes.

4.5 The Contractor shall as the Farmer's Agent order and purchase such inputs as may from time to time be authorised by the Farmer or his consultant. All records, vouchers, bills, cheques and other documents required in connection with the Farming Business shall be in the name of the Farmer.

5. Farmer's obligations

The Farmer shall at the expense of the Farming Business provide in a timely fashion in accordance with good farming practice and at reasonable cost all necessary seeds, fertilisers, sprays and other variable inputs for the efficient performance by the Contractor of his obligations hereunder.

6. Insurance

6.1 The Farmer shall at the expense of the Farming Business procure insurance cover to the reasonable satisfaction of the Contractor in respect of the following:

6.1.1 buildings, fixed machinery and plant referred to in the description of the Farm;

6.1.2 produce whilst growing and in store;

6.1.3 seeds, fertilisers and sprays and other sundry stores;

6.1.4 all other property on the Farm owned by or in the custody or control of the Farmer and used by the Farming Business;

6.1.5 all third party and occupiers' liability properly insurable by the Farmer.

6.2 The Contractor shall at his own expense procure insurance cover to the reasonable satisfaction of the Farmer in respect of the following:

6.2.1 the Contractor's machinery plant and all other property owned by him or in his custody against such loss or damage as the Contractor shall consider appropriate; and

6.2.2 the Contractor's liability for death or personal injury or for loss or damage to property arising out of or in the course of the Contractor's implementation of this Agreement.

7.   Non exclusivity

Nothing herein contained shall prevent the Farmer from carrying out or from engaging other contractors to carry out any operations reasonably required on the Farm (not being operations in contemplation herein as normal obligations of the Contractor).

8.   Remuneration

The Farmer shall in respect of each Accounting Period pay to the Contractor:

8.1.1   the Annual Fixed Contracting Charge plus value added tax by equal half yearly instalments in arrear on the payment dates in each year to be apportioned where necessary on a daily basis and paid on the termination of this Agreement if such determination does not fall on an Accounting Date;

8.1.2   a variable sum equal to the Bonus Percentage of the amount by which the Net Profits shall exceed in any Accounting Period the Base Figure such sum together with value added tax to be paid by a single instalment within twenty-eight days after the making up of the annual accounts PROVIDED that payment of the variable sum may be withheld by the Farmer either in whole or in part until such times as the crops for that Accounting Period shall have been actually sold and payment for them received.[5]

8.2   The Contractor shall be entitled to charge for the labour and machinery provided on a quarterly basis in arrears at the rate of 80% of the charges for farming operations set out in the then current issue of the Central Association of Agricultural Valuers Costings.[6]

9.   Banking

9.1   The Farmer shall maintain a separate banking account ('the No 2 Banking Account') for the Farming Business in his name with the Bankers.

9.2   Any sums introduced by the Farmer to such account otherwise than as receipts for crops grown or livestock produced on the Farm shall bear interest at 2% over the base lending rate of the Bankers such interest to be withdrawn by the Farmer on the Accounting Date.

9.3   On the expiration of each Accounting Period the Farmer shall withdraw from the No 2 Banking Account the Base figure.

9.4   The Farmer shall withdraw from such account the net profits of the Farming Business for each Accounting Period within twenty-eight days after the making up of the annual accounts and the sale of the crops (if later) and shall pay the sum due to the Contractor on that date in accordance with the provisions hereof.

10.   Records

10.1   The Contractor shall keep such records in respect of the Farming Business as may be required by the Farmer or the Farm Accountants with sufficient details so that all Quotas belonging either to the Farmer or the Farm and all compensation aid and grants payable to the Farmer under any statute or statutory or local regulation or bye-law or otherwise may be readily determined so that all statutes regulations or bye-laws are complied with and generally so that the rights of the Farmer can be accurately ascertained.

10.2   Proper books of account giving a true and fair view of the Farming Business shall be kept properly posted by the Farmer and such books shall be available for inspection by each of the parties and their respective advisers at all reasonable times either at the Farm or at the Farmer's usual place of business or at the offices of any consultant nominated by the Farmer.

11.   Restrictions

The Contractor shall not without the prior written approval of the Farmer except when duly authorised by the Farmer or the Farmer's Agent in writing (such authority being if the Farmer so requires of a general nature) enter into any contract or agreement on behalf of the Farmer draw, accept or endorse any bill on behalf of the Farmer or in any way pledge the credit of the Farmer or give any security or promise for the payment of money by the Farmer.

12.   Personal supervision

The Contractor hereby agrees with the Farmer that all work to be done or services to be performed by the Contractor under this Agreement shall be so done or performed by the Contractor personally or under his personal supervision.

13.   Licence to enter

The Farmer hereby gives leave to the Contractor to enter on the Farm specifically and exclusively for the purpose of carrying out the Contractor's obligations hereunder the Farmer himself remaining at all times in full occupation of the Farm and nothing in this Agreement shall give the Contractor any right to enter use or occupy the Farm other than by the licence of the Farmer for the purposes hereof.

14.   Cottages (where included in the Particulars)

The Farmer hereby agrees that:

14.1   Any employee of the Contractor employed on the Farm may occupy the service cottages during the currency of this Agreement and upon the termination of this Agreement the Contractor shall procure that suitable alternative accommodation shall be made available by the Contractor off the Farm for the occupier or occupiers aforesaid.

14.2   The Contractor may occupy one of the service cottages during the currency of this Agreement but not otherwise.

15.   Extra work

If the Contractor at the written request of the Farmer or the Farmer's Agent undertakes any operation which he is not obliged to carry out hereunder or if the Contractor with the written consent of the Farmer pays for any items properly payable by the Farmer hereunder the Farmer shall reimburse the Contractor for the costs thereof forthwith upon presentation by the Contractor of the appropriate invoice.

2 MANAGEMENT CONTRACTING AND SHARE FARMING

16.   Accounts

A profit and loss account giving a fair and accurate record of the Farming Business shall be promptly prepared by the Farm Accountants in respect of every Accounting Period during the currency of this Agreement and a copy of the same shall be supplied to the Contractor.

17.   Termination on short notice[7]

This Agreement may be terminated:

17.1   By the Farmer forthwith by giving notice in writing to the Contractor in any of the following events:

17.1.1   if there shall be any persistent breach or material breach or breaches by the Contractor of the terms of this Agreement;

17.1.2   if the Contractor shall after proper warning fail to comply with any lawful directions given by the Farmer in writing in accordance with the provisions stated above subject to weather conditions permitting and such failure continues for a period of seven days after the Contractor has been required to comply with such direction by written notice from the Farmer;

17.1.3   if the Contractor shall through illness, accident or any other cause be incapacitated or prevented from carrying on his duties under this Agreement for a continuous period of not less than three months or for not less than one hundred days in any continuous period of twelve months;

17.1.4   if the Contractor shall commit any act of bankruptcy or become bankrupt or make any composition or voluntary arrangement with his creditors or have any distress levied or any process by way of execution ordered against his property which shall not have been discharged within fourteen days;

17.1.5   if the Contractor becomes a patient within the meaning of the Mental Health Act 1983;

17.1.6   if the Contractor dies;

17.1.7   if the Contractor being a company enters into liquidation (whether compulsory or voluntary) other than for the purpose of amalgamation or reconstruction or if a receiver is appointed of the Contractor's undertaking.

17.2   In the event of the death of the Farmer by his personal representatives giving to the Contractor not less than six months' notice in writing.

17.3   By the Farmer giving to the Contractor not less than twelve months' notice in writing.[8]

17.4   Forthwith by the Contractor giving to the Farmer notice in writing in any of the following events:

17.4.1   if the Farmer being a Company enters into liquidation (whether compulsory or voluntary) other than for the purpose of amalgamation or reconstruction or if a receiver is appointed of the Farmer's undertaking;

17.4.2   if the Farmer being an individual commits any act of bankruptcy becomes bankrupt or makes any compulsory or voluntary arrangement with his creditors or has any distress levied or any process by way of execution ordered against his property which shall not have been discharged within fourteen days;

17.4.3   if there shall be any persistent or material breach or breaches by the Farmer of the terms hereof.

17.5   By the Contractor giving the Farmer not less than three months' notice in writing should the Contractor contract any debilitating chronic illness.

18.   Termination on full notice[9]

This Agreement may be determined by either party giving to the other not less than twelve months' notice in writing to expire on an Accounting Date in any year.

19.   Valuation[10]

19.1   On the termination of this Agreement and on the termination of each Accounting Period a valuation of growing crops and harvested crops shall be taken on the following bases:

19.1.1 growing crops shall be valued at the cost of production based on the sums paid or payable to the Contractor pursuant to clause 8.1.1 and 8.2 hereof together with the cost of seeds, fertilisers, sprays and other variable inputs and a fair allowance for enhancement where appropriate to be determined by the Farmer's Agent after consultation with the Contractor;

19.1.2 harvested crops shall be valued at open market value less any anticipated storage and other costs.

        [OR

19.1   On the termination of each Accounting Period a valuation of growing crops and harvested crops shall be taken on the following bases:

19.1.1 growing crops shall be valued at the cost of production based on the sums paid or payable to the Contractor pursuant to clause 8.1.1 and 8.2 hereof together with the cost of seeds, fertilisers, sprays and other variable inputs and a fair allowance for enhancement where appropriate to be determined by the Farmer's Agent after consultation with the Contractor;

19.1.2 harvested crops shall be valued at estimated open market value less any anticipated storage and other costs.

19.2   On the termination of this Agreement a valuation shall be taken on the following basis:

19.2.1 Stores shall be valued at actual cost.

19.2.2 The growing crops for harvest in the following year shall be valued at the cost of production based on the sums paid or payable to the Contractor pursuant to clause 8.1.1 and 8.2 hereof together with the cost of seeds, fertiliser, sprays and other variable inputs and a fair allowance for enhancement where appropriate to be determined by the Farmer's Agent after consultation with the Contractor.

19.2.3 Harvested crops and growing crops for harvest in the current season shall be valued at estimated open market value less any anticipated storage and other costs. When such crops have been harvested and/or sold then the net proceeds of sale thereof less the cost of cultivations, harvesting, storage, dressing and sale shall be brought into account in the preparation of the final accounts and the variable sum referred to in clause 8.1.2 shall be adjusted when the final results are known.]

19.2   The valuation shall be prepared by the Farm Accountants provided that in
[or 3]   the event of disagreement between the Farmer and the Contractor as to such Valuation clause 26 hereof shall apply.

2 MANAGEMENT CONTRACTING AND SHARE FARMING

20. Compensation on early termination[11]

If this Agreement shall be terminated for any reason other than the reasons specified in sub-clauses 17.1.1, 17.1.2 or 17.1.4 and on a date which is not an annual Accounting Date then the Contractor shall be entitled (in addition to a proportionate part of the Annual Fixed Contracting Charge) to a proportionate part of the Variable Sum referred to in clause 8.1.2 which would have been payable to the Contractor at the next making up of the annual accounts had this Agreement then been in existence. Such last mentioned proportionate part to be such sum as shall be fair and equitable having regard to all the circumstances of the case and to be payable in like manner as the Variable Sum.

21. Withdrawal of land

If the Farmer shall wish to use any part of the Farm for any non-agricultural purpose the Farmer may upon giving not less than three calendar months' notice in writing to the Contractor terminate this Agreement in relation to that part whereupon the net profits for the annual Accounting Period in which such partial termination shall be effected shall for the purpose of computing the Net Profits for that Accounting Period be adjusted to such figure as would have represented the Net Profits for that annual Accounting Period had this Agreement not been partially terminated as aforesaid. PROVIDED ALWAYS that if this Agreement shall by reason of one or more notices under this clause have been partially terminated in relation to an area amounting in aggregate to not less than one-half of the area of the Farm the Contractor may upon giving three months' notice in writing elect to treat this Agreement as having been terminated in full.

22. Profit adjustment

Any adjustment of the Net Profits that may fall to be made under the provisions of clause 21 shall be calculated as if the profits earned from any part of the Farm were the same as those earned from any other part of the Farm having an area equal to such first mentioned part.

23. Certificates[12]

All certificates as to the accounts of the Farm or the Net Profits or of any other matter which are by this Agreement to be given by the Farm Accountants shall in the absence of manifest error be final and binding upon both parties.

24. Relationship

It is hereby agreed and declared by the parties to this Agreement that nothing in this Agreement shall constitute a partnership between the Contractor and the Farmer or create a tenancy of the Farm or a licence for the exclusive occupation of the same.

25. Assignment

The Contractor shall not be entitled to assign or otherwise deal with the benefit of this Agreement.

26.   Disputes

In the event of a dispute between the Farmer and the Contractor touching the construction or effect of this Agreement or any matter relating or incidental thereto, either the Farmer or the Contractor may refer such dispute to a valuer local to the Farm and familiar with the type of farming carried on on the Farm agreed between the Farmer and the Contractor or in default of agreement appointed by the President for the time being of the Royal Institution of Chartered Surveyors. Such valuer shall act as an expert and not as an arbitrator and his decision shall be final and binding on the parties hereto and the costs of such appointment and valuation shall be in his award.

27.   Notices

27.1   Any notice or direction given in pursuance of the provisions of this Agreement shall be deemed to have been properly given to or served on the other party to whom it is addressed if it is sent in a prepaid letter by registered post or by recorded delivery service addressed to that other party at his last known address.

27.2   For the purposes of this Agreement any notice shall be deemed to have been given to the personal representatives of a deceased person notwithstanding that no grant of representation has been made in respect of his estate in England if the notice is addressed to that person by name or to his personal representatives by title and is sent by a prepaid letter by registered post or the recorded delivery service to the usual abode of the deceased person at his death.

28.   Value Added Tax

Where any sums payable pursuant to this Agreement are properly chargeable with value added tax the same shall be paid upon production of a suitably drawn value added tax invoice.

29.   Substitute contractors

If the Contractor does not perform the obligations on his part herein contained expeditiously then the Farmer may after notifying the Contractor in writing procure such person or persons as he may select to carry out such work and the reasonable cost of such work shall be charged against the remuneration due to the Contractor in accordance with this Agreement and any excess thereof over such remuneration then owing shall be forthwith recoverable from the Contractor.

30.   Meetings

Prior to the commencement of each Accounting Period the Farmer and the Contractor shall meet and the Farmer shall notify the Contractor of the farming programme during that period. A budget shall be prepared at the expense of the Farming Business and such other meetings as the Farmer shall reasonably request shall be held to review the progress of the Farming Business during the Accounting Period.

AS WITNESS the hands of the parties hereto the day and year first before written.

SCHEDULE

THE NET PROFITS OF THE FARMING BUSINESS

1.   The Net Profits of the Farming Business means the income thereof arising from sales (excluding sales of fixed assets or herd animals) and area aid and set-aside and premium payments under any European Union Scheme certified by the Farm Accountants utilising normal accounting practices after providing for all expenses and outgoings subject to the provisions of this Schedule utilising the valuation at the expiration of each Accounting Period and the termination of this Agreement referred to in clause 19 hereof and the valuation at the Commencement Date obtained by the Farmer.

2.   The expenses and outgoings of the Farming Business (without prejudice to the generality of the expression) include:

2.1   all rates and taxes including owners and occupiers drainage rates and other outgoings payable in respect of the Farm including levies other than income or corporation tax payable by the Farmer;

2.2   insurances maintained by the Farmer in respect of the Farm and the Farming Business;

2.3   repairs and maintenance of the Farm and the fixed equipment thereon belonging to the Farmer (including annual maintenance and clearance of ditches and drainage systems and mowing of banks) but not so as to put or place the Farm and the fixed equipment in a better state of repair and condition than the same were in on the Commencement Date;

2.4   all fees charged and remuneration of the Farmer's servants, agents or contractors including the Farmer's Agent (other than the remuneration payable to the Contractor under clause 8.1.2 hereof);

2.5   such provisions as the Farm Accountants consider necessary in respect of bad or doubtful debts;

2.6   the cost of seeds, fertilisers, sprays and other items provided by the Farmer at the expense of the Farming Business;

2.7   the expense of keeping the books of the Farming Business, computing interest and preparing the valuation at the commencement and expiration of each Accounting Period and preparing the accounts of the Farming Business;

2.8   interest withdrawn by the Farmer pursuant to clause 9.2;

2.9   interest incurred in respect of the Farmer's borrowing on the No 2 Banking Account;

2.10   fees and charges incurred in connection with any marketing arrangements and crop sale agreements;

2.11   the cost to the Farmer of labour and machinery provided by the Contractor and the cost of other work undertaken by other contractors to carry out any operations reasonably required on the Farm and which are not an improvement.

[Original]

SIGNED by the FARMER
in the presence of:

....

....

....

....

[Counterpart]

SIGNED by the CONTRACTOR
in the presence of:

....

....

....

....

---

1   This is a modest retainer figure and is not essential.
2   The Base Figure is the intended main return to the Farmer, ie the person providing the land. The
    Farmer will normally take a small share of the remaining profits.
3   If there are none, this should be deleted as well as clause 14 of the Agreement. Alternatively, it
    should be marked as not applicable and clause 14 left in.
4   This uncertainty may be unacceptable to the Contractor and is a matter of negotiation.
5   Advice needs to be taken on the fair bonus percentage from each party's advisers. The draft
    provides for payment to be withheld until the crops have been sold and payment received. This is
    advantageous to the Farmer. The draft provides by clause 9.3 for the Base Figure to be withdrawn
    at the end of the Accounting Period but this clause would mean that the Contractor's share of
    profit is not drawn out until cash is available. How acceptable this is to the Contractor may
    depend on whether he is receiving any cash during the course of the year for works specifically
    undertaken.
6   This clause would be fairly beneficial to the Contractor. Sometimes the Contractor will finance
    all the work throughout the harvest year. The risk of this is that the Contractor will be an
    unsecured creditor if the Farmer becomes insolvent. Payment rates vary with the parties' bargain.
7   It may be appropriate to vary this depending on whether the Contractor is a company or an
    individual.
8   The significance of this clause in particular is to ensure that for tax purposes the Farmer can obtain
    vacant possession within 12 months now extended by concession to 24 months. It will be
    remembered that, in order to obtain 100% agricultural relief for inheritance tax, this condition
    may in some circumstances have to be met.
9   If this clause is included then clause 17.3 will be deleted.
10 Alternatives are provided for a valuation at the termination of the Agreement or for a valuation
    with subsequent adjustments. The former means that certainty is available earlier. The latter may
    prolong uncertainty but it is probably fairer to both parties. It is particularly important to have the
    right result at the beginning and end of the Agreement.
11 Should there be further compensation for early termination based on profit foregone or cost of
    acquiring new tackle for the transaction? If so, provision must be made.
12 The contractor may not be too keen on the Farm Accountants as the final arbitrators but on the
    whole it is probably desirable to include this in the interest of avoiding too much argument.

2   SHARE FARMING AGREEMENT

THIS AGREEMENT is made the [*date*]

BETWEEN ....

(hereinafter called 'the Landowner') of the one part and ....

.... of ....

.... (hereinafter called 'the Share Farmer') of the other part.

WHEREAS

1.   The Landowner is the owner and occupier of ....
      .... farm.

2.   The Landowner and the Share Farmer have agreed to co-operate in the farming of certain parts of that farm for the benefit of their separate businesses.

NOW IT IS AGREED as follows:

1.   Share farming agreement
      The land described in Schedule 1 hereto and more particularly delineated and shown edged red on the plan annexed hereto (hereinafter called 'the land') shall be farmed by the Landowner and the Share Farmer for the separate benefit of each of them on the terms and conditions following.

2.   Woodlands game etc
2.1   No woodlands timber, minerals, game, wildfowl, wild birds or fish are included in this Agreement.
2.2   This Agreement is subject to the exercise by or under the authority of the owner of rights in respect of the matters set out in sub-clause 2.1 and of sporting rights in on or over the land.

3.   Commencement, duration and termination[1]
3.1   This Agreement shall commence on the [*date*] and shall continue until the [*date*] and unless terminated on that date by not less than twelve months' prior notice in writing given by either party to the other expiring on that date shall continue until terminated on any subsequent [*date*] by not less than twelve months' prior notice in writing as aforesaid.
3.2   Notwithstanding sub-clause 3.1 of this clause either party may terminate this Agreement by giving the other twenty-eight days' prior notice in writing in any of the following circumstances:
3.2.1   grave and persistent breach of the terms of this Agreement by the other provided that he has previously been given written notice specifying the breach and giving him a reasonable period to remedy the same if remediable;

3.2.2   the other being prevented from carrying out his obligations under this Agreement for a continuous period of not less than six months during the subsistence of this Agreement by illness accident or any other cause;

3.2.3   the other becoming bankrupt or making any composition or arrangement with his creditors.

3.3   Notwithstanding sub-clause 3.1 this Agreement may be terminated in the event of the death of the Landowner by his executors or administrators giving the Share Farmer not less than six months' notice in writing expiring on the [*date*] in any year but in the event of the Share Farmer suffering loss by reason of the termination under this sub-clause being earlier than it could have been under sub-clause 3.1 he shall be entitled to compensation for the loss, such compensation being limited to a maximum of £ . . . .

3.4   Notwithstanding sub-clause 3.1 in the event of the Share Farmer dying during the subsistence of this Agreement this Agreement shall terminate on the quarter day next occurring after a period of four months has expired from the date of his death.

3.5   Notwithstanding sub-clause 3.1 of this clause this Agreement may be terminated in the event of the Landowner entering into a contract to sell or otherwise dispose of the ownership of the whole or a substantial part of the land by giving the Share Farmer not less than six months' notice in writing expiring on the [*date*] in any year but in the event of the Share Farmer suffering loss by reason of termination under this sub-clause being earlier than it could have been under sub-clause 3.1 he shall be entitled to compensation for the loss, such compensation being limited to a maximum of £ . . . provided always that if such sale or disposition is completed before expiry of the notice referred to in this sub-clause the Landowner while himself remaining liable to perform all his obligations under this Agreement throughout its subsistence shall nevertheless procure that the transferee shall enter into an agreement in writing with the Share Farmer that the transferee will be personally liable thenceforth for all such obligations.

3.6   Notwithstanding sub-clause 3.1 this Agreement can be terminated by the Landowner at any time on giving eleven months' notice but in the event of the Share Farmer suffering loss by reason of termination under this sub-clause being earlier than it could have been under sub-clause 3.1 he shall be entitled to compensation for the loss, such compensation being limited to a maximum of £ . . . .

4.   Review in the event of change in cost structure of farming

Either the Landowner or the Share Farmer may if a significant change in the cost structure of farming occurs call for a review and revision of the terms of the Agreement as at [*date*] (the review date) in any year upon giving the other party not less than nine months' previous written notice and upon service of such notice the parties shall endeavour to agree by [*date*] of that year what amendment if any should take effect at the review date and in default of agreement the provisions of the Agreement shall remain unchanged.

2 MANAGEMENT CONTRACTING AND SHARE FARMING

5.   Occupation of the land
The land and every part of it shall remain in the possession and occupation of the Landowner throughout the subsistence of this Agreement. The Share Farmer shall have the right to occupy and use the land jointly with the Landowner for the purposes and during the currency of this Agreement only but neither the Share Farmer nor his servants or agents shall have exclusive possession of the land or any part of it as against the Landowner.

6.   Indemnity
Neither party shall hold himself out as partner of or agent for the other party and each party agrees to indemnify and to keep indemnified the other against all claims, demands, proceedings, costs and liabilities in respect of the activities or business of the indemnifier whether or not in relation to this Agreement.

7.   No tenancy partnership agency or employment
Nothing in this Agreement nor anything done in pursuance of this Agreement shall create or be deemed to create a tenancy, partnership, relationship of principal and agent or contract of employment between the parties.

8.   Farming policy
The parties shall carry on the share farming enterprise under this Agreement in accordance with the farming policy and cropping programme set out in Schedule 2 hereof.

9.   Share of inputs
9.1   The input costs including the provision of land buildings machinery and fixed equipment shall be provided by the parties in accordance with Schedule 3 hereto and any cost charge tax levy or other expense incurred by the Landowner or the Share Farmer shall be that of his respective business.

9.2   Livestock provided at the commencement of this Agreement additional stock and replacements purchased and the number of calves reared annually shall be in accordance with Schedule 2 hereof and no livestock shall otherwise be brought onto the land except with the express consent of both parties.

9.3   Each and every head of livestock on the land shall until sold under this Agreement belong as to . . . % to the Landowner and as to . . . % to the Share Farmer.

10.   Duties of share farmer
The Share Farmer agrees as follows:

10.1 To devote adequate time to the share farming enterprise for its efficient running. To manage the day-to-day farming of the land and animals efficiently and to a high standard of husbandry, and to keep the land clean and in good heart and to carry out the agreed farming policy and cropping programme referred to in clause 8 hereof including the livestock husbandry and all cultivations harvesting of crops and (subject to the agreed policy referred to in clause 14 hereof) marketing and sale of milk, livestock, crops and other produce and to provide such labour, plant, machinery, implements and transport necessary therefor.

10.2 To provide or pay for (as the case may be) the inputs required of him in accordance with Schedule 3 hereof and to purchase on behalf of and at the expense of the Landowner any items required from him in accordance with the said Schedule 3 in so far as the Landowner shall not have provided or purchased such items by the time they are required. At commencement of the Agreement to purchase his share of the Landowner's livestock in accordance with Schedule 6. To purchase (i) livestock in accordance with Schedule 2 hereof additional to the initial herd of dairy cows provided by the Landower and (ii) any replacements from an agreed or otherwise reputable supplier at the most favourable price obtainable ensuring that the animals are healthy and of good quality suitable for the farming policy required by this Agreement.

10.3 To carry out routine maintenance and repairs to the land buildings and fixed equipment (other than such as fall to be carried out by the Landowner under clause 11 hereof) including all fixtures and fittings together with all internal decorations and internal repairs to the houses and buildings, regular trimming and laying of hedges and cleaning of ditches. To carry out repairs and regular maintenance (the Landowner providing the materials thereof) to fences, hedges, gates, culverts, land, drains and roads and to repair and fully maintain the plant and machinery owned by the Landowner set out in Part (a) of Schedule 4 hereof.

10.4 To effect and maintain adequate policies of insurance to cover public and occupier's liability and to cover the plant and machinery and all property owned by him (whether solely or jointly) or in his possession and used or kept for the purposes of this Agreement (other than any required by this Agreement to be insured by the Landowner). To insure in the joint names of the Landowner (as to ... % ownership) all livestock kept or obtained under this Agreement. To refund to the Landowner ... % of the cost of insurance of severed crops covered under clause 11.3 hereof.

10.5 Not without the prior consent of the Landowner to take down any trees or to take up any hedges or fences and to comply with the conservation policies set out in Schedule 5 hereof.

10.6 To ensure to the best of his ability that the milk quota and all other quotas and subsidy allocations for the land and for production shall be maintained at the highest possible level and to avoid any act or omission that would prejudice the acquisition or maintenance of any quota at that level.

11. Duties of landowner

The Landowner agrees as follows:

11.1   To provide or pay for (as the case may be) the inputs required from him in accordance with Schedule 3 hereof.

11.2   To carry out routine external repairs to and painting of the buildings and within a reasonable time if reasonably necessary any major maintenance and repairs to the buildings and to provide materials for repairs to fences hedges gates culverts land drains and roads.

11.3   To effect and maintain adequate policies of insurance to cover public and occupier's liability and to cover the buildings and the growing and severed crops on the land and to pay to the Share Farmer . . . % of any insurance monies paid to the Landowner in respect of the growing or severed crops.

11.4   To pay . . . % of the cost of any livestock additional to the herd provided by him which is purchased to comply with the stocking policy set out in Schedule 2 hereof.

11.5   To pay to the Share Farmer . . . % of any premiums paid by the Share Farmer to insure livestock under this Agreement.

11.6   To avoid any act or omission that would prejudice the maintenance of any milk or other quota for the land or any production quota at the highest possible level.

11.7   To arrange for the performance of the share farming enterprise under this Agreement to be costed to provide a quarterly written schedule of performance and annual summary together with an annual inventory of live and dead stock. The cost of this service to be borne as to . . . % by the Landowner and . . . % by the Share Farmer.

12.   Ownership of growing crops and machinery

Growing crops on the land shall belong to the Landowner until severed but cannot be sold or otherwise disposed of by the Landower without the written consent of the Share Farmer and the plant machinery and equipment specified in Schedule 4 hereof shall belong as shown in that Schedule.

13.   Quotas

It is agreed by the Landowner and the Share Farmer as follows:

13.1   Throughout the term of this Agreement and any extension thereof a Quota Register for the Share Farming Agreement shall be maintained by the parties. The register shall record the initial quota provided by each party for the use in his separate business and any extra quota acquired by either party and all compulsory loss or suspension of quota.

13.2   At the commencement of this Agreement [   ] litres of milk quota shall be provided by the Landower and [   ] by the Share Farmer and shall be used throughout the term of the Share Farming Agreement on the land specified in the First Schedule hereto and on no other land.

13.3   On the termination of the Agreement the Landowner shall be entitled to retain his [   ] litres and any additional quota (less permanent cuts) recorded as his in the Quota Register referred to in sub-clause 13.1 above and to use such quota on any land in which he has an interest. The Share Farmer hereby undertakes to make no claim to that quota nor to any compensation in respect thereof.

13.4   Likewise on the termination of this Agreement the Share Farmer shall be entitled to retain his [   ] litres and any additional quota (less any permanent cuts) recorded as his in the said Quota Register and to use such quota on any land in which he has an interest. The Landowner hereby undertakes to make no claim to that quota nor to any compensation in respect thereof. OR

13.5   The Landowner shall make arrangements with the Intervention Board to lease [   ] litres of quota to the Share Farmer on an annual basis throughout the term of this Agreement. Such quota shall be used by the Share Farmer in his own business but the quota shall be used only on the land specified in the First Schedule.

13.6   If the regulations permitting such leasing should be changed or withdrawn then the Share Farmer may call for a review and revision of the terms of the Agreement by giving the Landowner not less than twelve months' prior notice in writing expiring on the 25th March notwithstanding that the full fixed term agreed has not expired.[2]

13.7   Both parties undertake to sign any documents required by the Intervention Board or similar regulatory body to enable an entry to be made on the Intervention Board Register (or that of a similar body) recording that the Landowner and the Share Farmer are joint suppliers under a Share Farming Agreement and to delete such an entry on the termination of the Agreement.

13.8   Should the Intervention Board or similar regulatory body succeed in an action taken against the Landowner alone for breach of the undertakings, warranties or indemnities given in the contract with the Intervention Board or similar body, then the Share Farmer will pay . . . % of any fine or payment unless the Landowner acted contrary to the express instructions of the Share Farmer.

13.8.1 Should the Intervention Board or similar regulatory body succeed in an action taken against the Share Farmer alone for breach of the undertakings, warranties or indemnities given in the contract with the Intervention Board or similar body, then the Landowner will pay . . . % of any fine or payment unless the Share Farmer has acted contrary to the express instructions of the Landowner.

14.   Share of gross output

The produce of the farm after severance shall belong as to . . . % to the Landowner and as to . . . % to the Share Farmer and shall be marketed and sold by the Share Farmer in accordance with a policy to be agreed between the parties at the best price reasonably obtainable and the gross receipts for the produce shall be paid to the parties in those percentages.

15.   Grants and subsidies

Any production grants or subsidies paid to either party in respect of livestock shall be shared between the parties . . . % being paid to the Landowner and . . . % to the Share Farmer.

16. Bank accounts

The parties shall maintain their own separate bank accounts and shall have no joint bank account in respect of this Agreement other than a joint account on which neither party shall be at liberty to draw opened at [*name and address of bank*] into which shall be paid gross receipts for sale of produce (other than such receipts which may from time to time be paid by purchasers directly to the parties in the shares referred to in clause 14 hereof); no other monies shall be paid into that joint account and the parties shall procure that all monies which are paid into that joint account shall be transferred forthwith by [*name of bank*] to the separate bank accounts of the parties in the shares referred to in clause 14 hereof.

17. Records and accounts

The Share Farmer shall keep proper and true records of all the farming operations carried out under this Agreement and shall if requested make them available for inspection by the Landowner or his agent at any reasonable time and each party shall keep proper and separate books of account in respect of his expenditure and receipts under this Agreement and each shall be separately registered for Value Added Tax.

18. Payment of accounts

18.1 Accounts in respect of inputs to be provided or paid for by each of the parties in accordance with Schedule 3 hereof shall be paid by the parties within one month of receipt of those accounts.

18.2 The parties shall endeavour to secure that separate invoices are submitted to each of them by any suppliers in respect of inputs required by each party by Schedule 3 hereof.

18.3 Where a supplier submits a single invoice in respect of inputs required by Schedule 3 to be provided by each of the parties separately then to comply with the requirements of HM Customs and Excise the party to whom the invoice is addressed must pay the bill. He shall then re-invoice the other party that party's share and Value Added Tax.

19. Disclosure of insurance

A copy of any policy of insurance required to be effected by a party under this Agreement shall be furnished to the other party if requested.

20. Meetings

The parties shall meet at least once in every three months to review the farming operations under this Agreement and after each harvest they shall review the farming policy for the following farming year. Notes shall be kept of decisions made at meetings.

21. Dwellinghouses

21.1 The Share Farmer shall be entitled during the subsistence of this Agreement to occupy rent free the dwellinghouse known as [*name of dwellinghouse*] for the purposes of carrying out his agricultural duties under this Agreement.

21.2 The Share Farmer shall pay any rates levied on that dwellinghouse during his occupation to the authority levying them and shall pay all other outgoings and shall keep the dwellinghouse clean and in full decorative repair internally and shall keep the garden clean and tidy.

21.3 The Landowner will provide the cottages known as [*names of cottages*] for occupation of the Share Farmer's employees provided that the employees:

21.3.1 pay the Landowner a rent of £251[3] (or greater agreed sum);

21.3.2 acknowledge receipt of the intention to grant Assured Shorthold Tenancies on Form 9 (or any prescribed form replacing Form 9);

21.3.3 sign the tenancy agreements relating to their properties in the form annexed hereto before entering into possession.

22. Surplus land

Any land becoming surplus to the requirements of the contract due to Government/EC regulations or directives shall either remain within the contract or be released from the contract for the sole use of the Landowner on his giving not less than six months' notice to the Share Farmer.

23. Arrangements at commencement

23.1 On the commencement of this Agreement the Share Farmer shall pay the Landowner:

23.1.1 in respect of the growing crops on the land the percentages of the costs as allocated to the Share Farmer in Schedule 3 hereof for any seeds sown, fertilisers, lime and sprays already expended in respect of those crops since severance or grazing of the last previous crop and likewise for costs so expended for labour, machinery, plant, electricity and water.

23.1.2 for the crops, stocks and stores in accordance with Schedule 6(a) hereto.

23.1.3 for any field machinery agreed to be taken over by the Share Farmer in accordance with Schedule 6(b) hereof.

23.1.4 for any livestock agreed to be taken over by the Share Farmer in accordance with Schedule 6(c) hereof.

24. Arrangements on termination

24.1 On the termination of this Agreement:

24.1.1 any growing crop shall belong to the Landowner but the Landowner shall repay to the Share Farmer the costs borne by the Share Farmer in respect of the growing crop for seeds, fertilisers, lime, sprays, labour, machinery, plant, electricity and water applied or used after the severance or grazing (as the case may be) of the last previous crop.

24.1.2 any crop severed under this Agreement and not yet disposed of and any seeds, fertilisers, lime and sprays acquired under this Agreement and still held in stock shall belong to the parties in the percentages set out in clause 14 hereof.

24.1.3 either of the parties may be given the first option to buy the interest in the livestock of the other.

2 MANAGEMENT CONTRACTING AND SHARE FARMING

24.1.4 Mr [*name*] shall have the option to purchase from Mr [*name*] the interest of Mr [*name*] in the livestock belonging to the parties under this Agreement provided that:

Mr [*name*] gives notice in writing before the termination date to Mr [*name*] of his intention to exercise the option and in exercising the option he purchases each and every head of livestock unless otherwise agreed.

24.1.5 If due notice to exercise the option referred to in sub-clause 24.1.4 is not given by Mr [*name*] then Mr [*name*] shall have the option to purchase from Mr [*name*] the interest of Mr [*name*] in that livestock provided that:

Mr [*name*] gives notice in writing not later than two weeks after the termination date to Mr [*name*] of his intention to exercise the option, and in exercising the option he purchases each and every head of livestock unless otherwise agreed.

24.1.6 Any livestock not acquired by one or other party under sub-clause 24.1.4 or 24.1.5 shall be sold by the Share Farmer on the expiration of two weeks from the termination date and the proceeds of sale shall be divided between the parties in the percentages referred to in clause 9.3 hereof.

24.1.7 Any unsold hay, silage, straw, feeding stuffs or produce produced from the land under this Agreement and any purchased feeding stuffs and other stores on the land acquired for the purposes of this Agreement and belonging to the Share Farmer solely or jointly shall become the property of the Landowner on the termination date but the Landowner shall make payment to the Share Farmer in respect thereof as set out in Schedule 6(a) hereof.

25. Rights and duties personal

Subject to sub-clause 3.5 hereof the rights and obligations of the parties under this Agreement shall be personal to them (or to their personal representatives) and shall not be assigned, transferred, mortgaged, charged or otherwise disposed of.

26. Disputes

In the event of any dispute arising as to any valuation required under this Agreement or as to any compensation payable under sub-clauses 3.3, 3.5 and 3.6 hereof either party may refer such dispute to be determined by arbitration under the Arbitration Act 1996 or any statutory modification or re-enactment thereof for the time being in force by a single arbitrator to be agreed upon by the parties or in default of agreement appointed by the President for the time being of the Royal Institution of Chartered Surveyors.

27. Costs

Each party shall bear his own costs of preparation and execution of this Agreement.

28.   No variation unless in writing

This Agreement contains the whole of the agreement between the parties and no variation shall be made unless it is made in writing and signed by or on behalf of both parties.

SCHEDULE 1

LAND AND BUILDINGS INCLUDED IN THE AGREEMENT AND PLAN

SCHEDULE 2

FARMING POLICY AND CROPPING PROGRAMME

SCHEDULE 3

INPUTS REQUIRED FROM EACH PARTY

Input	Landowner	Share Farmer
Land, Buildings, Farmhouse plus certain fixed machinery		
Maintenance of the above, rates and insurance		
Insurance of Growing Crops		
Materials for fencing, road and gate repairs		
Costings		
Labour		
Machinery and Plant		
Electricity and Water		
Telephone – miscellaneous		
Livestock Sundries		
Ownership of livestock and insurance		
Seeds, fertilisers and sprays		
Lime		

Insurance of crops in store

Purchased feed stuffs

A.I. – Vet. & Med.

SCHEDULE 4

OWNERSHIP OF PLANT AND EQUIPMENT

Part (a) The property of the Landowner

Part (b) The property of the Share Farmer

SCHEDULE 5

CONSERVATION POLICIES

SCHEDULE 6

VALUATION ON COMMENCEMENT AND TERMINATION OF THE AGREEMENT

(a) Crops Stocks and Stores

(b) Field and other Machinery

(c) Livestock

AS WITNESS the hands of the parties hereto the day and year first before written.

SIGNED by the LANDOWNER
in the presence of:

....

....

....

SIGNED by the SHARE FARMER
in the presence of:

}

....

....

....

....

---

1   The short notice provisions for the land owner are inserted for inheritance tax reasons (see footnote 8 on p 37).
2   The registration procedures with the Intervention Board and the formalities depend on the exact arrangements made between the parties.
3   This sum is the minimum needed to ensure that the tenancy is an assured shorthold tenancy.

2 MANAGEMENT CONTRACTING AND SHARE FARMING

CHAPTER 3: SALE AND ACQUISITION OF LAND

INDEX

3 SALE AND ACQUISITION OF LAND

CHAPTER 3: SALE AND ACQUISITION OF LAND

INTRODUCTION

Since this does not purport to be the definitive work on conveyancing in general, it is not really appropriate to provide full precedents of contracts, transfers, etc. Instead, there are provided samples of specific enquiries and specific contractual clauses of relevance in agricultural matters. It is assumed that the contract will also contain all necessary clauses relevant to the property itself, including the grant and reservation of rights and a general clause ensuring that the terms will remain binding beyond completion. Those clauses, so far as relevant, will be carried forward into the transfer or conveyance.

Pole v Peake (1998) *The Times*, 22 July relates to shooting rights and represents a cautionary tale. The Court of Appeal construed a reservation of shooting rights and confirmed that 'rearing' entitled the sportsmen to release birds onto the land. It did not matter if the shooting interfered with agricultural activity, so long as the rights were exercised with due care. Any purchase of land subject to a reservation of sporting rights should, therefore, be viewed with considerable concern.

In precedent 3, we have set out a miscellany of individual clauses, one or more of which may be relevant to the individual transaction. Aid schemes cause many practitioners particular problems. There is a wide variety of such schemes affecting agriculture; many of these involve undertakings and penalties on early termination, including the recovery of aid paid. It is therefore essential for the advisers to a seller of land to ascertain from their client details of any such schemes which are relevant, so that appropriate arrangements can be made.

We have also included an example of a Deed of Partition, appropriate to the situation where milk quota applies and the parties have different interests in the various properties. This is, however, merely an example.

PRECEDENTS

1   ENQUIRIES BEFORE CONTRACT

ENQUIRIES BEFORE CONTRACT

Property: ....

Parties: ....

....

Ref: ....   Ref: ....

Buyer's solicitors: ....   Seller's solicitors: ....

....

Dated: ....   Dated: ....

Replies (based on the knowledge of the Seller and, where relevant, of his solicitors) are requested to the following enquiries.

The replies are as follows:

Dwellings

1.   Are there any dwellings on the Property? If so, please:

1.1   specify which are sold with vacant possession;

1.2   in relation to each of the other dwellings, reply to the enquiries under the heading 'Dwellings' in the attached supplemental enquiries.

2.   Is any dwelling on the Property affected by an agricultural user restriction under any planning permission? If so, please give details.

3.   Please provide details of the Council Tax band of each dwelling on the Property and the current amounts payable.

4.   Has an improvement grant been received or approved for any dwelling during the last six years? If so, please:

4.1   state the date on which the local authority certified the dwelling as being fit for occupation after completion of the relevant works;

4.2   confirm that all the conditions of the grant were complied with throughout the period of five years beginning with the certified date and that no part of the improvement grant became or has become repayable.

5.   Is there a septic tank on or serving any part of the Property? If so, please mark its position on a plan, also showing the position of all associated pipes and the overflow.

Occupancy

6.   Please confirm that:

6.1   vacant possession of the whole will be given on completion;

6.2   no right of holdover will be required.

7.   If vacant possession of the whole will not be given:

7.1   please supply details of all persons other than the Seller now occupying or farming any part of the Property (other than any dwelling);

7.2   on what basis do those persons occupy or farm the part concerned?

8.   Please specify any sporting rights which are not in hand and supply full details of, and a copy of any relevant document relating to, the exercise of any such rights.

Rights of way

9.   Has any footpath or other public right of way on the Property been ploughed up? If so, please supply details and a copy of the relevant notice.

3 SALE AND ACQUISITION OF LAND

In-filling

10. Has there been any in-filling on the Property? If so, please:

10.1 supply full details, including the dates and the nature of the in-filling;

10.2 state the use to which the land had previously been put.

Flooding/subsidence

11. Please give details of:

11.1 any flooding that has affected the Property;

11.2 any subsidence or heave which has affected any structure on the Property.

Disease

12.1 Have any cattle which have been on the Property within the last six years suffered from bovine spongiform encephalopathy? If so, please give details.

12.2 Have any animals on the Property been affected by foot and mouth disease or any other notifiable disease? If so, please give details.

12.3 Is any part of the Property affected by disease, pests or persistent weeds, eg wireworm, rhizomania, blackgrass. If so, please supply details.

Employees

13. Are any employees of the Seller employed wholly or mainly on the Property? If so, in relation to each, please:

13.1 give his date of birth;

13.2 provide a copy of his contract of employment;

13.3 give full details of any terms of his employment which are not set out in the contract of employment.

Adverse matters

14.   Is the Seller aware of any past existing or proposed public or private rights of way claimed or exercised over the Property? If so, please supply full details, including copies of all orders and notices.

15.   Please supply full details of any of the following of which the Seller is aware:

15.1   any other rights or informal arrangements affecting the Property;

15.2   any restrictions affecting the Property, other than any referred to in the draft contract;

15.3   any other overriding interests as defined by the Land Registration Act 1926, s 70(1) (Note: If the title is unregistered, please reply as if it were registered).

16.   Does the Seller own or occupy any adjoining or nearby property? If so, please:

16.1   specify the property concerned;

16.2   supply details of all quasi-easements or analogous rights or privileges enjoyed by such property over or affecting the Property, with details of the part of that property which has the benefit of them.

17.   Is any part of the Property subject to any liability for chancel repair, corn rent or other unusual liability or payment? If so, please give full details.

Copyhold[1]

18.   Was any part of the Property formerly copyhold? If so, please supply details.

Planning

19.   Please supply a copy of each planning permission which relates to the Property or any part of it.

20.   In relation to each agricultural building please state whether it was erected or altered:

20.1   under a specific planning permission;

3 SALE AND ACQUISITION OF LAND

20.2 in reliance on the terms of the General Development Order.

21. If any part of the Property is used for a non-agricultural use (eg farm shop, cottage holiday lettings, commercial buildings etc), please supply full details.

22. Is there an established use certificate relating to any part of the Property or has there ever been an unsuccessful application for such a certificate? If so, please supply a copy with its plan (if any).

23. Is any building on the Property a listed building? If so, please:
23.1 specify the building;
23.2 supply a copy of the listing;
23.3 confirm that no listed items have been removed or altered;
23.4 supply a copy of any listed building consent obtained;
23.5 confirm that no works for which listed building consent was required have been carried out without such consent.

24. Is there any field/ancient monument on any part of the Property? If so, please supply particulars.

25. Is the Seller aware that any part of the Property is, or is likely to be, designated as an area of archaeological importance? If so, please give details.

Set-aside, area aid and quotas
26. Has the Property been registered for the Guaranteed Set-Aside Scheme? If so, please supply a copy of the registration form and of all relevant correspondence.

27. Has the land been registered for area aid under the Arable Area Payment Scheme ('the Scheme')? If so, please reply to the enquiries under the heading 'Land registered for Arable Aid' in the attached supplemental enquiries.

28. If the land has not been registered under the Scheme, please:

28.1 specify the use to which each part of the Property was put at 31.12.91;

28.2 supply details of the cropping during the period from 1.1.87 to 31.12.91 of any land in temporary grass on 31.12.91;

confirm that the land has not been deprived of previous eligibility.

29. Is the Buyer to receive the area aid payment for the current year? If so, please reply to the enquiries under the heading 'Aid payment to buyer' in the attached supplemental enquiries.

30. *Suckler cow and ewe premium quota*

Does the Property or the Seller have any suckler cow or ewe quota entitlement in respect of which the Buyer is to acquire any rights? If so, please:

30.1 supply copies of the latest forms in respect of any applications made under these schemes;

30.2 supply details of payments made, headage numbers and, where appropriate, details of any identification documents;

30.3 give details of all land farmed by the Seller in the United Kingdom, with details of the basis of occupation.

31. *Other quotas*

Does the Property have the benefit of any sugar beet or milk sale contract or milk quota? If so, please:

31.1 supply full details;

31.2 confirm that the Seller will co-operate for the Buyer's accession to the contracts and quota concerned.

Water and drainage

32. Is any water used on or for the Property obtained otherwise than from a main supply? If so, please:

3 SALE AND ACQUISITION OF LAND

32.1   supply a copy of the requisite water abstraction or other licence and any supplemental documents;

32.2   confirm that the conditions of the licence(s) have been fully complied with, or supply details of any breach;

32.3   confirm that the Seller will serve notice within 21 days of completion transferring the licence to the Buyer.

33.   If any non-mains water for which no licence is held by the Seller is used on the Property, please supply full details of:

33.1   the source of such water;

33.2   the amount consumed or used;

33.3   the use to which the water is put.

34.   Is there any dam or weir on the Property which requires an impounding licence? If so, please:

34.1   supply details and a copy of any licence held;

34.2   confirm that the conditions of the licence have been fully complied with, or supply full details of any breach.

35.   If payments are made pursuant to any licence relating to water, are they made at the full rate? If not, please supply details of the payments made and a copy of any relevant document.

36.   Are there any water meters or water abstraction meters serving the Property? If so, please:

36.1   supply a plan showing their position;

36.2   confirm that each of them is in good working order and condition.

37.   Is the Seller aware of any unsuccessful application for any licence relating to water? If so, please supply details.

38.   If the Property abuts upon a river, or if the Property is in any way affected by any watercourses, please:

38.1   confirm that the ownership of the entire watercourse passes with the Property so far as co-extensive;

38.2	confirm that there are no public or private rights along the co-extensive banks of the river or watercourse;
38.3	confirm that the fishing is in hand;
38.4	give the names and addresses of the appropriate River Authority and Drainage Board and say which of the river and watercourses they maintain;
38.5	give details of the rights of drainage into the river or watercourse.

39. Please confirm that on completion plans of the land drains on the Property will be handed over.

40. As to the drainage system serving the Property:

40.1 does the Seller have any reason to doubt the right to use it? If so, please give details.

40.2 who maintains the drains?

40.3 has the system been the subject of, or caused, any dispute? If so, please supply details.

Groundwater regulations

41. Please supply a copy of any authorisation under the Groundwater Regulations.

41.1 Please confirm that the Seller will serve notice within 21 days of completion transferring the authorisation to the Buyer.

41.2 Please supply details of disposal and tipping within the last 5 years and since 1 April 1999.

Environment

42. Has the Seller, or anyone to the Seller's knowledge, carried out any environmental audit, assessment or investigation of the Property? If so, please provide a copy.

3 SALE AND ACQUISITION OF LAND

43. Have any proceedings been instituted or has the Seller any knowledge
of contemplated proceedings in
respect of any environmental or
environment-related issues arising
from the use or activity on the
Property?

44. Has the Property been the subject of
any formal or informal investigation
by any regulatory body in respect of
any environmental or environment-
related issues arising from any use or
activity on the Property?

45. Please confirm that the Seller warrants that so far as he is aware the
Property has not been contaminated
or in any way affected by the deposit
or presence, however temporary, of
any hazardous or toxic material or
other pollutant whether such arose
on the Property or from any adjoining or neighbouring property.

46. Please supply copies of any docu-
mentary or other information produced by or on behalf of the Seller or
in the possession or control of the
Seller relating to any contamination
or pollution which is or may be
present in the Property or to the
actual or intended use of the Property
including any environmental or similar assessment.

47. In relation to the Property, or any
process or activity carried on there by
the Seller or anyone else now or in
the past, is the Seller aware of any
potential or actual civil or criminal
liability? If so, please provide full
details.

48.   Is the Seller aware of any circum-
            stances which might lead to the
            NRA, any Waste Regulation
            Authority, the Health and Safety
            Executive, or any other authority
            exercising any of its powers in respect
            of the Property? If so, please provide
            full details.

49.   Has any notice been served under
            s 51 of the Public Health Act 1936 in
            respect of either farm buildings or
            ancillary fixed plant (eg defective
            slurry tanks)? If so, please supply a
            copy.

50.   Is the Property affected by any matter
            under the Control of Pollution Act
            1974? If so, please give details.

51.   Is any part of the Property designated
            as an Environmentally Sensitive
            Area, a Nitrate Sensitive Area, a Site
            of Special Scientific Interest, a
            Nitrate Vulnerable Zone or any
            other special area or zone? If so,
            please provide copies of all relevant
            documents.

52.   Is the Property subject to any
            environmental land management
            scheme? If so, please supply a copy,
            with any other relevant documents.

53.   If the Property is in a Nitrate Vulner-
            able Zone please supply details of:
53.1   fertiliser;
53.2   manure;
            applied to the Property in the last 6
            years and since 19 December 1998
            on a field by field basis.

Genetically modified organisms
54.   Has any part of the Property been
            used for growing any plant which has
            been 'genetically modified' within
            the meaning of Part IV of the
            Environmental Protection Act 1990?

Woodlands

55.   Please supply full details of:

55.1   any Woodland Grant Scheme;

55.2   any other forestry grant;

55.3   any tree planting scheme carried out during the last five years.

56.   Please supply full details of all felling licences and felling directions affecting the Property and confirm that all their terms have been complied with.

Grants

57.   Except as already disclosed, has the Property or any part of it been included in any scheme under which moneys have been paid by way of grant or otherwise? If so, please reply to the enquiries under the heading 'Grants' in the attached supplemental enquiries.

Taxation

58.   Is any part of the purchase price subject to VAT? If so, please:

58.1   confirm that the purchase price stated in the draft contract is inclusive of VAT;

58.2   supply evidence of any relevant election to waive exemption from VAT.

59.   If no such waiver election has been made, please confirm that the Seller will not make such an election in relation to the Property.

60.   Are there any unused capital or agricultural buildings allowances? If so, please specify:

60.1   the nature and amount of the relevant expenditure;

60.2   the date the expenditure was incurred;

60.3   the allowances used to date.

Investment property

61. Is any part of the Property (other than a dwelling) occupied by anyone who may by virtue of that occupancy ('the letting') be entitled to claim a tenancy under the Agricultural Holdings Act 1986 ('AHA 1986') the Agricultural Tenancies Act 1995 or under Part II of the Landlord and Tenant Act 1954? If so, please reply to the enquiries under the heading 'Investment Property' in the attached supplemental enquiries.

General

62. *Boundaries*

62.1 Please specify (by reference to a plan or sketch) the boundary features and the ownership of each of them.

62.2 Of those not owned by the Seller, which (if any) has the Seller maintained or regarded as his responsibility to maintain?

62.3 Is the Seller aware of any alterations to the physical boundaries of the Property whether before or during his period of ownership? If so, please give details.

62.4 Is it necessary to enter upon any adjoining or neighbouring premises to maintain or repair any boundary feature or any building on the Property? If so, please give details and state:

62.4.1 by what right entry is obtained;

62.4.2 whether any neighbour has objected? If so, please give details.

62.5 Does the Seller own or occupy any adjoining property? If so, please specify.

63. *Disputes*

Please give details of the following of which the Seller is aware:

63.1 any dispute (whether resolved or not) relating to the Property;

63.2 any trespass or encroachment on the Property within the last three years;

3 SALE AND ACQUISITION OF LAND

63.3   any complaints or causes of complaint within the last three years relating to any adjoining or neighbouring property.

64.   *Notices*
Except where already supplied in reply to a previous enquiry, please give particulars of all notices, whether given or received, relating to the Property of which the Seller is aware.

65.   *Guarantees etc*
65.1   Are there any guarantees, warranties, or other arrangements relating to any improvement to, or treatment or repair of, the Property or any items included in the sale? If so, please:
65.1.1   supply copies together with copies of any documents and papers (including assignments) which may be relevant;
65.1.2   give details of any defects which have become apparent;
65.1.3   give details of any notice given or claims made in relation to any such document with a copy of any relevant document.
65.2   Please confirm that the Seller will assign (if appropriate) the benefit of any guarantees etc of which he has the benefit.

66.   *Services*
66.1   Does the Property have surface water and foul drainage, electricity, water and gas services?
66.2   Which of these are connected to the mains?
66.3   Is the water supply to the Property metered? If not, has the Seller received notification that compulsory metering is to be imposed?
66.4   Do any of the services pass through or over property not included in the sale? If so:
66.4.1   please give details of the routes;
66.4.2   by what right?

66.5   Please confirm that the Seller is not aware of any defect or want of repair in any of the services.

67.   *Fixtures, fittings and plant*

67.1   Please specify:

67.1.1   any fixtures fittings or plant on the Property which are not included in the sale;

67.1.2   any fixtures fittings or plant on the Property which, although not included in the sale, are available for purchase and say on what terms they may be acquired by the Buyer.

67.2   Please confirm that all items included in the sale or to be sold to the Buyer separately are the sole and absolute property of the Seller and are not subject to any hire purchase, credit sale, re-sale or other agreement or encumbrance.

67.3   If any items are to be removed, please confirm that all damage occasioned by their removal will be made good prior to completion.

68.   *Outgoings*

68.1   Please specify all outgoings (other than Council Tax) payable in respect of the Property.

68.2   Please confirm that all outgoings (including Council Tax) payable before completion have been or will be paid by then and receipts for those payments will be produced on completion.

---

1   This is likely to be relevant where there may be minerals within the property as it may affect the mineral rights. Reference should be made to the appropriate textbook.

3 SALE AND ACQUISITION OF LAND

2 SUPPLEMENTAL ENQUIRIES BEFORE CONTRACT

SUPPLEMENTAL ENQUIRIES BEFORE CONTRACT

Property: ....

Parties: ....

....

Ref: ....   Ref: ....

Buyer's solicitors: ....   Seller's solicitors: ....

....

Dated: ....   Dated: ....

Replies (based on the knowledge of the Seller and, where relevant, of his solicitors) are requested to the following enquiries.

The replies are as follows:

Dwellings

1.   Please supply:

1.1   full details (including age) of each occupier;

1.2   a copy of any document evidencing all or any of the terms of occupation.

2.   Insofar as they are not shown by any copy document supplied, please:

2.1   supply a plan of the area occupied, unless this is self-evident on the ground;

2.2   supply full details of any rights enjoyed or suffered by the dwelling;

2.3   specify the commencement date of the current occupation;

2.4   specify the period of the letting;

2.5   specify the respective repairing and other obligations undertaken by the owner and the occupier;

2.6   state who is responsible for emptying any septic tank;

2.7   give full details of any specific insurance.

3.   In relation to the rent or any other payment by the occupier:

3.1   how much is it?

3.2   on what dates is it payable?

3.3   is it payable in advance or in arrear?

3.4   please say when and how it was last fixed, and supply a copy of any relevant document;

3.5   have there been any arrears during the last twelve months? If so, please give details.

4.   If the tenancy was created before 15 January 1989 is the rent registered? If so, please supply a copy of the registration and any notice of increase.

5.   What was the rateable value of the dwelling on 31 March 1990?

6.   Has there been a succession to the tenancy? If so, please supply full details.

7.   Has the tenant been supplied with the statutory particulars of the local rent allowance scheme? If so, how?

8.   Has the landlord reeived payment of the tenant's rent allowance direct from the local authority?

9.   Has the Seller, or any predecessor in title, applied to the housing authority to rehouse the tenant, under the Rent (Agriculture) Act 1976, s 27? If so:

9.1   what was the result?

9.2   please supply copies of the MAFF assessment, the advice of the agricultural dwellinghouse advisory committee, and the decision of the authority.

IACS

Land registered for arable aid

10.   Please provide:

10.1   a copy of all relevant forms submitted to MAFF including field data printouts with the accompanying schedules and plan(s) for the last 3 years;

10.2   details of any queries raised by
        MAFF.

11.   Please:
11.1   supply a copy of the application form
        as submitted to MAFF;
11.2   confirm that all scheme rules have
        been complied with or give details of
        any breaches.

12.   In relation to land set-aside during
        the current or latest set-aside period,
        please:
12.1   specify any use for non-food crops;
12.2   specify any non-agricultural use;
12.3   supply details of any acts of cultiva-
        tion carried out during that period.

13.   Please provide details of:
13.1   the area of the Property taken up by
        any permanent structures above the
        surface;
13.2   any cables, pipelines, wires or other
        permanent installations placed on the
        Property within the last twelve
        months or to be placed thereon in
        future to the Seller's knowledge;
13.3   any compensation received for use of
        land, damage or loss of crops;
13.4   any islands within the Property aris-
        ing by reason of such installation,
        specifying whether they are:
13.4.1 sown;
13.4.2 inaccessible;
13.4.3 set-aside.

14. Please give details and a plan together with supporting claims to MAFF of any land on which fibre flax or hemp was grown and aid received under the fibre flax and hemp subsidy schemes in 1998, 1999 or 2000.

Aid payment to buyer

15. Is any of the land on which the Seller is claiming aid currently occupied by anyone other than the Seller? If so, please provide evidence that the occupier is obliged to observe the IACS Rules and comply with the conditions of the scheme.

16. Please supply details of the area aid payments to be received, giving the expected: amount; approximate dates of payment; and the payee.

17. Please confirm that, if so required by the Buyer, the Seller will enter into a written agreement to confirm the Buyer's entitlement to the payments.

18. Please confirm that, if the payment is received by the Seller, the Seller will forthwith pay the amount received to the Buyer.

19. Please confirm that the Seller will provide all necessary documents and sign all documents needed to assure the aid entitlement to the Buyer and ensure its due payment.

Grants

20. Please supply copies of any current scheme, together with details of the following:

20.1 works carried out in accordance with the scheme;

20.2 the dates of payment of the grant or other moneys, the amounts paid, and the payee;

20.3 the conditions imposed by the scheme and any further or subsequent conditions imposed;

20.4   any breaches of the conditions of the
        scheme with copies of all correspon-
        dence in connection therewith;
20.5   all moneys repaid in accordance with
        the scheme.

21.   In relation to any expired scheme,
        please confirm that:
21.1   the conditions of the scheme were
        fully complied with;
21.2   no grant or other moneys received
        under the scheme may become
        repayable.

Investment property
22.   Please supply:
22.1   full details (including age) of anyone
        occupying the whole or any part of
        the Property under the letting;
22.2   a copy of any document evidencing
        all or any of the terms of the letting.

23.   If the letting is of only part of the
        Property, then insofar as they are not
        shown by any copy document sup-
        plied, please:
23.1   supply a plan of the part of the
        Property comprised in the letting;
23.2   supply full details of any rights
        enjoyed or suffered by that part.

24.   Please:
24.1   specify the commencement date of
        the letting;
24.2   specify the period of the letting;
24.3   specify the respective repairing and
        other obligations undertaken by the
        owner and the occupier.

25.   In relation to the rent or any other
        payment by the occupier:
25.1   how much is it?
25.2   on what dates is it payable?
25.3   is it payable in advance or in arrear?
25.4   please say when and how it was last
        fixed, and supply a copy of any
        relevant document;
25.5   have there been any arrears during
        the last two years? If so, please give
        details.

26.   Have the owner and the occupier concluded any agreement as to the amount of the rent or any other sum which is to be payable for any future period? If so, please give particulars.

27.   If the occupier insures the Property or part concerned, please give particulars of the existing cover, stating the name and address of the insurers and any brokers, the policy number, the insured name(s), the risks covered, for what amount, the premium and the date to which insurance runs.

28.   Has any notice to quit relating to the Property or any part been served? If so, please supply a copy of the notice and any relevant details.

29.   Are there any outstanding matters arising from any notice served by the landlord:

29.1   under the Law of Property Act 1925, s 146?

29.2   under the AHA 1986, ss 26–28 and Schedule 3 Cases D, E and F or under the ATA 1995?
If so, please supply details.

30.   Please supply details of all agricultural tenancy successions.

31.   Please supply a list of, and all matters agreed as to:

31.1   tenant's fixtures on the Property;

31.2   tenant's improvements on the Property.

32.   Please supply copies of:

32.1   all licences or consents granted for any tenant's improvements that have been carried out or are to be carried out;

32.2   all notices to the Agricultural Land Tribunal or arbitrator for approval by the Tribunal or an arbitrator (AHA 1986, s 67) (ATA 1995, s 19).

3 SALE AND ACQUISITION OF LAND

33.   Have there been any other tenant's
           improvements for which consent was
           NOT granted? If so, please give full
           details.

34.   Has the owner refused any appli-
           cation for consent from the occupier?
           If so, please give details.

---

3   CONTRACT CLAUSES

There follows a range of optional clauses.

1.   **Area aid scheme**

1.1   The Property forms part of the land registered for area aid payments by the
           Seller.

1.2   Subject to paragraph 1.8 all area aid payments and set-aside payments in
           respect of the Property or any part thereof for . . . (whenever received) shall
           belong to the Seller.

1.3   The Buyer shall permit the staff and agents of the Ministry of Agriculture
           Fisheries and Food such access to the Property at such times as they may
           require in connection with the area aid payment scheme relating to the
           Property.

1.4   The Seller warrants to the Buyer as follows:

1.4.1   that he is not aware of any reason why any part of the Property (with the
           exception of permanent woodland spinneys cottages and gardens buildings
           and yards roads and ponds which amount to not more than . . . hectares in
           total) is not eligible for area aid payments;

1.4.2   that (save as aforesaid) no part of the Property was on 31 December 1991
           being used for any of the following purposes:
           −   permanent crops;
           −   woodland;
           −   non-agricultural use;
           −   as land which had already been entered into any scheme other than
                the area aid payment scheme;

1.4.3   that he has received no complaints or objections from the Ministry of
           Agriculture Fisheries and Food regarding his application for area aid
           payments for . . . ;

1.4.4   that he knows of no reason why he should not receive his . . . area aid
           payments without deduction or delay.

1.5   The Buyer shall be responsible for applying to register the Property for area
           aid payments under the said scheme for . . . and all area aid payments and
           set-aside payments in respect of the Property for . . . shall belong to the
           Buyer.

1.6 The Buyer shall comply with all the requirements of the area payments scheme in relation to the Property from the date of Completion or (where earlier) the date of entry by the Buyer.

1.7 The Seller warrants to the Buyer that the information on the Integrated Administration and Control System forms submitted to the Ministry of Agriculture Fisheries and Food was correct at the time such forms were submitted and further warrants that the Seller has duly complied with and will until Completion continue to comply with all requirements of the Integrated Administration and Control System in relation to the Property.

1.8 All instalments due under the Integrated Administration and Control System in respect of the Property for agrimonetary compensation for the years 1999 and 2000 shall if paid to the Seller forthwith on receipt be paid by the Seller to the Buyer.[1]

---

1 It is understood that payments will be made to the 1999 claimant in 2000 and 2001 and to the 2000 claimant in 2001. The Buyer may want a clause like this. Unless a retention is made, clearly the money is at risk!

---

1. Milk quota

1.1 It is the intention of the parties hereto that no milk quota shall pass with the Property or be transferred as a result of this transaction and each party agrees with the other not to claim the transfer of any milk quota.

1.2 If despite that intention milk quota is transferred then:

1.2.1 if it is transferred in pursuance of a claim made by the Buyer or any person claiming title under him the Buyer shall forthwith procure the transfer to the Seller without expense to the Seller of an equivalent amount of such quota to that lost by the Seller;

1.2.2 if it is transferred without any such claim the Buyer shall forthwith effect or procure the transfer to the Seller without expense to the Buyer/the Seller (*delete as appropriate*) of the milk quota so transferred;

1.2.3 if such transfer cannot be made for whatever reason the Buyer shall as soon as practicable after it has been ascertained that such transfer back cannot be made sell or (as the case may be) procure the sale of the milk quota in question at the best price reasonably obtainable at the time of such sale and account to the Seller for the net proceeds of sale thereof.

1.3 The Buyer will co-operate with the Seller in signing any forms and assisting in the granting of any tenancies to assist the sale by the Seller of any Milk Quota attached to the Holding.

1.4 The parties hereto shall co-operate to secure the results provided for in this clause.

3 SALE AND ACQUISITION OF LAND

Note. The Buyer should consider carefully such a clause; he may not have bargained for the creation of tenancies, even if he enters into a contracting agreement on the land, and his capital gains position may well be prejudiced.

1.   Sugar beet contract

1.1   If the Buyer is a registered grower the Seller will give up . . . tonnes of A and B sugar beet contract tonnage to the British Sugar Corporation immediately upon Completion so as to facilitate the grant of a replacement contract to the Buyer.

1.2   The Seller shall at the expense of the Buyer use such reasonable endeavours and execute such further documents as may reasonably be required to enable the Buyer to obtain the benefit of the said contract tonnage (less the appropriate deduction).

1.3   If the Buyer is not a registered grower he shall at his own expense use such reasonable endeavours and execute such further documents as may reasonably be required to enable the Seller to retain the said contract tonnage.

1.   Quotas – no transfer

It is not intended that the benefit of any quota or contract tonnage now held with or applicable to the Property or any part thereof should pass to the Buyer or with the Property and the Buyer shall do all such things and sign all such documents as the Seller may reasonably require to achieve that position.

1.   Tenantright

1.1   In addition to the Price the Buyer shall on Completion pay to the Seller the sum of . . . in respect of all items in the nature of tenantright.

1.   Tenantright – valuation by seller's agent

1.1   In addition to the Price the Buyer shall pay to the Seller a sum equal to the valuation of the items specified in the next sub-clause in accordance with The Agriculture (Calculation of Value for Compensation) Regulations 1978 to 1983 and the prices and recommendations of the Association of Agricultural Valuers and for the purposes of such valuation all appropriate notices shall be deemed to have been served the Seller shall be deemed to be the outgoing tenant and the Buyer shall be deemed to be the landlord of the Property under a yearly tenancy to which the Agricultural Holdings Act 1986 applies and of which the last year had commenced one year before the Completion Date.

1.2	The items to be so valued are:
1.2.1	seeds sown cost of cultivations (including beneficial cultivation to set-aside land) fertilisers and sprays applied growing crops residual manurial values and the unexpired value of lime and slag applied;
1.2.2	all sprays fertilisers seeds fuel and oil in store as at the date for valuation;
1.2.3	enhancement where appropriate.
1.3	The valuation shall be made as at the date on which the Buyer takes occupation of the Property or the part to which the valuation relates.
1.4	The amount of such valuation shall be assessed by the Seller's Agents whose valuation shall be final and binding on the parties hereto.
1.5	The amount payable under this clause shall be paid on Completion or within seven days of being ascertained (whichever is the later)/within seven days of being ascertained (*delete as appropriate*) (together with interest thereon at the contract rate from the date as at which the valuation is to be made until payment★) but neither party shall be entitled to delay Completion on the ground that the amount of such valuation has not by then been ascertained.

★delete if inapplicable

1. Tenantright – valuation by respective agents

1.1	In addition to the Price the Buyer shall pay to the Seller a sum equal to the valuation of the items specified in the next sub-clause in accordance with The Agriculture (Calculation of Value for Compensation) Regulations 1978 to 1983 and the prices and recommendations of the Association of Agricultural Valuers and for the purposes of such valuation all appropriate notices shall be deemed to have been served the Seller shall be deemed to be the outgoing tenant and the Buyer shall be deemed to be the landlord of the Property under a yearly tenancy to which the Agricultural Holdings Act 1986 applies and of which the last year had commenced one year before the Completion Date.
1.2	The items to be so valued are:
1.2.1	seeds sown cost of cultivations (including beneficial cultivation to set-aside land) fertilisers and sprays applied growing crops residual manurial values and the unexpired value of lime and slag applied;
1.2.2	all sprays fertilisers seeds fuel and oil in store as at the date for valuation;
1.2.3	enhancement where appropriate.
1.3	The valuation shall be made as at the date on which the Buyer takes occupation of the Property or the part to which the valuation relates.
1.4	Subject to the provisions of the next two following paragraphs of this sub-clause such valuation shall be made and agreed by the Seller's Agents and the Buyer's Agents.
1.4.1	Unless the Buyer's Agents are named in this Agreement the Buyer shall notify their name and address to the Seller's Agents in writing within five working days from the date hereof (as to which time shall be of the essence) and in default thereof the valuation shall be carried out by the Seller's Agents alone.

3 SALE AND ACQUISITION OF LAND

1.4.2   If the respective agents have not agreed the valuation within . . . weeks of the Seller's Agents submitting the claim to the Buyer's Agents the matter shall be referred to arbitration by a single arbitrator under the provisions of the Arbitration Act 1996 the arbitrator to be agreed between the respective agents or in default of such agreement to be nominated by the President for the time being of the Royal Institution of Chartered Surveyors upon the application of either party but at the joint and equal expense of the Seller and the Buyer.

1.5   The valuation made agreed or determined in accordance with this clause shall be final and binding on the parties hereto.

1.6   The amount payable under this clause shall be paid on Completion or within seven days of being ascertained (whichever is the later)/within seven days of being ascertained (*delete as appropriate*) (together with interest thereon at the contract rate from the date as at which the valuation is to be made until payment★) but neither party shall be entitled to delay Completion on the ground that the amount of such valuation has not by then been ascertained.

★delete if inapplicable

1.   No tenantright

1.1   No sum shall be payable by the Buyer in respect of any item in the nature of tenantright or otherwise beyond the Price.

1.   No dilapidations

The Buyer shall not be entitled to claim or make any deduction whatsoever for dilapidations or otherwise.

1.   Included items

1.1   Only the equipment and farm machinery detailed in the Schedule of Equipment/specified in the annexed inventory (*delete as appropriate*) (which the Seller warrants to be his own unencumbered property) is included in the sale★ and in particular there are excluded from the sale . . . ★

1.2   The sum of . . . (part of the Price) shall be apportioned to the equipment and machinery included in the sale.

★delete if inapplicable

1.   Excluded items

1.1   All items normally designated as tenant's fixtures (including . . .★) are excluded from the sale.

1.2   The items excluded from the sale insofar as they belong to the Seller may be removed by the Seller by Completion/[*date*] (*delete as appropriate*) but any such items not so removed by the Seller shall thereupon become the property of the Buyer without payment.

1.3   Insofar as such items do not belong to the Seller the Seller shall not be required to remove them and the provisions of sub-clause 2 of this clause shall not apply to them.

*delete if inapplicable

1.   Holdover – crops and storage

1.1   There are reserved out of the sale all crops growing on the Property at the date hereof together with the right for all appropriate persons with or without vehicles and equipment to come upon the Property after Completion from time to time up to and including [*date*] with or without equipment for any of the purposes of cultivating harvesting storing and removing such crops.

1.2   The Property will be left in the condition in which it is after the crops have been properly harvested.

1.3   There is also reserved the right to store and ventilate potatoes onions and corn in the buildings on the Property up to and including [*date*] together with full rights of access for all appropriate persons with or without vehicles and equipment for any of the purposes of depositing protecting inspecting conditioning and loading for delivery.

1.4   The Buyer shall provide such facilities labour fuel electricity and use of machinery as the Seller reasonably requires in connection with any of the rights reserved by this clause but shall be entitled to recover from the Seller the reasonable cost of such provision on written request with appropriate supporting documentation.

1.5   The crops shall be stored at the risk of the Seller and the Buyer shall not be liable for any loss or deterioration of the crops whether before or after harvest.

1.6   The Seller shall be responsible for and make good to the Buyer's reasonable satisfaction any damage done to the Property (including any buildings) by reason of the exercise of any of the rights reserved by this clause and shall compensate the Buyer in respect of any damage not capable of being made good*.

1.7   Neither the Seller nor any other person shall incur any liability whatsoever to the Buyer for any damage done to the Property (including any buildings) by reason of the exercise of any of the rights reserved by this clause*.

*delete if inapplicable

1.   Holdover – use and removal of buildings

1.1   For the period of ... months following Completion (or for such lesser period as the Seller may specify by notice in writing to the Buyer expiring not earlier than the date of that notice) the Seller reserves the right:

1.1.1   to use the Buildings or any of them in a similar way as heretofore for the purpose of ... ;

1.1.2   to dismantle and remove the Buildings or any of them;
           in each case together with all appropriate rights of access for himself his employees and contractors with or without vehicles and equipment at all times and for all reasonable purposes.

1.2   During the subsistence of the rights specified in sub-clause 1 of this clause:

1.2.1   the Seller shall discharge all outgoings in respect of the Buildings and shall indemnify the Buyer in respect thereof;

1.2.2   the Buildings and their contents shall be at the entire risk of the Seller who may (but shall not be under any obligation to) insure the Buildings or any of them.

1.3   Any of the Buildings not removed by the end of the period referred to in sub-clause 1 of this clause shall vest in the Buyer without payment at the expiration of that period.

1.   Stock/equipment sale

1.1   There is reserved the right to hold an auction sale of live and dead stock equipment and machinery in the enclosure numbered ... on the Ordnance Survey plan on or before [*date*] (in connection with which auction sale the Buyer undertakes to leave an agreed area within the said enclosure in stubble and unploughed until after the sale) and the right for all appropriate persons (including the purchasers of such stock equipment and machinery) to enter upon the Property with employees or contractors and any necessary equipment for the purpose of storing and removing the same at any time up to and including [*date*].

1.2   There is also reserved the right to store the said dead stock equipment and machinery in the buildings on the Property with all reasonable rights of access in connection therewith until [*date*] or if earlier seven days after the auction sale provided for in this clause.

1.3   Neither the Seller nor any other person shall incur any liability whatsoever to the Buyer for any damage done to the Property or any buildings thereon in the exercise or purported exercise of the rights reserved by this clause.

1.   Early entry – cultivation

1.1   On payment to the Seller of a further deposit equal to ten per cent of the Price the Buyer shall be permitted as licensee and not as tenant to enter on the Property/each cropping area forming part of the Property after it has been cleared of the current crop for the purpose of cultivating the crops on the Property/preparing the area concerned for and planting the following crop (*delete as appropriate*) but for no other purpose.

1.2 The Buyer shall:

1.2.1 ensure that in the exercise of the permission granted by this clause no damage or loss is occasioned to the Property or the Seller and as little inconvenience as practicable is occasioned to the Seller;

1.2.2 pay or indemnify the Seller against all outgoings and other expenses in respect of the Property or the part concerned (as the case may be) for the period during which that right is exercisable.

1.3 No interest shall be payable by the Buyer solely by reference to the permission granted by this clause.

1.4 The permission granted by this clause:

1.4.1 is personal to the Buyer save that he may exercise it by any employee or agricultural contractor of the Buyer;

1.4.2 ends on the earlier of the date for Completion and the rescission of this Agreement.

1. Early entry – buildings

1.1 On payment to the Seller of a further deposit equal to ten per cent of the Price the Buyer shall be permitted as licensee and not as tenant to store . . . in the buildings on the Property.

1.2 The Buyer shall:

1.2.1 be permitted all appropriate rights of entry on the Property with or without vehicles and equipment to enable him to exercise the permission granted by this clause but for no other purpose;

1.2.2 not alter the buildings in any way;

1.2.3 ensure that in the exercise of the permission granted by this clause no damage or loss is occasioned to the Property or the Seller and as little inconvenience as practicable is occasioned to the Seller;

1.2.4 pay or indemnify the Seller against all outgoings and other expenses (including the cost of electricity used) in respect of the buildings or their use for the period during which the permission is exercisable.

1.3 No interest shall be payable by the Buyer solely by reference to the permission granted by this clause.

1.4 The permission granted by this clause:

1.4.1 is personal to the Buyer save that he may exercise it by any employee or contractor of the Buyer;

1.4.2 ends on the earlier of the date for Completion and the rescission of this Agreement.

3 SALE AND ACQUISITION OF LAND

1.5   As from the date hereof the risk of damage to the buildings passes to the Buyer.[1]

---

1   Not required if there is a general provision that risk passes to the Buyer immediately.

---

1.   Drainage rates

The Buyer shall pay and indemnify the Seller in respect of the drainage rates payable in relation to those parts of the Property upon which the Buyer enters from and including the respective dates of entry and on the whole of the Property from and including the Completion Date.

1.   Dwellings – subject to occupancy

The dwellings on the Property are sold subject to the rights of their respective occupiers (as to which the Buyer shall raise no requisition objection or enquiry) and no warranty is given by the Seller that vacant possession of any of those dwellings may be obtained.

1.   Dwellings – occupiers to be relocated

1.1   The dwellings on the Property are occupied by ... and ... as tenants/ service occupiers.

1.2   Each of them has been given notice to vacate and the Seller shall use all reasonable endeavours (but so that whether or not any monetary payment is made shall be in the absolute discretion of the Seller) to re-locate the said tenants/occupiers so as to be able to give vacant possession of the said dwellings to the Buyer on Completion and on re-locating the last of those tenants/occupiers elsewhere shall give written notice of that fact to the Buyer.

1.3   If at Completion the tenancies/occupations (*delete as appropriate*) of the said dwellings or any of them are still subsisting the sale is subject to and with the benefit thereof.

1.   Dwellings – retention

1.1   If the Seller is unable to give vacant possession of any of the dwellings on the Property on Completion the sale and purchase shall nevertheless be completed but in relation to each dwelling of which vacant possession is not then given
EITHER

the Buyer shall be entitled to retain the sum of . . . pounds from the Price until he is notified in writing by the Seller that the dwelling concerned has been vacated by its present occupier whereupon the Buyer shall within . . . working days of the giving of that notice pay the said sum to the Seller without interest but if not paid within that period the said sum shall carry interest at the contract rate from the date of the giving of such notice until payment.

OR

the sum of . . . pounds shall be retained from the Price and invested in an account with . . . in the joint names of the Seller's Solicitors and the Buyer's Solicitors the interest whereon shall belong to the Buyer until such time as vacant possession is given whereupon the relevant sum or sums and any subsequent interest thereon shall forthwith be released to the Seller.

1.2 The Seller shall use all reasonable endeavours to obtain and deliver to the Buyer full vacant possession of the dwellings as soon as practicable.

1.3 Until the Retention End Date in relation to each dwelling the Seller shall be entitled to all rents and profits of but shall be responsible for all outgoings in respect of that dwelling (in each case apportioned where appropriate).

1.4 Until the Retention End Date the Buyer shall at the expense of the Seller/at his own expense insure the dwelling against the risks of . . ./the usual risks against which property of such type is customarily insured (*delete as appropriate*) (but in such manner as to preclude any right of subrogation against the Seller) but the Seller shall be responsible for and indemnify the Buyer against any damage to the dwelling to the extent that such damage is not:

1.4.1 covered by insurance otherwise than through any default of the Buyer;

1.4.2 due to any omission of the Buyer or any person on the Property with the express or implied consent of the Buyer.

1.5 Against a full indemnity as to costs the Seller may use the name of the Buyer in any appropriate proceedings for the recovery of possession of the dwelling.

1.6 By way of compensation or liquidated damages the Buyer shall be entitled to be paid/to retain out of the retention due to the Seller hereunder a sum calculated at the rate of . . . pounds for each week or part of a week after Completion/the expiry of . . . (*delete as appropriate*) for which vacant possession of the dwelling concerned was not available to the Buyer.

1.7 If vacant possession of the dwelling concerned has not been given by the time the retention payable to the Seller has been reduced to nil by the deductions authorised by clause . . . the Buyer shall be entitled to the whole of the retention in respect of that dwelling and the sale shall be deemed to have been subject to the occupancy of that dwelling.

1.8 For the avoidance of doubt it is hereby agreed that the Buyer shall be under no obligation to take any steps to secure vacant possession of the dwelling concerned but may nevertheless take such steps as he in his absolute discretion deems appropriate to that end.

3 SALE AND ACQUISITION OF LAND

1.   Dwellings – warranty against tenancy

The Seller warrants that none of the respective occupiers of the dwellings on the Property has or will acquire a tenancy thereof and that vacant possesion of the said dwellings will be given within .. months from the date hereof.

1.   Transfer of licences

The Seller will use all reasonable endeavours to procure that there will be handed over on Completion all current licences for the storage of petroleum spirit upon the Property and will execute and do or procure the execution and doing of all such other documents acts or things as may be required in order to procure the transfer of such licences to the Buyer.

1.   Lease-back

1.1   On Completion the Buyer shall grant to . . . and the Seller shall procure the acceptance by the said . . . of a tenancy of the Property upon the terms and conditions set forth in the Approved Draft Tenancy Agreement.

1.2   No sum shall be payable by the Buyer to the Seller in respect of any items in the nature of tenantright routine improvements or otherwise beyond the Price nor shall any sum in respect of any such matters be payable by the said . . . upon the grant to him of the said tenancy by the Buyer.

1.3   No sum shall be claimed debited or set off by the Buyer in respect of dilapidations.

1.4   All fixtures and fittings in the nature of tenant's fixtures and fittings are excluded from the sale as are all fixtures and fittings and buildings specified in the Approved Draft Tenancy Agreement as belonging to the tenant thereunder.

1.   Groundwater Regulations

The Seller agrees with the Buyer that the Seller will within twenty-one days of Completion serve notice on the Environment Agency pursuant to the Groundwater Regulations 1998 to transfer the authorisation applied for by/held by the Seller to the Buyer and will at the expense of the Buyer use such reasonable endeavours and execute such further documents as may reasonably be required to transfer the said authorisation to the Buyer. The Seller shall indemnify the Buyer against all costs claims demands and proceedings of whatsoever nature and howsoever arising from any breach of the Groundwater Regulations prior to Completion.

Note. This may need amendment once the authorisation is issued.

1. **Water licences**

1.1 The Seller hereby agrees with the Buyer that the Seller will within twenty-one days of completion serve notice on the Environment Agency to transfer to the Buyer the water licences affecting the property specified hereunder:

[*Specify water licences*]

1.2 The Seller shall indemnify the Buyer against all costs claims demands and proceedings of whatsoever nature and howsoever arising from any breach of the terms of the said Licences or any of them.

1. **Miscellaneous aid schemes**

1.1 The Buyer hereby agrees with the Seller within [*appropriate time-scale – usually 3 months*] to enter into an undertaking with the relevant authority to comply with the rules of [*scheme entered into by the Seller*].

1.2 The Seller agrees to hand over to the Buyer on completion all documents required by the Buyer to substantiate this entitlement to aid from the said scheme[s].

1. **Employees**

[*Note:* An appropriate clause about employees may be required if TUPE is likely to apply.]

Note. Many aid schemes provide for aid paid to be forfeited if the applicant ceases to farm the land unless a replacement undertaking is secured. The Seller's advisers should obtain details from their client of all such schemes. If a replacement undertaking can be secured, this should be covered in the contract.

Examples are:

Multiannual Set-aside Scheme;

Moorland Schemes (closed in 2000);

Nitrate Sensitive Areas (closed in 1998);

Habitat Schemes (closed in 1999);

Countryside Access (closed in 2000);

Woodlands;

Countryside Stewardship (old schemes);

Organic Farming (old schemes);

Environmentally Sensitive Areas (old schemes);

Schemes under the England Rural Development Programme:

– Energy Crops Scheme

– Countryside Stewardship

– Environmentally Sensitive Areas

– Organic Farming

– Processing and Marketing Grant Scheme

– Rural Enterprise Scheme.

If original documents are handed over, certified copies must be retained.

3 SALE AND ACQUISITION OF LAND

4   PRECEDENT 4: DEED OF PARTITION

THIS DEED OF PARTITION is made the [*date*]

BETWEEN [*name*] of [*address*] ('[*name*]') of the first part [*name*] of [*address*] ('[*name*]') of the second part [*name*] of [*address*] ('[*name*]') of the third part.

WHEREAS:

1.   The properties described in the Schedules hereto are held in fee simple by various of the parties hereto on trust as follows:

1.1   As to the property described in the First Schedule hereto (hereinafter called '[*name*]') for [*name*] absolutely.

1.2   As to the property described in the Second Schedule hereto (hereinafter called '[*name*]') as to one half share for [*name*] and one half share for [*name*] absolutely.

2.   There is attaching to the properties referred to in the said schedules a Wholesale Milk Quota ('the Quota') comprising ... litres in respect of which the Registered Producer is trading as '[*name*]'.

3.   It has been agreed between the parties hereto that the said properties in the Schedules hereto shall be partitioned among the parties hereto in manner herinafter appearing and further that the Quota shall be apportioned between the parties hereto based upon the areas used for milk production as follows namely as to ... litres which shall henceforth attach to [*name*], as to ... litres which shall henceforth attach to [*name*] and as to ... litres which shall henceforth attach to [*name*].

AND FURTHER that the parties hereto shall sign all necessary forms with the Intervention Board or other appropriate authority and do all necessary things to ensure the transfer of the Quota with the respective properties as hereinbefore referred to.

NOW THIS DEED WITNESSES as follows:

In pursuance of the said agreement and for the purpose of effecting the said Partition:

1.1   [*Name*] as beneficial owner hereby conveys ALL THAT freehold property containing ... acres or thereabouts being the property more particularly described in Part 1 of the First Schedule hereto for the purpose of identification only delineated on the plan annexed hereto and thereon edged red TO HOLD the same unto [*name*] for his own use and benefit absolutely subject as mentioned in Part 1 of the First Schedule.

1.2   [*Name*] as beneficial owner hereby conveys to [*name*] ALL THAT freehold property containing ... acres or thereabouts being the property more particularly described in Part 2 of the First Schedule hereto for the purpose of identification only delineated on the plan annexed hereto and thereon edged green TO HOLD the same unto [*name*] for his own use and benefit absolutely subject as mentioned in Part 2 of the First Schedule.

[Name] and [name] as trustees hereby convey and [name] as beneficial owner in respect of his one half share there hereby assigns unto [name] ALL THAT freehold property containing ... acres or thereabouts more particularly described in the Second Schedule TO HOLD the same unto [name] for his own use and benefit absolutely subject as mentioned in the Second Schedule.

1.4 In respect of the various properties the subject of this Deed of Partition there shall be apportioned thereto based upon the areas of land used for milk production for the benefit of the respective parties the following quantities of the Quota namely:

2.1 as to ... litres which shall henceforth attach to the land described in Part 1 of the First Schedule hereto;

2.2 as to ... litres which shall henceforth attach to the said land described in Part 2 of the First Schedule hereto;

2.3 as to ... litres which shall henceforth attach to the land described in the Second Schedule hereto.

3. For the purpose of giving effect to Clause 2 hereof the parties hereto will co-operate with each other in effecting such apportionment by signing all necessary forms and doing all necessary things required by the Intervention Board or other appropriate authority to effect such apportionment.

4. It is agreed by the parties that they will not make any further representations concerning apportionment of the said quota under the Dairy Produce Quotas Regulations 1997 ('the Regulations') or any statutory modification or re-enactment thereof or otherwise in respect of the said properties herein referred to and further that they will not seek to register any interest in that part of the Quota herein apportioned to the other or others of them nor make any claim with regard to such quota.

5. If notwithstanding the terms of this Deed, any claim is made outside the provisions of this Deed in respect of the Quota consequent upon the change of occupation arising from the partitioning of this land or otherwise resulting in apportionment of Quota in favour of one or more of the parties hereto pursuant to a decision of an Arbitrator appointed under the Regulations or otherwise the party or parties so claiming (as the case may be) will pay to the other party or parties the full value of the Quota thus transferred together with such sum (if any) as shall accurately represent the loss suffered by the other party or parties to include if appropriate costs incurred by any of the other parties in the acquisition of quota to replace any Quota so apportioned.

6. IT IS HEREBY certified that this transaction does not form part of a larger transaction or of a series of transactions in respect of which the amount or value of the aggregate amount of value exceeds £ ....

IN WITNESS whereof this Deed has been executed by the parties hereto the day and year first before written.

FIRST SCHEDULE

Part 1

ALL THAT land containing ... acres or thereabouts with the buildings thereon situate at [*address*] more particularly described in a Conveyance dated [*date*] and made between [*name*] (1) and [*name*] and [*name*] (2)

SUBJECT as therein mentioned AND SUBJECT ALSO to

FIRST SCHEDULE

Part 2

ALL THAT land containing ... acres or thereabouts situate at [*address*] aforesaid as more particularly described in a Conveyance dated [*date*] and made between [*name*] (1) and [*name*] and [*name*] (2) TOGETHER WITH but SUBJECT TO all rights and obligations and other matters more particularly contained or referred to in the said Conveyance.

SECOND SCHEDULE

ALL THAT land containing ... acres or thereabouts at [*address*] more particularly described in a Conveyance dated [*date*] and made between [*name*] of the one part and [*name*] of the other part TOGETHER WITH EXCEPT AND RESERVING and SUBJECT TO all rights obligations and other matters more particularly contained or referred to in [*details*].

SIGNED and delivered as a Deed by ⎱
the said [*name*] in the presence of: ⎰
....

....

....

....

SIGNED and delivered as a Deed by
the said [*name*] in the presence of:

}

....

....

....

....

SIGNED and delivered as a Deed by
the said [*name*] in the presence of:

}

....

....

....

....

3 SALE AND ACQUISITION OF LAND

CHAPTER 4: TENANCIES UNDER THE AGRICULTURAL HOLDINGS ACT 1986

INDEX

CHAPTER 4: TENANCIES UNDER THE AGRICULTURAL HOLDINGS ACT 1986

INTRODUCTION

Any new tenancies granted on or after 1 September 1995 can only be AHA 1986 tenancies in the circumstances specified in s 4 of the Agricultural Tenancies Act 1995. This will most commonly arise in the case of succession tenancies granted either by the Tribunal or by agreement. The terms of the new tenancy may depend to an extent on the terms of the original tenancy, in view of the provisions of ss 47 and 48 of the AHA 1986. However, as part of the negotiations in connection with the grant of a succession tenancy, it is often agreed that the terms of the tenancy will be updated and, for example, provisions relating to milk quota included, if not already provided for, and obligations in respect of repairs varied. It is imperative that the provisions of s 4 of the 1995 Act are met, otherwise the new tenancy will be a farm business tenancy. In some cases, the form of the old tenancy will be acceptable to the parties. A short form of new tenancy by reference to the terms of the old one is accordingly included.

Successions by agreement may be carried out either by surrender and grant of a new tenancy or by assignment. In the event of a surrender and grant the tenant must ensure that the formalities required by ATA 1995, s 4(1)(d) are met. If not, he will acquire only a farm business tenancy. This chapter contains a full length form of succession tenancy.

On a surrender and the grant of a new tenancy, the landlord may become entitled to 100% relief for inheritance tax purposes if he has owned the holding for seven years. The tenant, on the other hand, may have problems with capital gains tax and inheritance tax. There will be stamp duty on the new tenancy agreement.

In the case of an assignment, the landlord must ensure that the event is indeed a succession. If not, there will be a transfer of the tenancy without using one of the statutory successions referred to in s 37 of the AHA 1986. There will be no inheritance tax advantage (if appropriate) for the landlord. The tenant, on the other hand, will have capital gains tax and inheritance tax advantages and will pay no stamp duty if the appropriate certificate is included.

What can now constitute a succession by agreement depends upon when the tenancy was granted. For a tenancy granted before 12 September 1984, there must be a grant or assignment of the whole or a substantial part of the original holding to one eligible person. For a tenancy granted on or after 12 September 1984, the transaction can be a grant or assignment of all or part of the holding and can be to an eligible person or to an eligible person and another or others.

Where there is more than one tenant and the successor is related to one of them, the retirement route must be followed.

One of the items to be addressed in planning for succession will be the existing tenant's will. The tenant may designate in his will a named individual as the person he wishes to succeed under the AHA 1986, s 39(4).

If the family owns land in addition to renting it, the prospective applicant for a succession tenancy should not acquire land which would constitute a commercial unit. It may, therefore, be appropriate for a discretionary will to be drawn up, so that the prospective applicant will be only one of the potential beneficiaries. Under current law, if matters can be resolved within two years of the death, the discretionary will trust can be wound up in a tax-efficient manner.

New tenancy agreements may also be agreed in respect of AHA 1986 tenancies where the terms of an existing tenancy are reduced to writing. Again, great care must be taken with the form of the agreement to ensure that it does not create a new tenancy which would be a farm business tenancy but merely confirms the terms of the existing one.

Section 6 of the AHA 1986 applies where there is no written agreement embodying all the terms of the tenancy or there is an agreement but one or more of the matters specified in Schedule 1 to the Act is not included (section 6(1)). Either the landlord or the tenant may apply for the tenancy to be reduced to writing or for the missing term(s) to be recorded.

The matters to be included are set out in Schedule 1, but they are not all-embracing and other terms might have been agreed and could therefore be properly included. Schedule 1 provides the starting point. Although not included in Schedule 1, the model clauses as to repairs and insurance contained in the 1973 Regulations will apply unless some other repair obligation has been agreed and is recorded.

The precedent given (Precedent 3) is restricted to the matters contained in Schedule 1 but there may be other terms which the parties can agree.

As an unwritten tenancy will be assignable, it is essential that a landlord of such a tenancy serves a s 6 notice forthwith.

The tenancy should not be framed as a new letting. This will constitute a surrender and regrant not covered by Agricultural Tenancies Act 1995, s 4 and will convert the tenancy into a farm business tenancy.

A tenant under an oral tenancy may consider assignment to others or to a company. Any such assignment made after a s 6 notice is served will be void. It is not necessary to notify the landlord immediately.

Apart from a selection of conveyancing-related documents, we have also included a selection of more commonly used notices and a number of prescribed forms. It is hoped that this will be convenient for the practitioner. It cannot be stressed too highly, however, that the AHA 1986 is full of technicalities and no action should be taken, or omitted, without a proper understanding of the implications. In addition, there are tight time-limits with no opportunity of extension. Reference must therefore be made to the leading text-books, Scammell and Densham's *Law of*

Agricultural Holdings (Butterworths, 8th edn), and Muir, Watt and Moss *Agricultural Holdings* (Sweet & Maxwell, 14th edn), or if necessary to an expert skilled in the area of law. This should be done before the precedents in this book are used, rather than afterwards when a problem has arisen.

While every effort should be made to ensure that notices are correct, not every defect will invalidate the notice; see *Mannai Investment Co Limited v Eagle Star Life Assurance Co Limited* [1995] 1 WLR 1508 and subsequent cases. However, errors in prescribed forms, especially in respect of the warnings, are likely to be more strictly treated by the judiciary; see, for example, *Sabella v Montgomery* (1998) 09 EG 153.

When considering the diversification uses envisaged later in this book the tenant must be aware both of the restrictions in his tenancy agreement and the possibility of the landlord recovering possession under Case B if planning permission is obtained for non-agricultural use. Some comfort can be derived in respect of the former from *Pennell v Payne* (1995) 06 EG 152 where an unlawful sub-letting was held not to constitute an irremediable breach under Case E. However, there may be other avenues open to the landlord in appropriate cases.

4 TENANCIES UNDER THE AGRICULTURAL HOLDINGS ACT 1986

CHECKLIST

MATTERS TO BE CONSIDERED ON THE GRANT OF A SUCCESSION TENANCY

1.   Are there any tenant's improvements? If so, if they are to remain as tenant's improvements they should be recorded as such.

2.   Are there any tenant's fixtures? If so, it is as well to record the position at commencement.

3.   Are there any dilapidations? If so, these should be dealt with.

4.   What are the repairing obligations to be? The most likely alternatives are either a full repairing and insuring tenancy (whereby the tenant is responsible for everything) or a tenancy incorporating the statutory provisions set out in the Agriculture (Maintenance Repair and Insurance of Fixed Equipment) Regulations 1973 (SI 1973/1473 amended by SI 1988/281).

5.   Does the landlord own any adjoining land? If so, consider what provisions need to be incorporated.

6.   Is game to be included or reserved to the landlord?

7.   Will any rights of holdover be needed at the end of the tenancy?

8.   Are there any buildings? If so, what provision is to be made in the agreement?

9.   Is the farm a dairy farm? If so, careful consideration of the milk quota clauses will be needed.

10.   Is IACS provided for? If not, it should be.

11.   To what extent are the terms of the old agreement acceptable; how should change be sought?

12.   Are there any redundant items of fixed equipment? If so what?

13.   Is there a sugar beet contract? If so, what tonnage is attributable to the property?

14.   Is it a first or second succession?

PRECEDENTS

1   SUCCESSION TENANCY UNDER THE AHA 1986[1]

Particulars

DATE OF AGREEMENT	:	....
PARTIES	:	....
THE LANDLORD	:	....
of		....
THE TENANT	:	....
of		....
THE HOLDING	:	.... Farm

having an area of . . . or thereabouts more particularly described in the First Schedule hereto and shown for the purpose of identification only edged . . . on the plan annexed hereto

COMMENCEMENT DATE	:	....
TERM DATE	:	[*date*]
COMMENCING RENTAL	:	£ . . . per year payable in arrear/advance (*delete as appropriate*) on the Rent Days in each year
RENT DAYS	:	....
LANDLORD'S ADDRESS FOR SERVICE OF NOTICES (LANDLORD AND TENANT ACT 1987, SECTION 48(1))	:	....
REDUNDANT ITEMS	:	Those specified or subsequently deemed to be specified in the Second Schedule hereto
TENANT'S FIXTURES	:	Those specified in the Third Schedule hereto
MILK QUOTA – LITRES	:	....
– BUTTERFAT	:	....

1.   Interpretation
In this Agreement:

1.1   the attached Particulars are incorporated and unless the context otherwise requires expressions in the Particulars have the respective meanings set against them in the Particulars;

1.2   words importing one gender only include the other genders; words importing the singular include the plural number and vice versa;

1.3   words importing persons include corporations and vice versa;

1.4   the expression 'the Landlord' includes the person for the time beng entitled to the reversion immediately expectant on the Tenancy;

1.5   the expression 'the Tenant' includes the person for the time being entitled to the Tenancy;

1.6   where there are two or more persons included in the expression 'the Landlord' or 'the Tenant' the obligations of such persons under this Agreement shall be joint and several;

1.7   the expression 'the Tenancy' means the tenancy hereby created;

1.8   the expression 'the AHA 1986' means the Agricultural Holdings Act 1986;

1.9   the expression 'Relevant Quotas' means such quotas contracts premium rights or similar arrangements (as permitted by the context) as are from time to time attaching to or available in respect of the Holding or any crops produced thereon or to which the Tenant or any other person is entitled in respect of production on the Holding whether existing at the commencement of the Tenancy or introduced thereafter and 'Relevant Quota' shall be construed accordingly;

1.10   any reference to 'Holding' shall where the context admits include any part or parts thereof;

1.11   any provision not to do an act or thing shall import an obligation not to cause or permit such act or thing to be done;

1.12   any reference to a statutory provision regulation or code of practice shall be deemed to include any later provision substituted for or amending the same and any subsidiary provision made under powers thereby conferred;

1.13   the clause headings are for convenient reference only and shall not affect its construction.

2.   Letting
2.1   Subject as hereinafter mentioned and in consideration of the rent agreements and conditions hereinafter following the Landlord agrees to let and the Tenant agrees to take the Holding.

2.2   Part IV of the AHA 1986 shall apply to the tenancy hereby created.

2.3   The parties hereby agree that the tenancy hereby created is a first/second (*delete as appropriate*) succession and the tenant is both eligible and suitable within the meaning of Part IV of the AHA 1986.

3. Matters included in the holding

There are included with the Holding all appurtenances thereof and all fixtures and fittings thereon except any which the outgoing tenant is entitled to remove and any which are to be regarded as fixtures belonging to the Tenant (in respect of which section 10 of the AHA 1986 as hereinafter modified is to apply).

4. Matters affecting the holding

The Holding is let subject to:

4.1 the exceptions and reservations herein mentioned;

4.2 such public or private rights liabilities provisions agreements and other matters as affect the Holding;

4.3 the rights of the outgoing tenant (if any);

4.4 any existing tenancies or occupancies of any dwellings on the Holding.

5. Period of tenancy

The Tenancy shall commence on and include the Commencement Date and continue until the next following Term Date and (unless determined on the first anniversary of the Term Date) thereafter from year to year until determined.

6. Rent

The Holding is let at the Commencing Rental payable as specified in the Particulars on the Rent Days in each year the first (proportionate if appropriate) payment to be made on the First Rent Day and where the rent is otherwise payable in arrear the last payment shall if demanded be paid in advance on the Rent Day next preceding the termination of the Tenancy.

7. Exceptions and reservations

There are excepted and reserved out of the Holding:

7.1 *Game*

Subject to the provisions of the Ground Game Act 1880 (as amended by section 12 of the Wildlife and Countryside Act 1981) and the Ground Game (Amendment Act) 1906 all deer foxes game wildfowl woodcock snipe fish hares and rabbits and all birds listed in Part 1 of the Second Schedule to the Wildlife and Countryside Act 1981 and the nests and eggs of all birds in this clause referred to with the right for the purposes of shooting fishing hawking sporting taking preserving and rearing such wildlife and destroying pigeons and other pests to enter onto the Holding with such equipment and persons as the Landlord authorises [and also the right to hunt or permit hunting on foot or with horse and hound].

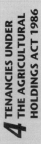
4 TENANCIES UNDER THE AGRICULTURAL HOLDINGS ACT 1986

7.2   *Water*

All springs of water or other wells ponds streams and water courses (including any underground water) with the right for the Landlord and all persons authorised by the Landlord to have access thereto and to take water therefrom by means of pumps and other constructions and equipment and pipes laid or to be laid on across or under the Holding or otherwise (subject to sufficient water being left for the Tenant for domestic and agricultural purposes other than irrigation).

7.3   *Timber*

All timber timber-like trees fruit trees tellers pollards saplings and underwood with the right for the Landlord and all persons duly authorised to make fell cut remove the same and to plant upon any coppice or woodland any quantity of young trees as the Landlord thinks fit including the right to enter the Holding for such purposes with or without motor vehicles plant and equipment but doing as little damage as practicable and paying the Tenant reasonable compensation for any damage done.

7.4   *Minerals*

All mines minerals quarries stones sand brick-earth clay gravel petroleum and its relative hydrocarbons and all other gases and substances in upon or under the Holding including the air space void created from time to time by the winning working getting and carrying away of any of such substances whether opened or unopened within upon or under the Holding together with the right for the Landlord and all persons authorised by the Landlord and his lessees and agents and all persons authorised by them or any of them with workmen and others from time to time and at all times hereafter whether by entry on the surface or by underground working to win work get and carry away the said substances and any like substances within upon or under any adjacent or other lands with full powers for those purposes:

7.4.1   to withdraw vertical and lateral support from the surface of the Holding and from any buildings or works now erected or hereafter to be erected thereon or from any crops standing thereon;

7.4.2   to sink pits or shafts open quarries and erect buildings and construct place and maintain any plant machinery equipment apparatus or materials in on or under the Holding;

7.4.3   to constitute any requisite access tracks roads or railways fences pipes drains sewers wires cables conduits or other apparatus in under or over the Holding;

7.4.4   to use the surface of the Holding for the temporary storage or deposit of any of the said substances or any waste;

7.4.5   to do all other things necessary or convenient for such purposes or any of them notwithstanding any subsidence or other injury or damage that may thereby be occasioned to the Holding or any building or works or crops as aforesaid or any other injury or damage or loss whatsoever arising whether directly or indirectly from any such working or operation as aforesaid which may be sustained by the Tenant save that the Landlord shall pay to the Tenant reasonable compensation for damage thereby done to the surface buildings or crops and shall allow an abatement of rent in respect of the surface land of the Holding of which the Tenant is deprived by reason of the exercise of any such rights and liberties as aforesaid.

7.5   *Roads*

The right at all times and for all purposes for the Landlord and the occupiers and tenants of any adjoining or neighbouring land of the Landlord and all other persons authorised by the Landlord or by such occupiers or tenants to use the roads tracks and footpaths within the Holding together with all other ways hitherto used or enjoyed across the Holding and in the case of each such road track or way so used (other than footpaths) either with or without animals vehicles implements machinery or plant.

7.6   *Services*

7.6.1   The right for the Landlord and the tenants or other occupiers of any adjoining or neighbouring land of the Landlord to the free passage of drainage water gas oil telecommunications and electricity from and to such other land through the watercourses channels drains sewers pipes cables and wires belonging to or running through the Holding.

7.6.2   The right for the Landlord and all persons authorised by the Landlord to erect lay maintain inspect repair renew and use within upon under or over the land comprised in the Holding telecommunications and electricity lines and cables and gas oil water drainage and sewage pipes and any necessary apparatus in connection therewith respectively with full power for the Landlord and such other persons as aforesaid and the agents and workmen of the Landlord and such other persons to enter onto the Holding for the purpose of inspecting repairing replacing and renewing such lines cables pipes and apparatus respectively doing as little damage as practicable and paying to the Tenant reasonable compensation for any damage done.

7.7   *Repairs*

The right to enter and execute repairs for which the Tenant is liable under any provision hereof and which he has failed to start within two months or complete within three months of being required so to do by written notice given by the Landlord and the whole of the proportionate part for which the Tenant is liable (as the case may be) of the expense thereof shall be payable by the Tenant forthwith after such repairs have been executed and shall be recoverable as rent in arrears. Provided that nothing in this clause shall relieve the Tenant from his liability under any provision hereof to execute repairs.

7.8   *Cultivation*
         The right after three days written notice to enter and execute acts of
         husbandry or cultivation which the Tenant after giving or receiving notice
         to quit is in the opinion of the Landlord or his agent neglecting or
         performing in a dilatory or otherwise unsatisfactory manner and to take
         such manure as the Landlord shall require for such purpose and the Tenant
         shall at the Tenant's entire expense provide accommodation for the
         Landlord's workmen and free of cost accommodation for any tractors
         machinery fertiliser seed or other items brought onto the Holding by the
         Landlord in exercise of this right.[2]

7.9   *Entry*
7.9.1   The right for the Landlord and all persons authorised by the Landlord
         (where appropriate with or without workmen animals carts motor vehicles
         plant machinery implements guns and other articles) to enter onto the
         Holding:
7.9.1.1 for the due and proper exercise and enjoyment of his rights hereunder;
7.9.1.2 for the due and proper performance of his obligations hereunder;
7.9.1.3 for any other reasonable purpose.
7.9.2   The right to permit any party involved in an arbitration under the AHA
         1986 or any other legal proceedings for which an inspection of the Holding
         is or may be relevant to inspect the Holding whether or not the Landlord is
         one of the parties to the arbitration or proceedings.

7.10   *Wayleaves*
7.10.1   The right to grant any wayleave contract easement or licence to any public
         or local authority or public utility company or other company or person
         with the right to authorise agents and servants of the grantee with or
         without motor vehicles plant and equipment to enter upon the Holding
         and carry out all appropriate works and in particular but without prejudice
         to the generality of the foregoing the right to run pipes drains conduits
         cables wires or other works (either already existing or any new ones) for the
         benefit of any adjoining or neighbouring land of the Landlord and the right
         to carry out works for the benefit of such adjoining or neighbouring land
         the grantee paying reasonable compensation for any damage done to the
         surface.
7.10.2   The benefit of all such contracts easements or licences existing at the date
         hereof or granted or made under this clause 7.10 and all rents and other
         payments reserved thereby (except annual payments made for disturbance
         to the occupier) and the benefit of any other similar agreements or
         contracts now or at any time affecting the Holding.

7.11   *Holdover*

If the Commencement Date falls between 1 July and 31 December the right of the Landlord and all persons authorised by the Landlord with or without motor vehicles plant and equipment to enter at any time or times upon the Holding for the purpose of storing any produce of the Holding on hard standings or in clamps or pies until 1 January immediately following the Commencement Date or in covered storage of adequate capacity until the following 25 March.

7.12   *Antiquities*

The right to all antiquities on the Holding together with the right for persons authorised by the Landlord to carry out scientific and research studies of whatsoever nature on the Holding the Landlord paying reasonable compensation for all damage occasioned thereby.

7.13   *Recordings*

The right for persons authorised by the Landlord to enter on the Holding with or without motor vehicles plant equipment cameras and visual and sound recording equipment and to use the Holding (other than the interiors of dwellings) for the purpose of making sound or visual recordings of whatever nature the Landlord paying reasonable compensation for any damage done.

8.   Tenant's agreements

The Tenant hereby agrees with the Landlord as follows:

8.1   *Rent*

8.1.1   To pay the Commencing Rent at the times and in the manner aforesaid.

8.1.2   To pay any additional yearly rents determined in accordance with section 13 of the AHA 1986 such additional rents to be paid (on the same basis as to period and timing as the Commencing Rent) on the Rent Days and with effect from the date of completion of the improvement to which such increase of rental values is attributable such date of completion for the purposes hereof being the date on which the said improvement is first capable of use as to which date the certificate of the Landlord's agents shall be conclusive.

8.1.3   To pay the rents referred to in clauses 8.1.1 and 8.1.2 hereof until a different rent is substituted therefor either by agreement or by arbitration under the provisions of the AHA 1986 which thereafter shall be the rent payable by the Tenant. In the event of a new rent for the Holding either being agreed or being determined by arbitration the same shall unless otherwise specifically agreed in writing be deemed to be made under this clause and not to create a new tenancy.

8.1.4   All such rents shall be paid to the Landlord free from all deductions whatsoever and without set off.

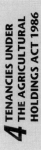

4 TENANCIES UNDER THE AGRICULTURAL HOLDINGS ACT 1986

8.2   *Interest*

To pay interest on any rent or other moneys payable to the Landlord hereunder which shall not have been paid by the due date for payment at the rate of four per cent above the base rate from time to time of such clearing bank as may be specified from time to time by the Landlord or if no such base rate is available at such other reasonably equivalent rate as the Landlord may from time to time specify.

8.3   *Outgoings*

To pay all present or future taxes rates (including drainage rates and drainage charges and water and sewer rates) assessments impositions and outgoings whatsoever of an annual or other recurring nature and whether chargeable on the Landlord or the Tenant) together with a proportionate part thereof from the commencement and/or up to the end of the Tenancy.

8.4   *Incoming*

To pay to the Landlord on demand the amount payable or to become payable by the Landlord to the outgoing tenant in respect of the Holding (compensation for disturbance and game damage if any excepted) together with the fees costs and stamp duty paid in connection therewith or (where there is no outgoing tenant) such sum as would have been payable as aforesaid had there been an outgoing tenant.

8.5   *Water expenses*

To reimburse to the Landlord on demand all charges costs and expenses reasonably incurred by the Landlord in connection with the provision or the improved provision of water to the Holding.

8.6   *Residence*

Personally to reside in the farmhouse and make the same his usual place of residence and personally to farm the Holding.

8.7   *Occupation*

8.7.1   Not to assign underlet or part with the possession of or share the occupation of the Holding PROVIDED THAT the Tenant may permit the occupation of cottages and gardens by persons employed regularly on the Holding but only if such occupation shall be as assured shorthold tenants without security of tenure.

8.7.2   Not to enter into any partnership agreement management agreement (whether under the Wildlife and Countryside Act 1981 or otherwise) contracting agreement importing a profit-sharing element or share-farming agreement in respect of the Holding.

8.7.3   Except as expressly required to do so by or under the provisions hereof not without the Landlord's written consent (such consent not to be unreasonably withheld) to enter into any scheme for setting aside land or imposing limitations on cropping or stocking or requirements for public access or any contract with a producer for growing specialist crops in respect of the Holding.

8.7.4   Not to place any tent or caravan upon the Holding nor to take in lodgers in the farmhouse or cottages on the Holding.

8.7.5   Not to let or sell any grass keeping or growing crops on the Holding not to take in on the Holding livestock belonging wholly or in part to any other person and not to enter into a contract of agistment with any other person in relation to the Holding.

8.8   *Charges*

To give written notice to the Landlord forthwith upon giving any charge over his farming stock under the Agricultural Credits Act 1928 or any other similar enactment or when bringing onto the Holding live or dead stock in which a third party has an interest under a hire purchase agreement or otherwise and on request to supply the Landlord with copies of all charges agreements and other arrangements made.

8.9   *Acknowledgement*

Not to give an acknowledgement as to the entitlement to any right of light or other easement over or in respect of the Holding.

8.10   *Water disposal*

Not to enter into any agreement or licence for the supply of water from any spring or well pond stream water course or underground water supply on the Holding to any adjoining or neighbouring premises.

8.11   *Recordings*

8.11.1   Not without the written approval of the Landlord to permit or authorise any person to take for hire or reward any film or other recording (in whatever form and whether of sight or sound) of or on the Holding or any natural or manmade feature thereon or anything done or occurring thereon but so that this shall not restrict the liberty of the Tenant to take such film or other recording as he shall think fit for the personal and domestic use and enjoyment of himself or his family and friends or in direct connection with his agricultural business.

8.11.2   Forthwith to pay to the Landlord any money received by the Tenant in consequence of any breach of this provision such money to be deemed for the purpose of calculating interest thereon to have become due on the date of the breach.

8.12   *Death of the tenant*

To take all such steps as are necessary to ensure that:

8.12.1   if the Tenant or any of them dies during the currency of the Tenancy written notice of such death and the date thereof shall be given to the Landlord within one month of such death;

8.12.2   Office or duly certified copies of all probates of wills letters of administration orders of court and other instruments affecting these presents or the Tenancy shall be served on the Landlord within one month from the respective dates thereof.

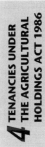

4 TENANCIES UNDER THE AGRICULTURAL HOLDINGS ACT 1986

8.13   *Proceedings*
         To permit the Landlord to take proceedings or do any other act in the name
         of the Tenant which the Landlord considers appropriate to preserve or
         protect his interest in the Holding and to cooperate with the Landlord in
         relation thereto the Landlord indemnifying the Tenant against any costs
         charges and expenses he may incur in connection with any such matter.

8.14   *Repairs*
8.14.1   To keep in good and substantial repair order and condition at all times
         during the Tenancy using the best and most suitable materials for the same
         all dwellings and other buildings on the Holding together with all fixtures
         and fittings drains sewers water supplies pumps fences live and dead hedges
         gates external boundary walls post stiles bridges culverts ponds water-
         courses ditches roads and yards in and upon the Holding or on other
         property but serving the Holding or which during the Tenancy may be
         erected or provided on the Holding or serve the Holding and to keep clean
         and in good working order all roofs valleys eaves guttering and down pipes
         gulleys and grease traps and without prejudice to the generality of the
         foregoing to do and perform all such acts and matters (except as to
         insurance against fire and other risks) which are the liability of a landlord or
         a tenant in accordance with Part I or Part II of the Schedule to the
         Agriculture (Maintenance Repair and Insurance of Fixed Equipment)
         Regulations 1973 (SI 1973/1473).
8.14.2   To replace and upon replacement adequately to paint gas–tar or creosote as
         may be proper all items of fixed equipment which need replacing from
         time to time.[3]

8.15   *Drainage*
         Without prejudice to the generality of the provisions of clause 8.14 hereof
         to maintain the drainage on all parts of the Holding requiring drainage in
         the most approved manner practised on lands of a similar nature in the
         district and in the case of field drains and outfalls to open up the land as
         necessary and to clean the drains and tiles as required.

8.16   *Common items*
         To pay to the Landlord on demand an appropriate proportion of the cost
         from time to time incurred by the Landlord in the maintenance and repair
         of all items used in common with adjoining or neighbouring property.

8.17   *Alterations*
         Not to carry out any alteration or make any addition to the farmhouse
         buildings or cottages (if any) or erect any new buildings or make any other
         improvement within the meaning of section 67 and the Seventh Schedule
         to the 1986 Act on the Holding except with the written consent of the
         Landlord or the approval of the Minister as thereby provided.

8.18   *Waste*

Not to commit any wilful or voluntary waste spoil or destruction on the Holding or do thereon anything which in the opinion of the Landlord may be or become a nuisance or annoyance to the Landlord or to the owners or occupiers of adjoining or neighbouring land.

8.19   *Ancient monuments*

Not in any way to interfere with or injure any tumulus stone circle or other ancient remain structure or monument (including known buried archaeological remains) or any actual or proposed Site of Special Scientific Interest (whether statutorily protected or not) and not to permit any person to enter on the Holding (with or without metal detectors tools hammers or other equipment) for the purpose of searching for or removing any object or specimen of antiquarian archaeological or scientific interest (save under the rights hereinbefore reserved to the Landlord) but if it shall come to the knowledge of the Tenant that any such object or specimen has been found or observed on the Holding forthwith to report the same to the Landlord in writing and to give such assistance as the Tenant reasonably can to enable possession therof to be given to the Landlord or as he shall direct.

8.20   *Damage*

Where damage results from the laying of pipelines sewers and other apparatus underground or from the erection of poles pylons and other apparatus above the ground to procure that such damage is fully made good and the Holding is fully restored.

8.21   *Record of condition*

To bear the cost of making any record of condition under section 22 of the AHA 1986 which the Tenant requires.

8.22   *Fire precautions*

To maintain adequate fire fighting equipment throughout the Holding and to comply in all respects with any requirements or recommendations made by a fire officer.

8.23   *Notices*

Forthwith to notify the Landlord in writing of any notice proposal or order served on him under or by virtue of any statutory provision and if so required to produce to the Landlord such notice proposal or order and allow the Landlord to make copies thereof.

8.24   *Legislation*

To observe and comply fully with the provisions of any statute order regulation rule direction code of practice or other thing which extends to or affects the Holding or anything done or omitted or to be done or omitted thereon.

8.25   *Insurance of crops and stock*

8.25.1   At all times during the Tenancy to insure in the joint names of the Landlord and the Tenant against destruction or damage by fire lightning aircraft explosion riot civil commotion malicious persons or theft (and including consequential loss relating to such loss destruction or damage) all live and dead farming stock and crops for the time being on the Holding to the full market value thereof (delivered to the Holding) or the cost of replacement (if greater) and so that every policy of insurance shall:

8.25.1.1 be effected with an insurance company approved in writing by the Landlord;

8.25.1.2 not be avoidable on account of the storing handling or keeping of petrol or any other inflammable substance on the Holding or for any other reason connected with the user of the Holding;

8.25.1.3 provide cover for the return to the land of the full equivalent manurial value of any crops destroyed or damaged insofar as the return thereof is required for the fulfilment by the Tenant of his obligations under this Agreement.

8.25.2   To lay out the insurance monies received by virtue of such insurance in replacement of live and dead farming stock and crops and the return of the appropriate manurial value to the Holding (as the case may be) and to make good any deficiency out of his own money.

8.25.3   To produce to the Landlord on demand the policy or policies of insurance and the receipt for the premium in respect of the current period of insurance.

8.25.4   If such insurance shall not be effected or maintained or if such policy or receipt shall not be produced in accordance with the terms hereof and the Landlord shall effect such insurance cover as the Landlord may determine to be appropriate to make good such default (which he is hereby authorised to do) to repay to the Landlord on demand all premiums paid for such purpose and all other expenses incurred by the Landlord in connection therewith.

8.26   *Landlord's insurance*

8.26.1   Not to do or suffer to be done on the Holding any act or thing which shall or may invalidate the Landlord's policy of insurance in respect of the Holding and/or any other property or cause the premium thereon to be increased or increase the risk of any insured peril to any of the buildings or fences for the time being on the Holding and/or any other property but to take full and proper precautions to protect the Holding from risk of any insured peril and in particular to take all responsible precautions when installing petrol oil gas or electric engines and when storing petrol paraffin oil or similar fuel or lubricants which shall be kept in proper containers and wherever possible in a detached building and in such cases to observe and perform every requirement of any statutory or other relevant provision.

8.26.2   To pay to the Landlord on demand a sum equal to the gross premium or premiums paid or payable by the Landlord for effecting or maintaining the insurance which he is hereby required to effect and maintain.

8.27   *Liability insurance*

8.27.1 At all times during the Tenancy to maintain adequate insurance in respect of all employer's risks for which the Tenant may be liable.

8.27.2 At all times during the Tenancy to maintain insurance in respect of all third party liability risks in respect of which liability may fall on the Landlord in relation to the Holding the policy or policies of such insurance to be in the joint names of the Landlord and the Tenant with an insurance company approved in writing by the Landlord and to provide cover in respect of each and every claim of not less than two million pounds or such higher sum as the Landlord may from time to time direct in writing.

8.27.3 To apply all monies received through such policies for the purpose in respect of which the same has been paid and to make good any deficiency out of his own money.

8.28   *Environmental practice*

8.28.1 Not to contravene any legislation intended to prevent or control pollution or to protect the environment which shall from time to time be in force and to comply with all such statutory or regulatory requirements or codes of practice from time to time and to use the Tenant's best endeavours to prevent the pollution of rivers water courses and water supplies and the air and land on the Holding.

8.28.2 When using spray chemicals to take all reasonable care to ensure that adjoining hedges trees and crops are not adversely affected and to make good or pay full compensation for any damage done.

8.28.3 In performing his obligations hereunder and his obligation to comply with the rules of good husbandry so far as possible to select chemicals and to adopt farming practices which cause the least harm to game birds wildlife (other then vermin and pests) and the environment.

8.29   *Trees*

        To use his best endeavours to protect from damage any trees coppice wood or underwood growing upon the Holding and in particular:

8.29.1 not to cut down cut top or lop or drive nails into or otherwise injure any trees growing on the Holding;

8.29.2 not to cut any tellars whether growing from stools or otherwise without the written consent of the Landlord;

8.29.3 to protect all trees from damage by livestock machinery or otherwise howsoever;

8.29.4 to prevent any waste occurring in relation to any trees on the Holding.

8.30   *Game*

8.30.1 To use his best endeavours to protect from damage all [foxes] game (other than ground game) wildfowl woodcock snipe fish and protected birds as hereinbefore referred to and their nests and eggs and not to interfere with measures taken by the Landlord or persons authorised by him to rear and preserve game.

4 TENANCIES UNDER THE AGRICULTURAL HOLDINGS ACT 1986

8.30.2 To warn off all poachers and trespassers and allow his name to be used in any proceedings which the Landlord may take against any poachers or trespassers (the Landlord indemnifying the Tenant against any costs charges and expenses he may thereby incur) and so far as possible to stop all encroachments.

8.30.3 Not to do any act or thing that may contravene the provisions of the Wildlife and Countryside Act 1981 and to give full written particulars to the Landlord within seven days of the receipt of any notice relating to the Holding served under or by virtue of that Act and upon request to produce the same to the Landlord.

8.30.4 Not to make or keep rabbit warrens on the Holding and to destroy any that may exist.

8.30.5 The period of twelve months mentioned in proviso (b) to sub-section (3) of section 20 of the AHA 1986 (within one month of the expiration of which any claim under the said section 20 for damage by game must be made) shall be the twelve calendar months ending on the sixth day of April in each year.

8.31 *Deleterious substances*

Not without the written consent of the Landlord to bring on to the Holding any material or substance inconsistent with the Tenant's obligations under this Agreement.

8.32 *Refuse*

8.32.1 Not to deposit any refuse waste redundant material or redundant machinery of any kind on the Holding.

8.32.2 Within seven days of receipt thereof to comply with any notice issued by the Landlord requiring removal from the Holding of any such material or item as is referred to in this clause in accordance with all statutory povisions relating to such removal then in force.

8.33 *User*

To use the Holding for the purposes of agriculture only and not to use the Holding for any other trade or for advertising purposes or for the holding of any show race match game or contest whether of animals birds vehicles or persons.

8.34 *Cultivation*

8.34.1 To cultivate and manage the Holding according to the best standard and system of cultivation used in the district and so as to comply with the rules of good husbandry as defined by section 11 of the Agriculture Act 1947 and so as not to impoverish or deteriorate the land and to leave the same clean and in good condition.

8.34.2 Except as permitted by or under any statutory provision not to change the system of cropping or type of farming without the witten consent of the Landlord (such consent not to be unreasonably withheld).

8.34.3 To take all reasonable precautions to prevent the introduction of eelworm rhizomania and other pests and diseases on the Holding and in particular not to grow on the same land during any period of four consecutive years more than one crop of potatoes and one crop of sugar beet including sugar beet grown for seed.

8.34.4 In the last year of the Tenancy to leave the arable land in a course normally practised in the district or as the Landlord shall otherwise direct in writing.

8.35 *Grass land*

8.35.1 To manage the grass land in the most approved manner and also to destroy and prevent from seeding and spreading all rushes thistles nettles thorns ragwort gorse and other weeds and to keep down moles and rats and other vermin and spread all molehills and ant hills.

8.35.2 Not to remove from the Holding any turf or topsoil without the previous written consent of the Landlord and forthwith to pay to the Landlord any money received by the Tenant in consequence of a breach of this provision such money to be deemed for the purpose of calculating interest thereon to have become due on the date of the breach.

8.35.3 Not to break up or convert into tillage any land which shall be considered permanent pasture and for this purpose (and for the purposes of paragraph 2 of the Second Schedule of the Agriculture Act 1947 and section 14 of the AHA 1986 or either of them) the whole of the land described in the Cultivation column of the First Schedule hereto as pasture meadow grass or ley and also any land subsequently laid to grass for which the Landlord has prescribed seeds shall be so considered.

8.35.4 The Tenant shall be at liberty to break up and convert into tillage any of the remainder of the grass land on the Holding PROVIDED THAT:

8.35.4.1 the Tenant shall at least one year before the termination of the Tenancy sow down to temporary pasture in a husbandlike manner with a seed mixture approved by the Landlord in writing the whole of the land so broken up so that such pasture is fully established before the termination of the Tenancy;

8.35.4.2 if the Tenant obtains the written consent of the Landlord he may sow down to temporary pasture in substitution for any grass land ploughed up an equal area of arable land elsewhere on the Holding upon such terms as the Landlord may direct in writing but such consent shall not imply any obligation upon the part of the Landlord to provide fencing or a water supply for such substituted land nor shall it imply the Landlord's consent to the provision of fencing or water supplied by the Tenant as an improvement under the terms of the Seventh Schedule of the AHA 1986;

8.35.4.3 [no compensation shall be payable to the Tenant in respect of any temporary pasture laid down by him in accordance with this clause.]

8.35.5 After giving or receiving notice to quit not to plough up temporary grass land sown more than five years prior to the end of the Tenancy without giving to the Landlord in writing the option to purchase the same at valuation.

8.35.6   If the Tenancy shall terminate between 1 January and 30 June in any year not to stock the new seeds after the 1 October immediately preceding such termination.

8.36   *Orchards*
To keep all orchards and gardens in a proper state of cultivation well manured and in good heart to protect from damage by cattle or otherwise howsoever and to prune at proper seasons all fruit trees and bushes and at his own expense to replace dead or worn out fruit trees with other fruit trees suitable to the district PROVIDED THAT the Tenant may at his option in lieu of replacing individual trees grub up and replace the whole or a substantial part of an orchard in accordance with a scheme approved in writing by the Landlord or in default of such approval found to be a reasonable scheme by arbitration hereunder.

8.37   *Manurial value crops*
Not to sell off or remove from the Holding any hay straw roots or green crops but annually to consume such produce on the Holding PROVIDED THAT the Tenant may except in the case of such produce grown in the last year of the Tenancy sell off and remove such produce on returning to the Holding the equivalent manurial value of the produce sold off.

8.38   *Records*
8.38.1   To keep upon the Holding and maintain a field book showing how every field or parcel thereof has been stocked cropped and cultivated in each year of the Tenancy and to make the same available to the Landlord at all reasonable times.
8.38.2   To supply a copy to the Landlord of any return or other form which the Tenant is required to make or complete pursuant to any United Kingdom or European Union requirements or directives and if so required by the Landlord to consult with the Landlord in regard to the completion of such return or form so as to preserve and safeguard in all respects the interest of the Landlord.
8.38.3   To keep true accounts of all crops or produce sold off and of the equivalent manurial value returned to the Holding and to produce such accounts to the Landlord or his agent forthwith upon receiving at any time a written request to do so.

8.39   *Boundaries*
Save in accordance with the rules of good husbandry not to alter or destroy any hedge fence or boundary on the Holding nor do anything whereby the size or shape of any field shall be rendered different from its present size or shape.

8.40   *Manure*
        To spread annually on the land all manure made on the Holding and at the termination of the Tenancy to leave the same on the Holding for the Landlord or his incoming tenant and at no time to remove or sell off from the Holding any farmyard manure.

8.41   *Disease*
        To give the Landlord immediate notification (to be confirmed in writing forthwith) of any outbreak or suspected outbreak of any notifiable disease of crops or livestock on the Holding.

8.42   *Burning*
        Not to burn any crop residues on land from which a crop has been harvested except in accordance with the provisions of any by-laws Regulations and Codes of Practice from time to time in force.

8.43   *Genetically modified organisms*
8.43.1 Not without the Landlord's previous consent in writing to grow or permit to be grown on the Holding any plant which has been 'genetically modified' within the meaning of Part VI of the Environmental Protection Act 1990.
8.43.2 In respect of any such plants grown on the Holding:
8.43.2.1 to observe all statutory provisions Regulations Codes of Practice and Guidelines;
8.43.2.2 to indemnify the Landlord against all claims proceedings and demands of whatsoever nature and howsoever arising from the presence of such plants on the Holding or the escape from the Holding of any 'organism' (within the meaning of Part VI of the Environmental Protection Act 1990) being part of or derived from such plants;
8.43.3 to use all reasonable endeavours to remove from the Holding on the determination of the tenancy all such plants and every part thereof.

8.44   *Groundwater Regulations*
        To comply with the provisions of the Groundwater Regulations 1998, SI 1998/2746 ('the Groundwater Regulations') and in particular:
8.44.1 to supply the Landlord with details of disposal and tipping on the Holding in each year to 31 March within one month of the expiration thereof;
8.44.2 to maintain an authorisation in respect of the Holding under the Groundwater Regulations;
8.44.3 to take all necessary steps to transfer such authorisation to the Landlord or the incoming occupier on the termination of the tenancy and to give notice of such transfer to the Environment Agency within 21 days thereof;
8.44.4 to indemnify the Landlord against all costs claims proceedings and demands of whatsoever nature and howsoever arising from any breach of the Groundwater Regulations.

8.45   *Nitrate Vulnerable Zones*
8.45.1 This clause applies if the farm is situated within a Nitrate Vulnerable Zone.

8.45.2   To retain all records required by the Action Programme for Nitrate Vulnerable Zones (England and Wales) Regulations 1997, SI 1997/1202 and on the termination of the tenancy to hand to the Landlord or the incoming occupier such records for the period of 5 years preceding the end of the tenancy (but not prior to 19 December 1998).

8.45.3   To comply with the provisions of the said Regulations and to indemnify the Landlord against all claims proceedings and demands of whatever nature and howsoever arising from any failure to comply therewith.

8.46   *Farm Assurance Schemes*

8.46.1   At all times at his own expense to ensure that the requirements of the Farm Assurance Schemes specified in Schedule 7 or any schemes replacing the same are met in respect of the Holding and the crops produced thereon.

8.46.2   If the Tenant wishes to register the Holding or the Tenant for the purposes of any Farm Assurance Scheme to comply at his own expense with the requirements thereof including any works required in respect of any fixed equipment on the Holding.

8.46.3   At his own expense to ensure that the requirements of any Farm Assurance Scheme available in respect of crops grown on the Holding are met.

8.46.4   On the expiration of the tenancy to hand to the Landlord all records required as evidence that the Tenant has complied with the requirements of all such Schemes.[4]

8.47   *Sewage sludge*

8.47.1   Not to use or permit to be used sludge as defined in the Sludge (Use in Agriculture) Regulations 1989 on the Holding or any part thereof.
         OR

8.47.2   Not to use or permit to be used sludge as defined in the Sludge (Use in Agriculture) Regulations 1989 on the Holding or any part thereof otherwise than:

8.47.2.1 in accordance with the said Regulations;

8.47.2.2 in accordance with any Code of Practice or Guidelines relating thereto from time to time published by the Government or any Government Ministry or Agency;

8.47.2.3 after obtaining the Landlord's consent in writing and in compliance with any conditions specified in writing by the Landlord.

8.48   *Health and safety*

8.48.1   To comply in respect of the Holding and the Tenant's activities thereon with the Regulations relating to Health and Safety at Work and all Codes of Practice in respect thereof for the time being in force.

8.48.2   Forthwith to notify the Landlord of any defects under the Health and Safety Regulations in respect of the Holding or any areas used by the Tenant in common with other persons.

8.48.3   To indemnify the Landlord in respect of any liability arising in respect of the Holding under the Health and Safety Regulations and in respect of any areas used in common to reimburse the Landlord a fair payment according to user of the costs of any works required to be undertaken by the Landlord to comply with such Regulations.

8.49   *Water abstraction licence*
8.49.1   Where a previous occupier of the Holding held a licence to abstract water to give notice to the Water Authority of the change of occupancy of the Holding within one month from the date on which the Tenant becomes the occupier in order to preserve the licence to abstract water.
8.49.2   Not to allow to lapse any licence taken over from a previous occupier of the Holding or granted during the Tenancy.
8.49.3   On the termination of the Tenancy to make such application for the continuance or renewal of the licence as may be requisite for the time being under regulations then in force to preserve the licence for the benefit of the Landlord or his nominee without payment.

8.50   *IACS*
          In each year to register the Holding or the Tenant (as the case may be) under all relevant schemes or arrangements for area aid set-aside or other compensatory payments established by the United Kingdom or the European Union and to supply to the Landlord on demand copies of all applications for such registration and any other documents relating thereto.

8.51   *Arable Area Scheme*
          To comply with the requirements of the Arable Area Scheme under European Union Council Regulation 1251/99 and of any substituted or similar scheme.

8.52   *Milk quota*
          If milk quota shall have been transferred from the Landlord or outgoing tenant to the Tenant on the commencement of the Tenancy (details of such quota being set out in the Particulars):
8.52.1   To fulfil and maintain such quota with no less litres (subject only to generalised cuts) and the same butterfat by milk produced on the Holding.
8.52.2   [Not to use any land not comprised in the Holding for the production of milk or ancillary purposes.]
8.52.3   To procure on the termination of the Tenancy the transfer of such quota without payment to the Landlord or his nominee and to sign all requisite forms for that purpose.
8.52.4   To pay to the Landlord the value of any such quota not transferred to the Landlord or his nominee as aforesaid such value to be the open market value thereof on the date of termination.

4 TENANCIES UNDER THE AGRICULTURAL HOLDINGS ACT 1986

8.52.5   Not to sign any contract for the supply of milk from the Holding without ensuring appropriate provisions for the continuation of the acquisition of milk from the Holding in the event of the Tenancy being terminated and on the termination of the Tenancy to use his best endeavours to transfer any contract for the supply of milk to the Landlord or his nominee if the Landlord so requires.

8.52.6   In relation to the period which falls both prior to the termination of the Tenancy and within the milk quota year current at that termination not to produce a quantity of milk which is greater than the due proportion for that period as indicated on the monthly quota statement relating to the Holding.

8.52.7   If the Tenant produced a quantity of milk in excess of the proportion calculated in accordance with clause 8.52.6 to indemnify the Landlord and any other occupier of the Holding against any levy liability payable in respect of such excess.

8.53   *Relevant Quotas*

8.53.1   At all times during the Tenancy to do all such acts and things as shall be required (including producing a sufficient quantity of any relevant product and signing and lodging within any applicable statutory or other time-limits such documents as are required) to maintain all Relevant Quotas.

8.53.2   To notify the Landlord in writing of any changes in the level of any of the Relevant Quotas within seven days of the Tenant becoming aware of any such change.

8.53.3   To use his best endeavours to obtain for the Holding suitable quotas contracts premium rights or similar arrangements under any new scheme introduced after the commencement of the Tenancy.

8.53.4   At all times during the Tenancy to carry out all obligations imposed on the Tenant as occupier or producer or quota or contract owner in regard to notices compliance with directions payments of levies maintenance of records or otherwise in connection with every Relevant Quota.

8.53.5   Forthwith to furnish to the Landlord all information which the Landlord may reasonably request concerning allocation of any Relevant Quota or concerning other farming activities of the Tenant which may affect or tend to affect the allocation of any Relevant Quota whether such farming activities are carried out by the Tenant directly or indirectly and whether they relate to the Holding or to other land.

8.53.6   If the Landlord at any time or times wishes to agree or record any figures facts or calculations concerning any Relevant Quota and the relative rights of the parties thereto under any United Kingdom or European scheme legislation or directive from time to time in force then to endeavour to agree the same with the Landlord and in default of agreement the matter shall be referred to arbitration either in accordance with the arbitration provisions of such scheme legislation or directive or hereunder.

8.53.7   Not so to dispose of transfer lend lease or otherwise deal with the whole or any part of a Relevant Quota as to result in the Relevant Quota concerned lapsing or reducing during the Tenancy or the Relevant Quota concerned being transferred off the Holding or otherwise becoming unavailable for use on the Holding on the termination of the Tenancy.

8.53.8   Not by any direct or indirect act or omission in respect of any land or property not included in the Holding to allow any Relevant Quota to pass to any other person whatsoever or become attached to land not comprised in the Holding.

8.53.9   On quitting the Holding to take all such steps as may be required to procure the transfer to the Landlord or such person as the Landlord shall in writing require as his successor in respect of each of the Relevant Quotas without charge or payment.

8.54   *General indemnity*
        Without prejudice to any right or remedy of the Landlord in relation to the Tenant's obligations hereunder at all times to keep the Landlord indemnified against all actions claims and liabilities arising out of or in connection with any of those obligations.

8.55   *Crops on termination*
        At the termination of the Tenancy to leave upon the Holding all the unconsumed hay straw roots or green crops (other than peas beans potatoes sugar beet carrots or other vegetable crops) produced on the Holding during the last year of the Tenancy.

8.56   *Vacant possession*
        To take every available measure (including the giving of any necessary notice) to enable vacant possession of the whole of the Holding (including any cottages or houses comprised therein) to be given to the Landlord upon the termination of the Tenancy whether by notice forfeiture or otherwise.

9.   Landlord's agreements
        The Landlord hereby agrees with the Tenant as follows:

9.1   *Tenantright*
        To pay to the Tenant on quitting the value to an incoming tenant of all items in the nature of tenantright such value to be calculated in accordance with the Agriculture (Calculation of Value for Compensation) Regulations 1978 save that the Landlord may set off:

9.1.1   any sum due to the Landlord for rent breaches of agreement waste or otherwise;

9.1.2   if the year of quitting shall not coincide with a year during which the external painting or internal painting and decoration must be executed then a due proportion of the cost of such painting or decoration the deduction for external painting being one-fifth and that for internal painting papering and decorating one-seventh of the estimated total cost in respect of each year that has elapsed since the last repainting papering or decorating or since the commencement of the Tenancy (whichever shall be the later);[5]

9.1.3   the estimated cost of such repairs and replacements to the Landlord's fixed equipment as may in the opinion of the Landlord be required at the time of quitting.

9.2   *Insurance*
To insure the farmhouse cottages (if any) and farm buildings (except the buildings and fixtures belonging to the Tenant and any Redundant Items) against destruction or damage by fire and such other risks as the Landlord shall choose and in the event of destruction or damage by an insured risk (except to the extent that such insurance shall have been vitiated by some act or default of the Tenant or any person for whose acts or defaults the Tenant may be responsible) to reinstate or replace the same if its reinstatement or replacement is required for the fulfilment of his responsibilities to manage the Holding in accordance with the rules of good estate management (and in the event of any shortfall in the insurance monies, to make good the same from his own resources).

9.3   *Quiet enjoyment*
To permit the Tenant on paying the rent and performing and observing the several agreements by the Tenant herein contained peaceably to hold the Holding without any lawful interruption by the Landlord or any person deriving title under him.

10.   Repairs and insurance
The Landlord and the Tenant hereby agree that the Fourth Schedule annexed hereto shall apply to the Tenancy and hereby agree with each other to comply with their respective obligations therein contained.

11.   Provisos and conditions
Provided always and it is hereby agreed and declared as follows:

11.1   *Re-entry*
If at any time:
11.1.1   the rent or any other payment due to the Landlord from the Tenant hereunder is in arrear for more than fourteen days after any of the days appointed for payment thereof (whether formally demanded or not); or
11.1.2   there shall be a breach of any of the agreements by the Tenant herein contained or implied; or

11.1.3 the Tenant or any of them shall become insolvent for the purposes of the AHA 1986 or if the interest of the Tenant or any of them under this Agreement shall be taken in execution or if any execution shall be levied on the goods or chattels of the Tenant or any of them or if any stock or crops on the Holding shall be taken under a bill of sale or sold under the authority of a charge made under the Agricultural Credits Act 1928 or the Tenant shall be convicted of stealing sheep or cattle; or

11.1.4 a receiver or administrator is appointed in respect of the Tenant's goods property or undertaking or any part thereof;
and if the Landlord shall give to the Tenant at least two months' written notice of such non-payment breach or event stating in such notice that the Landlord accordingly relies upon this sub-clause then in any or every such case it shall be lawful for the Landlord or any person authorised by him in that behalf at any time thereafter to re-enter upon the Holding or upon any part thereof in the name of the whole and thereupon the Tenancy shall absolutely determine without prejudice to the right of action or other remedies of the Landlord in respect of any breach of any of the agreements by the Tenant or any of them herein contained.[6]

11.2 *Insolvency*

If the Tenant shall be insolvent for the purposes of the AHA 1986 or a receiver or administrator shall be appointed as aforesaid it shall be lawful for the Landlord at any time upon giving to the Tenant no less than three months' previous notice in writing to expire at any time to resume possession and determine the Tenancy.

11.3 *Distress*

Upon seizure by the Landlord under distress for rent the Landlord shall not be obliged to sell any hay straw silage or crops (except the crops which the Tenant is permitted to sell under the terms hereof without returning an equivalent manurial value to the Holding) upon the terms that the same may be removed from the Holding but may exercise the power of sale on distrained goods conferred by statute by selling the same subject to the condition that such produce shall be consumed on the Holding or subject to some other condition which shall secure that the manurial value of such hay straw or crops shall be returned to the Holding. Upon any such seizure and sale it shall be lawful for the Landlord to grant to any purchaser of such hay straw or crops and for such period or periods as the Landlord may think fit the use of such part or parts of the Holding as the Landlord may think necessary or proper for the purpose of harvesting storing consuming or otherwise dealing with such hay straw or crops and without making any compensation to the Tenant in respect thereof.

11.4 *Tenant's fixtures*

11.4.1 The Tenant's right to and in respect of fixtures erected by him or acquired on entry shall be limited to those given to him by section 10 of the AHA 1986.

11.4.2   If the Tenant shall not within two calendar months after the termination of the Tenancy have removed from the Holding any fixtures or fittings to which section 10 of the AHA 1986 applies and in relation to which the Landlord has not given written notice of his intention to purchase under that section such fixtures or fittings shall on the expiration of that period immediately become the property of the Landlord without payment.

11.5   *Redundant items*

11.5.1   The items specified in the Second Schedule hereto are agreed as obsolete or redundant to the farming of the Holding.

11.5.2   If at any time or times during the continuance of the Tenancy either party shall wish to treat any buildings or other items of fixed equipment on the Holding (other than those included in the Second Schedule hereto) as obsolete or redundant to the proper requirements of the Holding then in default of agreement such party shall be entitled on giving two months' written notice to the other to have the question whether such buildings or other items of fixed equipment or any of them are obsolete or redundant referred to arbitration under the AHA 1986 and if it shall be agreed or if such arbitration shall award that such buildings or other items of fixed equipment or any of them are obsolete or redundant then as from the date of such agreement or award (as the case may be) the buildings or other items of fixed equipment so agreed or awarded to be obsolete or redundant shall be deemed to be included in the said Second Schedule.

11.5.3   In relation to the items specified or deemed to be included in the Second Schedule both parties shall be relieved from all liability to repair or insure the same save that the Tenant shall keep them in a safe condition.

11.5.4   The Tenant may use any redundant buildings or other items of fixed equipment at his own risk and without any obligation (save as aforesaid) to carry out any repairs to them but he must keep them in a clean and tidy condition.

11.5.5   The Landlord shall have the right at any time or times (whether or not the Tenant is using them in accordance with the immediately preceding sub-clause) if he shall so desire to enter and remove any obsolete or redundant fixed equipment at his own expense.

11.6   *Cottages*

If any of the cottages or other houses or premises comprised in the Tenancy shall at any time have been unoccupied for a continuous period of not less than six months (other than by reason of the temporary absence of an employee or former employee of the Tenant who can demonstrate an intention to return) or occupied in breach of the provisions hereof then it shall be lawful for the Landlord to give to the Tenant not less than three months' written notice to expire at any time to resume possession and determine the Tenancy as to the part of the Holding comprising the said cottage house or premises and its curtilage and appurtenances. In respect of any such property the Landlord may require the Tenant (at the Tenant's expense) to apply to the Court for the purpose of obtaining such orders as may be necessary to secure vacant possession thereof and relief ancillary thereto.[7]

11.7   *Termination for non agricultural use*

It shall be lawful for the Landlord at any time or times upon giving to the Tenant not less than three months' previous written notice to expire at any time to resume possession and determine the Tenancy as to the whole or any part of the Holding for any purpose not being the use of the Holding or such part for agriculture and whether the use thereof for any of such purposes is to be made by the Landlord or by a purchaser lessee assignee or other person deriving title from or through the Landlord.

11.8   *Determination as to part*

If there shall be a determination of the Tenancy as to any part of the Holding (whether under the foregoing provisions hereof or by surrender or otherwise) then subject to any contrary agreement the Tenant shall have the same rights as to compensation and to a proportionate reduction of rent as would have been applicable had such determination been by notice to quit pursuant to section 31 of the AHA 1986 but without the need to serve any notice required by that section and in the event of the parties hereto failing to agree as to the amount of such compensation or proportionate reduction of rent the same shall be determined by arbitration hereunder.

11.9   *Rent reviews*

11.9.1 As between the parties hereto paragraph 4(2) of Schedule 2 to the AHA 1986 shall be read and construed as if there were added at the end thereof:

'An increase or reduction of rent by reason of the determination of the tenancy as to part of the Holding (whether by notice to quit surrender or otherwise) or the addition of land to the Holding in either case whether with or without a variation in the amount actually payable'.

11.9.2 If the arbitrator on any subsequent rent review shall decline jurisdiction under section 12 of the AHA 1986 the question of the rent payable in respect of the Holding shall be referred to arbitration hereunder and it shall be determined as nearly as may be on the same basis as it would have been determined under that section but without the need to serve any notices required by that section.

11.10   *Termination on non agricultural use by tenant*

If the Tenant shall at any time not be using any part or parts of the Holding for agriculture then it shall be lawful for the Landlord at any time or times upon giving to the Tenant not less than three months' previous written notice to expire at any time to resume possession and determine the Tenancy as to such part or parts of the Holding.

11.11   *Severed reversion*

If at any time the reversionary estate expectant on the Tenancy shall be severed then for the purposes of rent reviews section 12 of the AHA 1986 shall be read and construed as if the words 'or a severed part of the reversionary estate therein' were added after the word 'holding' where it first occurs in that section and as if the words 'or a severed part of the reversionary estate therein (as the case may be)' were added after the word 'holding' where it subsequently occurs in that section.

11.12   *Set-off*

The Landlord shall be entitled to set off against and deduct from any moneys which may at any time be payable by the Landlord to the Tenant in respect of the Holding any moneys which may be payable to the Landlord by the Tenant in respect of the Holding whether such sum so payable by or to the Landlord shall be of a liquidated character or not.

11.13   *Misdescription*

In the event of the description of the Holding in the First Schedule hereto being by reference to an Ordnance Survey plan or areas the fact that Ordnance Survey areas are measured to the centre of the hedge shall not in the case of the boundary of the Holding be taken to indicate that the Holding ends at the centre of the hedge.

11.14   *Custom*

The rights of the parties under this Agreement or otherwise in respect of the Tenancy shall not depend on or be affected by any custom of the country.

11.15   *Perennial crops*

Nothing herein contained shall be deemed to be a consent within the meaning of the AHA 1986 to the making of any improvement nor shall the Holding be deemed to be let as a market garden but if the Tenant shall wish to remove (except from the gardens and orchards of the farmhouse and cottages) any asparagus rhubarb or other perennial crop or any fruit bushes planted or purchased by him before the termination of the Tenancy he shall first give to the Landlord written notice of such his wish three months before the end of the Tenancy and to the extent that the Landlord shall not have agreed in writing to purchase them by valuation within one month of receiving such notice the Tenant may remove such items but shall make good and replace the surface of the soil.

11.16   *Arable area payments*

On the termination of the Tenancy:

11.16.1   Arable and set-aside area aid payments due and not by then received shall be payable to the Landlord and the Tenant shall sign all requisite forms authorising payment to the Landlord;

11.16.2   Any such aid received by the Tenant shall be forthwith paid over to the Landlord;

11.16.3   Any payment due from the Landlord to the Tenant in respect of tenantright shall be calculated having regard to the receipt by the Landlord of the aid payment but pending receipt of such payments there shall be retained by the Landlord an amount equal to such payments which shall be paid over to the Tenant forthwith on receipt thereof by the Landlord;

11.16.4   Neither party shall do or omit anything which may prejudice the aid payments;

11.16.5   Any documents required to secure the aid payments shall be handed by the Tenant to the Landlord on the termination of the Tenancy;

11.16.6   In the event of the Tenancy terminating during any set-aside period any contract for the sale of non food crops on set-aside land shall be assigned to the Landlord or his nominee and all requisite notices shall be submitted in the appropriate time-scale.

11.17   *Value added tax*

Where under the terms of this Agreement the Tenant is obliged to make any payment to the Landlord which attracts value added tax (or any tax replacing it) the Tenant shall be responsible for the payment of such value added tax (or any tax replacing it).

11.18   *Sale*

In the event of the sale of the Holding the responsibility for the Landlord's obligations hereunder shall pass to the purchaser and no action shall lie against the Landlord for their non–observance after the date on which the rent accrues to the purchaser.

11.19   *Notices*

Where any notice is required under this Agreement to be given by or to the Landlord such notice may be given by or to his duly authorised agent any notice (including notices to quit) to be given by either party under this Agreement may be served in the manner provided by section 93 of the AHA 1986 or as regards any notice to the Tenant by being sent to him by registered post or recorded delivery to the farmhouse or by handing it to the Tenant or his agent or by affixing the notice to some conspicuous part of the Holding and any notice to the Tenant shall be sufficient though the same is not addressed to the Tenant by name but only addressed to him by the description of the Tenant of the Holding.

4 TENANCIES UNDER THE AGRICULTURAL HOLDINGS ACT 1986

11.20   *Arbitration*

All questions valuations and claims hereafter in dispute between the Landlord and the Tenant under this Agreement not compulsorily referred to arbitration by any statutory provision shall be referred to arbitration under the provisions of the Arbitration Act 1996 by a single arbitrator to be appointed in default of agreement by the President for the time being of the Royal Institution of Chartered Surveyors.

FIRST SCHEDULE

THE HOLDING

| | Ordnance Survey | | | | Area | |
Parish	Sheet No	Enclosure No	Field Name	Cultivation	Hectares	Acres

SECOND SCHEDULE

REDUNDANT ITEMS

THIRD SCHEDULE

TENANT'S FIXTURES

FOURTH SCHEDULE

General provisions and limitations

1.   Nothing contained in this Agreement shall oblige either the Landlord or the Tenant:

1.1   to maintain repair replace or insure any item of fixed equipment which is specified or deemed to be included in the Second Schedule;

1.2   to execute any work if and so far as the execution of such work is rendered impossible (except at prohibitive or unreasonable expense) by reason of subsidence of any kind or by the blocking of outfalls which are not under the control of either the Landlord or the Tenant.

2.   The Landlord shall not be obliged to execute repairs or replacements or to insure buildings or fixtures which are the property of the Tenant or to execute repairs or replacements rendered necessary by the wilful or negligent act or omission of the Tenant or any member of his household or any of his employees licensees or invitees.

The landlord's rights and obligations

3. To execute all repairs and replacements to the following parts of the farmhouse cottages and farm buildings on the Holding namely:

3.1 the main walls and exterior walls (including walls of open and covered yards and garden walls) of whatever construction (but excluding the interior covering of such walls save to the extent that such interior covering has been adversely affected by any default by the Landlord in carrying out his obligations) and the chimney stacks including the pots. But at his own option the Landlord may substitute a stockproof fence for any garden wall and thereafter paragraph 12.1.2 of this Schedule shall apply to such substituted fence;

3.2 the roofs (subject to the provisions of paragraphs 10 and 14.1 of this Schedule);

3.3 the timbers carrying the roofs ceilings and floors;

3.4 the floors doors windows and skylights including the frames (except glass glass substitute locks sashcords and fastenings);

3.5 the staircases of the farmhouse and cottages including banisters and hand rails (but not ladders);

3.6 the eaves guttering and downpipes.

4. To execute all repairs and replacements to the water supply pipes laid underground on the Holding (subject to the provisions of paragraph 14.2 of this Schedule).

5. Save to the extent that replacement is rendered necessary by any failure by the Tenant to comply with his obligations to replace the following items when they or any of them are beyond repair:

5.1 the electric wiring system of the premises (except the fittings);

5.2 the soil drains sewers gulleys manholes inspection chambers cesspools septic tanks filter beds and sewage disposal apparatus (excepting the covers tops and gratings of these items and the media of any filter bed);

5.3 the wells boreholes reservoirs pumphouses and pumping equipment;

5.4 the bridges (but not culverts) and cattle grids.

6. When in the opinion of the Landlord it shall be necessary and in a proper workmanlike manner to paint gas-tar creosote or otherwise effectively treat with a preservative material (at the option of the Landlord) the whole of the exterior wood and ironwork on the Holding including the inside of all external doors and windows opening outwards of the farm buildings usually so dealt with but subject to the provisions of paragraph 15 of this Schedule.

4 TENANCIES UNDER THE AGRICULTURAL HOLDINGS ACT 1986

7. If the Tenant does not start work on the repairs or replacements for which he is liable under paragraphs 9–17 of this Schedule within two months or if he fails to complete them within three months of receiving from the Landlord a written notice (not being a notice requiring him to remedy a breach of the terms of the Tenancy by doing work of repair maintenance or replacement in a form prescribed under the Agricultural Holdings (Forms of Notice to Pay Rent or to Remedy) Regulations 1987, SI 1987/711 specifying the necessary repairs or replacements and calling on him to execute them the Landlord may enter and execute such repairs or replacements and recover the reasonable cost from the Tenant forthwith.

The tenant's rights and obligations

8. To pay to the Landlord on demand:
8.1 any sum recoverable by the Landlord under paragraph 7 of this Schedule;
8.2 a proportion not exceeding one-half of the reasonable cost of:
8.2.1 repairs and replacements executed by the Landlord to the items specified in paragraph 4 of this Schedule;
8.2.2 exterior painting tarring creosoting or treatment with other preservative material executed by the Landlord in accordance with paragraph 6 of this Schedule.

9. To repair so long as practicable and to use his best endeavours to keep clean and in good repair until worn out the items specified in paragraph 5 of this Schedule.

10. To provide free of charge suitable straw or reed and spars for the repair or renewal of thatch.

11. To replace anything mentioned in paragraph 5 of this Schedule which has worn out or otherwise become incapable of repair if the need for replacement arises out of the Tenant's failure to repair it.

12. Except insofar as such liabilities fall to be undertaken by the Landlord under the foregoing provisions of this Schedule:
12.1 To put keep and leave clean and in good tenantable repair order and condition:
12.1.1 the farmhouse cottages and farm buildings on the Holding;
12.1.2 all fences live and dead hedges gates gate posts and irons field walls posts stiles culverts covers and gratings (to inspection pits septic tanks cesspits filter beds wells and boreholes) the media in filter beds troughs taps tanks and all water pipes and fittings fixed above ground.
12.2 To keep in good tenantable repair all roads yards (including the concrete or other surfaces thereof) watercourses sluices ditches ponds underdrains and outfalls.
12.3 To keep clean and in good working order all roof valleys eaves guttering and downpipes and also to use carefully so as to protect from wilful reckless or negligent damage all items for the repair or replacement of which the Landlord is responsible under the provisions of this Schedule and report in writing immediately to the Landlord any damage however caused to items for the repair or replacement of which the Landlord is responsible.

12.4   To replace and repair and, upon replacement or repair, adequately to paint, gas-tar or creosote or otherwise effectively treat with a proper and adequate preservative material all items of fixed equipment and to do any work where such replacement, repair or work is rendered necessary by the wilful or negligent act or omission of the Tenant or any member of his household or any of his employees licensees or invitees or by damage caused by the Tenant's stock.

13.   As often as may be requisite and in any case at intervals of not more than seven years properly to clean colour whiten paper and paint limewash or otherwise treat with materials of suitable quality the inside of the farmhouse cottages and farm buildings which have been previously so treated including the internal structural steelwork of farm buildings (whether open-sided or not) and including the inside of all doors and windows of the farmhouse and cottages opening outwards and in the last year of the Tenancy to limewash the inside of all farm buildings which have previously been limewashed.

14.1   To renew all broken or cracked tiles or slates and replace all slipped tiles or slates from time to time as the damage occurs but so that the Tenant shall not be required to carry out in any one year of the Tenancy such works to a cost greater than £. . .

14.2   To repair or renew any burst or damaged waterpipes underground as the damage occurs but so that the Tenant shall not be required to carry out in any one year of the Tenancy such works to a cost greater than £. . .

15.   To put keep and leave clean and in good repair and condition the interior and exterior of all chitting houses or other glasshouses (including all glass thereof) and to paint with at least two coats to the interior and exterior wood and iron work at least once in every five years and so to leave the same at the end of the tenancy.

16.   To cut trim or lay a proper proportion of the hedges in each year of the Tenancy so as to maintain them in good and sound condition.

17.   To dig out scour and cleanse all ponds water courses ditches and grips as may be necessary to maintain them at sufficient width and depth and to keep clear and free from obstructions all field drains and their outlets.

AS WITNESS the hands of the parties hereto the day and year first before written.

SIGNED by the LANDLORD in the
presence of: ....

....

....

....

4 TENANCIES UNDER THE AGRICULTURAL HOLDINGS ACT 1986

SIGNED by the TENANT
in the presence of:

}

....

....

....

....

---

1   This tenancy is a traditional tenancy agreement updated to some extent which fits in with the
    concept of a succession tenancy; practitioners may prefer the format of the farm business tenancy
    agreement (see p 000) but must be careful to include clauses relevant only to 1986 Act tenancies
    from this precedent and exclude clauses relevant only to 1995 Act tenancies from that precedent.
    A number of the clauses are contentious, particularly from the point of view of the tenant, and
    would need careful consideration and instructions.
        Note that stamp duty is based on rent.
2   The tenant may regard this clause as particularly unreasonable.
3   If clause 10 is included, this clause will be deleted. Clause 8.14 assumes the tenant is responsible
    for all repairs.
4   The tenant may regard this clause as unreasonable.
5   This sub-clause will only be appropriate if clause 10 applies.
6   The need for notice to give the tenant time to make all appropriate end of tenancy claims,
    otherwise the clause will be void: *Parry v Million Pigs Ltd* (1980) 260 EG 281.
7   This clause may well be unenforceable, certainly as regards recovering possession, but is often
    seen.

---

2   SUCCESSION TENANCY UNDER THE AHA 1986 – SHORT FORM BY REFERENCE

THIS TENANCY AGREEMENT is made this [*date*]

BETWEEN [*name*] of [*address*] ('the Landlord')

AND [*name*] of [*address*] ('the Tenant')

In the following terms:

1.   This tenancy is an agreed succession to the tenancy which commenced on
        the [*date*] pursuant to a Tenancy Agreement made on the [*date*] between
        the Landlord (1) and [*name*] (2) ('the Principal Agreement') in respect of
        ALL THAT property situate at and known as [*Holding details*] ('the
        Holding').

2.   The Landlord hereby lets the Holding to the Tenant on a tenancy from
        year to year commencing on the [*date*] at an initial rental of [*sum in words*]
        pounds (£. . .) per annum payable on the days and in the manner set out in
        the Principal Agreement.

3.   Part IV of the Agricultural Holdings Act 1986 is to apply to this tenancy.

4.   For the purposes of the Agricultural Holdings Act 1986 this agreed
        succession is the first/second (*delete as appropriate*) succession.

5.   This tenancy is subject to the terms conditions covenants and provisions contained in the Principal Agreement as if the same had been repeated herein.

AS WITNESS the hands of the parties hereto the day and year first before written.

SIGNED by the said LANDLORD in the presence of: } ....

....

....

....

SIGNED by the TENANT in the presence of: } ....

....

....

....

Note. Stamp duty based on rent.

3   ASSIGNMENT OF TENANCY

THIS ASSIGNMENT is made the [*date*]

BETWEEN [*name*] of [*address*] ('the Assignor') of the first part [*name*] of [*address*] ('the Assignee') of the second part and [*name*] of [*address*] ('the Landlords') of the third part.

NOW THIS DEED WITNESSES as follows:

1.   Definitions and interpretation
1.1   'the Property' means the property more particularly described in the Schedule;
1.2   'the Tenancy Agreement' means an Agreement ... and includes any deeds or documents supplemental thereto whether or not expressed to be so;
1.3   words importing one gender shall be construed as importing any other gender;
1.4   words importing the singular shall be construed as importing the plural and vice versa;
1.5   where any party comprises more than one person the obligations and liabilities of that party under this assignment shall be joint and several obligations and liabilities of those persons;
1.6   the clause headings do not form part of this assignment and shall not be taken into account in its construction and interpretation.

2.   Recitals
2.1   By the Tenancy Agreement [*name*] let the Property to [*name*] for a term beginning on [*date*] and continuing from year to year until determined as therein mentioned.
2.2   The Assignor is desirous of retiring and assigning all his interest in the Property and the Tenancy Agreement to the Assignee.
2.3   The Assignee is the ... of the Assignor and is a person who if the Assignor had died immediately before the date of this deed would have been a close relative of the Assignor for the purposes of the Agricultural Holdings Act 1986.
2.4   The Landlords are now the landlords of the Property.
2.5   The current annual rent is £ ....
2.6   The Assignor has agreed with the Assignee for the assignment of the tenancy created by the Tenancy Agreement to the Assignee.
2.7   The Tenancy Agreement contains a provision prohibiting the Assignor from assigning the tenancy thereby created.

2.8 The Assignor has applied to the Landlord for consent to the assignment on the basis that such assignment will constitute a first/second succession for the purposes of Part IV of the Agricultural Holdings Act 1986 and on that basis notwithstanding but without prejudice to the provision in the Tenancy Agreement prohibiting assignment the Landlords have agreed to grant such consent in the manner hereinafter appearing to enable the Assignor to assign the whole of his estate and interest in the Property to the Assignee.

3. Licence to assign

The Landlords grant to the Assignor licence to assign the whole of the Assignor's estate and interest in the Property to the Assignee.

4. Assignment

In pursuance of the said agreement and in consideration of the covenents by the Assignee contained in clause 5 the Assignor hereby assigns to the Assignee ALL THAT the Property and the Assignor with full title guarantee hereby releases to the Assignee all that his interest in the Property and in the said tenancy created by the Tenancy Agreement TO HOLD to the Assignee from the date hereof during the continuance of the tenancy created by the Tenancy Agreement as yearly tenant in the place of the Assignor SUBJECT TO the performance and observance of the terms and conditions of the said tenancy.

5. Covenant for indemnity[1]

With the object and intention of affording to the Assignor a full and sufficient indemnity but not further or otherwise the Assignee covenants with the Assignor that he and his successors in title will:

5.1 during the tenancy pay the rents reserved under the Tenancy Agreement and perform all the terms and conditions on the part of the tenant therein contained; and

5.2 keep the Assignor and his successors in title indemnified against all actions and claims demands losses costs damage and liabilities whatsoever arising by reason of any breach of the terms and conditions of the Tenancy Agreement.

6. Covenant with landlords

The Assignee covenants with the Landlords that at all times hereafter during the remainder of the tenancy created by the Tenancy Agreement the Assignee shall pay the rent reserved by and observe and perform the covenants on the part of the tenant and the conditions contained in the Tenancy Agreement.

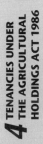

4 TENANCIES UNDER THE AGRICULTURAL HOLDINGS ACT 1986

7.   Non-waiver

Nothing herein contained shall waive or be deemed to waive any breach of the obligations of the Assignor under the Tenancy Agreement which may have occurred prior to the date hereof or authorise or be deemed to authorise any further assignment and the covenants on the part of the tenant and conditions contained in the Tenancy Agreement shall continue in full force and effect.

8.   First/Second succession

The parties hereby agree that this Assignment shall be treated as a first/second succession for the purposes of Part IV of the Agricultural Holdings Act 1986 and that the Assignee is both eligible and suitable within the meaning of the said Act.

9.   Stamp duty

It is hereby certified that the transaction hereby effected falls within Category L in the Schedule to the Stamp Duty (Exempt Instruments) Regulations 1987.

IN WITNESS whereof this Deed has been executed by the parties hereto the day and year first before written.

SCHEDULE

THE PROPERTY

SIGNED and delivered as a Deed by   }
the said [*name*] in the presence of: }
                                                              ....

....

....

....

SIGNED and delivered as a Deed by
the said [*name*] in the presence of: }

....

....

....

....

SIGNED and delivered as a Deed by
the said [*name*] in the presence of: }

....

....

....

....

SIGNED and delivered as a Deed by
the said [*name*] in the presence of: }

....

....

....

....

---

1   Or a release by the Landlords may be negotiated.

---

4   AGREEMENT RECORDING TERMS OF TENANCY[1]

THIS AGREEMENT is made the [*date*]

BETWEEN:

(1) [*name*] of [*address*]
    ('the Landlord'); and

(2) [*name*] of [*address*]
    ('the Tenant').

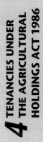

4 TENANCIES UNDER THE AGRICULTURAL HOLDINGS ACT 1986

WHEREAS:

1.   The Tenant is the tenant from year to year of the agricultural holding known as [*name*] ('the Holding') situate at [*address*] and containing ... acres or thereabouts and being [the land registered with absolute title at H.M. Land Registry under the title number ...] TOGETHER WITH all the Landlord's fixtures and fittings on the Holding.

2.   The Landlord and the Tenant desire to record the terms of the tenancy in writing.

NOW IT IS AGREED as follows:

1.   The Holding is held on a tenancy from year to year until it shall be determined on [*date*] by either party giving to the other at least twelve months' previous notice in writing.

2.   Rent
           Annual rent of £ ... is payable in advance/arrears on the [*date*] and the [*date*] in each year.

3.   Agreement by the tenant
           The Tenant agreed with the Landlord as follows:

3.1   *To pay outgoings*
           to pay all existing and future rates taxes assessments and outgoings of any kind charged or imposed upon the Holding or upon the owner or occupier thereof;

3.2   *Return of manurial values in the event of the destruction by fire of harvested crops grown on the holding for consumption on it*
           to return to the Holding the full equivalent manurial value of the crops destroyed insofar as the return is required for the fulfilment of the Tenant's responsibilities to farm in accordance with the rules of good husbandry;

3.3   *Insurance*
           to insure against damage by fire all dead stock on the Holding and such harvested crops as are grown on the Holding for consumption on it;

3.4   *Assignment*
           not to assign sublet or part with possession of the Holding or any part of it without the Landlord's consent in writing.

4.   Right of re-entry
4.1   If at any time:
4.1.1   the rent or any part of it is in arrear for at least 21 days after becoming due; or
4.1.2   there is any breach or non-observance by the Tenant of any of the covenants and conditions contained in this Agreement,

then the Landlord may without previously demanding any rents that may be due (after giving the Tenant two calendar months' notice) re-enter immediately upon the Holding or any part of it in the name of the whole and the tenancy is then to determine absolutely without prejudice to the rights of the Landlord in respect of any breach or non-observance of any of the agreements contained above and on the part of the Tenant to be performed and observed or any other rights and remedies of the Landlord.

AS WITNESS the hands of the parties hereto the day and year first before written.

SIGNED by the said [*name*]
in the presence of:

....

....

....

....

SIGNED by the said [*name*]
in the presence of:

....

....

....

....

---

1   Probably chargeable to stamp duty by reference to the rent.
As repairs are not mentioned, the model clauses (SI 1973/1473 amended by SI 1988/281) will apply.

4 TENANCIES UNDER THE AGRICULTURAL HOLDINGS ACT 1986

5 REQUEST TO ENTER WRITTEN AGREEMENT UNDER AHA 1986, SECTION 6

AGRICULTURAL HOLDINGS ACT 1986

SECTION 6, SCHEDULE 1

TO: [*addressee's name and address*]

HOLDING: [*details of Holding and number*]

In accordance with section 6(1) of the Agricultural Holdings Act 1986 I/we [*Landlord's/Tenant's/Agents' name and address (as the case may be)*] [*on behalf of* [*name*] *(as the case may be)*] request you to enter into a written agreement embodying the terms of the tenancy under which I/you (*delete as applicable*) hold the Holding and containing provision for all the matters included in Schedule 1 to the said Act.

Dated ....

Signed ....
       Duly Authorised Signatory
       on behalf of the Landlord/Landlord

OR

Signed ....
       Duly Authorised Signatory
       on behalf of the Tenant/Tenant

6 ASSIGNMENT OF AN ORAL TENANCY[1]

THE ASSIGNMENT is made the [*date*]

BETWEEN:

(1) [*name*]
of [*address*] ('The Assignor')
(2) [*name*]
of [*address*] ('The Assignee')

NOW THIS DEED WITNESSES as follows:

1.   Definitions and interpretation
1.1   'the Property' means the property more particularly described in the Schedule;

1.2   words importing one gender shall be construed as importing any other gender;

1.3   words importing the singular shall be construed as importing the plural and vice versa;

1.4   where any party comprises more than one person the obligations and liabilities of that party under this assignment shall be joint and several obligations and liabilities of those persons;

1.5   the clause headings do not form part of this assignment and shall not be taken into account in its construction and interpretation.

2.   Recitals

2.1   The Assignor has since on or about the [*date*] been the tenant of the Property from year to year by virtue of an oral agreement made between (1) [*name*] and (2) the Assignor.

2.2   The landlord of the property is now [*name*].

2.3   The current annual rent is £ . . . .

2.4   The Assignor has agreed with the Assignee for the assignment of the Assignor's term and interest in the Property to the Assignee.

3.   Assignment

In pursuance of the said agreement and in consideration of the covenants by the Assignee contained in clause 4 the Assignor hereby assigns to the Assignee ALL THAT the Property and the Assignor with full title guarantee hereby releases to the Assignee all that his interest in the Property and in the said tenancy created by the said oral agreement TO HOLD to the Assignee for all of the yearly tenancy now vested in the Assignor SUBJECT TO the performance and observance of the terms and conditions of the said tenancy.

4.   Covenant for indemnity

With the object and intention of affording to the Assignor full and sufficient indemnity but not further or otherwise the Assignee covenants with the Assignor that he and his successors in title will:

4.1   during the tenancy pay the rents reserved under the tenancy and perform all the terms and conditions of the tenancy; and

4.2   keep the Assignor and his successors in title indemnified against all actions and claims demands losses costs damages and liabilities whatsoever arising by reason of any breach of the terms and conditions of the tenancy.

5.

It is hereby certified that the transaction hereby effected falls within category L in the Schedule to the Stamp Duty (Exempt Instruments) Regulations 1987.[2]

IN WITNESS whereof this Deed has been executed by the parties hereto the day and year first before written.

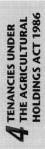

4   **TENANCIES UNDER THE AGRICULTURAL HOLDINGS ACT 1986**

SCHEDULE

THE PROPERTY

ALL THAT parcel of land situate at [*address*] in the County of [*county*] extending to
some . . . acres or thereabouts and shown for the purposes of identification edged red
on the plan annexed hereto.

SIGNED and delivered as a Deed by
the said [*name*] in the presence of:

....

....

....

SIGNED and delivered as a Deed by
the said [*name*] in the presence of:

....

....

....

---

1   No stamp duty if appropriate certificate can be inserted.
2   This assumes a gift. If for value, a certificate of value for stamp duty should be inserted. If a
    change of trustees, Certificate A will be appropriate.

7 SURRENDER AGREEMENT MAKING PROVISION FOR TRANSFER OF MILK QUOTA TO THIRD PARTIES[1]

THIS AGREEMENT made the [*date*]

BETWEEN:

(1) [*name*] of [*address*] in the County of [*county*] ('the Landlord')
(2) [*name*] of [*address*] ('the Tenant').

WHEREAS:

1.   By an agreement for tenancy commencing on or about the [*date*] and made between the Landlord of the one part and the Tenant of the other part ALL THAT agricultural holding known as [*name of holding*] in the County of [*county*] comprising some . . . acres or thereabouts ('the Holding') was let to the Tenant on a tenancy from year to year.

[2.   The Tenant is the Registered Producer (in the name of [*name*]) for Intervention Board purposes in respect of . . . litres of wholesale milk quota ('the milk quota') and it has been agreed that the Tenant shall be permitted to transfer the milk quota to one or more third parties retaining the net proceeds of sale free from any claim by or on behalf of the Landlord in respect of same and further that the Landlord shall assist the Tenant to effect the said transfer or transfers by signing all necessary documentation as required by the Tenant.]

[3.   It has been further agreed between the parties that the Landlord will sign all necesary forms and do all necessary things to ensure the transfer of the milk quota to the Tenant or as he shall direct.]

4.   It is further agreed between the parties as hereinafter appearing.

NOW IT IS HEREBY AGREED as follows:

1.   In consideration of the sum of £. . . and of the agreements on the part of the Landlord hereinafter contained and set out the Tenant with full title guarantee shall on the [*date*] (the 'Surrender Date') surrender the Holding to the Landlord on the terms of a Deed of Surrender (the 'Deed of Surrender') in the form annexed hereto to the intent that the Tenant's interest in the same shall become merged and extinguished in the freehold reversion.

2.   Forthwith on the exchange of this agreement the Tenant will execute the Deed of Surrender.

2.1   As soon as practicable after the date hereof and in any event before the Surrender Date the Landlord will execute the Deed of Surrender (or duplicate thereof).

2.2   Until the Surrender Date the Deed of Surrender shall be held by the Landlord's Agent subject to the terms of this agreement.

TENANCIES UNDER THE AGRICULTURAL HOLDINGS ACT 1986

3.   The rent payable by the Tenant to the Landlord during the period from the date hereof to the Surrender Date shall be the sum of £... per acre per annum such rental to be paid half yearly in advance on the [*date*] and [*date*] in each year the first payment to be made on the date hereof in respect of the period from the date hereof to the payment date next following.

4.   The Landlord shall pay to the Tenant by way of tenantright the agreed sum of £....

4.1   The Tenant shall pay to the Landlord in respect of dilapidations the sum of £....

[5.   The Tenant shall transfer to one or more third parties as the Tenant shall decide the milk quota the Tenant retaining the net proceeds of sale thereof free from any claim by or on behalf of the Landlord AND FURTHER the Landlord shall assist the Tenant to effect the transfer or transfers by signing all necessary documentation and at the Tenant's expense doing all necessary things to ensure the transfer of the milk quota upon being requested so to do by the Tenant and shall consent to the grant of subtenancies provided that each of them expires on or before the Surrender Date.]

5.1   The Landlord shall not make any futher representations concerning the milk quota pursuant to the Dairy Produce Quotas Regulations 1997 (SI 1997/733) ('the Regulations') or otherwise nor shall he seek to register any interest in the milk quota nor make any claim with regard thereto.

5.2   If notwithstanding the terms of this Agreement, any claims are made outside the provisions of this Agreement in respect of the milk quota consequent upon the termination of the Tenancy Agreement or otherwise resulting in an apportionment of the same in favour of the Landlord pursuant to a decision of an Arbitrator appointed under the Regulations or otherwise the Landlord will pay to the Tenant or other party or parties all lawfully recoverable losses reasonably and properly incurred by the Tenant or the other party or parties in the acquisition of milk quota of comparable butterfat base and usage to replace the milk quota together with (but without prejudice to the generality hereof) all costs incurred in such acquisition.

6.   The Tenant agrees that he is and will remain liable on the covenants contained in the Tenancy Agreement until the Surrender Date.

7.   Any provision of this agreement to which full force and effect has not been given by the Surrender Date shall continue in full force and effect after the Surrender Date.

8.   The provisions of this agreement shall bind the parties their successors in title assigns personal representatives and any insolvency practitioner appointed in respect of the affairs of any of them.

AS WITNESS the hands of the parties hereto the day and year first before written.

SIGNED by the said [*name*]
in the presence of:

}

....

....

....

....

SIGNED by the said [*name*]
in the presence of:

}

....

....

....

....

---

1   No stamp duty if surrender later – surrender may be stampable.

In light of *Johnson v Morton* [1978] All ER 37 it has been suggested that a Surrender Agreement is a contracting out of the Act and unenforceable. So far as the authors are aware this contention has never been proved and Surrender Agreements are still entered into in practice. They are useful where the parties wish to agree terms for a surrender prior to the event.

---

8   DEED OF SURRENDER [WITH TRANSFER OF MILK QUOTA TO THIRD PARTY[1]]

THIS DEED OF SURRENDER made the [*date*]

BETWEEN:

(1)   [*name*]
      ('the Tenant')
(2)   [*name*]
      ('the Landlord')

WHEREAS:

1.   The Tenant is the Tenant of (inter alia) certain premises situate and known as land at [*address*] as the same is for identification purposes only delineated and edged red on the plan annexed hereto (the 'Holding') being part of the property comprised in a Tenancy Agreement (the 'Tenancy Agreement') made in or about the [*date*] between the Landlord of the one part and the Tenant of the other part.

2.   The reversion immediately expectant upon the determination of the tenancy under the tenancy agreement and the supplemental agreement (the 'Tenancy') is now vested in the Landlord.

[3.   The Tenant is the registered producer (in the name of [*name*]) for Intervention Board purposes in respect of ... Litres of wholesale milk quota ('the Milk Quota') and it has been agreed that the Tenant shall be permitted to transfer the Milk Quota to one or more third parties retaining the net proceeds of sale free from any claim by or on behalf of the Landlord in respect thereof and further that the Landlord shall assist the Tenant to effect the said transfer or transfers by signing all necessary documentation required by the Tenant in connection therewith.]

4.   The Tenant has agreed to surrender to the Landlord the Holding on the terms hereinafter appearing.

NOW THIS DEED WITNESSES as follows:

1.   In consideration of the sum of £... receipt of which is hereby acknowledged and the agreements on the part of the Landlord hereinafter contained and set out and in consideration of the premises the Tenant with full title guarantee hereby surrenders the Holding to the Landlord with vacant possession to the intent that the Tenant's interest in the Holding shall forthwith become merged and extinguished in the freehold reversion.

2.1   The Landlord shall pay to the Tenant by way of tenantright the agreed sum of £ ....

2.2   The Tenant shall pay to the Landlord in respect of dilapidations the sum of £ ....

[3.1   The Tenant shall transfer to one or more third parties as the Tenant shall decide the Milk Quota the Tenant retaining the net proceeds of sale in respect of same free from any claim by or on behalf of the Landlord AND FURTHER the Landlord shall assist the Tenant to effect the transfer or transfers by signing all necessary documentation and at the Tenant's expense doing all necessary things to ensure the transfer of the Milk Quota upon being requested so to do by the Tenant.]

3.2   The Landlord shall not make any futher representations concerning the Milk Quota pursuant to the Dairy Produce Quotas Regulations 1997 or otherwise nor shall it seek to register any interest in the Milk Quota nor make any claim with regard thereto.

3.3   If notwithstanding the terms of this Agreement any claims are made outside the provisions of this Agreement in respect of the Milk Quota consequent upon the termination of the Tenancy Agreement or otherwise resulting in an apportionment of the same in favour of the Landlord pursuant to a decision of an Arbitrator appointed under the Dairy Produce Quotas Regulations 1997 or otherwise the Landlord will pay to the Tenant or other party or parties all lawfully recoverable losses reasonably and properly incurred by the Tenant or the other party or parties in the acquisition of milk quota of comparable butterfat base and usage to replace the Milk Quota together with (but without prejudice to the generality hereof) all reasonable and proper costs incurred in such acquisition.

4.   Subject to the provisions hereinbefore contained the parties hereby release each other from all obligations claims and liabilities arising out of or in consequence of the Tenancy Agreement.

5.   This Surrender shall bind the parties their successors in title and assigns and any insolvency practitioner appointed in respect of the affairs of either of them.

6.   It is certified that the transaction hereby effected does not form part of a larger transaction or series of transactions in respect of which the amount or value or the aggregate amount of value of the consideration exceeds £ ....[1]

IN WITNESS whereof this Deed has been executed by the parties hereto the day and year first before written.

SIGNED and delivered as a Deed by
the said [*name*] in the presence of: } ....

....

....

....

SIGNED and delivered as a Deed by
the said [*name*] in the presence of: } ....

....

....

....

---

1   No stamp duty if suitable certificate of value.

9   DEED OF SURRENDER OF WHOLE BY PERSONAL REPRESENTATIVES OF DECEASED TENANT[1]

THIS DEED OF SURRENDER is made the [*date*]

BETWEEN [*name*] and [*name*] both of [*address*] (herinafter called 'the Personal Representatives') of the one part and [*name*] of [*address*] (hereinafter called 'the Landlord') of the other part

WHEREAS:

1.   By an Agreement for Tenancy dated the [*date*] (hereinafter called 'the Tenancy Agreement') and made between [*name*] (1) and [*name*] (2) the farmhouse land and buildings at [*address*] containing . . . acres or thereabouts delineated and edged red on the plan annexed hereto (hereinafter called 'the Property') were demised and let to the said [*name*] on an agricultural tenancy from year to year.

2.   The Landlord is now the owner of the reversion immediately expectant upon the determination of the tenancy under the Tenancy Agreement in respect of that part of the Property.

3.   The said [*name*] died on or about the [*date*].

4.   The Personal Representatives are the Personal Representatives of the said [*name*] and in such capacity have agreed to surrender to the Landlord the agricultural tenancy of the Property on the terms hereinafter appearing.

NOW THIS DEED WITNESSES as follows:

1.   In consideration of the covenant on the part of the Landlord hereinafter contained the Personal Representatives hereby surrender and assign to the Landlord the said tenancy and all other (if any) the estate right or interest of themselves and the said [*name*] in the Property to the intent that their interest and that of the said [*name*] in the Property shall forthwith become merged and extinguished in the freehold reversion.

2.   The Landlord and the Personal Representatives hereby respectively release all (if any) claims whatsoever one against the other (save as hereinafter provided) in respect of the Property and each and every part thereof to which they may respectively have been entitled by virtue of the provisions of the Tenancy Agreement or the Agricultural Holdings Act 1986 or otherwise howsoever.

3.   The Landlord covenants to pay to the Personal Representatives the sum of £. . . in respect of the agreed tenantright.[2]

4.   The Personal Representatives covenant to pay to the Landlord the sum of £. . . in respect of the agreed dilapidations.[2]

5.   This surrender shall bind the parties their successors in title and assigns and any insolvency practitioner appointed in respect of the affairs of any of them.

6.   In this Deed words importing the masculine gender only shall include the feminine and neuter genders and words importing the singular number shall include the plural number and where there are two or more persons mentioned in the expressions the Landlord or the Personal Representatives the obligations of such persons under this deed shall be joint and several.

7.   [Certificate of value – stamp duty.]

IN WITNESS whereof this Deed has been executed by the parties hereto the day and year first before written.

SIGNED and delivered as a Deed by
the said [*name*] in the presence of: } ....

....

....

....

SIGNED and delivered as a Deed by
the said [*name*] in the presence of: } ....

....

....

....

SIGNED and delivered as a Deed by
the said [*name*] in the presence of: } ....

....

....

....

---

1 No stamp duty if certificate of value.

2 It is thought that it is not possible to contract out of liability to pay compensation under these heads. If none is to be paid, each should be quantified at £1.

10   DEED OF SURRENDER OF PART FOR BOUNDARY ADJUSTMENT[1]

THIS DEED OF SURRENDER is made the [*date*]

BETWEEN:

[*name*] of [*address*] ('the Tenant') of the one part and [*name*] of [*address*] ('the Landlord') of the other part

SUPPLEMENTAL to the Tenancy Agreement short details of which are contained in the First Schedule hereto ('the Tenancy').

WHEREAS:

1.   The term granted by the Tenancy is vested in the Tenant.

2.   The reversion immediately expectant upon the termination of the term granted by the Tenancy is now vested in the Landlord.

3.   The property described in the Second Schedule hereto ('the surrendered land') is part of the land let by the tenancy.

4.   It has been agreed by the parties that the Tenant will surrender all his estate and interest in the surrendered land to the Landlord and the Landlord will accept such surrender upon the terms hereinafter mentioned.

NOW THIS DEED WITNESSES as follows:

1.   IN CONSIDERATION of the said agreement the Tenant as beneficial owner HEREBY SURRENDERS AND ASSIGNS unto the Landlord all the surrendered land to the intent that the interest granted by the Tenancy insofar as it relates to the surrendered land (but not further or otherwise) shall merge and be extinguished in the reversion immediately expectant thereon.

2.   IT IS HEREBY AGREED that if any claims to compensation accrue by statute or otherwise to the Tenant pursuant hereto in respect of the surrendered land (whether for tenantright disturbance improvements or otherwise) such claims shall be deemed to be equal to the claims of the Landlord to compensation for dilapidations or otherwise in respect of the surrendered land and accordingly no payment shall be made by either party to the other in respect of any such matters.

3.   IT IS HEREBY AGREED AND RECORDED that the surrender hereby effected amounts to an adjustment of boundaries in accordance with paragraph 6 of Schedule 2 to the Agricultural Holdings Act 1986 and is accordingly to be disregarded for the purposes of paragraph (b) of sub-paragraph (1) of paragraph 4 of the said Schedule 2.[2]

4.   [Certificate of value – stamp duty.]

IN WITNESS whereof this Deed has been executed by the parties hereto the day and year first before written.

FIRST SCHEDULE

DETAILS OF THE TENANCY

DATE   PARTIES   PROPERTY

SECOND SCHEDULE

SURRENDERED LAND

SIGNED and delivered as a Deed by
the said [*name*] in the presence of: }

....

....

....

....

SIGNED and delivered as a Deed by
the said [*name*] in the presence of: }

....

....

....

....

---

1   No stamp duty if suitable certificate of value.
2   Unless the adjustment referred to is a true boundary adjustment, or no rent charge is made, paragraph 6 referred to in this clause is likely to be inapplicable, see *Mann v Gardner* (1990) 66 P&CR 1. This means that an attempt should be made to coordinate the surrender with a rent review or a separate agreement made concerning the next rent review date. Otherwise, the three-yearly review period under paragraph 4 of Schedule 2 will recommence.

4 TENANCIES UNDER THE AGRICULTURAL HOLDINGS ACT 1986

11   NOTICE UNDER LTA 1987, SECTION 48

LANDLORD AND TENANT ACT 1987 SECTION 48

NOTICE[1]

To: [*name*]

Re: [*Holding address and number*]

NOTICE IS GIVEN in accordance with section 48 of the Landlord and Tenant Act 1987 that your Landlord's name and address for service of proceedings and notices in respect of your tenancy agreement [*a copy of which is annexed hereto*] is:

....

....

....

....

....

All notices and proceedings may be served personally on the Landlord at the above address or care of his agents.

Signed ....

Dated ....

---

1   If the holding includes a dwelling, the rent is not technically 'due' unless a notice in these terms has been served on the tenant or at least an adequate address for service in the UK appears on the face of the Tenancy Agreement. This may, therefore, preclude an effective notice to pay under Case D, but the subsequent notice to quit must be challenged within one month.

12 PERMISSION TO ERECT FIXTURE UNDER AHA 1986, SECTION 10

AGRICULTURAL HOLDINGS ACT 1986

SECTION 10

Re: the Holding known as [*Holding address, details and number*]

To: [*Tenant's name and address*]

Pursuant to section 10 of the Agricultural Holdings Act 1986 I HEREBY CONSENT to the erection on the above holding of the fixture details of which are set out in the Schedule hereto upon the terms and conditions of the said Schedule.

SCHEDULE

1.   The Fixture(s):   [*description of fixture*]

2.   Terms and conditions:

2.1   The Fixture shall be considered a Tenant's Fixture under the provisions of the said section 10.

2.2   No compensation shall be payable to the Tenant under sections 64 and 66 of the said Act at the termination of the Tenancy.

2.3   The Fixture is to be sited in a position approved by me or my representative.

2.4   The Tenant must at his own expense keep the Fixture in good repair and (where appropriate) decoration at all times.

2.5   The Tenant will not cause any undue damage or disturbance in the erection or removal of the Fixture and must make good at his own expense any damage caused.

2.6   This Consent is conditional upon the Tenant obtaining all necessary Planning and By-Law approvals in respect of the Fixture and the Tenant will comply at his own expense with any conditions attached to such approvals and will not commence work on the erection of the Fixture until all such approvals have been obtained and conditions precedent attached thereto complied with.

Dated ....

Signed ....   Signed ....
        Duly Authorised Signatory on   Tenant
        behalf of [*Landlord's name*
        and address]

13   DEMAND FOR ARBITRATION OF RENT UNDER AHA 1986, SECTION 12

AGRICULTURAL HOLDINGS ACT 1986

SECTION 12

To: [*addressee's name and address*]

Holding: [*details of Holding and number*]

TAKE NOTICE THAT I DEMAND in accordance with section 12 of the Agricultural Holdings Act 1986 that the question of the rent to be paid in respect of the Holding of which you are the *tenant/landlord* (*delete as applicable*) as from the [*date*] being the next termination date within the meaning of sub-section (4) of the said section be referred to arbitration under the Act.

THIS NOTICE is given without prejudice to any other notice or act in connection with the tenancy which has been or may after the date of this notice be given or done by me or on behalf of me or any other involved party.

Dated: ....

Signed: ....
          Landlord

OR

Signed: ....
          Tenant

---

14   MEMORANDUM OF RENT REVIEW

AGRICULTURAL HOLDINGS ACT 1986

MEMORANDUM OF RENT REVIEW[1]

Landlord: [*Landlord's name and address*]

Tenant: [*Tenant's name and address*]

Holding: [*details of Holding and number*]

Tenancy Agreement: [*date of and parties to Tenancy Agreement*]

MEMORANDUM

IT IS MUTUALLY AGREED that the rent payable in respect of the Holding shall with effect from the [*date*] be increased to [*sum*] Pounds ($£$ ...) per annum.

Save in respect of the rent increase, the subject of this Memorandum, the Tenancy Agreement shall remain in full force and effect.

Dated: ....

Signed: ....
   Landlord

Signed: ....
   Tenant

---

1   Consider the stamp duty implications of this Agreement. If the rent is increased, the increase will
    be stampable.

---

15   MEMORANDUM OF RENT INCREASE AFTER LANDLORD'S IMPROVEMENT

AGRICULTURAL HOLDINGS ACT 1986

MEMORANDUM OF RENT INCREASE AFTER LANDLORD'S IMPROVEMENT[1]

Landlord:	[*Landlord's name and address*]
Tenant:	[*Tenant's name and address*]
Holding:	[*details of Holding and number*]
Tenancy Agreement:	[*date of and parties to Tenancy Agreement*]

MEMORANDUM

In consideration of the Landlord having carried out in agreement with the Tenant on the Holding the Improvement specified in the Schedule below it has been agreed between the parties that (pursuant to section 13 of the Agricultural Holdings Act 1986) the rent payable in respect of the Holding shall with effect from the [*date*] be increased to [*sum*] Pounds (£ ...) per annum.

Save in respect of the rent increase, the subject of this Memorandum, the Tenancy Agreement shall remain in full force and effect and for the avoidance of any doubt it is agreed that the proviso for re-entry herein contained shall apply in respect of any non-payment of the rental herein referred to or any part thereof as it does to the rental referred to in the Tenancy Agreement.

SCHEDULE

Dated: ....

Signed: ....
   Landlord

Signed: ....
   Tenant

16   LANDLORD'S CONSENT TO TENANT'S IMPROVEMENT

AGRICULTURAL HOLDINGS ACT 1986

SECTION 67

Re: the Holding known as [*Holding address, details and number*]

To: [*Tenant's name and address*]

Pursuant to section 67 of the Agricultural Holdings Act 1986 I HEREBY CONSENT to the making on the above Holding of the Improvement details of which are set out in the Schedule hereto upon the terms and conditions of the said Schedule.

SCHEDULE

1.   The Improvement: [*description of improvement*]

2.   Terms and conditions:

2.1   The Improvement is to be created at the Tenant's own risk and expense.

2.2   At the termination of the Tenancy the Improvement shall become the sole property of the Landlord and compensation of One Pound (£1.00) shall be payable to the Tenant in respect thereof.

2.3   The Tenant must at his own expense keep the Improvement repaired and maintained at all times.

2.4   The Tenant will not cause any undue damage or disturbance in the creation of the Improvement and must make good at his own expense any damage caused.

2.5   This Consent is conditional upon the Tenant obtaining all necessary Planning and By-Law approvals in respect of the Improvement and the Tenant will comply at his own expense with any conditions attached to such approvals and will not commence work on the creation of the Improvement until all such approvals have been obtained and conditions precedent attached thereto complied with.

Dated ....

Signed ....   Signed ....
          Landlord   Tenant

This is an extreme agreement on compensation. Often a write-off period based on cost reduced on a straight line basis over a period of years (say 10 or 20) will be agreed.

If consent is obtained from the Landlord or an arbitrator for the carrying out of an improvement and no compensation is agreed, s 66 of the 1986 Act provides that the quantum of compensation is 'an amount equal to the increase attributable to the improvement in the value of the agricultural holding as a holding having regard to the character and situation of the holding and the average requirements of tenants reasonably skilled in husbandry.'

There may therefore be situations where a tenant may wish to seek arbitration under s 67(3) if a landlord is prepared to consent to an improvement but on terms which the tenant regards as unreasonable.

17   NOTICE OF INTENTION TO CLAIM COMPENSATION UNDER AHA 1986, SECTION 72

AGRICULTURAL HOLDINGS ACT 1986

SECTION 72

To: [*Tenant's name and address*]

Re: [*Holding address, details and number*]

Date:

We, [*name*] [*address*] as agent for [*Landlord's name and address*], give you notice of our intention on your quitting the above Holding on the termination of your tenancy to claim compensation under section 72 of the Agricultural Holdings Act 1986 for the general deterioration such as is mentioned in that section of that Act.

....

Duly Authorised Signatory
on behalf of the Landlord

18   NOTICE OF INTENTION TO CLAIM COMPENSATION ON TERMINATION OF TENANCY PURSUANT TO AHA 1986, SECTION 83

AGRICULTURAL HOLDINGS ACT 1986

SECTION 83

Re: the Holding known as [*Holding address details*]

To: [*Landlord or Tenant's name and address*]

Pursuant to s 83 of the Agricultural Holdings Act 1986 I HEREBY GIVE YOU NOTICE that it is my intention to make against you the claims set out in the Schedule hereto arising out of the termination of the tenancy of the above Holding.

SCHEDULE

[*Nature of claim*]   [*Statutory provision or term of agreement under which claim is made*]

Dated ....

Signed ....
      Landlord/Tenant

---

19   NOTICE OF INTENTION TO RE-ENTER OR FORFEIT

NOTICE OF INTENTION TO RE-ENTER OR FORFEIT

To: [*Tenant's name and address*]

Holding: [*details of Holding and number*]

Landlord: [*Landlord's name and address*]

Tenancy Agreement: An agreement dated [*date*] and made between [*name*] (1) and [*name*] (2).

WHEREAS on [*date*] you were/[*name*] was (*delete as applicable*) adjudged bankrupt.

AND WHEREAS under the provisions of clause [*forfeiture clause*] of the Tenancy Agreement it was provided that in such event it would be lawful for the Landlord after giving not less than [*figure*] weeks/months (*delete as applicable*) notice to re-enter the Holding and thereupon the tenancy thereof should automatically determine.

NOW IN PURSUANCE of the provisions of the said clause [*forfeiture clause*] of the Tenancy Agreement I GIVE YOU NOTICE that by reason of your/[*name*]'s (*delete as applicable*) bankruptcy I intend to enforce the right of re-entry or forfeiture that has thereby arisen on [*date*] (being a date not less than [*as before*] weeks/months (*delete as applicable*) from the date of this Notice) and will do so by action or otherwise as I see fit AND THEREUPON your tenancy of the Holding shall absolutely determine (subject as may be set out in the said clause [*forfeiture clause*] of the Tenancy Agreement).

Dated ....

Signed ....
      Landlord

20 NOTICE TO QUIT TO PERSONAL REPRESENTATIVES

AGRICULTURAL HOLDINGS ACT 1986

SECTION 26 AND SCHEDULE 3, PART I, CASE G

To: The Personal Representatives of the late [*deceased Tenant's name*]

Holding: [*details of Holding and number*]

I GIVE YOU NOTICE to quit the Holding which was held by the late [*deceased tenant's name*] as tenant until his/her (*delete as applicable*) death on or about the [*date*] (and which you now hold as his/her (*delete as applicable*) Personal Representatives) on [*date*] or at the expiration of the year of the tenancy which shall expire next after the end of twelve months from the service of this notice.

In accordance with Case G in Schedule 3 to the Agricultural Holdings Act 1986 this notice to quit is given by reason of the death of [*deceased tenant's name*] who immediately before his/her (*delete as applicable*) death was the sole (or sole surviving) tenant under the contract of tenancy of the Holding.

Dated ....

Signed ....
          Landlord
_____

21 NOTICE TO TENANT TO PAY RENT DUE IN THE PRESCRIBED FORM UNDER SI 1987/711

AGRICULTURAL HOLDINGS ACT 1986

SCHEDULE 3, PART I, CASE D

NOTICE TO TENANT TO PAY RENT DUE

Re: the holding known as [*Holding address, details and number*]

To: [*Tenant's name and address*]

IMPORTANT – FAILURE TO COMPLY WITH THIS NOTICE MAY BE RELIED ON AS REASON FOR A NOTICE TO QUIT UNDER

CASE D. IF YOU WANT YOUR TENANCY TO CONTINUE YOU MUST ACT QUICKLY. READ THE NOTICE AND ALL THE NOTES CAREFULLY. IF YOU ARE IN ANY DOUBT ABOUT THE ACTION YOU SHOULD TAKE, GET ADVICE IMMEDIATELY – EG FROM A SOLICITOR, SURVEYOR, OR CITIZENS ADVICE BUREAU

1.   I hereby give you notice that I require you to pay within two months from the date of service of this Notice★ the rent due in respect of the above holding as set out below.

★*Note*. This Notice may not be served before the rent is due.

Particulars of Rent Not Paid:

[*Date When Due*]   [*Amount Due*]

2.   This Notice is given in accordance with Case D in Part I of Schedule 3 to the Agricultural Holdings Act 1986, and failure to comply with it within the period specified above may be relied on as a reason for a notice to quit under Case D.

3.   Your attention is drawn to the Notes following the signature to this Notice.

Signed .... Date ....

(If signed by any person other than the landlord of the Holding, state in what capacity or by what authority the signature is affixed.)

Address ....

....

....

....

NOTES

1.   You cannot at this stage refer to arbitration either your liability to comply with this Notice to pay rent or any other question as to the validity of the Notice. You will, however, be entitled to do so later if a notice to quit is served on you on the ground that you have failed to comply with this Notice to pay rent. That is the *only* opportunity you will have to challenge this Notice.

2.   At that stage under article 9 of the Agriculture Holdings (Arbitration on Notices) Order 1987 (SI 1987/710) you have one month after the service of the notice to quit within which you can serve on your landlord a notice in writing requiring the question to be determined by arbitration under the Agricultural Holdings Act 1986 (c 5).

3.   You will then have three months from the date of service of that notice in which to appoint an arbitrator by agreement or (in default of such an agreement) to make an application under paragraph 1 of Schedule 11 to that Act for the appointment of an arbitrator. If this is not done by you or your landlord your notice requiring arbitration ceases to be effective (see article 10 of that Order).

22   NOTICE TO TENANT TO REMEDY BREACH OF TENANCY BY DOING WORK OF REPAIR, MAINTENANCE OR REPLACEMENT

AGRICULTURAL HOLDINGS ACT 1986

SCHEDULE 3, PART I, CASE D

NOTICE TO TENANT TO REMEDY BREACH OF TENANCY BY DOING WORK OF REPAIR, MAINTENANCE OR REPLACEMENT

Re: the Holding known as [*Holding details/address*]

To: [*name and address of Tenant*]

IMPORTANT – FAILURE TO COMPLY WITH THIS NOTICE MAY BE RELIED ON AS REASON FOR A NOTICE TO QUIT UNDER CASE D. IF YOU WANT YOUR TENANCY TO CONTINUE YOU MUST ACT QUICKLY. READ THE NOTICE AND ALL THE NOTES CARE-FULLY. IF YOU ARE IN ANY DOUBT ABOUT THE ACTION YOU SHOULD TAKE, GET ADVICE IMMEDIATELY – EG FROM A SOLICITOR, SURVEYOR OR CITIZENS ADVICE BUREAU.

1.   I hereby give you notice that I require you to remedy within .. months* from the date of service of this Notice the breaches, set out below, of the terms or conditions of your tenancy, being breaches which are capable of being remedied of terms or conditions which are not inconsistent with your responsibilities to farm the Holding in accordance with the rules of good husbandry.

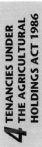

4 TENANCIES UNDER THE AGRICULTURAL HOLDINGS ACT 1986

★Note. This period must be a reasonable period for the tenant to remedy the breaches and must in any event be not less than six months.

---

2.   This Notice requires the doing of the work of repair, maintenance or replacement specified below.

          Particulars of breaches of terms or conditions of tenancy:

[*Term or condition of tenancy*]   [*Particulars of breach and work required to remedy it*]

3.   This Notice is given in accordance with Case D in Part I of Schedule 3 to the Agricultural Holdings Act 1986, and failure to comply with it within the period specified above may be relied on as a reason for a notice to quit under Case D.

4.   Your attention is drawn to the Notes following the signature to this Notice.

Signed .... Date ....

(If signed by any person other than the landlord of the Holding, state in what capacity or by what authority the signature is affixed.)

                              Address ....

                              ....

                              ....

                              ....

NOTES

In these Notes 'the Order' means the Agricultural Holdings (Arbitration on Notices) Order 1987 (SI 1987/710).

What to do if you wish —
  (a)   to contest your liability to do the work, or any part of the work, required by this Notice to remedy (Question (a)); or
  (b)   to request the deletion from this Notice to remedy of any item or part of an item of work on the ground that it is unnecessary or unjustified (Question (b)); or
  (c)   to request the substitution in the case of any item or part of an item of work of a different method or material for the method or material which this Notice to remedy would otherwise require to be followed or used (Question (c)).

1. Questions (a), (b) and (c) mentioned in the heading to these Notes can be referred to arbitration under article 3(1) of the Order. To do so you must serve a notice in writing upon your landlord within one month of the service upon you of this Notice to remedy. The notice you serve upon your landlord should specify –
    (a) if you are referring Question (a), the items for which you deny liability;
    (b) if you are referring Question (b), the items you wish to be deleted;
    (c) if you are referring Question (c), the different methods or materials you wish to be substituted;
    and in each case should require the matter to be determined by arbitration under the Agricultural Holdings Act 1986 (c 5). You will not be able to refer Question (a), (b), or (c) to arbitration later, on receipt of a notice to quit. This action does not prevent you settling the matter in writing by agreement with your landlord.

Carrying out the work

2. If you refer any of these Questions (a), (b) and (c) to arbitration, you are not obliged to carry out the work which is the subject of the reference to arbitration unless and until the arbitrator decides that you are liable to do it; but you must carry out any work which you are not referring to arbitration.

3. If you are referring Question (a) to arbitration you may wish to carry out any of the work which is the subject of that reference to arbitration without waiting for the arbitrator's award. If you do this and the arbitrator finds that you have carried out any such work which you were under no obligation to do, he will determine at the time he makes his award the reasonable cost of any such work which you have done and you will be entitled to recover this from your landlord (see article 8 of the Order). This provision does not apply in the case of work referred to arbitration under Question (b) or Question (c).

What to do if you wish to contest any other question arising under this Notice to remedy

4. If you wish to contest any other question arising under this Notice other than Question (a), (b) or (c), such as whether the time specified in the Notice to do work is a reasonable period in which to carry out the work, you should refer the question to arbitration in either of the following ways, according to whether or not you are also at the same time referring Question (a), (b) or (c) to arbitration –
    (a) If you are referring Question (a), (b) or (c) to arbitration, then you *must* also refer to arbitration at the same time any other question relevant to this Notice which you may wish to dispute.
        To do this, you should include in the Notice to your landlord referred to in Note 1 above a statement of the other questions which you require to be determined by arbitration under the Agricultural Holdings Act 1986 (see article 4(1) of the Order).
    (b) If you are not referring Question (a), (b) or (c) to arbitration, but wish to contest some other question arising under this Notice to remedy, you may refer that question to arbitration either now, on receipt of this Notice, or later, if you get a notice to quit.

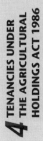

To refer the question to arbitration now, you should serve on your landlord *within one month* after the service of this Notice to remedy a notice in writing setting out what it is you require to be determined by arbitration under the Agricultural Holdings Act 1986 (see article 4(2)(a) of the Order).

Alternatively, you have one month after the service of the notice to quit within which you can serve on your landlord a notice in writing requiring the question to be determined by arbitration under the 1986 Act (see article 9 of the Order). You will then have three months from the date of service of that notice in which to appoint an arbitrator by agreement or (in default of such an agreement) to make an application under paragraph 1 of Schedule 11 to that Act for the appointment of an arbitraror. If this is not done by you or your landlord your notice requiring arbitration ceases to be effective (see article 10 of that Order).

Warning

5. Notes 1 to 4 above outline the only opportunities you have to challenge this Notice to remedy.

Extensions of time allowed for complying with this Notice to remedy

6. If you refer to arbitration now any question arising from this Notice to remedy, the time allowed for complying with the Notice will be extended until the termination of the arbitration. If the arbitrator decides that you are liable to do any of the work specified in this Notice to remedy, he will extend the time in which the work is to be done by such period as he thinks fit (see article 6(2) of the Order).

Warning as to the effect which any extension of the time allowed for complying with this Notice to remedy may have upon a subsequent notice to quit

7. If your time for doing the work is extended as mentioned in note 6 above, the arbitrator can specify a date for the termination of your tenancy should you fail to complete the work you are liable to do within the extended time. Then, if you did fail to complete that work within the extended time, your landlord could serve a notice to quit upon you expiring on the date which the arbitrator had specified, and the notice would be valid even though that date might be less than twelve months after the next term date, and might not expire on a term date. The arbitrator cannot, however, specify a termination date which is less than six months after the expiry of the extended time to do the work. Nor can he specify a date which is earlier than would have been possible if you had not required arbitration on this notice to remedy and had failed to do the work (see article 7 of the Order).

23 NOTICE TO TENANT TO REMEDY BREACH OF TENANCY (NOT BEING A NOTICE REQUIRING THE DOING OF ANY WORK OF REPAIR, MAINTENANCE OR REPLACEMENT)

AGRICULTURAL HOLDINGS ACT 1986

SCHEDULE 3, PART I, CASE D

NOTICE TO TENANT TO REMEDY BREACH OF TENANCY (NOT BEING A NOTICE REQUIRING THE DOING OF ANY WORK OF REPAIR, MAINTENANCE OR REPLACEMENT

Re: the Holding known as [*Holding details/address*]

To: [*name and address of Tenant*]

IMPORTANT – FAILURE TO COMPLY WITH THIS NOTICE MAY BE RELIED ON AS REASON FOR A NOTICE TO QUIT UNDER CASE D. IF YOU WANT YOUR TENANCY TO CONTINUE YOU MUST ACT QUICKLY. READ THE NOTICE AND ALL THE NOTES CAREFULLY. IF YOU ARE IN ANY DOUBT ABOUT THE ACTION YOU SHOULD TAKE, GET ADVICE IMMEDIATELY – EG FROM A SOLICITOR, SURVEYOR OR CITIZENS ADVICE BUREAU.

1. I hereby give you notice that I require you to remedy within ... months from the date of service of this Notice the breaches, set out below, of the terms or conditions of your tenancy, being breaches which are capable of being remedied of terms or conditions which are not inconsistent with your responsibilities to farm the Holding in accordance with the rules of good husbandry.

    Particulars of breaches of terms or conditions of tenancy:
    [*Term or condition of tenancy*]   [*Particulars of breach*]

2. This Notice is given in accordance with Case D in Part I, Schedule 3 to the Agricultural Holdings Act 1986 and failure to comply with it within the period specified may be relied on as a reason for a notice to quit under Case D.

3. Your attention is drawn to the Notes following the signature to this Notice.

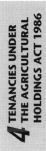

4 TENANCIES UNDER THE AGRICULTURAL HOLDINGS ACT 1986

Signed .... Date ....

(If signed by any person other than the landlord of the Holding, state in what capacity or by what authority the signature is affixed.)

Address ....

....

....

....

NOTES

1.   You cannot at this stage refer to arbitration either your liability to comply with this Notice to pay rent or any other question as to the validity of the Notice. You will, however, be entitled to do so later if a notice to quit is served on you on the ground that you have failed to comply with this Notice to pay rent. That is the *only* opportunity you will have to challenge this Notice.

2.   At that stage under article 9 of the Agricultural Holdings (Arbitration on Notices) Order 1987 (SI 1987/710) you have one month after the service of the notice to quit within which you can serve on your landlord a notice in writing requiring the question to be determined by arbitration under the Agricultural Holdings Act 1986 (c 5).

3.   You will then have three months from the date of service of that notice in which to appoint an arbitrator by agreement or (in default of such an agreement) to make an application under paragraph 1 of Schedule 11 to that Act for the appointment of an arbitrator. If this is not done by you or your landlord your notice requiring arbitration ceases to be effective (see article 10 of that Order).

24   DESIGNATION FOR INCLUDING IN A WILL

'I hereby designate [*name*] as the person whom I wish to succeed me as Tenant of [*holding details*] comprised in a Tenancy Agreement made the [*date*] between [*name of landlord*] of the one part and [*name of tenant*] of the other part'

25 APPLICATION FOR DIRECTION GIVING ENTITLEMENT TO TENANCY

Ref No: ....
(to be inserted by the Secretary)

AGRICULTURAL LAND TRIBUNAL

APPLICATION FOR DIRECTION GIVING ENTITLEMENT TO TENANCY OF AGRICULTURAL HOLDING

APPLICATION FOR DETERMINATION THAT APPLICANT BE TREATED AS AN ELIGIBLE PERSON

[in completing this form it is important to refer to the notes]

PART A

To be completed by all applicants

To the secretary of the Agricultural Land Tribunal for the .... Area

1. I .... *[block capitals]*

    of .... *[address]*
    hereby apply under section 20(1) of the Agriculture (Miscellaneous Provisions) Act 1976 for a direction entitling me to a tenancy of the holding specified in paragraph 2 below.§

2. The holding in respect of which the application is made is known as:

    ....
    and consists of:
    (a) .... hectares of arable land (including temporary grass)
         (Ordnance Survey Field Nos ....);
    (b) .... hectares of permanent pasture
         (Ordnance Survey Field Nos ....);
    (c) .... hectares of rough grazing
         (Ordnance Survey Field Nos ....);
    (d) .... hectares of other land (including orchards)
         (Ordnance Survey Field Nos ....).

TOTAL .... hectares .... ANNUAL RENT £ ....

3. The current year of the tenancy of the holding expires on *[date]*

4. The holding includes the following buildings *[give a general description]*:

    ....

†5. The holding forms part of a larger agricultural unit known as and consisting of [*give a general description*]:

....

6. The application arises on the death of [*name*] formerly the tenant of the holding referred to in paragraph 2, who died on [*date*][1]

His/her tenancy was:

....

†(a) granted before [12 July 1984];

†(b) obtained on or after [12 July 1984] by virtue of a direction of the Agricultural Land Tribunal under section 20 of the 1976 Act;

†(c) granted on or after [12 July 1984] following a direction of the Agricultural Land Tribunal under section 20 of the 1976 Act but commenced before the relevant time for the purposes of section 23 of that Act;§

†(d) granted on or after [12 July 1984] by a written contract of tenancy indicating that the succession provisions in Part II of the 1976 Act should apply;§

†(e) granted on or after [12 July 1984] to a person who, immediately before that date, was a tenant of the holding or of any agricultural holding which comprised the whole or a substantial part of the land comprised in the holding.

7. The landlord of the holding is ....
of .... [*address*]

†8. I am the sole person validly designated by the deceased tenant of the holding in his will as the person he wished to succeed him as tenant of the holding. A copy of the relevant part of the will in which I am designated is attached [*attach a copy of or extract from the will marking the relevant passage*].[2]

9.
†(a) I am the *wife/*husband/*brother/*sister/*child of the deceased tenant.[3]

†(b) I was treated by the deceased tenant as a child of the family in relation to his marriage to ....[4]
on .... [*give date of marriage*].

†10.
(a) During the seven years ending with the date of death of the deceased tenant my only or my principal source of livelihood was derived from:

*(i) my agricultural work on the holding, or on a agricultural unit of which the holding forms a part;

*(ii) his/his and my agricultural work on the holding, or on an agricultural unit of which the holding is a part;

during the following period(s) and in the following manner [*give details of the way livelihood derived from agricultural work on the holding*][5]

†(b)   During the period(s) specified in paragraph 10(a) I had the following source(s) of livelihood other than those derived from the holding or from an agricultural unit of which the holding forms a part [*give details of other sources of livelihood*]:

†(c)   During the period(s) specified in paragraph 10(a) I had no other source of livelihood.

†11.   During the seven years ending with the date of death of the deceased tenant I attended a full-time course at .... [*name of university, college or other establishment of further education*] during the following period(s) [*give details of time spent at university*]:[5, 6] During this period/these periods I studied the following subjects and obtained the following qualifications [*give details of subjects studied and any qualifications obtained*]:

†12.

(a)   The following agricultural land is occupied by me, my spouse or a company under my control, the control of my spouse or our joint control as owner–occupier/tenant/licensee, whether alone or jointly with others [*give particulars of any land occupied, including area and any land occupied jointly with others*]:

†(b)   The following agricultural land is occupied by a person under a licence or such a[7] tenancy as is mentioned in paragraph 2(1)(a) to (d) of Schedule 3A to the 1976 Act[8] granted by ★me and/or ★my spouse and/or ★a company controlled by me and/or my spouse †together with one or more other persons, being at the time it was granted a person or persons entitled to occupy the land otherwise than under a tenancy, or in a capacity, falling within paragraph 2(1)(a) to (f) of that Schedule[8] [*give particulars of any land occupied, including area*]:§

†(c)   I apply under paragraph 4(2) of Schedule 3A to the 1976 Act for the net annual income from the following agricultural land which is:§
★(i)   jointly occupied;
★(ii) deemed by virtue of paragraph 6(2) of that Schedule to be jointly occupied;

by me and one or more other persons (not being only my spouse or a company under my control, the control of my spouse or our joint control) to be treated as limited to my appropriate share of that net annual income [*give particulars of any land in joint occupation or deemed joint occupation*]:[9]

13.   I was born on [*date*]

14.   I claim to be a suitable person to receive the tenancy of this holding because:[10]
....

PART B

To be completed if you think that you may not fully satisfy the requirements of paragraph 10(a)

15.   Further to the application set out in the preceding paragraphs of this Form, I, ... [*block capitals*] of the above address also apply under section 21(2) of the 1976 Act for a determination that I am to be treated as an eligible person for the purposes of Part II of that Act.[11]§

16.

(a)   During the seven years ending with the date of death of the deceased tenant my livelihood was derived from:

....

★(i)   my agricultural work on the holding referred to in paragraph 2, or on an agricultural unit of which the holding forms a part;

★(ii)   his/his and my agricultural work on the holding referred to in paragraph 2, or on an agricultural unit of which the holding forms a part;

to a material extent during the following period(s) and in the following manner [*give details of the extent to which livelihood was derived from agricultural work on the holding*]:[12]

†(b)   During the period(s) specified in paragraph 16(a) I had the following sources of livelihood other than those derived from the holding or from an agricultural unit of which the holding forms a part [*give details of other sources of livelihood*]:

†(c)   During the period(s) specified in paragraph 16(a) I had no other source of livelihood.

†17.   During the seven years ending with the date of death of the deceased tenant I attended a full-time course at .... [*name of university, college or other establishment of further education*] during the following period(s) [*give details of time spent at university, etc*]:[6]

During this period/these periods I studied the following subjects and obtained the following qualifications [*give details of subjects studied and any qualifications obtained*]:

....

†18.   I claim that, because of the following circumstances, it is fair and reasonable for me to be able to apply under section 20 of the 1976 Act for a direction entitling me to a tenancy of the holding referred to in paragraph 2:[13]§

PART C

To be completed by all applicants

19.   I attach the following documents which I intend to produce in support of my case:

(a)   two[14] copies of a 6 inch to one mile or 1/10,000[15] map of the holding described in paragraph 2 above (and of the other land referred to in paragraph 5);

(b)   two[14] copies of:[16]

     ....

20.   The persons whom I shall notify of this application/these applications are:[17]

     (a)   the landlord of the holding whose name and address are:

     (b)   ....

     (c)   ....

     (d)   ....

21.

     (a)   The following is/are the personal representative(s) of the deceased tenant or (if there are no personal representatives) the person or persons responsible for the management of the holding on behalf of the deceased's estate:[18]

        Names(s) ....

        Address(es) ....

        ....

        ....

     (b)   The following person(s) is/are or may be interested in the outcome of this application:[18]

        Names(s) ....

        Address(es) ....

        ....

        ....

        Nature of interest ....

        Date ....   Signed[19] ....

NOTES

1.   Formal proof of the date of death will be required at the hearing.

2.   This paragraph should be completed only if the applicant received a specific bequest of the deceased's tenancy under his will or is specifically named in the will as the person whom the deceased tenant wished to succeed him as tenant of the holding. It will be necessary for a grant of probate or administration to be obtained from the Family Division of the High Court in respect of the will before the tribunal can hear any claim to be a designated applicant. Where an applicant establishes that he is so designated under the deceased tenant's will, no other application will be considered unless the tribunal determine that the designated applicant is not an eligible person or is not a suitable person to become the tenant of the holding.

3.   Formal proof of the relationship to the deceased, eg by production of marriage or birth certificates, may be required at the hearing. Adopted children should complete this sub-paragraph, and not paragraph 9(b) following.

4.   Paragraph 9(b) may apply where the applicant was the step-child or foster child of the deceased or was otherwise treated by him as his child. An outline should be given of the circumstances relied on as establishing that the applicant was treated by the deceased as his child in relation to the marriage. Production

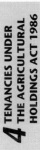

TENANCIES UNDER THE AGRICULTURAL HOLDINGS ACT 1986

of the relevant marriage certificate and any relevant birth certificate may be required at the hearing.

5.   To qualify under paragraph 10(a)(i) the applicant should have derived his only or principal source of livelihood from his agricultural work on the holding (or on a larger unit of which the holding forms part) during a total of five years of the seven years ending with the death of the deceased tenant. Paragraph 10(a)(ii) is available only to a widow of the deceased tenant. The total of five years may be made up of one continuous period, or one or more separate periods. A period of full-time education at a university etc, may, in the circumstances set out in note 6, count towards the five-year period of earning a livelihood from the holding, and reference should be made to paragraph 11 and note 6 in deciding whether the requirements of this paragraph can be satisfied. An applicant who cannot satisfy the requirements of paragraph 10(a) fully but who believes he can satisfy them to a material extent should not complete paragraphs 10 and 11 but should complete instead paragraph 15, together with paragraphs 16, 17 (if relevant) and 18 in Part B of the Form. The Notes to those paragraphs should also be consulted. Where an applicant is in any doubt as to whether or not he can satisfy the requirements of paragraph 10 fully, he is advised to complete paragraphs 10 and 11 (if relevant) and Part B of the Form.

6.   Any period or periods (up to an aggregate total of three years) during the seven years ending with the date of death of the deceased tenant during which the applicant was attending a full-time course at a university, college or other establishment of further education will be treated as a period throughout which his only or principal source of livelihood was derived from his agricultural work on the holding. Any subject may have been studied.

7.   Land occupied by the applicant's spouse or by a company controlled by that person or jointly by that person and the applicant should not be included in paragraph 12 where either of the parties has obtained a decree of judicial separation or a decree nisi of divorce or of nullity of marriage and in each case that decree remains unrescinded. In addition, land should not be included in paragraph 12 if it is occupied by the applicant, his spouse or a controlled company:

    (a)   under a tenancy approved under section 2(1) of the Agricultural Holdings Act 1948 or under such a tenancy relating to the use of land for grazing or mowing as is referred to in the proviso to that provision;

    (b)   under a tenancy for more than one year but less than two years;

    (c)   under a tenancy not falling within (a) or (b) above and not having effect as a contract of tenancy;

    (d)   under a tenancy to which section 3 of the 1948 Act does not apply by virtue of section 3B of that Act;

    (e)   as a licensee; or

    (f)   as an executor, administrator, trustee in bankruptcy or person otherwise deriving title from another person by operation of law.

However, where the applicant occupies land in accordance with (a) to (e) above under a licence or tenancy granted to him by his spouse or by a body corporate controlled by him, that land should be included in paragraph 12.‡

8. Paragraph 2(1)(a) to (f) of Schedule 3A to the Agriculture (Miscellaneous Provisions) Act 1976 is set out in note 7.§

9. If the applicant occupies land jointly with one or more other persons (not being only his spouse or a company under the control of the applicant or his spouse or under their joint control), or if the applicant is deemed to occupy land jointly with one or more such persons, he may in either case complete the application set out in paragraph 12(c) of the Form for the net annual income which the land is or was capable of producing to be treated as limited to his appropriate share.

10. All matters relied on as supporting the claim to be a suitable person to become the tenant of the holding should be summarised. These should include details of the applicant's training and practical experience of agriculture, physical health, financial standing and any educational qualifications not already listed in paragraph 11 or 17.

11. This paragraph should be completed (together with paragraphs 16, 17 (if relevant) and 18) in any case where the applicant, while otherwise meeting the conditions contained in paragraphs (a) and (c) of the definition of 'eligible person' in section 18(2) of the 1976 Act cannot fully satisfy the conditions as to deriving his principal or main source of livelihood from the holding contained in paragraph (b) of that subsection. (It is also necessary for the application set out in paragraph 1 of the Form to be completed in addition to completing this paragraph.) An applicant who fully satisfies the requirements of paragraph 10(a) need not complete this paragraph or paragraphs 16, 17 and 18.

12. The applicant should state to what extent he has derived his livelihood from his agricultural work on the holding (or on a larger unit of which the holding forms part) during a total of five years of the seven years ending with the death of the deceased tenant. Paragraph 16(a)(ii) applies only to a widow of the deceased tenant. The total of five years may be made up of one continuous period, or one or more separate periods. A period of full-time education at a university, etc, may in certain circumstances count in relation to the five-year period as a period in which a livelihood was derived from agricultural work on the holding, and paragraph 17 should also be completed where relevant.

13. A summary should be given of matters relied on as establishing that it is fair and reasonable that the applicant should be entitled to apply under section 20 of the 1976 Act for a tenancy of the holding, though not fully satisfying the conditions specified in paragraph (b) of the definition of 'eligible person' in section 18(2) of that Act. The length of time the applicant has lived on the holding, details of work done by him on the holding (apart from those already given in paragraph 16) and any special circumstances which have prevented him from qualifying in full as an eligible person under paragraph (b) of the definition of 'eligible person' should be given. (Note 5 describes the requirements needed to qualify fully under paragraph (b) of the definition.)

4 TENANCIES UNDER THE AGRICULTURAL HOLDINGS ACT 1986

14. By virtue of art 11(1) of the Agricultural Land Tribunals (Succession to Agricultural Tenancies) Order 1984, two copies of the application and of any map and document must be sent to the secretary.

15. A larger scale map may be used if preferred. Ordnance Survey Field Numbers must be marked on the map.

16. Mention any other document which is attached to this application.

17. The applicant is required to send to the landlord of the holding, and to every other person who to his knowledge has made or may be able to make an application for a tenancy of the holding, notice of this application in Form 3 (Succession on Death) which is set out in the Appendix to the Agricultural Land Tribunals (Succession to Agricultural Tenancies) Order 1984. The applicant should enter the name and address of the landlord at (a) and the names and addresses of appropriate other persons (if any) respectively at (b), (c) and (d), etc.

18. This information is required by art 5(2) of that Order.

19. If signed by any person other than the applicant himself, he should state in what capacity or by what authority he signs.§

---

* Strike out whichever is inapplicable.

† Strike out if inapplicable.

§ The prescribed form still refers to the 1976 Act now repealed. Some ALTs have modified the form pursuant to art 1(3) of the Agricultural Land Tribunal (Succession to Agricultural Tenancies) Order 1984, SI 1984/1301. It is necessary to check with the appropriate ALT for details. It is perhaps safer, if time permits, to contact the secretary of the relevant ALT and request copies of the necessary forms from him/her.

‡ Although not referred to in the prescribed form, s 40 and Sch, para 32 to ATA 1995 added a letting under a farm business tenancy for less than five years (including a periodic tenancy).

---

26 REPLY TO APPLICATION FOR DIRECTION GIVING ENTITLEMENT TO TENANCY

Rule 6

Ref No: ....
(to be inserted by the Secretary)

AGRICULTURAL LAND TRIBUNAL

REPLY TO APPLICATION FOR DIRECTION GIVING ENTITLEMENT
TO TENANCY OF AGRICULTURAL HOLDING

REPLY TO APPLICATION FOR DETERMINATION THAT APPLICANT BE TREATED AS AN ELIGIBLE PERSON

To the secretary of the Agricultural Land Tribunal for the .... Area

I, ...*[block capitals]*

of .... *[address]*

landlord of .... *[name or description of holding]*

having received a copy of the application bearing the above reference number reply as follows:

1. The facts stated in paragraphs 1, 2, 4 and 7 of the application are, to the best of my knowledge, information and belief, correct† except that:
    ....

†2. I dispute the claim of the applicant to be an eligible person[1] on the following grounds:
    ....

3. I dispute the claim of the applicant to be treated as an eligible person[2] on the following grounds:
    ....

4. I have the following comments on the suitability of the applicant to become the tenant of the above holding:
    ....

5. I attach two copies of the following relevant documents:[3]
    ....

6. I consider the application to be invalid by reason of:[4]
    ....

Date ....   Signed[5] ....

TAKE NOTICE THAT IF YOU DO NOT REPLY IN THIS FORM WITHIN ONE MONTH OF THE DATE OF SERVICE ON YOU OF THE ATTACHED APPLICATION, THEN, SUBJECT TO SECTION 20(7) OF THE AGRICULTURE (MISCELLANEOUS PROVISIONS) ACT 1976, YOU WILL NOT BE ENTITLED AT THE HEARING OF THE APPLICATION TO DISPUTE ANY MATTER ALLEGED IN IT.§

NOTES

1. The paragraphs of the application which (where completed) will be relevant to the applicant's claim to be an eligible person are paragraphs 9, 10, 11 and 12.

2. The paragraphs of the application which (where completed) will be relevant to the applicant's claim to be treated as an eligible person are paragraphs 15, 16, 17 and 18.

4 TENANCIES UNDER THE AGRICULTURAL HOLDINGS ACT 1986

3. By virtue of art 11(1) of the Agricultural Land Tribunals (Succession to Agricultural Tenancies) Order 1984, two copies of this reply and of any document which you wish to submit to the tribunal must be sent to the secretary. If you disagree with any map or plan attached to the application, your reply should be accompanied by two copies of a 6 inch to one mile or 1/10,000 (or larger) map showing what you consider to be the true position and marking the Ordnance Survey Field Numbers.

4. If you consider that, for any reason, the applicant is not legally entitled to make this application, you should state succinctly the grounds on which you rely.

5. If signed by any person other than the landlord himself, he should state in what capacity or by what authority he signs.

---

† Strike out if inapplicable.

§ The prescribed form still refers to the 1976 Act now repealed. Some ALTs have modified the form pursuant to art 1(3) of the Agricultural Land Tribunal (Succession to Agricultural Tenancies) Order 1984, SI 1984/1301. It is necessary to check with the appropriate ALT for details. It is perhaps safer, if time permits, to contact the secretary of the relevant ALT and request copies of the necessary forms from him/her.

---

27 APPLICATION FOR CONSENT TO OPERATION OF NOTICE TO QUIT

FORM 2 (SUCCESSION ON DEATH)

Rule 4(1)

Ref No: ....
(to be inserted by the Secretary)

AGRICULTURAL LAND TRIBUNAL

APPLICATION FOR CONSENT TO OPERATION OF NOTICE TO QUIT

To the secretary of the Agricultural Land Tribunal for the .... Area

1. I, ...[*block capitals*]

of ....[*address*]

hereby apply under section 22(1) of the Agriculture (Miscellaneous Provisions) Act 1976 for the consent of the tribunal to the operation of a notice to quit which I gave to§

.... and ....

being the personal representative(s) of ....[*block capitals*] deceased, formerly of ....[*address*]

I was officially notified of his/her death by .... on ....

2.   The notice to quit was served on [*insert date*] .... in respect of the holding known as ....

3.   An application (bearing reference number ....) to the tribunal under Part II of the 1976 Act or a tenancy of this holding was made on ....

Full particulars of the holding are set out in that application †(as amended in reply to that application dated ....).

4.   I apply for the tribunal's consent to the operation of the notice to quit in the event of an applicant under the application referred to in paragraph 3, or any other such applicant, being determined by the tribunal to be a suitable person to become the tenant of the holding.

5.   The grounds upon which I make this application are those provided by paragraph(s) .... of section 3(3) of the Agricultural Holdings (Notices to Quit) Act 1977 as read with section 22(2) of the 1976 Act, as amended. (It is important to refer to note 1.)§

6.   The main facts on which I will base my case are:
....

7.   If I obtain possession of the land I intend:
       ★(a)   to farm it myself.
       ★(b)   to let it to another tenant [*state name and address if known*].
       ★(c)   [*state any other intention*]

†8.   The future tenant referred to in paragraph 7(b)[2] at present farms other land consisting of:
       (a)   .... hectares of arable land (including temporary grass) (Ordnance Survey Field Nos ....);
       (b)   .... hectares of permanent pasture (Ordnance Survey Field Nos ....);
       (c)   .... hectares of rough grazing (Ordnance Survey Field Nos ....);
       (d)   .... hectares of other land (including orchards) (Ordnance Survey Field Nos ....).

       TOTAL .... hectares.

9.   I attach the following documents which I intend to produce in support of my case:
       (a)   two copies[3] of a 6 inch to one mile or 1/10,000[4] map of the land described in paragraph 8[5] above;
       (b)   two copies[3] of:[6]

Date ....   Signed[7] ....

4 TENANCIES UNDER THE AGRICULTURAL HOLDINGS ACT 1986

NOTES

1. The applicant must state on which paragraph or paragraphs of the subsection he intends to rely. The five paragraphs state as follows:

   (a) that the carrying out of the purpose for which the landlord proposes to terminate the tenancy is desirable in the interests of good husbandry as respects the land to which the notice relates, treated as a separate unit;

   (b) that the carrying out thereof is desirable in the interests of sound management of the estate of which the land to which the notice relates forms part or which that land constitutes (see note 5 below);

   (c) that the carrying out thereof is desirable for the purposes of agricultural research, education, experiment or demonstration, or for the purposes of the enactments relating to smallholdings or allotments;

   (d) that greater hardship would be caused by withholding than by giving consent to the operation of the notice;

   (e) that the landlord proposes to terminate the tenancy for the purpose of the land's being used for a use, other than for agriculture, not falling within Case B in section 2(3) of the Agricultural Holdings (Notices to Quit) Act 1977.§

   If, under paragraph (d) above, the applicant intends to rely on hardship to a person or persons other than himself, he should set out in paragraph 6 the name of every person who will be so affected, and the relationship of that person to himself, and should state the nature of the hardship on which he relies.

2. Paragraph 8 need not be completed if the name of the future tenant is unknown. Where land is described, a map should be provided (see note 5 below).

3. By virtue of art 11(1) of the Agricultural Land Tribunal (Succession to Agricultural Tenancies) Order 1984, two copies of the application and of any map and document must be sent to the secretary.

4. A larger scale map may be used if preferred. Ordnance Survey Field Numbers must be marked on the map.

5. Where it is intended to give evidence about any land other than that which is the subject of the notice to quit, it must be shown either on the map produced or on a separate map of a scale of 6 inch to one mile or 1/10,000 (or larger).

6. Mention any other document which is attached to this application.

7. If signed by any person other than the applicant himself, he should state in what capacity or by what authority he signs.

---

* Strike out whichever is inapplicable.

† Strike out if inapplicable.

§ The prescribed form still refers to the 1976 Act now repealed. Some ALTs have modified the form pursuant to art 1(3) of the Agricultural Land Tribunal (Succession to Agricultural Tenancies) Order 1984, SI 1984/1301. It is necessary to check with the appropriate ALT for details. It is perhaps safer, if time permits, to contact the secretary of the relevant ALT and request copies of the necessary forms from him/her.

28   REPLY TO APPLICATION FOR CONSENT TO OPERATION OF NOTICE TO QUIT

FORM 2R (SUCCESSION ON DEATH)

Rule 7

Ref No: ....
(to be inserted by the Secretary)

AGRICULTURAL LAND TRIBUNAL

REPLY TO APPLICATION FOR CONSENT TO OPERATION OF NOTICE TO QUIT

To the secretary of the Agricultural Land Tribunal for the .... Area

I, ...*[block capitals]*

of ....*[address]*

having applied to the tribunal on .... for a direction entitling me to a tenancy of
.... and having received a copy of the application
(bearing the above reference number) for the tribunal's consent to the operation of a
notice to quit, reply as follows:
....

1.   The facts stated in the first three paragraphs of the application are correct†
     except that:
     ....

2.   My main reasons for resisting the application are:
     ....

†3. The landlord is not acting fairly and reasonably because:[1]
     ....

4.   I attach copies of the following relevant documents:[2]
     ....

Date ....   Signed[3] ....

TAKE NOTICE THAT IF YOU DO NOT REPLY IN THIS FORM WITHIN
ONE MONTH OF THE DATE OF SERVICE ON YOU OF THE
ATTACHED APPLICATION BY THE LANDLORD OF THE HOLDING
FOR THE TRIBUNAL'S CONSENT TO THE OPERATION OF THE
LANDLORD'S NOTICE TO QUIT, THE TRIBUNAL MAY GIVE THAT
CONSENT SUMMARILY AND SUMMARILY DISMISS YOUR OWN
APPLICATION TO BE GRANTED A TENANCY OF THE HOLDING,
WITHOUT HEARING YOUR CASE.

4 TENANCIES UNDER THE AGRICULTURAL HOLDINGS ACT 1986

NOTES

1.   The tribunal must withhold consent if, in all the circumstances, it appears that a fair and reasonable landlord would not insist on possession. If you have any special reasons for saying the landlord is acting unfairly or unreasonably which do not appear under paragraph 2, you should state them under paragraph 3.

2.   By virtue of art 11(1) of the Agricultural Land Tribunals (Succession to Agricultural Tenancies) Order 1984, two copies of the reply and of any document which you wish to submit to the tribunal must be sent to the secretary. If you disagree with any map or plan attached to the application, your reply should be accompanied by two copies of a 6 inch to one mile or 1/10,000 (or larger) map showing what you consider to be the true position and marking the Ordnance Survey Field Numbers.

3.   If signed by any person other than the applicant himself, he should state in what capacity or by what authority he signs.

---

† Strike out if inapplicable.

---

29   APPLICATION FOR DIRECTION GIVING ENTITLEMENT TO TENANCY

FORM 5 (SUCCESSION ON RETIREMENT)

Rule 23(1)

Ref No: ....
(to be inserted by the Secretary)

AGRICULTURAL LAND TRIBUNAL

APPLICATION FOR DIRECTION GIVING ENTITLEMENT TO TENANCY OF AGRICULTURAL HOLDING

[in completing this form it is important to refer to the notes]

To the secretary of the Agricultural Land Tribunal for the .... Area

1.   I, ...*[block capitals]*

of ....*[address]*

hereby apply under paragraph 5(1) of Schedule 2 to the Agricultural Holdings Act 1984 for a direction entitling me to a tenancy of the holding specified in paragraph 2 below.§

2.   The holding in respect of which the application is made is known as .... and consists of:

(a)   ....hectares of arable land (including temporary grass)
(Ordnance Survey Field Nos ....);

(b)   ....hectares of permanent pasture
(Ordnance Survey Field Nos ....);

(c)   ....hectares of rough grazing
(Ordnance Survey Field Nos ....);

(d)   ....hectares of other land (including orchards)
(Ordnance Survey Field Nos ....).

TOTAL .... hectares .... ANNUAL RENT £..........

3.   The current year of the tenancy of the holding expires on ....[*date*]

4.   The holding includes the following buildings [*give a general description*]:
....

†5.   The holding forms part of a larger agricultural unit known as and consisting of
[*give general description*]:
....

6.   The landlord of the holding is[*name*]

of ....[*address*]

The tenant(s) of the holding is/are ....[*name(s)*]

of ....[*address(es)*].

7.   This application arises as a result of a retirement notice given by the tenant(s) to
the landlord on ....[*date*]

8.   I am the nominated successor.

9.

†(a)   I am the *wife/*husband/*brother/*sister/*child of the tenant [*where
there is more than one tenant, specify which*].[1]

†(b)   I am treated by the tenant [*where there is more than one tenant, specify which*]
as a child of the family in relation to his marriage to ......[2] on ......[*give
date of marriage*].

10.

(a)   During the seven years ending with the date on which the tenant(s) gave
the retirement notice to the landlord, my only or principal source of
livelihood was derived from:

(i)*   my agricultural work on the holding, or on an agricultural unit of
which the holding forms a part;

(ii)*   the tenant's/the tenant's and my [*where there is more than one tenant,
specify which*] agricultural work on the holding, or on an
agricultural unit of which the holding forms a part;

during the following period(s) and in the following manner [*give details
of the way livelihood derived from agricultural work on the holding*]:[3]
....

(b)★　During the period(s) specified in paragraph 10(a) I had the following source(s) of livelihood other than those derived from the holding or from an agricultural unit of which the holding forms a part [*give details of other sources of livelihood*]:

....

(c)★　During the period(s) specified in paragraph 10(a) I had no other source of livelihood.

†11.　During the seven years ending with the date on which the tenant(s) gave the retirement notice to the landlord I attended a full-time course at ....
[*name of university, college or other establishment of further education*] during the following period(s) [*give details of time spent at university, etc*]:[4]

....

During this period/these periods I studied the following subjects and obtained the following qualifications [*give details of subjects studied and any qualifications obtained*]:

....

†12.

(a)　The following agricultural land is occupied by me, my spouse or a company under my control, the control of my spouse or our joint control as owner-occupier/tenant/licensee, whether alone or jointly with others [*give particulars of any land occupied, including area and any land occupied jointly with others*]:[5]

†(b)　The following agricultural land is occupied by a person under a licence or such a tenancy as is mentioned in paragraph 2(1)(a) to (d) of Schedule 3A to the Agriculture (Miscellaneous Provisions) Act 1976[6] granted by ★me and/or ★my spouse and/or ★a company controlled by me and/or my spouse †together with one or more other persons, being at the time it was granted a person or persons entitled to occupy the land otherwise than under a tenancy, or in a capacity, falling within paragraph 2(1)(a) to (f) of that Schedule[6] [*give particulars of any land occupied including area*]:§

....

†(c)　I apply under paragraph 4(2) of Schedule 3A to the 1976 Act, as applied by paragraph 1(4)(b) of Schedule 2 to the 1984 Act, for the net annual income from the following agricultural land which is:
(i)★　jointly occupied;
(ii)★　deemed by virtue of paragraph 6(2) of the said Schedule 3A, as applied by the said paragraph 1(4)(b), to be jointly occupied;
by me and one or more other persons (not being only my spouse or a company under my control, the control of my spouse or our joint control) to be treated as limited to my appropriate share of that net annual income [*give particulars of any land in joint occupation or deemed joint occupation*]:[7]

....

13.　I was born on ....[*date*]

14.　I claim to be a suitable person to receive the tenancy of this holding because:[8]

....

5.   I attach the following documents which I intend to produce in support of my case:
     (a)   two[9] copies of a 6 inch to one mile or $1/10,000$[10] map of the holding described in paragraph 2 above (and of the other land referred to in paragraph 5);
     (b)   two[9] copies of the retirement notice;
     (c)   two[9] copies of:[11]

16. I shall notify the landlord of this application.[12]

Date ....   Signed[13] ....

                                            Signature of retiring tenant(s) ....

                                            ....

                                            ....

                                            ....

NOTES

1.   Formal proof of the relationship to the tenant, eg by production of marriage or birth certificates, may be required at the hearing. Adopted children should complete this sub-paragraph, and not paragraph 9(b) following.

2.   Paragraph 9(b) may apply where the applicant is the step-child or foster child of the tenant or is otherwise treated by him as his child. An outline should be given of the circumstances relied on as establishing that the applicant is treated by the tenant as his child in relation to the marriage. Production of the relevant marriage certificate and any relevant birth certificate may be required at the hearing.

3.   To qualify under paragraph 10(a)(i) the applicant should have derived his only or principal source of livelihood from his agricultural work on the holding (or on a larger unit of which the holding forms part) during a total of five years of the seven years ending with the date on which the tenant(s) gave the landlord the retirement notice. Paragraph 10(a)(ii) is available only to a tenant's wife. The total of five years may be made up of one continous period, or one or more separate periods. A period of full-time education at a university etc, may, in the circumstances set out in note 4, count towards the five-year period of earning a livelihood from the holding, and reference should be made to paragraph 11 and note 4 in deciding whether the requirements of this paragraph can be satisfied.

4.   Any period or periods (up to an aggregate total of three years) during the seven years ending with the date on which the tenant(s) gave the retirement notice to the landlord during which the applicant was attending a full-time course at a university, college or other establishment of further education will be treated as a period throughout which his only or principal source of livelihood was derived from his agricultural work on the holding. Any subject may have been studied.

4 TENANCIES UNDER THE AGRICULTURAL HOLDINGS ACT 1986

5.   Land occupied by the applicant's spouse or by a company controlled by that person or jointly by that person and the applicant should not be included in paragraph 12 where either of the parties has obtained a decree of judicial separation or a decree nisi of divorce or of nullity of marriage and in each case that decree remains unrescinded. In addition, land should not be included in paragraph 12 if it is occupied by the applicant, his spouse or a controlled company:

(a)   under a tenancy approved under section 2(1) of the Agricultural Holdings Act 1948 or under such a tenancy relating to the use of land for grazing or mowing as is referred to in the proviso to that provision;

(b)   under a tenancy for more than one year but less than two years;

(c)   under a tenancy not falling within (a) or (b) above and not having effect as a contract of tenancy;

(d)   under a tenancy to which section 3 of the 1948 Act does not apply by virtue of section 3B of that Act;

(e)   as a licensee; or

(f)   as an executor, administrator, trustee in bankruptcy or person otherwise deriving title from another person by operation of law.

However, where the applicant occupies land in accordance with (a) to (e) above under a licence or tenancy granted to him by his spouse or by a body corporate controlled by him, that land should be included in paragraph 12.‡

6.   Paragraph 2(1)(a) to (f) of Schedule 3A to the Agriculture (Miscellaneous Provisions) Act 1976 is set out in note 5.§

7.   If the applicant occupies land jointly with one or more other persons (not being only his spouse or a company under the control of the applicant or his spouse or under their joint control), or if the applicant is deemed to occupy land jointly with one or more such persons, he may in either case complete the application set out in paragraph 12(c) of the Form for the net annual income which the land is or was capable of producing to be treated as limited to his appropriate share.

8.   All matters relied on as supporting the claim to be a suitable person to become the tenant of the holding should be summarised. These should include details of the applicant's training and practical experience of agriculture, physical health, financial standing and any educational qualifications not already listed in paragraph 11.

9.   By virtue of art 28 of the Agricultural Land Tribunals (Succession to Agricultural Tenancies) Order 1984, two copies of the application and of any map and document must be sent to the secretary.

10.   A larger scale map may be used if preferred. Ordnance Survey Field Numbers must be marked on the map.

11.   Mention any other document which is attached to this application.

12.   The applicant is required to send to the landlord of the holding notice of this application in Form 6 (Succession on Retirement) which is set out in the Appendix to the Agricultural Land Tribunals (Succession to Agicultural Tenancies) Order 1984.

13.   If signed by any person other than the applicant himself, he should state in what capacity or by what authority he signs.

---

* Strike out whichever is inapplicable.

† Strike out if inapplicable.

§ The prescribed form still refers to the 1976 Act now repealed. Some ALTs have modified the form pursuant to art 1(3) of the Agricultural Land Tribunals (Succession to Agricultural Tenancies) Order 1984, SI 1984/1301. It is necessary to check with the appropriate ALT for details. It is perhaps safer, if time permits, contacting the secretary of the relevant ALT and requesting copies of the necessary forms from him/her.

‡ Although not referred to in the prescribed form, s 40 and Sch, para 32 to ATA 1995 added a letting under a farm business tenancy for less than five years (including a periodic tenancy).

---

30   REPLY TO APPLICATION FOR DIRECTION GIVING ENTITLEMENT TO TENANCY

FORM 5R (SUCCESSION ON RETIREMENT)

Rule 25

Ref No: ....

(to be inserted by the Secretary)

AGRICULTURAL LAND TRIBUNAL

REPLY TO APPLICATION FOR DIRECTION GIVING ENTITLEMENT
TO TENANCY OF AGRICULTURAL HOLDING

To the secretary of the Agricultural Land Tribunal for the .... Area

I, ...*[block capitals]*

of ....*[address]*

landlord of ....*[name or description of holding]*

having received a copy of the application bearing the above reference number reply as follows:

....

1.   The facts stated in paragraphs 1, 2, 4, 6, and 7 of the application are, to the best of my knowledge, information and belief, correct† except that:

....

4 TENANCIES UNDER THE AGRICULTURAL HOLDINGS ACT 1986

†2.   I dispute the claim of the applicant to be an eligible person[1] on the following grounds:

    ....

3.   I have the following comments on the suitability of the applicant to become the tenant of the above holding:

    ....

†4.   I claim that greater hardship would be caused by the tribunal giving the direction sought by the applicant than by refusing his application and my reasons for this claim are:

    ....

†5.   The tenancy is the subject of a notice to quit Case ★B/★C/★D/★E/★F served on ....[*date*].

    †(For Case C only) The notice to quit is founded on a certificate granted in accordance with an application made on ....[*date*].

    †(For Case D only) The notice to quit is founded on a notice given for the purposes of that Case on ....[*date*].

6.   I attach two copies of the following relevant documents:[2]

    ....

7.   I consider the application to be invalid by reason of:[3]

    ....

Date ....   Signed[4] ....

TAKE NOTICE THAT IF YOU DO NOT REPLY IN THIS FORM WITHIN ONE MONTH OF THE DATE OF SERVICE ON YOU OF THE ATTACHED APPLICATION, THEN, SUBJECT TO PARAGRAPH 5(5) OF SCHEDULE 2 TO THE AGRICULTURAL HOLDINGS ACT 1984, YOU WILL NOT BE ENTITLED AT THE HEARING OF THE APPLICATION TO DISPUTE ANY MATTER ALLEGED IN IT.§

NOTES

1.   The paragraphs of the application which (where completed) will be relevant to the applicant's claim to be an eligible person are paragraphs 9, 10, 11 and 12.

2.   By virtue of art 28 of the Agricultural Land Tribunals (Succession to Agricultural Tenancies) Order 1984, two copies of this reply and of any document which you wish to submit to the tribunal must be sent to the secretary. If you disagree with any map or plan attached to the application, your reply should be accompanied by two copies of a 6 inch to one mile or 1/10,000 (or larger) map showing what you consider to be the true position and marking the Ordnance Survey Field Numbers.

3.   If you consider that, for any reason, the applicant is not legally entitled to make his application, you should state succinctly the grounds on which you rely.

4.   If signed by any person other than the landlord himself, he should state in what capacity or by what authority he signs.

★   Strike out whichever is inapplicable.

†   Strike out if inapplicable.

§   The prescribed form still refers to the 1984 Act now repealed. Some ALTs have modified the form pursuant to art 1(3) of the Agricultural Land Tribunals (Succession to Agricultural Tenancies) Order 1984, SI 1984/1301. It is necessary to check with the appropriate ALT for details. It is perhaps safer, if time permits, contacting the secretary of the relevant ALT and requesting copies of the necessary forms from him/her.

---

31   NOTICE OF APPLICATION FOR ENTITLEMENT TO TENANCY

FORM 3 (SUCCESSION ON DEATH)

Rule 5(1)

Ref No: ....

(to be inserted by the Secretary)

AGRICULTURAL LAND TRIBUNAL

NOTICE OF APPLICATION FOR ENTITLEMENT TO TENANCY
UNDER PART II OF THE AGRICULTURE (MISCELLANEOUS
PROVISIONS) ACT 1976§

To: ....*[name]*

of ....*[address]*

I, ...*[block capitals]*

of ....*[address]*

hereby give you notice that I applied on ....*[date of application]*

under Part II of the above-named Act for a direction entitling me to a tenancy of the agricultural holding known as ....*[address]*

[address or brief description of holding] in succession to ....

[name of deceased tenant of the holding] who died on ....

Dated ....   Signed ....

A copy of the full application will in due course be sent to the landlord and any other applicants by the secretary of the tribunal.

§   The prescribed form still refers to the 1976 Act now repealed. Some ALTs have modified the
    form pursuant to art 1(3) of the Agricultural Land Tribunals (Succession to Agricultural
    Tenancies) Order 1984, SI 1984/1301. It is necessary to check with the appropriate ALT for
    details. It is perhaps safer, if time permits, to contact the secretary of the relevant ALT and
    requesting copies of the necessary forms from him/her.

32   REPLY TO APPLICATION FOR DIRECTION GIVING ENTITLEMENT TO TENANCY

FORM 4 (SUCCESSION ON DEATH)

Rule 8

Ref No: ....

(to be inserted by the Secretary)

AGRICULTURAL LAND TRIBUNAL

REPLY TO APPLICATION FOR DIRECTION GIVING ENTITLEMENT TO TENANCY OF AGRICULTURAL HOLDING

To the secretary of the Agricultural Land Tribunal for the .... Area

I, ...*[block capitals]*

of ....*[address]*

having received a copy of the application of ....

(hereinafter called 'the applicant') bearing the above reference number, reply as follows:

....

1.   The facts stated in the first seven paragraphs of the application are correct†
     except that:
     ....

2.   *I accept the applicant's claim to be a designated applicant, as stated in
     paragraph 8 of the application.

     OR

     *I dispute the applicant's claim to be a designated applicant, as stated in
     paragraph 8 of the application, on the following grounds:
     ....

3.   I do not dispute any of the matters stated in paragraphs 9–13, 16 and 17 of the
     application† except that:
     ....

4.   I claim to be a more suitable person than the applicant to be granted a tenancy of the holding; and I base this claim on the following grounds:

....

†5.   The applicant and I †(and ....) have agreed to request the landlord's consent to a direction entitling us to a joint tenancy of the holding.

Date ....   Signed ....

---

*   Strike out whichever is inapplicable.
†   Strike out if inapplicable.

---

33   NOTICE OF APPLICATION FOR ENTITLEMENT TO TENANCY

FORM 6 (SUCCESSION ON RETIREMENT)

Rule 24

Ref No: ....
(to be inserted by the Secretary)

AGRICULTURAL LAND TRIBUNAL

NOTICE OF APPLICATION FOR ENTITLEMENT TO TENANCY UNDER SCHEDULE 2 TO THE AGRICULTURAL HOLDINGS ACT 1984

To: ....*[name]*

of ....*[address]*

I, ...*[block capitals]*

of ....*[address]*

hereby give you notice that I applied on ....*[date of application]*

under Schedule 2 to the above-named Act for a direction entitling me to a tenancy of the agricultural holding known as .... [*address or brief description of holding*] in succession to [*name of present tenant(s) of the holding*] who served on you his/their retirement notice on ....*[date]*.

Date ....   Signed ....

A copy of the full application will in due course be sent to you by the secretary to the tribunal.

CHAPTER 5: TENANCIES UNDER THE AGRICULTURAL TENANCIES ACT 1995

INDEX

CHAPTER 5: TENANCIES UNDER THE AGRICULTURAL TENANCIES ACT 1995

INTRODUCTION

FARM BUSINESS TENANCIES

All tenancies created after 1 September 1995 will be farm business tenancies unless they fall within one of the exceptions set out in the 1995 Act, s 4. Most short-term tenancies are dealt with by land agents on standard forms, but a short form of agreement is included for information. However, some tenancies exist for a much longer period, for example 20 or 30 years. These arise either from sale and lease-back arrangements or where, for some reason, the parties want to substitute something rather like a 1986 Act tenancy but are forced to do so by means of a farm business tenancy. Accordingly, a long form of agreement is also included. Clearly, the variety of possible terms is extremely great.

The Act provides that a tenancy for a term of more than two years shall continue as a tenancy from year to year unless, at least 12 months but less than 24 months before the term date, a written notice has been given by either party to the other of his intention to terminate the tenancy (s 5).

A tenancy from year to year will be terminable only by notice of at least 12 but less than 24 months, taking effect at the end of a year of the tenancy. Similarly, the notice to operate the break in a long lease containing a break clause must be at least 12 but less than 24 months in length.

Tenancies for two years or less will expire without any notice. Periodic tenancies shorter than yearly tenancies will not be covered by the rules and will therefore be subject to the usual common law notice period.

If a break clause is to be included, it is important to consider in what circumstances either party may wish to break the tenancy. For example, if the tenant dies, his executors might wish to bring the tenancy to an end. Again, unless there is an opportunity to terminate a fixed term in the event of the death of the tenant, his death will not *ipso facto* lead to the termination of the tenancy. The landlord may therefore wish to have a right to break in these circumstances. Every case must be negotiated.

The rent clause will need careful consideration. Generally speaking, if the tenancy lasts for more than three years, the statutory review procedure contained in the 1995 Act, ss 9–14 will apply. If this is not intended, it is necessary to contract out, but the provisions of the Act are restrictive. The parties are free to agree that the rent should not be reviewed at all (s 9(a)). If this is what they intend, they must say so in the agreement.

The rent can also be varied either by a specified amount or in accordance with a formula, but not subject to the exercise by any person of a value judgment in respect of the holding (s 9(b)). The agreement must, if a formula is adopted, state that otherwise the rent is to remain fixed. Should the formula fail, it is possible that one can revert to the statutory review procedure. However, this is not certain. If a formula is to be adopted, the drafting is extremely important and it is essential that the parties understand the implications.

It is possible for the parties to agree what date should be the rent review date for purposes of statutory reviews (s 10(4) and (5)). However, if a formula is adopted, the rent review procedure must also be written into the agreement.

Although the 1995 Act lays down certain rules that cannot be avoided, in many other respects, for example repairs, there are no underlying rules and regulations. Accordingly, it is important when drafting an agreement to make sure that everything the parties need has been included. Farm business tenancies need to be very much bespoke.

PRECEDENTS

1   LANDLORD'S NOTICE COMPLYING WITH NOTICE CONDITION

AGRICULTURAL TENANCIES ACT 1995

SECTION 1(4)(a)

[name and identification of holding by
address, ordnance survey number or plan]

TO
[Name and address]

I, *[name and address of Landlord]*, give you notice that I intend the proposed tenancy of
the above Holding to be and remain a Farm Business tenancy.

Signed: ....

Dated: ....

2 TENANT'S NOTICE COMPLYING WITH NOTICE CONDITION

AGRICULTURAL TENANCIES ACT 1995

SECTION 1(4)(a)

*[name and identification of holding by
address, ordnance survey number or plan]*

TO
[Name and address]

I, *[name and address of Tenant]*, give you notice that I intend the proposed tenancy of the above Holding to be and remain a Farm Business tenancy.

Signed: ....

Dated: ....

Note. Contrary to popular belief in some quarters, these notices are not essential when dealing with FBTs in connection with milk quota transfers. It is important to remember that, if notices are used, there need to be two, one served by landlord on tenant and vice versa. It is *not* sufficient for a landlord to serve notice on a tenant and ask that it be receipted and returned. This will not satisfy the requirements of the Act.

---

3 FARM BUSINESS TENANCY AGREEMENT (SHORT FORM)[1]

Particulars

DATE OF AGREEMENT   :   ....

THE LANDLORD   :   ....

       of ....

       ....

THE TENANT   :   ....

       of ....

       ....

COMMENCEMENT DATE   :   ....

TERM DATE : [*date*]

TERM : The period of [*no*] years from and including the Commencement Date/The period from and including the Commencement Date to and including the next following Term Date and thereafter from year to year until determined in accordance with clause [*no*] (*delete as appropriate*)

RENT : [£ ...] per year (or such other yearly amount as may be substitued from time to time). (*delete if inapplicable*)

RENT INSTALMENTS : Equal instalments (except in respect of a broken period) payable in arrear/advance (*delete as appropriate*) on the Rent Days.

RENT DAYS : [*date*] and [*date*] in each [*period*]

PERMITTED USE : Use in the trade or business of agriculture.

REVIEW DATE : Any day which is a day next following a Term Date and which complies with the conditions set out in paragraph (b) of section 10(6) of the 1995 Act.

THIS FARM BUSINESS TENANCY AGREEMENT is made on the Date of Agreement

BETWEEN

(1)   [*Landlord's name*]
(2)   [*Tenant's name*]

1.   Particulars and definitions

1.1   The attached Particulars are incorporated in this Agreement and to the extent allowed by the context the expressions in the left-hand column of the Particulars have the respective meanings shown opposite them;

1.2   In this Agreement to the extent allowed by the context the following phrases have the respective meanings set under them:

1.2.1   'the Fixed Equipment'
the buildings structures fixtures and fittings (if any) affixed to and any works constructed on in or over the Holding from time to time except any which are to be regarded as belonging to the Tenant.

1.2.2   'the Holding'
the property described in the Holding Description Schedule.

1.2.3   'Insured Risks'
such risks in relation to the insurance concerned as the Landlord may from time to time reasonably require.

1.2.4   'the Tenancy'
the tenancy hereby created.

1.2.5 'the 1995 Act'

the Agricultural Tenancies Act 1995.

2. Interpretation

In this Agreement to the extent allowed by the context:

2.1 'the Holding' includes any part of the Holding;

2.2 'the Landlord' includes whoever for the time being owns the interest in the Holding which gives the right to possession of it at the end of the Tenancy;

2.3 'the Tenant' includes the Tenant's successors in title;

2.4 'Value Added Tax' includes any substituted or additional tax of a similar nature;

2.5 unless stated otherwise any reference to a sum of money is to that sum exclusive of Value Added Tax and any Value Added Tax charged on it is payable in addition;

2.6 a right given to the Landlord to enter the Holding extends to anyone the Landlord authorises to enter and includes the right to bring workmen and appliances onto the Holding for the stated purposes;

2.7 authority given to a person to enter the Holding after giving notice extends if the circumstances justify it to entry after giving less notice than specified or without giving any notice;

2.8 any obligation not to do any act or thing includes an obligation not to cause or allow anyone else to do that act or thing;

2.9 whenever any party in relation to the Tenancy comprises two or more persons the obligations of that party may be enforced against any one of those persons alone or against all or some of them jointly;

2.10 the act or default of any person on the Holding with the express or implied consent of the Tenant shall be deemed the act or default of the Tenant;

2.11 words importing the singular number include the plural and vice versa; words importing persons include corporations and vice versa; words importing only one gender include the other genders;

2.12 any reference to this Agreement includes its schedules;

2.13 any reference to a page clause or schedule is to that page clause or schedule of this Agreement;

2.14 the clause and paragraph headings are for convenient reference only and shall not affect its construction;

2.15 any reference to a statute regulation order or code of practice includes any later provision substituted for or amending the same and any subsidiary provision made under powers thereby conferred.

3. Letting

EITHER

The Landlord lets to the Tenant ALL THAT the Holding TO HOLD the same unto the Tenant for the Term (subject to any provision for earlier determination herein contained) on the terms of this Agreement YIELD-ING AND PAYING therefor the Rent in accordance with the provisions of this Agreement.

OR

3.1 The Landlord lets to the Tenant ALL THAT the Holding TO HOLD the same unto the Tenant for the Term (subject to any provision for earlier determination herein contained) on the terms of this Agreement YIELD-ING AND PAYING therefor the Rent in accordance with the provisions of this Agreement.

3.2 Either the Landlord or the Tenant may determine the Tenancy by giving to the other notice in writing of not less than twelve nor more than twenty-four months expiring on the second or any subsequent Term Date.

4. Tenant's covenants
The Tenant covenants with the Landlord:

4.1 *Rent*
To pay the Rent by the Rent Instalments on the Rent Days.

4.2 *Outgoings*
To pay all existing and future rates taxes assessments and outgoings of any kind charged or imposed upon the Holding or upon the owner or occupier thereof.

4.3 *Value added tax*
To pay all Value Added Tax which may be payable on any taxable supply made to the Tenant in relation to the Tenancy or on any payment by the Landlord which the Tenant is required to reimburse to the Landlord.

4.4 *Insurance*
4.4.1 To insure the Fixed Equipment against damage or destruction by the Insured Risks to the full cost of rebuilding and reinstatement (including the cost of demolition and fees) and to have the interest of the Landlord duly noted on the policy.

4.4.2 If so required by the Landlord to produce reasonably satisfactory evidence that the insurance required by this clause is in force.

4.5 *Repair*[2]
4.5.1 At all times to maintain and keep in good repair and condition and (where appropriate) neat and tidy the Holding and all fixtures and fittings (whether belonging to the Landlord or the Tenant) on it or on any other property but serving the Holding.

4.5.2 To keep clear and free from obstruction all land drains and ditches on the Holding.

4.5.3 To keep all boundary features on the Holding in such state as is adequate for their purpose and (in the case of hedges) reasonably cut back.

4.5.4 To pay to the Landlord on demand an appropriate proportion of the costs from time to time incurred by the Landlord in the maintenance and repair of any items used in common with any adjoining or neighbouring property.

4.6   *Good husbandry*
          To farm in accordance with the requirements of good husbandry so as to
          keep the land at all times in good heart and condition.

4.7   *Permitted use*
          To use the Holding for the Permitted Use only and in particular not to use
          any part of the Holding as a market garden.

4.8   *Alteration*
          The Tenant shall not on the Holding:
4.8.1   commit waste of any kind;
4.8.2   plant any trees coppice saplings pollards or underwood;
4.8.3   make any alteration any addition or any tenant's improvement falling
          within the provisions of Part III of the 1995 Act other than any routine
          improvement as defined in section 19(10) of the 1995 Act.[3]

4.9   *Statutory obligations*[4]
          At the Tenant's own expense to do everything in relation to the Holding or
          its use which is required to comply with any statutory or other obligation
          (whether such obligation is imposed on the owner or the occupier) and in
          particular those relating to:
4.9.1   the health safety and welfare of the persons using or employed on or about
          or visiting the Holding;
4.9.2   waste effluent manure or other matter or thing of a noxious dangerous or
          offensive nature.

4.10   *Not to obstruct roadway*
          Not to obstruct any roadway or track by which access to and from the
          Holding or any neighbouring property is gained.

4.11   *No nuisance*
          Not to do or allow to remain upon the Holding anything which may be or
          become or cause a nuisance disturbance inconvenience injury or damage to
          the Landlord or the owner or occupier of any neighbouring property.

4.12   *Adverse rights*
          To take all reasonable steps to prevent any right over the Holding being
          acquired and to prevent trespass on the Holding.

4.13   *Indemnity – loss*
4.13.1   Not to do or omit to do on or near the Holding any act or thing which may
          render the Landlord liable to pay any penalty damages compensation costs
          charges or expenses or to carry out any work of whatever nature.
4.13.2   At all times to keep the Landlord fully indemnified against all losses claims
          actions and liabilities arising (whether directly or indirectly) as a result of
          any act or default of the Tenant.

4.14   *Dilapidations notice*

To pay to the Landlord on an indemnity basis all expenses incurred by the Landlord in the preparation and service of a notice under section 146 of the Law of Property Act 1925 or in relation to proceedings under section 146 or 147 of that Act notwithstanding that forfeiture is avoided otherwise than by relief granted by the Court.

4.15   *Alienation*

Not without the consent of the Landlord to assign underlet charge or part with possession of the whole or any part of the Holding or permit anyone else to occupy the whole or any part of the Holding.

4.16   *Notices*

To give full particulars to the Landlord of any notice direction order or proposal relating to the Holding made given or issued to the Tenant within seven days of receipt and to take all necessary steps to comply with it.

4.17   *Yield up*

On the determination of the Tenancy to yield up the Holding in such repair and so cultivated as to be in accordance with the terms of this Agreement and with vacant possession.

[4.18   *Costs of agreement*

On the signing hereof to reimburse the Landlord the legal costs and expenses incurred by the Landlord of and incidental to the preparation of this Agreement and a counterpart thereof.]

5.   Landlord's agreement

The Landlord agrees with the Tenant to permit the Tenant on paying the Rent and performing and observing the several obligations of the Tenant in relation to the Tenancy peaceably and quietly to hold and enjoy the Holding during the Tenancy without any interruption or disturbance from or by the Landlord or any person claiming under or in trust for the Landlord.

6.   Re-entry

At any time after the happening of any of the events specified in the following paragraphs of this clause 6 it shall be lawful for the Landlord after giving two months' notice to the Tenant of his intention to do so to re-enter the Holding or any part thereof in the name of the whole and thereupon the Tenancy shall absolutely determine but without prejudice to any right of action or remedy of the Landlord in respect of any antecedent breach by the Tenant of any of his obligations in relation to the Tenancy namely:

6.1   if any rent hereby reserved is unpaid for fourteen days after becoming due (whether legally demanded or not);

6.2   if the Tenant at any time fails or neglects to perform or observe any of his obligations in relation to the Tenancy;

6.3   if the Tenant has any distress or process of execution levied on his goods.
         EITHER (Company Tenant)

6.4   if the Tenant:

6.4.1   enters into liquidation whether compulsorily or voluntarily (not being a
         voluntary liquidation for the sole purpose of reconstruction or amalga-
         mation of a solvent company);

6.4.2   suffers an administrative receiver to be appointed;

6.4.3   enters into a voluntary arrangement as defined in section 1 of the
         Insolvency Act 1986;

6.4.4   does anything which would entitle a receiver to be appointed to take
         possession of any of its assets;

6.4.5   does anything which would entitle any person to present a petition for
         winding up the Tenant or apply for an administration order in relation to
         the Tenant;

6.4.6   ceases to exist or is dissolved,
         OR (Individual Tenant)

6.4   if the Tenant:

6.4.1   is unable to pay a debt or has no reasonable prospect of being able to pay a
         debt within the meaning of section 268 of the Insolvency Act 1986;

6.4.2   makes an application to the court for an interim order under section 253 of
         the Insolvency Act 1986;

6.4.3   makes any assignment for the benefit of or enters into any arrangement
         with his creditors either by composition or otherwise;

6.4.4   does anything which would entitle a petition for a bankruptcy order to be
         made against him,

         EITHER

7.   Rent review

         For the purposes of Part II of the 1995 Act the Review Date from and
         including which the Rent may be varied is the Review Date.

         OR

8.   No rent review

         The Rent specified in the Particulars shall be payable throughout the Term
         and there shall be no review.

[9.   Break clause][5]

10.   Custom

         The rights of the parties under this Agreement or otherwise in respect of
         the Tenancy shall not depend upon or be affected by any custom of the
         country.

11.   Certificate

         It is hereby certified that there is no agreement for lease to which this
         document gives effect.

IN WITNESS whereof this Deed has been executed by the parties hereto the day
and year first before written.

THE HOLDING DESCRIPTION SCHEDULE

ALL THAT farm shortly described as [*address*] and more particularly described below by reference to the Ordnance Survey Plan (. . . Edition) of the district,

TOGETHER with the benefit of any rights which are appurtenant to the Holding or which are reasonably needed for its proper enjoyment by the Tenant and capable of grant by the Landlord,

SUBJECT TO any rights which are expressly excepted or reserved out of the Holding and any rights or quasi–rights which have been enjoyed until now over the Holding by any occupier of any neighbouring property or the Landlord,

SUBJECT ALSO TO any subsisting obligations under any covenants affecting the Holding but with any subsisting benefit under any such covenants.

OS No   Area (hectares)

SIGNED and delivered as a Deed by
the said [*name*] in the presence of: }   ....

....

....

....

SIGNED and delivered as a Deed by
the said [*name*] in the presence of: }   ....

....

....

....

EXECUTED and delivered as a Deed
for and on behalf of [*name*] (Director)   }
and [*name*] (Secretary)   ....

1 Stamp duty based on rent.
2 The Tenant must consider the implication of a fully repairing tenancy: for a short term this would be inappropriate if there were buildings and fixed equipment.
3 This should help the Landlord in any negotiations if the Tenant wishes to carry out improvements. Clearly, the Tenant must consider the implications.
4 With increasing environmental restrictions the Tenant may need to consider this clause carefully before agreeing.
5 See comments in Introduction. If a break clause is to be included, see Precedent 4, cls 6.9 and 6.10.

4   FARM BUSINESS TENANCY AGREEMENT (LONG FORM)[1]

Particulars

DATE OF AGREEMENT	:	....
THE LANDLORD	:	....
		of ....
		....
THE TENANT	:	....
		of ....
		....
THE SURETY	:	....
		of ....
		....
TITLE GUARANTEE	:	Full/Limited/Limited except that the covenant implied by section 3(3) of the Law of Property (Miscellaneous Provisions) Act 1994 shall apply only to a charge incumbrance or third party right created by the Landlord personally (*delete as appropriate*)
COMMENCEMENT DATE	:	....
TERM DATE	:	[*date*]
TERM	:	The period of ... years from the Commencement Date/The period from the Commencement Date to the day preceding the next following Term Date and thereafter from year to year until determined in accordance with clause 2.2 (*delete as appropriate*)

BREAK DATE : [*date*]/the anniversary of the first Term Date during the Term/the ... and ... anniversaries of the first Term Date during the Term (*delete as appropriate*) [Note: Delete Clause 2.2 if appropriate]

INITIAL HOLDING RENT : [£ ...] per year

RENT DAYS : [*date*] and [*date*]

RENT SUSPENSION PERIOD : [   ] years

RESOLUTION OF DISPUTES
BY : Arbitrator/expert (*delete as appropriate*)

GRAIN HOLDOVER DATE : [*date*] next following the termination of the Tenancy

SUGAR BEET HOLDOVER
DATE : [*date*] next following the termination of the Tenancy

POTATO/ONION
HOLDOVER DATE : [*date*] next following the termination of the Tenancy

VALUATION ASSOCIATION : Central Association of Agricultural Valuers

LANDLORD'S ADDRESS : ....
FOR SERVICE OF NOTICES   ....
(LANDLORD AND TENANT   ....
ACT 1987, SECTION 48(1))   ....

*SUGAR BEET CONTRACT : [   ] (*delete if inapplicable*)
TONNAGE

*LANDLORD'S MILK QUOTA
          – LITRES : [   ]
          – BUTTERFAT : [   ]
and any milk quota subsequently transferred to the Tenant without payment but as to the whole subject to any addition or reduction due to any general adjustment (*delete if inapplicable*)

*TENANT'S MILK QUOTA
                – LITRES   :   [   ]
                – BUTTERFAT   :   [   ]
                                                        and any milk quota subsequently trans-
                                                        ferred to the Holding by the Tenant at his
                                                        expense in accordance with the provisions
                                                        hereof but as to the whole subject to any
                                                        addition or reduction due to any general
                                                        adjustment (*delete if inapplicable*)

THIS FARM BUSINESS TENANCY AGREEMENT is made on the Date of
Agreement

BETWEEN

(1)   The Landlord;
(2)   The Tenant;
(3)   The Surety.

1.   Particulars definitions and interpretation
1.1   The attached Particulars are incorporated in this Agreement and unless the
          context otherwise requires the expressions in the left-hand column of the
          Particulars have the respective meanings set against them in the Particulars.
1.2   In this Agreement unless the context otherwise requires the following
          phrases shall have the respective meanings set under them:
1.2.1   *the Fixed Equipment*
          the buildings structures fixtures and fittings (if any) affixed to and any works
          constructed on in over or under the Holding from time to time except any
          which the outgoing tenant is entitled to remove and any which are to be
          regarded as belonging to the Tenant;
1.2.2   *the Holding*
          the premises described in the Holding Description Schedule including the
          Fixed Equipment TOGETHER WITH the rights specified in the
          Schedule of Rights Granted but EXCEPT AND RESERVING the rights
          specified in the Schedule of Reservations;
1.2.3   *the Holding Rent*
          the yearly rent payable in accordance with paragraph 1 of the Rents
          Schedule;
1.2.4   *the Holdover Buildings*
          the grain drying and storage buildings and bins on the Holding at the
          termination of the Tenancy;
1.2.5   *the Holdover Plant*
          all drying plant conveyors and other machines and machinery in the
          Holdover Buildings;

1.2.6   *IACS*

the Integrated Administration and Control System or any alternative scheme for the support of agricultural incomes or the control of agricultural production or the restriction of land use which may be introduced in addition thereto or in substitution therefor and administered by the Ministry or the European Commission or any other public or statutory body whether jointly or individually;

1.2.7   *the Insured Risks*

fire storm lightning tempest flood aircraft in peacetime and articles dropped therefrom impact explosion earthquake subsidence riot malicious damage and civil commotion (or such of them as the Landlord may from time to time specify in writing in relation to any particular insurance) and such other risks (including terrorism) as the Landlord in his discretion from time to time specifies by notice in writing to the Tenant;

1.2.8   *the Interest Rate*

Four per centum per annum above the base lending rate from time to time of [*name*] Bank plc or in the event of that base rate ceasing to be published such other rate as the Landlord shall reasonably specify by notice in writing to the Tenant;

1.2.9   *the Land*

the land comprised in the Holding but excluding the Fixed Equipment;

1.2.10   *the Landlord's Surveyor*

any qualified person or corporation (including an employee of the Landlord) appointed by or acting for the Landlord to perform the function of a surveyor or manager for any purpose of this Agreement;

1.2.11   *the Ministry*

the Ministry of Agriculture Fisheries and Food or (as the case may be) the Welsh Office Agricultural Department or any substitute Ministry for either and shall include where the context so admits the authority responsible for administering IACS or any alternative scheme as aforesaid introduced in addition thereto or in substitution therefor;

1.2.12   *the Planning Acts*

the Town and Country Planning Act 1990, the Planning (Listed Buildings and Conservation Areas) Act 1990, the Planning (Hazardous Substances) Act 1990, the Planning (Consequential Provisions) Act 1990 and the Planning and Compensation Act 1991;

1.2.13   *Redundant Items*

those items which are redundant to the farming of the Holding as specified or subsequently deemed to be specified in the Schedule of Redundant Items;

1.2.14   *the Referee*

the person appointed as an arbitrator or independent expert (as the case may be) in accordance with the clause of this Agreement headed 'Resolution of Disputes';

1.2.15   *Relevant Quotas*
         such quotas (including sheep and suckler cow premium quota rights but
         excluding the Tenant's Milk Quota) contracts premium quota rights or
         similar arrangements (as permitted by the context) as are from time to time
         attaching to or available in respect of the Holding or any produce thereof or
         to which the Tenant or any other person is entitled in respect of such
         produce whether existing at the commencement of the Tenancy or
         introduced thereafter and 'Relevant Quota' shall be construed
         accordingly;

1.2.16   *Restricted Use*
         Use for agricultural purposes/as a dairy farm/as an arable farm/in
         accordance with a system of farming approved in writing by the Landlord
         (*delete as appropriate*);

1.2.17   *Restricted Use Period*
         The first [*no*] months/years (*delete as appropriate*) of the Term;

1.2.18   *the Tenancy*
         the tenancy hereby created;

1.2.19   *Tenant's Fixtures*
         those specified in the Schedule of Tenant's Fixtures and any other tenant's
         fixtures affixed to the Holding during the Tenancy;

1.2.20   *the 1995 Act*
         the Agricultural Tenancies Act 1995.

1.3   In this Agreement unless the context otherwise requires:

1.3.1   words importing one gender only include the other genders; words
         importing the singular include the plural number and vice versa; words
         importing persons include corporations and vice versa;

1.3.2   the expression 'the Landlord' includes the person for the time being
         entitled to the reversion immediately expectant on the Tenancy;

1.3.3   the expression 'the Tenant' includes the person for the time being entitled
         to the Tenancy;

1.3.4   the expression 'the Surety' includes the personal representatives of the
         named Surety;

1.3.5   where there are two or more persons included in the expression 'the
         Landlord' 'the Tenant' or 'the Surety' the obligations of such persons under
         this Agreement shall be joint and several;

1.3.6   any reference to 'the Holding' includes any part or parts thereof;

1.3.7   any matter 'referred for decision under this Agreement' shall be determined
         in accordance with the clause of this Agreement headed 'Resolution of
         Disputes';

1.3.8   any reference to any tax includes that tax as from time to time amended or
         extended and any tax by which it is replaced;

1.3.9   any provision not to do an act or thing imports an obligation not to cause or
         permit such act or thing to be done;

1.3.10   any reference to a statutory provision regulation or code of practice
         includes any later provision substituted for or amending the same and any
         subsidiary provision made under powers thereby conferred;

1.3.11   the clause and paragraph headings are for convenient reference only and
         shall not affect its construction.

2.   Letting

2.1   The Landlord lets to the Tenant with the Title Guarantee ALL THAT the Holding TO HOLD the same unto the Tenant for the Term (subject to any provision for earlier determination herein contained) on the terms of this Agreement YIELDING AND PAYING therefor the rents specified in the Rents Schedule.

2.2   *Optional* [Either the Landlord or the Tenant may determine the Tenancy by giving to the other notice in writing of not less than twelve nor more than twenty-four months expiring on the day preceding the second or any subsequent Term Date both the Commencement Date and the expiry date being included in the Term].

3.   Matters affecting the holding

The Holding is let subject to:

3.1   such public or private rights liabilities provisions agreements and other matters as affect the Holding;

3.2   the rights of the outgoing tenant (if any);

3.3   any existing tenancies or occupancies of any dwellings on the Holding.

4.   Tenant's covenants

The Tenant hereby covenants with the Landlord to the intent that the obligations shall continue throughout the Tenancy as follows:

4.1   *Pay rent*

To pay the rents specified in the Rents Schedule at the times and in the manner therein provided and if the Landlord so requires to make any payment or payments of such rents by banker's standing order or direct debit to such account as the Landlord from time to time notifies to the Tenant in writing.

4.2   *Pay VAT*

To pay within fourteen days after demand (against a proper Value Added Tax invoice where appropriate) all Value Added Tax which may be payable on any taxable supplies made to the Tenant under or in connection with this Agreement (including Value Added Tax or replacement tax on any rent payable hereunder).

4.3   *Pay outgoings*

4.3.1   To pay all existing and future rates taxes assessments and outgoings of every kind (whether or not of a novel nature) which are now or may at any time hereafter during the Tenancy be charged or imposed upon the Holding or upon the owner or occupier thereof except only such as the Landlord is by law bound to pay notwithstanding any contract to the contrary and any taxation payable either by reason of the Landlord's ownership of the Holding or in respect of any dealing with the Landlord's reversion in the Holding.

4.3.2   If any payment falling within sub-clause 1 of this clause is payable in respect of or calculated by reference to both the Holding and other property the Tenant shall pay a proper and reasonable proportion thereof.

4.4   *Pay interest and costs of recovery*
4.4.1   In relation to any rent or other sum due to the Landlord but unpaid for seven days to pay interest at the Interest Rate from the time when such rent or other sum became due (whether formally demanded or not) until the time when it is actually paid (as well after as before any judgment) and the aggregate of such sum and interest shall at the option of the Landlord be recoverable by action or as rent in arrear.
4.4.2   To pay costs and disbursements incurred by the Landlord in seeking to recover any rent or other payment in arrear by any appropriate steps including instructing a bailiff to levy distress for that rent (whether or not any distress in the event be levied).

4.5   *Pay incoming valuation*
         To pay to the Landlord:
4.5.1   the amount payable by the Landlord to the outgoing tenant in respect of the Holding (except only any compensation for disturbance and game damage and any compensation in respect of milk quota unless otherwise expressly agreed);
4.5.2   (where there is no outgoing tenant) such sum as would have been payable under sub-clause 1 of this clause had there been an outgoing tenant such payment to be made within fourteen days of the Tenant being notified by the Landlord in writing of the amount payable under this clause.

4.6   *Notice of charges*
         To give notice in writing to the Landlord forthwith upon giving any charge over his farming stock under the Agricultural Credits Act 1928 or any other similar enactment and on request to supply the Landlord with copies of all charges given.

4.7   *Death of tenant*
         To take all such steps as are necessary to ensure that:
4.7.1   if the Tenant or any of them dies during the currency of the Tenancy notice in writing of such death and the date thereof is given to the Landlord within one month of the death;
4.7.2   an office or duly certified copy of any probate of a will letters of administration order of court or other instrument affecting the Holding or the Tenancy is served on the Landlord within one month from the date thereof.

4.8   *Landlord's proceedings*
         To permit the Landlord to take proceedings or do any other act in the name
         of the Tenant which the Landlord considers appropriate to preserve or
         protect his interest in the Holding and to co-operate with the Landlord in
         relation thereto the Landlord indemnifying the Tenant against any costs
         charges and expenses the Tenant may incur in connection with any such
         matter.

4.9   *Insuring dealing and other obligations in schedules*
         To comply at all times with the obligations of the Tenant:
4.9.1   as to insurance contained in the Insurance Schedule;
4.9.2   as to dealings with the Holding contained in the Dealings Schedule;
4.9.3   as to holdover to the Tenant contained in the Holdover Schedule;
4.9.4   as to any other matter not otherwise specifically provided for or contained
         in any other schedule to this Agreement.

4.10   *Waste*
4.10.1   Not to commit any wilful or voluntary waste spoil or destruction on the
         Holding.
4.10.2   To prevent any encroachment easement or footpaths from being made in
         or acquired over the Holding.
4.10.3   Not to give any acknowledgement as to the entitlement to any right or
         easement over or in respect of the Holding.
4.10.4   Where damage results from the laying underground of any pipeline sewer
         or other apparatus or from the erection of any pole pylon or other apparatus
         above the ground to procure that without delay such damage is fully made
         good and the Holding is fully restored.
4.10.5   Not to do or omit any act or thing in relation to the Holding (including the
         making of any application or the giving of any notice of any kind) which
         may:
4.10.5.1 render the Landlord liable for the payment of any tax chargeable by
         reference to the realisation of development value;
4.10.5.2 entitle any authority to acquire the Holding or take any other step adverse
         to the interest of the Landlord under any then existing statute or subsidiary
         legislation.

         EITHER

4.11   *Repairs*
4.11.1   At all times during the Tenancy to keep in good and substantial repair order
         and condition (which where appropriate includes keeping the same clean
         and properly decorated and/or protected) all items from time to time on
         the Holding or on other property but serving the Holding which are stated
         in the Repairs Schedule to be the responsibility of the Tenant using the best
         and most suitable materials for the purpose.
4.11.2   The provisions of sub-clause 1 of this clause shall not apply to:
4.11.2.1 any Redundant Item;

4.11.2.2 any repair or replacement which is required by reason of loss or damage by any risk against which the Landlord has or should have insured in accordance with the provisions of this Agreement save to the extent that any such insurance has been vitiated by some act or default of the Tenant or any person for whose acts or defaults the Tenant may be responsible.

OR

4.11   *Repairs*

4.11.1   At all times during the Tenancy to keep in good and substantial repair order and condition (which where appropriate includes keeping the same clean and properly decorated and/or protected) all items (other than any Redundant Items) from time to time on the Holding or on other property but serving the Holding using the best and most suitable materials for the purpose.

4.12   *Common items*

To pay to the Landlord on demand an appropriate proportion of the cost from time to time incurred by the Landlord in the maintenance and repair of all items used in common with adjoining or neighbouring property.

4.13   *Alterations*

4.13.1   Not to carry out any alteration or make any addition to the farmhouse buildings or cottages (if any) or erect any new buildings or make any other improvement on the Holding.

4.13.2   Before making any permitted Tenant's Improvement to use his best endeavours to obtain any grant subsidy or other payment which may be available in respect thereof under any local national or European scheme.

4.13.3   To indemnify the Landlord against any liability to any adjoining owner or occupier or the local authority or any member of the public which may be incurred by reason of the execution by or on behalf of the Tenant of any works which the Tenant is permitted or required to carry out on the Holding.

4.13.4   To remove (and make good all damage occasioned by such removal) any erection addition or alteration made by the Tenant without the consent required by this Agreement or in respect of which the permission of the planning authority is refused withdrawn or lapses within one month after being required in writing by the Landlord to do so.

4.14   *Planning*

4.14.1   To comply in all respects with the provisions and requirements of the Planning Acts and all licences consents permissions and conditions (if any) granted or imposed thereunder so far as the same relate to or affect the Holding or any operations works acts or things already or hereafter to be carried out executed done or omitted thereon or the use thereof for any purpose and at all times hereafter to keep the Landlord fully indemnified against all liabilities actions costs claims losses and expenses in respect of any act matter or thing contravening any of those provisions and requirements.

4.14.2   As often as occasion requires at the expense in all respects of the Tenant to obtain all such licences consents and permissions and serve all such notices as may be required for the carrying out by the Tenant of any operation on the Holding or the institution or continuance by the Tenant thereon of any act or use which may constitute development within the meaning of the Planning Acts.

4.14.3   Not to make any application for planning permission without the previous consent in writing of the Landlord and to deliver to the Landlord within five days after the service or giving of the same a copy of any notice or application served or given by the Tenant on or to any planning authority under the Planning Acts.

4.14.4   To pay and satisfy any charge that may hereafter be imposed under the Planning Acts in respect of the carrying out or maintenance by the Tenant of any such operations or the institution or continuance by the Tenant of any such use as aforesaid.

4.14.5   Notwithstanding any consent which may be granted by the Landlord under this Agreement not to carry out or make any alteration or addition to the Holding or any change of use thereof before any requisite planning permission has been produced to the Landlord and acknowledged by the Landlord in writing as satisfactory to the Landlord PROVIDED that the Landlord may refuse so to express satisfaction with any such planning permission on the ground that the period thereof or anything contained therein or omitted therefrom in the reasonable opinion of the Landlord or the Landlord's Surveyor would be or be likely to be prejudicial to the Landlord's interest in the Holding whether during or following the expiration of the Tenancy.

4.14.6   Unless the Landlord otherwise directs to carry out before the termination of the Tenancy any works stipulated to be carried out on the Holding by a date subsequent to that termination as a condition of any planning permission wholly or partly implemented during the Tenancy.

4.14.7   If and when called upon so to do to produce to the Landlord or the Landlord's Surveyor all such plans documents and other evidence as the Landlord may reasonably require in order to satisfy the Landlord that the provisions of this covenant have been complied with in all respects.

4.14.8   Not to do or omit any act matter or thing in on or respecting the Holding which is required to be done or omitted (as the case may be) by the Planning Acts or to do or suffer to be done any act or thing which contravenes any provision of those Acts and at all times to keep the Landlord fully indemnified against all liabilities actions costs claims losses and expenses in respect of any such matter or thing contravening the provisions of the Planning Acts.

4.15   *Legislation*
To observe and comply fully with the provisions of any statute order regulation rule direction code of practice or other thing which extends to or affects the Holding or anything done or omitted or to be done or omitted thereon by the Landlord or the Tenant in relation to the Holding.[2]

4.16   *Notices*
         In relation to any direction notice proposal or order served on him under or
         by virtue of any statutory provision or otherwise:
4.16.1   forthwith to give the Landlord notice in writing thereof and if so required
         to produce to the Landlord such direction notice proposal or order and
         allow the Landlord to make copies thereof;
4.16.2   to comply immediately with and give sufficient effect to every such
         direction notice or order and keep the Landlord fully indemnified against
         all liabilities actions costs claims losses and expenses arising out of or in
         connection with the same.

4.17   *Fire precautions*
4.17.1   To maintain adequate fire fighting equipment throughout the Holding and
         to comply in all respects with any requirements or recommendations made
         by the insurers or a fire officer or other authority.
4.17.2   To keep the Holding supplied and equipped with proper and suitable fire
         fighting and extinguishing apparatus and appliances appropriate to the use
         of and the business carried on on the Holding.

4.18   *Environmental practice*
4.18.1   To use the Tenant's best endeavours to prevent pollution of whatever kind
         on the Holding or any neighbouring land.
4.18.2   When using spray chemicals to take all reasonable care to ensure that
         hedges trees and crops on the Holding or any adjacent property are not
         adversely affected and to make good or pay full compensation for any
         damage done.
4.18.3   In performing his obligations hereunder and his obligation to comply with
         the rules of good husbandry so far as possible to select chemicals and to
         adopt farming practices which cause the least harm to game birds wildlife
         (other than vermin and pests) and the environment.

4.19   *Ancient monuments*
         Not in any way to interfere with or injure any tumulus stone circle or other
         ancient remains structure or monument (including known buried archae-
         ological remains) or any actual or proposed site of special scientific interest
         (whether statutorily protected or not) and not to permit any person to enter
         on the Holding (with or without metal detectors tools hammers or other
         equipment) for the purpose of searching for or removing any object or
         specimen of antiquarian archaeological or scientific interest (save under the
         rights hereby reserved to the Landlord) but if it comes to the knowledge of
         the Tenant that any such object or specimen has been found or observed on
         the Holding forthwith to report the same to the Landlord in writing and to
         give such assistance as the Tenant reasonably can to enable possession
         thereof to be given to the Landlord or as he shall direct.

4.20   *Refuse*
4.20.1   Not to deposit any refuse waste redundant material or redundant
         machinery of any kind on the Holding.

4.20.2 Within seven days of receipt thereof to comply with any notice issued by the Landlord requiring removal from the Holding of any such material or item as is referred to in this clause in accordance with all statutory provisions relating to such removal then in force.

4.21 *Recordings*

4.21.1 Not without the written approval of the Landlord to permit or authorise any person to take for hire or reward any film or other recording (in whatever form and whether of sight or sound) of or on the Holding or any natural or man-made feature thereon or anything done or occurring thereon but so that this provision shall not restrict the liberty of the Tenant to take such film or other recording as he thinks fit for the personal and domestic use and enjoyment of any of himself his family and friends or in direct connection with his agricultural business.

4.21.2 Forthwith to pay to the Landlord any money received by the Tenant in consequence of any breach of this provision such money to be deemed for the purpose of calculating interest thereon to have become due on the date of the breach.

4.22 *Non-permitted users*

4.22.1 Not to use the Holding for any illegal or immoral purpose.

4.22.2 Not to carry on on the Holding any offensive noisome noxious or dangerous occupation or activity.

4.22.3 Not to do on the Holding any act matter or thing whatsoever which may be or become a nuisance or annoyance or cause damage disturbance or inconvenience to the Landlord or the owner or occupier of any adjoining or neighbouring property or the users of any road abutting the Holding.

4.22.4 Not to hold on the Holding any sale by auction or public meeting.

4.22.5 Not to use the Holding for any trade other than the Restricted Use or for advertising purposes or for the holding of any show race match game or contest whether of animals birds vehicles or persons.

4.22.6 Not to place any tent or caravan upon the Holding nor to take in lodgers in the farmhouse or other dwellings on the Holding.

4.22.7 Not to burn any crop residues on land from which a crop has been harvested.

4.23 *Personal farming and residence*

Personally to farm the Holding and reside in the farmhouse and make the same his usual place of residence but if the Tenant comprises more than one person residency by one of them shall satisfy this residence requirement.

4.24 *User*

During the Restricted Use Period to use the Holding only for the Restricted Use.

4.24.1 Not at any time to change the use of the Holding without the Landlord's consent in writing but any such consent shall not be deemed to be a consent for the purposes of this Agreement or of sections 17 and 18 of the 1995 Act to any Tenant's Improvement.

4.24.2   In the last year of the Tenancy to farm and cultivate the Holding in accordance with such reasonable requirements as are notified to him in writing by the Landlord but subject thereto:

4.24.2.1 to leave the arable land in a course normally practised in the district;

4.24.2.2 at the termination of the Tenancy to leave upon the Holding all the unconsumed hay straw roots or green crops (other than peas beans potatoes sugar beet carrots or other vegetable crops) produced on the Holding during the last year of the Tenancy.

4.25   *Cultivation*

4.25.1   To cultivate and manage the agricultural land on the Holding according to the best standards and system of cultivation used in the district and so as to comply with the rules of good husbandry as defined by section 11 of the Agriculture Act 1947 and so as not to impoverish or deteriorate the agricultural land and to leave the same clean and in good condition.

4.25.2   To take all reasonable precautions to prevent the introduction of any pest or disease on the Holding and in particular not to grow on the same land during any period of four consecutive years more than one crop of potatoes and one crop of sugar beet (including sugar beet grown for seed).

4.25.3   Not to make or keep rabbit warrens on the Holding and to destroy any that may exist.

4.25.4   When so required by and at the expense of the Landlord to have taken a proper analysis of the soil of the Holding (or such part of it as may be specified by the Landlord) by the Ministry or such other body as the Landlord may specify.

4.26   *Grass land*

4.26.1   To manage the grass land in a proper manner and also to destroy and prevent from seeding and spreading all rushes thistles nettles thorns gorse ragwort and other weeds and to keep down moles and rats and other vermin and spread all molehills and ant hills.

4.26.2   Not to remove from the Holding any turf or topsoil without the consent in writing of the Landlord and forthwith to pay to the Landlord any money received by the Tenant in consequence of a breach of this provision such money to be deemed for the purpose of calculating interest thereon to have become due on the date of the breach.

4.26.3   Not to break up or convert into tillage any land which is considered permanent pasture and for this purpose (and for the purposes of paragraph 2 of the Second Schedule to the Agriculture Act 1947) there shall be so considered the whole of the land described in the Cultivation column of the Holding Description Schedule as pasture meadow grass or ley and also any land subsequently laid to grass for which the Landlord has prescribed seeds.

4.26.4   The Tenant shall be at liberty to break up and convert into tillage any of the remainder of the grass land on the Holding PROVIDED THAT:

4.26.4.1 the Tenant shall at least one year before the termination of the Tenancy sow down to temporary pasture in a husbandlike manner with a seed mixture approved in writing by the Landlord the whole of the land so broken up so that such pasture is fully established before the termination of the Tenancy;

4.26.4.2 with the consent in writing of the Landlord the Tenant may sow down to temporary pasture in substitution for any grass land ploughed up an equal area of arable land elsewhere on the Holding upon such terms as the Landlord may direct in writing but such consent shall not imply any obligation on the part of the Landlord to provide fencing or a water supply for such substituted land nor shall it imply the Landlord's consent to the provision of fencing or water supplied by the Tenant as an improvement under the terms of section 17 of the 1995 Act;

4.26.4.3 no compensation shall be payable to the Tenant in respect of any temporary pasture laid down by him in accordance with this clause.

4.26.5 After giving or receiving notice to quit not to plough up temporary grass land sown more than five years prior to the end of the Tenancy.

4.26.6 If the Tenancy terminates between 1 January and 30 June in any year not to stock the new seeds after 1 October immediately preceding such termination.

4.26.7 Not to sell off or remove but to consume on the Holding all grasses and clover and forage crops (whether harvested or not) and all fodder straw and roots grown on the Holding in the last year of the Tenancy or remaining unconsumed from previous years and to leave for the use of the Landlord or incoming tenant all such grasses clover and forage crops fodder straw and roots remaining unconsumed on the Tenant quitting the Holding.

4.26.8 To return to the Holding the full equivalent manurial value of any grasses clover or forage plants (whether green or conserved) or any fodder straw roots or other produce of the Holding sold or removed from it at any time prior to the last year of the Tenancy.

4.26.9 To spread annually on the Holding all farmyard manure and compost produced and made on the Holding and at the termination of the Tenancy to leave carefully stored all such farmyard manure and compost not already spread.

4.27 *Trees*

To use his best endeavours to protect from damage any trees coppice wood or underwood growing on the Holding and in particular:

4.27.1 not to cut down cut top or lop or drive nails into or otherwise injure trees growing on the Holding;

4.27.2 not to cut any tellars whether growing from stools or otherwise without the consent in writing of the Landlord;

4.27.3 to protect all trees from damage by livestock machinery or otherwise howsoever;

4.27.4 not without the Landlord's consent in writing to plant with trees any area of the Holding not so planted at the commencement of the Tenancy.

4.28   *Orchards*

To keep all orchards and gardens in a proper state of cultivation well manured and in good heart to protect from damage by livestock or otherwise howsoever and to prune at proper seasons all fruit trees and bushes and at his own expense to replace dead or worn out fruit trees with other fruit trees suitable to the district PROVIDED THAT the Tenant may at his option in lieu of replacing individual trees grub up and replace the whole or a substantial part of an orchard in accordance with a scheme approved in writing by the Landlord.

4.29   *Game*

4.29.1   To use his best endeavours to protect from damage all animals fish and protected birds (with their nests and eggs) reserved by the relevant paragraph of the Schedule of Reservations and not to interfere with measures taken by the Landlord or persons authorised by him to rear and preserve game.

4.29.2   To warn off all poachers and trespassers and allow his name to be used in any proceedings which the Landlord may take against any poachers or trespassers (the Landlord indemnifying the Tenant against any costs charges and expenses he may thereby incur) and so far as possible to stop all encroachments.

4.30   *Boundaries*

Save in accordance with the rules of good husbandry and with the Landlord's prior written consent not to alter or destroy any hedge fence or boundary on the Holding nor do anything whereby the size or shape of any field is rendered different from its present size or shape.

4.31   *Records*

4.31.1   To keep on the Holding and maintain a field book showing how every field or parcel thereof has been stocked cropped and cultivated in each year of the Tenancy and to make the same available to the Landlord at all reasonable times.

4.31.2   To supply a copy to the Landlord of any return or other form which the Tenant makes or completes pursuant to any local national or European Union requirement or directive and if so required by the Landlord to consult with the Landlord in regard to the completion of such return or form to the extent required to preserve and safeguard in all respects the interest of the Landlord.

4.31.3   To keep true accounts of all crops or produce sold off and of the equivalent manurial value returned to the Holding and to produce such accounts to the Landlord forthwith upon receiving at any time a request in writing to do so.

4.32   *Disease*

4.32.1   To give the Landlord immediate notification (to be confirmed in writing forthwith) of any outbreak or suspected outbreak of any notifiable disease of crops or livestock on the Holding.

4.32.2   To comply at his own expense with any recommendation from time to time made by any appropriate authority or qualified person (including the Landlord's veterinary surgeon) for the prevention or treatment of any such disease.

4.32.3   Not to bring any diseased plant material or animal on to the Holding and to compensate the Landlord for all losses incurred as a result of any diseased plant material or animal being on the Holding.

4.33   *Water*

4.33.1   On entering the Holding to give all necessary notices and make all necessary applications and payments to preserve any existing licence granted in respect of the Holding under the Water Resources Act 1991 or any similar enactment and subsequently to continue the licence in force during the Tenancy and not at any time by any act or omission to jeopardise the licence nor to surrender it without the consent in writing of the Landlord.

4.33.2   On the termination of the Tenancy to make such application for the continuance or renewal of the licence as may be requisite for the time being under regulations then in force to preserve the licence for the benefit of the Landlord or his nominee without payment.

4.33.3   Not to enter into any agreement or licence for the supply of water from any spring or well pond stream watercourse or underground water supply on the Holding to any adjoining or neighbouring premises.

4.33.4   To reimburse to the Landlord on demand all charges costs and expenses reasonably incurred by the Landlord in connection with the provision or the improved provision of water to the Holding.

4.34   *New schemes*

          Except as expressly required to do so by or under the provisions hereof not without the Landlord's consent in writing to enter into any voluntary scheme or arrangement for setting aside land or imposing limitations on cropping stocking or production or requirements for public access.

4.35   *IACS*

4.35.1   Promptly to give to the Landlord a copy of any document submitted to the Ministry under IACS relating to the Holding and a copy of any communication received from the Ministry concerning any such document.

4.35.2   To confirm in writing to the Landlord no later than one month before the closing date in any year for applications under IACS whether or not he has submitted or will be submitting an area aid application under IACS for that year.

4.35.3   To submit prior to the deadline date in each year a properly completed area aid application under IACS and to take such steps as are required to ensure that all payments due under IACS are received and that the requirements relevant to the Holding are met.

4.35.4   Not without the prior consent in writing of the Landlord:

4.35.4.1 to set-aside any part of the Holding in excess of an area which will (viewing the Holding as a holding on its own) constitute the minimum percentage required to be set-aside in order to be eligible for area aid and set-aside payments under IACS;

4.35.4.2 to enter into any non-rotational or long term set-aside option forming part of IACS which involves diversification of land out of agricultural production for more than one annual cropping season;

4.35.4.3 to enter into any form of agreement which involves the transfer to the Tenant of the set-aside commitments of another producer;

4.35.4.4 to transfer any or all of the Tenant's own commitment to set-aside land required to be so set-aside in order to be eligible for payments under IACS.

4.35.5 Not to apply for any part of the Holding to cease to be eligible for arable area aid payments.

4.35.6 To allow the Landlord and any person authorised by the Landlord or the Ministry to enter on any part of the Holding at all reasonable times for any reasonable purpose in connection with IACS.

4.35.7 If the Tenancy terminates prior to the deadline date for submission of an area aid application in any calendar year and the Landlord so requests in writing to withdraw any such application made by the Tenant.

4.35.8 On the termination of the Tenancy:

4.35.8.1 if so required by the Landlord to hand over to the Landlord all documents required to ensure that area aid and set-aside payments are made in full;

4.35.8.2 to sign and submit any documents reasonably required by the Landlord to secure any aid payment and to assign to the Landlord or any person nominated by the Landlord any contract for the sale of any non-food crops on set-aside land and to join in the giving of all requisite notices within any applicable time-limits;

4.35.8.3 to authorise the Ministry to pay any area aid and set-aside payments payable thereafter to the Landlord and forthwith to pay to the Landlord any such payments received by or on behalf of the Tenant or anyone deriving title under the Tenant.

4.35.9 Forthwith on the Landlord's request to instruct the Ministry to give such information to the Landlord as the Landlord may require in respect of the Holding any return made for the purpose of IACS and any representations made by or to the Ministry in respect thereof. The Tenant hereby appoints the Landlord as his agent for the purpose of obtaining any such information as is referred to in this sub-clause.[3]

4.36 *Genetically modified organisms*

4.36.1 Not without the Landlord's previous consent in writing to grow or permit to be grown on the Holding any plant which has been 'genetically modified' within the meaning of Part VI of the Environmental Protection Act 1990.

4.36.2 In respect of any such plants grown on the Holding:

4.36.2.1 to observe all statutory provisions Regulations Codes of Practice and Guidelines;

4.36.2.2 to indemnify the Landlord against all claims proceedings and demands of whatsoever nature and howsoever arising from the presence of such plants on the Holding or the escape from the Holding of any 'organism' (within the meaning of Part VI of the Environmental Protection Act 1990) being part of or derived from such plants;

4.36.3 to use all reasonable endeavours to remove from the Holding on the determination of the tenancy all such plants and every part thereof.

4.37   *Groundwater Regulations*

To comply with the provisions of the Groundwater Regulations 1998, SI 1998/2746 ('the Groundwater Regulations') and in particular:

4.37.1 to supply the Landlord with details of disposal and tipping on the Holding in each year to 31st March within one month of the expiration thereof;

4.37.2 to maintain an authorisation in respect of the Holding under the Groundwater Regulations;

4.37.3 to take all necessary steps to transfer such authorisation to the Landlord or the incoming occupier on the termination of the tenancy and to give notice of such transfer to the Environmental Agency within 21 days thereof;

4.37.4 to indemnify the Landlord against all costs claims proceedings and demands of whatsoever nature and howsoever arising from any breach of the Groundwater Regulations.

4.38   *Nitrate Vulnerable Zones*

4.38.1 This clause applies if the farm is situated within a Nitrate Vulnerable Zone.

4.38.2 To retain all records required by the Action Programme for Nitrate Vulnerable Zones (England and Wales) Regulations 1997, SI 1997/1202 and on the termination of the tenancy to hand to the Landlord or the incoming occupier such records for the period of five years preceding the end of the tenancy (but not prior to 19 December 1998).

4.38.3 To comply with the provisions of the said Regulations and to indemnify the Landlord against all claims proceedings and demands of whatever nature and howsoever arising from any failure to comply therewith.

4.39   *Farm assurance schemes*

4.39.1 At all times at his own expense to ensure that the requirements of the Farm Assurance Schemes specified in Schedule 7 or any schemes replacing the same are met in respect of the Holding and the crops produced thereon.

4.39.2 If the Tenant wishes to register the Holding or the Tenant for the purposes of any Farm Assurance Scheme to comply at his own expense with the requirements thereof including any works required in respect of any fixed equipment on the Holding.

4.39.3 At his own expense to ensure that the requirements of any Farm Assurance Scheme available in respect of crops grown on the Holding are met.

4.39.4 On the expiration of the Tenancy to hand to the Landlord all records required as evidence that the Tenant has complied with the requirements of all such Schemes.[4]

4.40   *Sewage Sludge*

4.40.1   Not to use or permit to be used sludge as defined in the Sludge (Use in Agriculture) Regulations 1989 on the Holding or any part thereof.
          OR

4.40.2   Not to use or permit to be used sludge as defined in the Sludge (Use in Agriculture) Regulations 1989 on the Holding or any part thereof otherwise than:

4.40.2.1 in accordance with the said Regulations;

4.40.2.2 in accordance with any Code of Practice or Guidelines relating thereto from time to time published by the Government or any Government Ministry or Agency;

4.40.2.3 after obtaining the Landlord's consent in writing and in compliance with any conditions specified in writing by the Landlord.

4.41   *Health and safety*

4.41.1   To comply in respect of the Holding and the Tenant's activities thereon with the Regulations relating to Health and Safety at Work and all Codes of Practice in respect thereof for the time being in force.

4.41.2   Forthwith to notify the Landlord of any defects under the Health and Safety Regulations in respect of the Holding or any area used by the Tenant in common with other persons.

4.41.3   To indemnify the Landlord in respect of any liability arising in respect of the Holding under the Health and Safety Regulations and in respect of any areas used in common to reimburse the Landlord a fair payment according to user of the costs of any works required to be undertaken by the Landlord to comply with such Regulations.

4.42   *Relevant quotas*

4.42.1   At all times during the Tenancy to do all acts and things (including producing a sufficient quantity of any relevant product and signing and lodging within any applicable time-limits such documents as are required) which may be required to maintain all Relevant Quotas.

4.42.2   Not to do or omit to do anything during the Tenancy which results or may result in all or any part of a Relevant Quota being reduced lost or charged or whereby it is removed from the Holding whether permanently or temporarily.

4.42.3   To notify the Landlord in writing of any change in the level of any Relevant Quota within seven days of the Tenant becoming aware of that change.

4.42.4   To use his best endeavours to obtain for the Holding any new or further Relevant Quota which becomes available under any local national or European scheme whether existing at or introduced after the commencement of the Tenancy and which is suitable for the Holding.

4.42.5   At all times during the Tenancy to carry out all obligations imposed on the Tenant as occupier or producer or quota or contract owner in regard to notices compliance with directions payments of levies maintenance of records or otherwise in connection with every Relevant Quota.

4.42.6 Forthwith to furnish to the Landlord (in writing if required) all information which the Landlord may reasonably request concerning any Relevant Quota or concerning other farming activities of the Tenant which may affect or tend to affect any Relevant Quota whether such farming activities are carried out by the Tenant directly or indirectly and whether they relate to the Holding or to other land.

4.42.7 If the Landlord at any time or times wishes to agree or record any figures facts or calculations concerning any Relevant Quota and the relative rights of the parties thereto under any local national or European scheme legislation or directive from time to time in force then to endeavour to agree the same with the Landlord and in default of such agreement the matter shall (unless referred to arbitration in accordance with the arbitration provisions of such scheme legislation or directives) be referred for decision under this Agreement.

4.42.8 Not so to dispose of transfer lend lease or otherwise deal with the whole or any part of a Relevant Quota as to result in the Relevant Quota concerned lapsing or reducing during the Tenancy or the Relevant Quota concerned being transferred off the Holding or otherwise becoming unavailable for use in full on the Holding on the termination of the Tenancy.

4.42.9 Not by any direct or indirect act or omission in respect of any land or property not included in the Holding to allow any Relevant Quota or the benefit of any Relevant Quota to pass to any other person whatsoever or become attached to land not comprised in the Holding.

4.42.10 Not to make or permit anyone claiming on his behalf or through him to make any claim either during or at or following termination of the Tenancy which may result in any Relevant Quota or any part thereof ceasing to belong to or be available for the Landlord or the Holding and if as a result of any such claim a Relevant Quota or any part thereof is lost to the Landlord or the Holding to indemnify the Landlord against all losses which the Landlord suffers thereby including (but not necessarily limited to) all costs incurred in the acquisition of replacement Relevant Quota which is comparable in all respect to that lost.

4.42.11 On quitting the Holding to take all such steps as may be required to procure the transfer of each of the Relevant Quotas to the Landlord or such person as the Landlord nominates in writing as his successor in each case without charge or payment save in respect of livestock quotas.

4.43 *Landlord's Milk Quota*
In relation to the Landlord's Milk Quota (if any):

4.43.1 to fulfil and maintain such quota with no less litres (subject only to generalised cuts) and the same butterfat by milk produced on the Holding;

4.43.2 not to use any land not comprised in the Holding for the production of milk or ancillary purposes;

4.43.3   not to sign any contract for the supply of milk from the Holding without ensuring appropriate provisions for the continuation of the acquisition of the same quantity of milk from the Holding in the event of the Tenancy being terminated and on the termination of the Tenancy to use his best endeavours to transfer any contract for the supply of milk to the Landlord or his nominee if the Landlord so requires;

4.43.4   in relation to the period which falls both prior to the termination of the Tenancy and within the milk quota year current at that termination not to produce a quantity of milk which is greater than the due proportion for that period as calculated by apportioning the litreage for that quota year on a daily basis subject to any appropriate adjustment for seasonal variations;

4.43.5   if the Tenant produces a quantity of milk in excess of the proportion calculated in accordance with sub-clause 4 of this clause to indemnify the Landlord and any other occupier of the Holding against any levy payable in respect of such excess;

4.43.6   forthwith on demand to give to the Landlord copies of any documentation relating to the Landlord's milk quota.

4.44   *Livestock quotas*
          Before quitting the Holding on the termination of the Tenancy to offer to transfer such livestock quota as he may then have to the Landlord or as the Landlord directs at a price to be agreed between them or failing agreement as to price at the then current market price prevailing in open market transfers between a willing seller and a willing buyer but if the Landlord does not accept the Tenant's offer to transfer the livestock quota to him in full or in part within fourteen days of the receipt of such offer the Tenant may then permanently transfer the same on the open market.[4]

4.45   *Indemnities*
4.45.1   To indemnify the Landlord against all solicitors' surveyors' architects' and agents' costs and fees and all other expenses properly incurred by the Landlord in connection with:

4.45.1.1 any application by the Tenant for any consent or approval under or pursuant to the terms of this Agreement whether or not such consent is given;

4.45.1.2 the preparation and service of all notices and schedules relating to wants of repair on the Holding whether the same be served during or after the termination of the Tenancy and in particular of all notices under section 146 or 147 of the Law of Property Act 1925 notwithstanding that forfeiture is avoided otherwise than by relief granted by the court.

4.45.2   To indemnify the Landlord against all liabilities actions costs claims losses and expenses arising out of or in connection with a breach of any obligation of the Tenant herein contained or implied and such indemnity shall extend to and cover all costs and expenses incurred by the Landlord in connection with any steps which the Landlord may (but without being in any way obliged so to do) take to remedy any such breach and shall be without prejudice to any other right or remedy of the Landlord in respect of such breach.

4.45.3   To indemnify the Landlord against all liabilities actions costs claims losses and expenses instituted or arising out of or in connection with the use or occupation of the Holding the existence of any article in or about the Holding or the execution or omission of any works upon the Holding except and insofar as the same may be due to the Landlord's own act or default or the act or default of any employee or agent of the Landlord.

4.45.4   To indemnify the Landlord against the Landlord's Solicitors' costs of and incidental to the preparation and completion of this Agreement and a counterpart hereof and the stamp duties thereon.

4.46   *Re-letting*

To permit the Landlord during the six months immediately preceding the termination of the Tenancy to affix and retain without interference upon any part of the Holding a notice for re-letting the same and at any time during the Tenancy a notice for the sale of the Landlord's reversion in the Holding and to permit all persons with the authority in writing of the Landlord or the Landlord's agents at all reasonable times of the day to view the Holding.

4.47   *Yielding up*

4.47.1   In the last year of the Tenancy to permit (to the extent required by the Landlord) the Landlord or his ingoing tenant to enter on directly after harvest and cultivate any part of the land from time to time cleared of crops before the termination of the Tenancy without any reduction or abatement of the Holding Rent by reference to such entry.

4.47.2   To take every available measure (including the giving of any necessary notice) to enable vacant possession of the whole of the Holding (including any cottage or house comprised therein) to be given to the Landlord upon the termination of the Tenancy whether by notice forfeiture or otherwise.

4.47.3   On the termination of the Tenancy (whether by notice forfeiture or otherwise) to return to the Landlord the Holding as to the Land in good heart and condition and as to the Fixed Equipment in good repair and (where appropriate) decorated in accordance with the provisions of the Repairs Schedule.

5.   Landlord's agreements

The Landlord hereby agrees with the Tenant as follows:

5.1   *Compensation*

To pay to the Tenant on quitting the compensation specified in the Compensation Schedule save that the Landlord may set off:

5.1.1   any sum due to the Landlord for rent breaches of agreement or otherwise;

5.1.2   if the year of quitting does not coincide with a year during which the external painting or internal painting and decoration must be executed then a due proportion of the cost of such painting or decoration the deduction for external painting being one-fifth and that for internal painting papering and decorating one-seventh of the estimated total cost in respect of each year that has elapsed since the last repainting papering or decorating or since the commencement of the Tenancy (whichever is the later);

5.1.3   the estimated cost of such repairs and replacement to the Fixed Equipment as may in the opinion of the Landlord be required at the time of quitting.

5.2   *Insuring repairing and other obligations in schedules*
To comply at all times with the obligations of the Landlord:

5.2.1   as to insurance contained in the Insurance Schedule;

5.2.2   as to repairs contained in the Repairs Schedule;

5.2.3   as to allowing the Tenant to holdover after the termination of the Tenancy contained in the Holdover Schedule;

5.2.4   as to any other matter not otherwise specifically provided for or contained in any other schedule to this Agreement.

5.3   *Make good damage*
Save to the extent otherwise expressly or impliedly provided in the reservation concerned to cause as little damage as practicable in the exercise of the reservations herein contained and to pay reasonable compensation for any damage caused.

5.4   *Quiet enjoyment*
To permit the Tenant on paying the rents hereby reserved and performing and observing the several covenants by the Tenant herein contained peaceably to hold the Holding without any lawful interruption by the Landlord or any person deriving title under him.

6.   Provisos and conditions
Provided always and it is hereby agreed and declared as follows:

6.1   *Re-entry*
If at any time:

6.1.1   the rent or any other payment due to the Landlord from the Tenant hereunder is in arrear for more than fourteen days after any of the days appointed for payment thereof (whether formally demanded or not); or

6.1.2   there is a breach of any of the covenants by the Tenant herein contained or implied; or

6.1.3   the Tenant or any of them becomes insolvent if the interest of the Tenant or any of them under this Agreement is taken in execution or if any execution is levied on the goods or chattels of the Tenant or any of them or if any stock or crops on the Holding is taken under a bill of sale or sold under the authority of a charge made under the Agricultural Credits Act 1928 or the Tenant or any of them is convicted of stealing sheep or cattle; or

6.1.4   a receiver or administrator is appointed in respect of the goods property or undertaking of the Tenant or any of them or any part thereof;

and if the Landlord gives to the Tenant at least two months' notice in writing of such non-payment breach or event stating in such notice that the Landlord accordingly relies upon this sub-clause then in any or every such case it shall be lawful for the Landlord or any person authorised by him in that behalf at any time thereafter to re-enter upon the Holding or upon any part thereof in the name of the whole and thereupon the Tenancy shall absolutely determine without prejudice to the right of action or other remedies of the Landlord in respect of any breach of any of the covenants by the Tenant herein contained.

6.2   *Non-waiver*

The demand for or acceptance of rent by the Landlord or anyone acting on his behalf shall not constitute or be construed as a waiver of any breach of the Tenant's obligations under this Agreement or of the Landlord's remedies in respect thereof.

6.3   *Distress*

Upon seizure by the Landlord under distress for rent the Landlord shall not be obliged to sell any hay straw silage or crops (except any crops which the Tenant is permitted to sell under the terms hereof without returning an equivalent manurial value to the Holding) upon the terms that the same may be removed from the Holding but may exercise the power of sale on distrained goods conferred by statute by selling the same subject to the condition that such produce shall be consumed on the Holding or subject to some other condition which secures that the manurial value of such hay straw or crops is returned to the Holding. Upon any such seizure and sale it shall be lawful for the Landlord to grant to any purchaser of such hay straw or crops and for such period or periods as the Landlord may think fit the use of such part or parts of the Holding as the Landlord may think necessary for the purpose of harvesting storing consuming or otherwise dealing with such hay straw or crops and without making any compensation to the Tenant in respect thereof.

6.4   *Exclusion of implied rights*
        Nothing herein contained shall by implication of law or otherwise operate
        to confer on the Tenant any easement right or privilege whatsoever (except
        those hereby expressly granted) over or against any adjoining or other
        property belonging to the Landlord which might restrict or prejudicially
        affect such adjoining or other property for any present or future use or
        purpose nor shall the Tenant be entitled to compensation for any damage
        or disturbance caused by or suffered through any present or future use of or
        operation on such adjoining or other property.

6.5   *Provisions in Schedules*
        The provisions of the several Schedules to this Agreement (in addition to
        the respective obligations of the parties hereto under those schedules) shall
        have effect and be enforceable between the parties hereto.

6.6   *Tenant's fixtures*
6.6.1   The fixtures and fittings (if any) specified in the Schedule of Tenant's
        Fixtures are fixtures belonging to the Tenant which the Tenant is entitled
        under section 8 of the 1995 Act to remove subject to the provisions of that
        section.
6.6.2   Any Tenant's Fixtures which the Tenant does not on or before the
        termination of the Tenancy remove from the Holding shall immediately
        and without more become the property of the Landlord unless the
        Landlord otherwise elects in which case:
6.6.2.1 the Landlord shall notify the Tenant in writing of such election;
6.6.2.2 the Tenant shall forthwith remove such fixtures and fittings from the
        Holding and make good any damage occasioned as a result for which
        purposes the Landlord shall afford reasonable access; and
6.6.2.3 if the Tenant fails so to remove such fixtures and fittings within one month
        from the date of the Landlord having so notified him the Landlord shall be
        entitled to arrange the removal of such fixtures and fittings and the cost of
        so doing shall be recoverable by the Landlord from the Tenant by action or
        as if it were rent in arrears.

6.7   *Redundant items*
6.7.1   The items specified in the Schedule of Redundant Items are agreed as
        obsolete or redundant to the farming of the Holding.

6.7.2   If at any time or times during the Tenancy either party wishes to treat any building or other item of fixed equipment on the Holding (other than those included in the Schedule of Redundant Items) as obsolete or redundant to the proper requirements of the Holding then in default of agreement such party shall be entitled on giving two months' written notice to the other to have the question whether such buildings or other items of fixed equipment or any of them are obsolete or redundant referred for decision under this Agreement and if it is agreed or awarded that such building or other item of fixed equipment is obsolete or redundant then as from the date of such agreement or award (as the case may be) the building or other item of fixed equipment so agreed or awarded to be obsolete or redundant shall be deemed to be included in the Schedule of Redundant Items.

6.7.3   In relation to the items specified or deemed to be included in the Schedule of Redundant Items both parties shall be relieved from all liability to repair or insure the same save that the Tenant shall keep them in a safe condition.

6.7.4   The Tenant may use any redundant building or other item of fixed equipment at his own risk and without any obligation (save as aforesaid) to carry out any repairs to such building or item but he must keep it in a clean and tidy condition.

6.7.5   The Landlord may at any time or times enter and remove at his own expense any obsolete or redundant building or item of fixed equipment whether or not the Tenant is using it in accordance with the immediately preceding sub-clause.

6.8   *Record of condition*
6.8.1   If any party requires any record of condition of the Holding or of anything on the Holding to be made that party shall bear the cost of making the record.

6.9   *Break clause – landlord*
         The Landlord may by notice in writing of between twelve and twenty-four months (expiring at any time except as otherwise provided) terminate this Agreement to the extent and subject to the provisions of this clause:
6.9.1   as to the entire Holding by notice expiring on the Break Date or any of the Break Dates if there is more than one;
6.9.2   as to the entire Holding by notice given within three months after the death of the Tenant or the last surviving Tenant or if later within two months after receiving notice of that death in accordance with the provisions of this Agreement;
6.9.3   as to the entire Holding by notice given at any time after the Tenant (or any of them) has become insolvent;

6.9.4   as to any dwelling comprised in the Tenancy which has at any time been unoccupied for a continuous period of not less than six months (other than by reason of the temporary absence of an employee or former employee of the Tenant who can demonstrate an intention to return) or occupied in breach of the provisions hereof by notice given at any time before the dwelling has become again occupied in accordance with the provisions hereof. In respect of any such property the Landlord may require the Tenant (at the Tenant's expense) to apply to the court for the purpose of obtaining such orders as may be necessary to secure vacant possession thereof and relief ancillary thereto;

6.9.5   as to the whole or any part of the Holding for any purpose not being the use of the Holding or such part for agriculture and whether the use thereof for such purpose is to be made by the Landlord or by a purchaser lessee assignee or other person deriving title from or through the Landlord;

6.9.6   as to any part of the Holding which the Tenant is at the time the notice is given using for any purpose other than agriculture.

6.10   *Break clause – tenant*
         The Tenant may terminate this Agreement by written notice of between twelve and twenty-four months given to expire on the Break Date or any of the Break Dates if there is more than one.

6.11   *Determination as to part*
         If there is a termination of the Tenancy as to any part of the Holding (whether under the foregoing provisions hereof or by surrender or otherwise) then subject to any contrary agreement the Tenant shall be entitled to a reduction of the Holding Rent proportionate to that part of the Holding and in respect of any depreciation of the value to him of the residue of the Holding caused by the severance or by the use to be made of the part severed and in the event of the parties hereto failing to agree as to the amount of such reduction of the Holding Rent the same shall be referred for decision under this Agreement.

6.12   *Set-off*
6.12.1   The Tenant shall not be entitled to exercise any right of set-off against any rents or other moneys payable by the Tenant pursuant to this Agreement.
6.12.2   The Landlord shall be entitled to set off against any sum payable by the Landlord to the Tenant in respect of the Holding any moneys payable to the Landlord by the Tenant in respect of the Holding in each case whether of a liquidated character or not.

6.13   *Custom*
         The rights of the parties under this Agreement or otherwise in respect of the Tenancy shall not depend on or be affected by any custom of the country.

6.14   *Tenant's Milk Quota*

6.14.1   The Tenant's Milk Quota shall belong to the Tenant free from any interest of the Landlord or any third party or parties claiming through him or on behalf of the Landlord.

6.14.2   The Tenant shall not transfer any Tenant's Milk Quota to the Holding whether at the commencement of the Tenancy or subsequently without obtaining the Landlord's prior consent in writing which shall not be unreasonably withheld.

6.14.3   If at any time during the Tenancy the Tenant wishes to dispose of all or any part of the Tenant's Milk Quota by way of permanent transfer he shall first give the Landlord notice in writing of his intention so to do and the Landlord may within 14 days thereafer notify the Tenant in writing of his wish to acquire such quota or part thereof in which event such quota or part shall be purchased by the Landlord at the then current market value thereof AND the Landlord and the Tenant shall sign all necessary forms and do all necessary things to ensure the transfer of the same to the Landlord or as he directs with all due despatch.

6.14.4   The Tenant shall be free to sell any such quota which the Landlord does not duly notify the Tenant he wishes to purchase to one or more third parties and the Landlord and the Tenant shall sign all necessary forms and do all necessary things to ensure the transfer of the same with all due despatch.

6.14.5   During the last fifteen months of the Tenancy the Tenant may transfer the Tenant's Milk Quota or any part of it to another holding or holdings and the Landlord hereby consents to the Tenant transferring such quota to such alternative holding or holdings free from any claim by the Landlord or anyone claiming on his behalf or through him and confirms that he will sign all necessary documents and do all necessary things to ensure the transfer to such alternative holding or holdings including (notwithstanding the other terms of this Agreement) the creation of any interests in land which may be required for this purpose so long as they do not attract any security of tenure in any form they have been created by documentation which has first been approved in writing by the Landlord and they terminate prior to the end of the Tenancy.

6.14.6   If at the determination of the Tenancy any part of the Tenant's Milk Quota remains available to the owner or occupier of the land formerly comprised in the Tenancy the Landlord shall pay to the Tenant the market value of such quota valued as at the date of the termination of the Tenancy.

6.14.7   Unless agreed by the parties the market value of any quota required to be ascertained for the purposes of this clause shall be determined by an independent expert to be appointed failing agreement by the President of the Royal Institution of Chartered Surveyors.

6.14.8   The Landlord confirms that except in accordance with the provisions of this Agreement neither he nor his successors in title shall make any claim in respect of the Tenant's Milk Quota either during or at the termination of the Tenancy howsoever determined.

6.15   *Sale*
In the event of the sale of the Holding the responsibility for the Landlord's obligations hereunder shall pass to the purchaser and no action shall lie against the vendor for their non–observance after the date on which the rent accrues to the purchaser.

6.16   *Notices and agency*
6.16.1 Where any notice is required under this Agreement to be given by or to the Landlord such notice may be given by or to his duly authorised agent any notice (including notices to quit) to be given by either party under this Agreement may be served in the manner provided by section 36 of the 1995 Act or as regards any notice to the Tenant by being sent to him by registered post or recorded delivery to the farmhouse or by handing it to the Tenant's agent or by affixing the notice to some conspicuous part of the Holding and any notice to the Tenant shall be sufficient though the same is not addressed to the Tenant by name but only addressed to him by the description of the Tenant of the Holding.
6.16.2 Any right or power under this Agreement granted to the Landlord shall be exercisable by the Landlord or the Landlord's duly authorised agent or servant.

6.17   *Resolution of disputes*
6.17.1 Any question valuation or claim which is in dispute between the Landlord and the Tenant arising out of this Agreement and not compulsorily referred to arbitration by any statutory provision shall (except as hereby otherwise expressly provided) be decided by an arbitrator or expert as stated in the Particulars.
6.17.2 Any dispute to be decided by an arbitrator shall be referred to arbitration under the provisions of the Arbitration Acts 1950 to 1979 by a single arbitrator and any matter to be decided by an expert shall be referred to an independent expert.
6.17.3 Either party may give notice in writing to the other of his intention to refer the matter to the Referee pursuant to the provisions of this clause.
6.17.4 The parties may agree on the identity of the Referee in which event they shall jointly appoint him but in the absence of such agreement within one month of the serving of the notice of intention either party may apply to the President for the time being of the Royal Institution of Chartered Surveyors for the appointment of a suitably qualified person to act as the Referee.
6.17.5 The Referee's decision shall be final and binding on the parties.
6.17.6 The fees and expenses of the Referee and (as the case may be) of the President of the Royal Institution of Chartered Surveyors shall be borne equally or as the Referee otherwise decides in his discretion.
6.17.7 If the Referee dies or becomes unable or unwilling to act or fails to deliver a decision within four months (or such other period as the parties agree in writing and notify to the Referee) of his appointment the procedure set out in this clause shall be repeated and may be repeated as often as is necessary to achieve the resolution of the dispute.

7. Farm business tenancy

The parties hereto acknowledge that prior to the execution of this Agreement notices were served under s 1(4) of the 1995 Act and that it is intended that the Tenancy shall be and remain at all times a Farm Business Tenancy within the meaning of the 1995 Act.

8. Surety's covenants

The Surety in consideration of the letting of the Holding having been made at the request of the Surety hereby covenants with the Landlord as follows:

8.1   The Tenant will observe and perform all the Tenant's obligations contained or implied in this Agreement as well after as before any disclaimer of this Agreement by a liquidator or trustee in bankruptcy and during any extension or continuance of the Term and that in case of default in such observance and performance of any of those obligations as aforesaid the Surety will pay and make good to the Landlord on demand all losses damages costs and expenses thereby arising or incurred by the Landlord PROVIDED ALWAYS and the parties hereby agree that any neglect or forbearance of the Landlord in endeavouring to obtain payment of any rent when the same becomes payable or to enforce performance of any of the Tenant's obligations contained or implied in this Agreement and any time which may be given to the Tenant by the Landlord or any variation in the terms of this Agreement which may be agreed between the Landlord and the Tenant shall not release or exonerate or in any way affect the liability of the Surety under this covenant.

8.2   If during the Tenancy the Tenant (being a corporation) enters into liquidation or (being an individual) becomes bankrupt and the liquidator or the trustee in such bankruptcy (as the case may be) disclaims this Agreement or if this Agreement is determined by forfeiture or by the exercise of the Landlord's right of re-entry hereunder and if the Landlord within the period of six months after such disclaimer forfeiture or determination serves upon the Surety a notice in writing so to do the Surety will accept from the Landlord a lease of the Holding for a term equal in duration to the residue remaining unexpired of the Term at the time of such disclaimer forfeiture or determination such new lease to take effect from the date of such disclaimer forfeiture or determination and to reserve the same rents and to contain the like Landlord's and Tenant's covenants respectively and the like provisos agreements and conditions in all respects (including the proviso for re-entry) as are reserved and contained in this Agreement.

9. Certificate

It is hereby certified that there is no Agreement for Lease to which this Lease gives effect.

IN WITNESS whereof this Deed has been executed by the parties hereto the day and year first before written.

THE HOLDING DESCRIPTION SCHEDULE

ALL THAT farm shortly described as [*description*] and more particularly described below by reference to the Ordnance Survey plan (County Series Edition)/(Metric Edition sheets [*nos*]) (*delete as appropriate*) of the district.

	Ordnance Survey				Area	
Parish	Sheet No	Enclosure No	Field Name	Cultivation	Hectares	Acres

THE SCHEDULE OF RIGHTS GRANTED

THE SCHEDULE OF RESERVATIONS

There are excepted and reserved out of the Holding:

1.   Game

Subject to the provisions of the Ground Game Act 1880 (as amended by section 12 of the Wildlife and Countryside Act 1981) and the Ground Game (Amendment) Act 1906 all deer foxes game wildfowl woodcock snipe fish hares and rabbits and all birds listed in Part 1 of the Second Schedule to the Wildlife and Countryside Act 1981 and the nests and eggs of all birds referred to in this paragraph with the right for the purposes of shooting fishing hawking sporting taking preserving and rearing such wildlife and destroying pigeons and other pests to enter onto the Holding with such equipment and persons as the Landlord authorises and also the right to hunt or permit hunting on foot or with horses and hounds.

2.   Water

All springs of water or other wells ponds streams and water courses (including any underground water) with the right for the Landlord and all persons authorised by the Landlord to have access thereto and to take water therefrom by means of pumps and other constructions and equipment and pipes laid or to be laid on across or under the Holding or otherwise (subject to sufficient water being left for the Tenant for domestic and agricultural purposes other than irrigation).

3.   Timber

All timber timber-like trees fruit trees tellers pollards saplings and underwood with the right for the Landlord and all persons duly authorised to make fell cut and remove the same and to plant upon any coppice or woodland such quantity of young trees as the Landlord from time to time thinks fit including the right to enter the Holding for such purposes with or without motor vehicles plant and equipment.

4.   **Minerals**

All mines minerals quarries stones sand brick-earth clay gravel petroleum and its relative hydrocarbons and all other gases and substances in upon or under the Holding including the air space void created from time to time by the winning working getting and carrying away of any of such substances whether opened or unopened within upon or under the Holding together with the right for the Landlord and all persons authorised by the Landlord and his lessees and agents and all persons authorised by them or any of them with workmen and others from time to time and at all times thereafter whether by entry on the surface or by underground working to win work get and carry away the said substances and any like substances within upon or under any adjacent or other lands with full powers for those purposes:

4.1   to withdraw vertical and lateral support from the surface of the Holding and from any buildings or works now erected or hereafter to be erected thereon or from any crops standing thereon;

4.2   to sink pits or shafts open quarries and erect buildings and construct place and maintain any plant machinery equipment apparatus or materials in on or under the Holding;

4.3   to construct any requisite access tracks roads or railways fences pipes drains sewers wires cables conduits or other apparatus in under or over the Holding;

4.4   to use the surface of the Holding for the temporary storage or deposit of any of the said substances or any waste;

4.5   to do all other things necessary or convenient for such purposes or any of them notwithstanding any substance or other injury or damage which may thereby be occasioned to the Holding or any building or works or crops as aforesaid or any other injury or damage or loss whatsoever arising whether directly or indirectly from any such working or operation as aforesaid which may be sustained by the Tenant save that the Landlord shall pay to the Tenant reasonable compensation for damage thereby done to the surface buildings or crops and shall allow an abatement of rent in respect of the surface land of the Holding of which the Tenant is deprived by reason of the exercise of any such rights and liberties as aforesaid.

5.   **Roads**

The right at all times and for all purposes for the Landlord and the occupiers and tenants of any adjoining or neighbouring land of the Landlord and all other persons authorised by the Landlord or by such occupiers or tenants to use the roads tracks and footpaths within the Holding together with all other ways hitherto used or enjoyed across the Holding and in the case of each such road track or way so used (other than footpaths) either with or without animals vehicles implements machinery or plant.

6.   Services

6.1   The right for the Landlord and the tenants or other occupiers of any adjoining or neighbouring land of the Landlord to the free passage of drainage water gas oil telecommunications and electricity from and to such other land through the watercourses channnels drains sewers pipes cables and wires belonging to or running through the Holding.

6.2   The right for the Landlord and all persons authorised by the Landlord to erect lay maintain inspect repair renew and use within upon under or over the land comprised in the Holding telecommunications and electricity lines and cables and gas oil water drainage and sewage pipes and any necessary apparatus in connection therewith respectively with full power for the Landlord and such other persons as aforesaid and the agents and workmen of the Landlord and such other persons to enter onto the Holding for the purpose of inspecting repairing replacing and renewing such lines cables pipes and apparatus respectively.

7.   Repairs

The right to enter and execute repairs for which the Tenant is liable under any provision hereof and which he has failed to start within two months or complete within three months of being required so to do by notice in writing given by the Landlord and the whole or the proportionate part for which the Tenant is liable (as the case may be) of the expense thereof shall be payable by the Tenant forthwith after such repairs have been executed and shall at the option of the Landord be recoverable by action or as rent in arrears PROVIDED THAT nothing in this paragraph shall relieve the Tenant from his liability under any provision hereof to execute repairs.

8.   Cultivation

The right after three days' written notice to enter and execute acts of husbandry or cultivation which the Tenant after giving or receiving notice to quit is in the opinion of the Landlord or his agent neglecting or performing in a dilatory or otherwise unsatisfactory manner and to take such manure as the Landlord shall require for such purpose and the Tenant shall at the Tenant's entire expense provide accommodation for the Landlord's workmen and free of cost accommodation for any tractors machinery fertiliser seed or other items brought onto the Holding by the Landlord in exercise of this right.[4]

9.   Entry

9.1   The right for the Landlord and all persons authorised by the Landlord (where appropriate with or without workmen animals carts motor vehicles plant machinery implements guns and other articles):

9.1.1   for the due and proper exercise and enjoyment of his rights hereunder;

9.1.2   for the due and proper performance of his obligations hereunder;

9.1.3   to make good any breach by the Tenant of any of his obligations under this Agreement;

9.1.4   for any other reasonable purpose.

9.2   The right to permit any party involved in any arbitration or other legal proceedings for which an inspection of the Holding is or may be relevant to inspect the Holding whether or not the Landlord is one of the parties to the arbitration or proceedings.

10.   Wayleaves

10.1   The right to grant any wayleave contract easement or licence to any public or local authority or public utility company or other company or person with the right to authorise agents and servants of the grantee with or without motor vehicles plant and equipment to enter upon the Holding and carry out all appropriate works and in particular but without prejudice to the generality of the foregoing the right to run pipes drains conduits cables wires or other works (either already existing or any new ones) for the benefit of any adjoining or neighbouring land of the Landlord and the right to carry out works for the benefit of such adjoining or neighbouring land.

10.2   The benefit of all such contracts easements or licences existing at the date hereof or granted or made under this paragraph and all rents and other payments reserved thereby (except annual payments made for disturbance to the occupier) and the benefit of any other similar agreements or contracts now or at any time affecting the Holding.

11.   Holdover

If the Commencement Date falls between 1 July and 31 December the right for the Landlord and all persons authorised by the Landlord with or without motor vehicles plant and equipment to enter at any time or times upon the Holding for the purpose of storing any of the following crops produced on the Holding in appropriate buildings or on appropriate sites on the Holding nominated by the Landlord until the next following respective dates set opposite them:

      Grain   :   the Grain Holdover Date
      Sugar Beet   :   the Sugar Beet Holdover Date
      Potatoes and/or Onions   :   the Potato/Onion Holdover Date

on the same respective terms (*mutatis mutandis*) as those set out in the Holdover Schedule (*delete if inapplicable*).

12.   Antiquities

The right to all antiquities on the Holding together with the right for persons authorised by the Landlord to carry out scientific and research studies of whatsoever nature on the Holding.

13.   Recordings

The right for persons authorised by the Landlord to enter on the Holding with or without motor vehicles plant equipment cameras and visual and sound recording equipment and to use the Holding (other than the interiors of dwellings) for the purpose of making sound or visual recordings of whatever nature.[4]

THE RENTS SCHEDULE

Part 1

The Holding Rent

EITHER

1.   **Amount**
The Holding Rent shall be the Holding Rent specified in the Particulars which shall be payable throughout the Term and there shall be no review.
OR

1.   **Amount**

1.1   The Holding Rent for the first [   ] years of the Term shall be the Initial Holding Rent specified in the Particulars.

1.2   The Holding Rent payable for the next following [   ] year[s] of the Term shall be £ . . . . (*repeat this sub-clause as necessary*)

1.3   If at any time at which a variation of the Holding Rent is due to take place under the provisions of this paragraph legislation restricts the right to vary the Holding Rent then the Holding Rent shall be varied on the day following the removal of the legislative restriction to the same amount as that to which it would have been at that time had the legislative restriction not been imposed.

1.4   Except as provided in this clause the Holding Rent shall not be capable of variation.
OR

1.   **Amount**

1.1   In this paragraph:

1.1.1   'Review Date' means (subject to sub-paragraph 1.5) [*date*] and every [   ] anniversary thereof during the Term.

1.1.2   'Review Period' means successively:

1.1.2.1   each period of the Term beginning on a Review Date and ending on the day before the next Review Date;

1.1.2.2   the period of the Term commencing on the last Review Date and ending on the expiry of the Term.

1.1.3   'Base Figure' means the figure of the Index for [*date*].

1.1.4   'Index' means the 'All Items' Index of Retail Prices published by the Department of Employment or any successor Ministry or Department.

1.2   The Holding Rent payable for the first years of the Term shall be the Initial Rent specified in [*clause*].

1.3   During each successive Rent Period the Holding Rent shall be the particular amount which bears the same direct proportion to the Initial Rent as the figure of the Index for the month preceding the relevant Review Date bears to the Base Figure.

1.4 If the reference base used to compile the Index changes after the date hereof the figure taken to be shown in the Index after the change shall be the figure which would have been shown in the Index if the reference base current at the date hereof had been retained.

1.5 If on any Rent Day the Holding Rent payable remains unquantified by reason of non-publication of the relevant data or is otherwise undetermined the Tenant shall pay rent at the rate contractually payable immediately prior to the relevant Review Date and within fourteen days of publication of the relevant data or determination the Tenant shall pay to the Landlord the amount of the shortfall and/or the Landlord shall repay to the Tenant the amount of any arrears. (*delete as appropriate*)

1.6 If at the relevant Review Date legislation restricts the right of either party to require a review of the rent payable hereunder then the day following the removal of the legislative restriction shall be treated for all purposes as the relevant Review Date.

1.7 After each occasion on which the Reviewed Rent is determined pursuant to this paragraph a record or memorandum thereof shall be made and signed by or on behalf of the Landlord and the Tenant in such manner and form as the Landlord may require the parties paying their own costs of this procedure.

1.8 Except as provided in this paragraph the rent hereunder shall not be capable of variation.

OR

1. Amount

The Holding Rent shall be the Initial Holding Rent specified in the [*place specified*] or any rent substituted therefor in accordance with the provisions of the 1995 Act.

2. Payment

The Holding Rent shall be paid without any deductions whatsoever by equal payments in advance on the Rent Days the first payment (being a proportionate amount in respect of the period from the Commencement Date to the next Rent Day) to be made on the date of this Agreement.

3. Suspension

If the Landlord has or should have effected insurance against loss of rent and if any part of the Holding is damaged or destroyed by any of the Insured Risks so as to be unfit for occupation and use then (save to the extent that the relevant insurance has been vitiated by some act or default of the Tenant or any person for whose acts or defaults the Tenant may be responsible) a fair proportion of the Holding Rent (assessed according to the nature and extent of the damage sustained) shall be suspended until the part of the Holding concerned is again rendered fit for occupation and use or (if earlier) the expiration of the Rent Suspension Period calculated from the date of such damage or destruction and any dispute concerning this paragraph shall be referred for decision under this Agreement,

Part 2

The Insurance Rent

1. **Amount**

The Insurance Rent is a sum equal to the gross premium or premiums which the Landlord from time to time pays to effect or maintain the insurance which he is required to effect and maintain under this Agreement.

2. **Payment**

The Insured Rent shall be paid without deduction within fourteen days after demand in writing.

THE INSURANCE SCHEDULE

Part 1

(Landlord's Obligations)

The obligations of the Landlord in respect of insurance are:

1. **Property**

To insure and keep insured the undermentioned items (except any buildings and fixtures belonging to the Tenant and any Redundant Items) against destruction or damage by any of the Insured Risks and in the event of destruction or damage by an Insured Risk (except to the extent that such insurance has been vitiated by some act or default of the Tenant or any person for whose acts or defaults the Tenant may be responsible) to reinstate or replace the same if its reinstatement or replacement is required for the fulfilment of his responsibilities to manage the Holding in accordance with the rules of good estate management:

Dwellings;
Other buildings;
Fixed equipment;
Plant and machinery.

2.   Rent

If the Landlord in his discretion so decides or if the Tenant so requires by notice in writing to the Landlord to insure and keep insured the Holding against loss of the Holding Rent for the Rent Suspension Period by reason of damage or destruction due to an Insured Risk.

Part 2

(Tenant's Obligations)

The obligations of the Tenant in respect of insurance are:

1.   The Premises

To insure and keep insured the undermentioned items (except any buildings and fixtures belonging to the Tenant and any Redundant Items) against destruction or damage by any of the Insured Risks and in the event of destruction or damage by an Insured Risk to reinstate or replace the same:

Dwellings;

Other buildings;

Fixed equipment;

Plant and machinery.

2.   Crops and stock

2.1   To insure and keep insured against loss destruction or damage by any of the Insured Risks (including consequential loss relating to such loss destruction or damage) all live and dead farming stock and crops for the time being on the Holding to the full market value thereof or the cost of replacement (if greater) and so that every policy of such insurance shall:

2.1.1   not be avoidable on account of the storing handling or keeping of petrol or any other inflammable substance on the Holding or for any other reason connected with the use of the Holding;

2.1.2   provide cover for the return to the land of the full equivalent manurial value of any crops destroyed or damaged insofar as the return thereof is required for the fulfilment by the Tenant of his obligations under this Agreement.

3.   Liabilities

3.1   To maintain adequate insurance in respect of all employer's risks for which the Tenant may be liable.

3.2   To maintain insurance in respect of all third party liability risks in respect of which liability may fall on the Landlord in relation to the Holding the policy or policies of such insurance to provide cover in respect of each and every claim of not less than two million pounds or such higher sum as the Landlord may from time to time direct in writing.

4.   Landlord's insurance

In relation to each insurance in respect of the Holding and/or any other property effected by the Landlord:

4.1   not to effect any insurance cover against any risks covered by the policy effected by the Landlord;

4.2   not to do on the Holding any act or thing which shall or may invalidate such insurance or cause such insurance to be offered on less favourable terms or cause the premium thereon to be increased or increase the risk of any insured peril to any part of the Holding and/or any other property but to take full and proper precautions to protect the Holding and/or any other property against risk from any Insured Risk;

4.3   save as permitted by any relevant insurance not to store or bring on the Holding any articles of a specifically combustible inflammable radio-active or dangerous nature and in particular to take all responsible precautions when installing petrol oil gas or electric engines and when storing petrol paraffin oil or similar fuel or lubricants which shall be kept in proper containers and where reasonably practicable in a detached building and in such cases to observe and perform every requirement of any statutory or other relevant provision;

4.4   to indemnify the Landlord against any excess payable in relation to any claim made.

5.   Tenant's insurance

In relation to each insurance effected by the Tenant:

5.1   to ensure that it is effected in the joint names of the Landlord and the Tenant with an insurer approved in writing by the Landlord;

5.2   to produce to the Landlord on demand the policy or policies of insurance and the receipt for the premium in respect of the current period of insurance;

5.3   to apply all money received through any such policy for the purpose in respect of which the same has been paid and to make good any deficiency out of his own money.

6.   Repay premiums

6.1   If any insurance which the Tenant is obliged to maintain hereunder is not effected or maintained or if the policy or premium receipt relating to it is not produced in accordance with the terms hereof and the Landlord effects such insurance cover as the Landlord may determine to be appropriate to make good such default (which he is hereby authorised to do) to repay to the Landlord on demand all premiums paid for such purpose and all other expenses incurred by the Landlord in connection therewith.

THE REPAIRS SCHEDULE

Part 1

(Landlord's Repairing Obligations)

The Landlord shall be responsible for the maintenance repair and replacement of the following:

1. **Dwellings**
    Roofs (including chimneys)
    External walls
    Ceilings and internal plastering
    Ceilings and floor joists
    Floors
    Staircases
    Doors
    Windows and skylights
    Gutters and downpipes
    Baths, toilets and other sanitary fittings
    Electrical installations including fittings
    Water pipes
    Foul drainage systems
    Boilers and heating apparatus
    Internal decorations and treatments
    External decorations and treatments
    Fire detection and security systems

2. **Other buildings and fixed equipment**
    Roofs (including chimneys)
    Structural frames and walls
    Cladding
    Floors
    Doors and gates
    Windows
    Staircases and fixed ladders
    Gutters and downpipes
    Electrical installation including fittings
    Water supplies and fittings
    Foul drainage system
    Fixtures and fittings
    External decorations and treatments
    Internal decorations and treatments
    Timber and other infestations

3.   External work and services
Rainwater drainage systems
Foul drainage systems
Sewage disposal
Slurry systems
Water supply systems
Electrical supply systems
Gas supply systems
Garden walls and fences
Yard walls, fences and gates
Roads and yards
Cattle grids
Field gates and posts
Bridges and culverts
Field drains, ditches and associated works
Field boundaries
Watercourses, ponds, lakes and associated systems
Signs and notices

Part 2

(Tenant's Repairing Obligations)

The Tenant shall be responsible for the repair and maintenance of the following:

1.   Dwellings
Roofs (including chimneys)
External walls
Internal walls
Ceilings and internal plastering
Ceiling and floor joists
Floors
Staircases
Doors
Windows and skylights
Gutters and downpipes
Baths, toilets and other sanitary fittings
Electrical installations including fittings
Water pipes
Foul drainage systems
Boilers and heating apparatus
Internal decorations and treatments
External decorations and the treatments
Fire detection and security systems

2. **Other buildings and fixed equipment**
   Roofs (including chimneys)
   Structural frames and walls
   Cladding
   Floors
   Doors and gates
   Windows
   Staircases and fixed ladders
   Gutters and downpipes
   Electrical installation including fittings
   Water supplies and fittings
   Foul drainage system
   Fixtures and fittings
   External decorations and treatments
   Internal decorations and treatments
   Timber and other infestations

3. **External works and services**
   Rainwater drainage systems
   Foul drainage systems
   Sewage disposal
   Slurry systems
   Water supply systems
   Electrical supply systems
   Gas supply systems
   Garden walls and fences
   Yard walls, fences and gates
   Roads and yards
   Cattle grids
   Field gates and posts
   Bridges and culverts
   Field drains, ditches and associated works
   Field boundaries
   Water courses, ponds, lakes and associated systems
   Signs and notices

THE DEALINGS SCHEDULE

The Tenant's obligations in this Schedule are:

1.	If any dwelling on the Holding (other than any farmhouse) is not required by the Tenant for occupation by a Person employed on the Holding but the Tenant wishes the dwelling to remain in the Holding so as to be available in the future for a person employed on the Holding then on giving the Landlord written notice thereof the Tenant may let the dwelling on an assured shorthold tenancy under the provisions of the Housing Act 1988 for a fixed term not exceeding twelve months at a full market rent.

2.	Not to make any contract for any producer to grow a specialist crop on the Holding except on condition that such contract:

2.1	is in writing and signed by both parties before the producer enters upon the Holding;

2.2	does not confer on the producer any interest greater than a tenancy for a period of less than two years;

2.3	does not confer on the producer any security of tenure;

2.4	does not (or if more than one contract is granted all the contracts together do not) relate to a greater area in any one year than one-fifth of the total arable area of the Holding;

2.5	does not relate to any part of the last year of the Tenancy except with the consent in writing of the Landlord.

3.	Save as permitted by the preceding paragraphs of this Schedule:

3.1	not to assign charge or underlet any part or parts (as opposed to the whole) of the Holding;

3.2	not to part with the possession of or share the occupation of the Holding or any part or parts thereof.

4.	Not to assign the Holding as a whole without the previous consent in writing of the Landlord but such consent shall not be unreasonably withheld.

5.	Upon every assignment to procure:

5.1	that the assignee enters into a direct covenant with the Landlord to pay the rents and observe and perform the covenants and conditions on the part of the Tenant herein contained;

5.2	if the assignee is a limited liability company and if the Landlord reasonably so requires to procure that a guarantor or guarantors of adequate standing enter into direct covenants with the Landlord in a form similar to those in the clause headed 'Surety's Covenants'.

6.	Not to underlet the whole of the Holding without the previous consent in writing of the Landlord which shall not be unreasonably withheld PROVIDED THAT:

6.1	the rent for the Holding to be reserved by the underlease shall not be less than the Holding Rent and shall be the best rent obtainable without taking a fine or premium;

6.2   the underlease shall contain such provisions as are requisite to secure that it is in all respects consistent with the provisions hereof including in particular provision for the review of the rent thereby reserved at the same time as the review of the Holding Rent hereunder provision that the Landlord shall approve the amount of any reviewed rent and an absolute prohibition against any further underletting.

7.   To use his best endeavours to enforce the performance and observance of all the covenants and conditions on the part of the undertenant contained in such underlease.

THE SCHEDULE OF TENANT'S FIXTURES

(Tenant's Fixtures and Fittings)

THE SCHEDULE OF TENANT'S IMPROVEMENTS

THE SCHEDULE OF REDUNDANT BUILDINGS

THE HOLDOVER SCHEDULE

Part 1

Grain

1.   Where at the termination of the Tenancy grain produced on the Holding is being stored in the Holdover Buildings the Landlord shall permit the Tenant to continue to use the Holdover Buildings and Holdover Plant for the purpose of drying and storing that grain until the Grain Holdover Date or (if earlier) until all his grain has been removed from the Holding and to have appropriate access with or without vehicles to the Holdover Buildings.

2.   The Tenant shall reimburse the Landlord for the actual cost of fuel or electricity consumed and the cost of any men employed by the Landlord (and approved by the Tenant) who operate the Holdover Plant and/or load the grain.

3.   During the period of holdover under this Part of this Schedule the Landlord shall be responsible for the insurance of the Holdover Buildings and the Holdover Plant but not for the grain therein.

4.   The Landlord shall pay compensation for any damage arising from the negligence of the Landlord or any employee of his but subject thereto the Tenant shall be liable for the cost of any repair required to remedy any breakdown in the Holdover Plant.

5.   The Landlord shall be entitled to defer until the end of the period of holdover under this Part of this Schedule the payment to the Tenant of all compensation to which he is entitled for any of the Holdover Buildings or for any of the Holdover Plant which the Landlord has elected to acquire at valuation and any valuation of such items shall take into account the use of the Holdover Buildings and the Holdover Plant by the Tenant under this Part of this Schedule and any expenditure on repairs during the period of holdover under this Part of this Schedule.

6.   The Landlord shall be entitled to have all capital or other tax allowances apportioned from the date of termination of the Tenancy.

Part 2

Sugar Beet

7.   After the termination of the Tenancy the Landlord shall permit the Tenant to enter upon the Holding to raise the remainder of the his crop of sugar beet and cart the same to heaps on convenient sites at the road or drove-side in a good and husbandlike manner.

8.   The work of lifting and carting off shall be completed by the Sugar Beet Holdover Date next following the termination after which date the Landlord shall have the right to harvest and cart off any unharvested beet receiving payment for such work in accordance with the current prevailing agricultural contractors' charges in the district.

9.   The Tenant shall be responsible for arranging the loading and delivery of his crop to the factory and for the removal of the beet from the heaps.

Part 3

Potatoes and/or Onions

10.   After the termination of the tenancy the Landlord shall permit the Tenant to enter on the Holding to lift cart away and store the last year's crop of potatoes and/or onions with the right to retain possession of any appropriate store or field clamp together with sufficient accommodation for grading and loading equipment tractors and vehicles with access to bag and cart away the potatoes and/or onions from the store or clamp until the Potatoes/Onions Holdover Date or (if earlier) until all his potatoes/onions have been removed from the Holding.

11.   If the Tenant has not completely removed the potatoes and/or onions and any clamps from all parts of the Holding by that date he shall pay for the cost of their removal or disposal irrespective of whether or not the potatoes and/or onions have been sold.

Part 4

General

12.   No rent or other charge shall be payable by the Tenant for any right of holdover under this Schedule.

13.   At the end of the relevant holdover period the Tenant shall leave all parts of the Holding used in connection with the holdover in a clean and tidy condition.

14.   In this Schedule references to 'the Landlord' shall where the context requires or permits include any incoming tenant.

THE COMPENSATION SCHEDULE

(Tenant's Compensation on Termination)

1.   On the termination of this Agreement the Tenant shall be entitled to receive compensation in respect of the matters and on the terms and conditions set out in and subject to the provisions of Part III of the 1995 Act.

2.   Such compensation shall be calculated having regard to the methods of practice and prices of the Valuation Association.

3.   Where the Tenant has submitted an IACS form and any area aid or set-aside aid payable in consequence thereof has not been paid:

3.1   the Landlord may retain from the compensation due to the Tenant a sum equal to the estimated amount of such aid pending payment;

3.2   for the purposes of calculating the compensation payable to the Tenant under this paragraph the Landlord agrees with the Tenant that:

3.2.1   the value which may be attributed to the growing crops or severed or harvested crops and produce shall include a sum to reflect a fair proportion of the payments payable under IACS in respect of these crops;

3.2.2   the compensation shall include a sum to reflect a fair proportion of the payments payable under IACS which relate to the Holding (including set-aside) but which do not relate to a specific crop.

4.   Where sheep belonging to the Tenant have become acclimatised hefted or settled on the Holding the Tenant shall be entitled to receive compensation in the amount of a sum equal to the increase attributable to such acclimatisation hefting or settlement in the value of the Holding at the termination of this Agreement as land comprised in a tenancy.

5.   Where the Landlord requires by notice in writing to the Tenant given at any time prior to the termination of this Agreement that the Tenant leaves on the Holding severed crops unconsumed hay straw silage and farmyard manure the Tenant shall be entitled on leaving such items on the Holding to compensation equal to the market value of the items left subject to paragraph 3.1 above.

SIGNED and delivered as a Deed by
the said [*name*] in the presence of:
            }   ....

....

....

....

SIGNED and delivered as a Deed by
the said [*name*] in the presence of:
            }   ....

....

....

....

EXECUTED and delivered as a Deed
for and on behalf of [*name*] (Director)
and [*name*] (Secretary)
            }   ....

---

1   Stamp duty based on rent and term.
2   The Tenant must carefully consider his position before agreeing to this.
3   A formal authority to MAFF, signed by the occupier, to disclose information direct to the Landlord would be advisable.
4   The Tenant may regard this clause as unreasonable.

5   TENANT'S NOTICE TO TERMINATE FIXED TERM TENANCY OF OVER TWO YEARS

AGRICULTURAL TENANCIES ACT 1995

SECTION 5

THE HOLDING

[*name and identification of Holding, by address, ordnance survey numbers or plan*]

TO LANDLORD
[*name and address*]

I, [*name and address of Tenant*], give you notice that I intend to terminate the tenancy of the above Holding dated [*date*] and made between (1) [*name*] and (2) [*name*] on [*date*], being the date fixed by the lease for the expiry of the term granted by the lease.

Signed: ....

Dated: ....

Note: This will be used in cases where the fixed term is more than two years. If not so terminated, the tenancy will continue as a tenancy from year to year.

6 LANDLORD'S NOTICE TO TERMINATE PERIODIC TENANCY

AGRICULTURAL TENANCIES ACT 1995

SECTION 6

THE HOLDING

[*name and identification of Holding, by address, ordnance survey numbers or plan*]

TO TENANT
[*name and address*]

I, [*name and address of Landlord*], give you notice that I intend to terminate the tenancy of the above Holding dated [*date*] and made between (1) [*name*] and (2) [*name*] on [*date*], or at the expiration of the year of your tenancy which expires next after the end of twelve months from the date of service of this notice.

Signed: ....

Dated: ....

———————————————

7   TENANT'S NOTICE TO TERMINATE PERIODIC TENANCY

AGRICULTURAL TENANCIES ACT 1995

SECTION 6

THE HOLDING

*[name and identification of Holding, by
address, ordnance survey numbers or plan]*

TO LANDLORD
[name and address]

I, *[name and address of Tenant]*, give you notice that I intend to terminate the tenancy of the above Holding dated *[date]* and made between (1) *[name]* and (2) *[name]* on *[date]*, or at the expiration of the year of my tenancy which expires next after the end of twelve months from the date of service of this notice.

Signed: ....

Dated: ....

8   TENANT'S NOTICE EXERCISING OPTION TO TERMINATE TENANCY OR PART OF TENANCY OF OVER TWO YEARS

AGRICULTURAL TENANCIES ACT 1995

SECTION 7

THE HOLDING

[*name and identification of Holding, by
address, ordnance survey numbers or plan*]

TO LANDLORD
[*name and address*]

I, [*name and address of Tenant*], in accordance with Clause [*no*] of the Tenancy Agreement of the above Holding dated [*date*] and made between (1) [*name*] and (2) [*name*] hereby exercise the option to terminate the tenancy [as to the whole of the Holding] [as to that part of the Holding shown edged red on the plan attached to this notice] on the [*date*].

Signed: ....

Dated: ....

──────────────────────────

9 LANDLORD'S NOTICE EXERCISING OPTION TO TERMINATE TENANCY OR RESUME POSSESSION OF PART IN TENANCY OF OVER TWO YEARS

AGRICULTURAL TENANCIES ACT 1995

SECTION 7

THE HOLDING

[*name and identification of Holding, by*
address, ordnance survey numbers or plan]

TO TENANT
[*name and address*]

I, [*name and address of Landlord*], in accordance with Clause [*no*] of the Tenancy Agreement of the above Holding dated [*date*] and made between (1) [*name*] and (2) [*name*] hereby exercise the option to terminate the tenancy [as to the whole of the Holding] [as to that part of the Holding shown edged red on the plan attached to this notice] on the [*date*].

Signed: ....

Dated: ....

_____

10   TENANT'S NOTICE DEMANDING STATUTORY REVIEW OF RENT

AGRICULTURAL TENANCIES ACT 1995

SECTION 10

THE HOLDING

[*name and identification of Holding, by
address, ordnance survey numbers or plan*]

TO LANDLORD
[*name and address*]

I, [*name and address of Tenant*], demand that the question of rent to be paid in respect of the above Holding as from [*date*] shall be referred to arbitration in accordance with Section 10 of the Agricultural Tenancies Act 1995.

Signed: ....

Dated: ....

_____

11   LANDLORD'S NOTICE DEMANDING STATUTORY REVIEW OF RENT

AGRICULTURAL TENANCIES ACT 1995

SECTION 10

THE HOLDING

[*name and identification of Holding, by address, ordnance survey numbers or plan*]

TO TENANT
[*name and address*]

I, [*name and address of Landlord*], demand that the question of rent to be paid in respect of the above Holding as from [*date*] shall be referred to arbitration in accordance with Section 10 of the Agricultural Tenancies Act 1995.

Signed: ....

Dated: ....

_____

12   LANDLORD'S NOTICE OF PROPOSAL TO APPOINT AN ARBITRATOR

AGRICULTURAL TENANCIES ACT 1995

SECTION 28

THE HOLDING

*[name and identification of Holding, by
address, ordnance survey numbers or plan]*

TO TENANT
[name and address]

I, *[name and address of Landlord]*, propose to apply to the President of RICS for the appointment of an arbitrator by him to settle the dispute specified below unless within two months from the service of this notice you and I have appointed an arbitrator by agreement.

[brief details of dispute]

Signed: ....

Dated: ....

_____

13 TENANT'S NOTICE OF REFERENCE OF DISPUTE TO THIRD PARTY

AGRICULTURAL TENANCIES ACT 1995

SECTION 29

THE HOLDING

[name and identification of Holding, by address, ordnance survey numbers or plan]

TO LANDLORD
[name and address]

I, *[name and address of Tenant]*, in accordance with Clause *[no]* of the Tenancy Agreement dated *[date]* made between (1) *[name]* and (2) *[name]* have made a reference to *[specify third party named in Tenancy Agreement]* to settle the dispute specified below.

[brief details of dispute]

Signed: ....

Dated: ....

_____

14   LANDLORD'S NOTICE OF REFERENCE OF DISPUTE TO THIRD PARTY

AGRICULTURAL TENANCIES ACT 1995

SECTION 29

THE HOLDING

[*name and identification of Holding, by
address, ordnance survey numbers or plan*]

TO TENANT
[*name and address*]

I, [*name and address of Landlord*], in accordance with Clause [*no*] of the Tenancy
Agreement dated [*date*] made between (1) [*name*] and (2) [*name*] have made a
reference to [*specify third party named in Tenancy Agreement*] to settle the dispute
specified below.

[*brief details of dispute*]

Signed: ....

Dated: ....

_____

CHAPTER 6: RESIDENTIAL TENANCIES

INDEX

RESIDENTIAL
TENANCIES

6

CHAPTER 6: RESIDENTIAL TENANCIES

INTRODUCTION

It is well known that agricultural workers who occupy property as part of their terms of employment are often protected from eviction under the Rent (Agriculture) Act 1976 or the Housing Act 1988. This means that possession can be recovered only in the event that the cottage is required in accordance with the provisions of the relevant Act. Sometimes, however, farmers are still prepared to allow occupiers to move into cottages on this basis.

There may be an inheritance tax advantage. Properties let on shorthold are likely to be treated as investments rather than business or agricultural property and are, therefore, non-relievable, although cf *Farmer v IRC* [1999] STC (SCD) 321. Moreover, where the farmer is a tenant he may well be barred by his tenancy agreement from sub-letting, although he is sometimes permitted to allow his employees into occupation. In any event, if the farmer is a tenant, it is essential to refer to the principal tenancy agreement to ensure that one is not in breach, despite the comfort afforded by *Pennell v Payne* [1995] QB 192.

It is important to note that, despite the general removal of notice requirements with effect from 28 February 1997, under the Housing Act 1996, notices are still required for assured shorthold lettings to agricultural workers.

As a tenancy at a rent of £250 per annum or less does not constitute an assured tenancy, the occupier under a letting on this basis will acquire protection as an agricultural occupant under the Housing Act 1988. A rent of more than £250 per annum is therefore required. Clearly, payment of rent by an employee has income tax disadvantages, since income tax will be charged on the portion of salary needed to pay the rent and the rent itself is not relievable.

6 RESIDENTIAL TENANCIES

CHECKLIST 1

ASSURED SHORTHOLD TENANCY AGREEMENTS – NOTES ON DRAFTING

As to all cases:

1. As most assured shorthold tenancies are granted for a fixed term, the standard draft assumes that the tenancy will be on that basis. The term can be of any length (but see paragraph 2).

2. In most cases, it is no longer necessary to serve a notice (under section 20 of the Housing Act 1988) before the tenancy begins. The exception is where the letting would otherwise qualify as an assured agricultural occupancy, ie a letting made in consequence of 'the occupier's employment in agriculture') as to which see point 15 below.

3. The rent must still in all cases be above the statutorily prescribed minimum (currently £250 per year).

4. In the case of a fixed-term tenancy, provision can be made for the Tenant to terminate the tenancy before the end of the term. If that is required, a suitable sub-clause can be drafted. That sub-clause should be inserted as clause 2.2 with standard clause 2 being renumbered as sub-clause 2.1.

5. Similarly, provision can be made for the Landlord to terminate early – a separate clause will be required. The notice to be served to terminate the contractual tenancy is the same as that required to terminate the statutory tenancy.

6. Delete the Address for Service line in the Particulars if that address would be the same as the Landlord's address.
    Clause 8.5 should also be amended if and as required.

7. If there is no deposit, delete:
    (a) the reference to it in the Particulars;
    (b) clause 6.3;
    (c) clause 7.4;
    (d) clause 8.3;
    (e) the words between [and] in clause 8.4.

8. If no interest is to be charged on late payment, delete:
    (a) the reference to the Interest Rate in the Particulars;
    (b) clause 6.6.

9. If there are no contents or furniture, clause 4 and the Contents Schedule can be deleted.

10. If there is no schedule of condition, clause 5 can be deleted.

11. If rent is to be paid in arrear, amend clause 6.1.

12. If the tenant is not paying any of the costs of the agreement, delete clause 6.8.

13. If there is no septic tank, delete clause 6.11 and amend the second version of clause 7.2 if that version is used.

14. Select the appropriate alternative from the two versions of clause 7.2, or amend as appropriate. If the second alternative is selected and clause 7.2.3 is left in, delete clause 6.11.

As to agricultural occupiers only

15. The letting can be 'in consequence of the occupier's employment in agriculture' even if the Landlord is not the employer.

16. A preliminary notice in the statutorily prescribed form must be served *before* the tenancy is entered into or the Tenant is allowed into possession.

CHECKLIST 2

ASSURED SHORTHOLD TENANCY AGREEMENTS – GUIDANCE NOTES ON COMPLETION (EXCEPT AGRICULTURAL OCCUPANTS)

Documents

Original and counterpart Tenancy Agreement. They are in the same form, except as to who signs them – see below.

Completion of tenancy agreement

(All the details to be filled in are on the Particulars page at the front of the Agreement).

1.   The Date of Agreement should be written in on the Particulars page and the front sheet of both copies. This is the date on which the documents are completed. The Date of Agreement and the date of commencement of the tenancy need not necessarily coincide.

2.   If any of the following details have not been pre-arranged and are therefore not already typed in, they should be added in words (not figures) on both copies:

> The Rent;
> The Rent Days;
> The Deposit; and
> The Term.

3.   The Landlord (or his agent) signs the original Tenancy Agreement at the end of the document where his initials are pencilled, in the presence of an independent witness (not the Tenant). The witness should sign, print his or her name and add his or her address in the places indicated.

4.   The Tenant signs the counterpart Tenancy Agreement at the end of that document where his initials are pencilled, in the presence of an independent witness (not the Landlord). The witness (who can be the same person who has witnessed the Landlord's signature) should sign, print his or her name and add his or her address in the spaces indicated.

5.1   If there is an Inventory attached to the Tenancy Agreement and counterpart, the Landlord (or his agent as to the Agreement) and the Tenant (as to the counterpart) should also sign and date the Inventory.

5.2   If there is a separate Inventory (where there is one referred to in the Tenancy Agreement), it needs to be prepared in duplicate. Each copy should have endorsed on it:

> 'This is the Inventory referred to in the Tenancy Agreement made [*date*] between (1) [*the Landlord*] and (2) [*the Tenant*]'.

One copy of the Inventory should be signed by the Landlord (or his agent) and the other by the Tenant(s). The two copies should then be exchanged so that each party is holding an Inventory signed by the other.

6.   The Landlord (or his agent) should finish up with:
6.1   the counterpart Tenancy Agreement (and any attached inventory) signed by the Tenant;
6.2   any separate Inventory signed by the Tenant;
6.3   the Tenant's remittance for the first rent payment (and the deposit if there is one); and
6.4   the Tenant's payment for the legal costs for the preparation of the documents (if applicable), which should be forwarded to the Landlord's solicitors.

7.   The Tenant finishes up with:
7.1   the original Tenancy Agreement signed by or on behalf of the Landlord;
7.2   any separate Inventory signed by or on behalf of the Landlord.

8.   The counterpart Agreement and any Inventory should be retained in a safe place for future reference. The counterpart agreement is liable for £5 stamp duty. The tenancy agreement is liable to *ad valorem* stamp duty.

Timing

Although it is no longer essential that the Tenancy Agreements are completed and exchanged before the Tenant is allowed into occupation of the property, it is still highly desirable that they should be. Otherwise, completion of the Tenancy Agreement can be left undone, which may give room for confusion and dispute.

Rent paid weekly

If the rent is paid weekly, the Tenant must be issued with a rent book.

6 RESIDENTIAL TENANCIES

CHECKLIST 3

ASSURED SHORTHOLD TENANCY AGREEMENTS – GUIDANCE NOTES ON COMPLETION (AGRICULTURAL OCCUPANTS ONLY)

Documents

1.   Housing Act 1988 Notice (original and duplicate).

2.   Tenancy Agreement (original and counterpart).

Order of steps

The order should be:

1.   Sign and serve the notice.

2.   Sign and complete the Tenancy Agreement.

3.   Allow the Tenant into occupation of the property.

If this order is not to be *strictly* complied with, it is necessary to please check with the Landlord's solicitors before proceeding. Failure to comply with the statutory requirements will have very serious adverse consequences.

Notice

1.   If the commencement date of the tenancy has not been pre-arranged, and is therefore not already typed in, the commencement date should be written in section 2 on both copies of the Notice.

2.   The Landlord (or his agent) signs and dates both copies of the Notice in section 4.

3.   The Tenant should sign and date the duplicate of the Notice by way of receipt.

Tenancy agreement

(All the details to be filled in are on the Particulars page at the front of the Agreement).

4.   The Date of Agreement should be written in on the Particulars page and the front sheet of both copies. This is the date on which the documents are completed. The Date of Agreement and the date of commencement of the tenancy need not necessarily coincide, but:

4.1   the Date of Agreement must not pre-date the date on which the Notice is served;

4.2   the date of commencement of the tenancy must not be earlier than the Date of Agreement.

5.   If any of the following details have not been pre-arranged and are therefore not already typed in, they should be added in words (not figures) on both copies:

>   The Rent;
>   The Rent Days;
>   The Deposit; and
>   The Term

(the dates inserted must agree with the dates in the Notice).

6.   The Landlord (or his agent) signs the original Tenancy Agreement at the end of the document where his initials are pencilled, in the presence of an independent witness (not the Tenant). The witness should sign, print his or her name and add his or her address in the places indicated.

7.   The Tenant signs the counterpart Tenancy Agreement at the end of that document where his initials are pencilled, in the presence of an independent witness (not the Landlord). The witness (who can be the same person who has witnessed the Landlord's signature) should sign, print his or her name and add his or her address in the spaces indicated.

7.1   If there is an Inventory attached to the Tenancy Agreement and counterpart, Landlord (or his agent) (as to the Agreement) and the Tenant (as to the counterpart) should also sign and date the Inventory.

7.2   If there is a separate Inventory (where there is one referred to in the Tenancy Agreement) it needs to be prepared in duplicate. Each copy should have endorsed on it:

>   'This is the Inventory referred to in the Tenancy Agreement made [*date*] between (1) [*the Landlord*] and (2) [*the Tenant*]'.

One copy of the Inventory should be signed by the Landlord (or his agent) and the other by the Tenant(s). The two copies should then be exchanged so that each party is holding an Inventory signed by the other.

8.   The Landlord (or his agent) should finish up with:

8.1   the receipted duplicate Notice;

8.2   the counterpart Tenancy Agreement (and any attached inventory) signed by the Tenant;

8.3   any separate Inventory signed by the Tenant;

8.4   the Tenant's remittance for the first rent payment (and the deposit if there is one; and

8.5   the Tenant's payment for the legal costs for the preparation of the documents (if applicable), which should be forwarded to the Landlord's solicitors.

9.   The Tenant finishes up with:
9.1   the original Notice;
9.2   the original Tenancy Agreement signed by or on behalf of the Landlord;
9.3   any separate Inventory signed by or on behalf of the Landlord.

10.   The counterpart Agreement, Notice and any Inventory should be retained in a safe place for future reference. The counterpart Agreement is liable to £5 stamp duty. The tenancy agreement is liable to *ad valorem* stamp duty.

Rent paid weekly

If the rent is paid weekly, the Tenant must be issued with a rent book.

PRECEDENTS

1 ASSURED SHORTHOLD TENANCY

Particulars

DATE OF AGREEMENT	:	....
THE LANDLORD	:	....
Full Name	:	....
Address	:	....
Address for Service	:	....
THE TENANT	:	....
Full name	:	....
THE PROPERTY	:	The property described in the Property Schedule
THE RENT	:	£ ... per calendar month/week★
THE RENT DAYS	:	The ... day of each month/... of each week★
THE DEPOSIT	:	£ ...
THE TERM	:	From [*date*] to [*date*] (both dates inclusive)
INTEREST RATE	:	Four per cent above the published base rate from time to time of ... Bank plc

★ *delete as appropriate*

AN AGREEMENT made on the Date of Agreement.

BETWEEN

1.   The Landlord and

2.   The Tenant.

WHEREBY IT IS AGREED as follows:

1.   Definitions and interpretation
       In this Agreement:
1.1   the attached Particulars are incorporated and to the extent allowed by the context the expressions in capitals in the left-hand column of the Particulars have the respective meanings shown opposite them;

6 RESIDENTIAL TENANCIES

1.2 'the Landlord' includes whoever for the time being owns the interest in the Property which gives the right to possession of it at the end of this tenancy;

1.3 'Interest' means a sum calculated at the Interest Rate compounded on each usual quarter day and to be paid both before and after judgment or arbitration award;

1.4 'the Regulations' means the regulations set out in the Regulations Schedule and all other reasonable regulations of which the Landlord gives the Tenant written notice;

1.5 whenever there is more than one tenant all their obligations can be enforced against all or some of them jointly or against each of them individually;

1.6 a reference to an Act of Parliament refers to that Act as it applies at the date of this Agreement and any later amendment or re-enactment of it;

1.7 any reference to this Agreement includes its schedules;

1.8 any reference to a page clause or schedule is to that page clause or schedule of this Agreement;

1.9 any agreement by the Tenant not to do any act or thing includes an agreement not to allow anyone else to do that act or thing;

1.10 any obligation to pay money refers to a sum exclusive of Value Added Tax and any Value Added Tax charged on it is payable in addition;

1.11 a right given to the Landlord to enter the Property extends to anyone the Landlord authorises to enter and includes the right to bring workmen and applicances onto the Property for the stated purpose;

1.12 authority given to a person to enter the Property after giving notice extends if the circumstances justify it to entry after giving less notice than specified or without giving any notice.

2. Letting

The Landlord lets the Property to the Tenant for the Term.

3. Assured shorthold tenancy

The Property is let on an assured shorthold tenancy as defined in section 20 of the Housing Act 1988 (as amended) so the Landlord is entitled to resume possession in accordance with section 21 of that Act.

4. Furnished letting

If the Property is let furnished or with any contents the provisions of the Contents Schedule apply.

5. Schedule of condition

If there is a schedule of condition which either is attached to this Agreement or is signed by or on behalf of the parties and identified as being the Schedule of Condition for the purposes of this Agreement then nothing in this Agreement shall require the Tenant to do any work to put any part of the Property specified in that schedule into any better condition than that recorded in the schedule.

6. Tenant's obligations

The Tenant's obligations are:

6.1 *Pay rent*

To pay the Rent in advance on the Rent Days (by banker's order if so required by the Landlord) except the first payment (of only a proportion if appropriate) which is to be made on the Date of Agreement.

6.2 *No set-off*

Not to reduce any payment of the Rent by making any deduction from it or by setting off any sum against it.

6.3 *Pay deposit*

To pay to the Landlord the Deposit when this Agreement is signed and whenever required to do so to pay to the Landlord any sum needed to bring the Deposit up to the full amount.

6.4 *Pay rates etc*

6.4.1 To pay promptly to the authorities or companies to whom they are due all rates taxes and outgoings relating to the Property or its owner or occupier including any which are imposed after the date of this Agreement (even if of a novel nature).

6.4.2 To make good forthwith to the Landlord any loss of relief against the payment of the standard council tax or any similar property tax relating to the Property or its occupier which the Landlord may suffer after the end of the tenancy but which he would not have suffered if no such relief had been allowed to the Tenant in respect of a period during the tenancy for which the property was unoccupied.

6.5 *Pay for services*

To pay promptly all charges (including meter and standing charges) for the supply of water electricity and gas to the Property and the use of any telephone there and immediately following the signing of this Agreement to notify the respective supply companies of his liability to pay such accounts and to enter into all such contracts as may be required to obtain such supplies.

6.6 *Pay interest*

To pay Interest from the due date until payment on any sum paid more than seven days after it falls due.

6.7 *Pay fees*

To pay all expenses (including solicitors' and surveyors' fees and disbursements) which the Landlord incurs in preparing and serving:

6.7.1 a notice under section 146 of the Law of Property Act 1925 even if forfeiture is avoided without a court order;

6.7.2 a schedule of dilapidations recording failure to give up possession of the Property in the appropriate state of repair when the tenancy ends.

6.8   *Pay costs of agreement*
        To pay all/one half of★ the expenses (including solicitors' and surveyors'
        fees and disbursements) which the Landlord incurs in connection with the
        negotiation and completion of this Agreement subject to a limit of . . .
        pounds excluding Value Added Tax.★ (*delete as appropriate*)

6.9   *Repair property*
        Not to damage the Property (except by fair wear and tear) and to keep in
        good repair all parts of the Property and all additions to it except that the
        Tenant is not obliged to:
6.9.1   do any repairs which are the Landlord's responsibility under this
        Agreement or under a statutory provision which applies despite any
        agreement to the contrary;
6.9.2   make good any damage caused by a risk against which the Landlord is
        insured at the relevant time unless the insurance moneys are withheld
        because of any act or omission of the Tenant or anyone on the Property
        with the Tenant's consent.

6.10   *Repair appliances*
6.10.1 To keep all smoke and other alarms on the Property in full working order at
        all times checking them not less often than once a month and replacing
        batteries as required.
6.10.2 To do all repairs and make all replacements which fall within the Tenant's
        liability under the general law to keep the Premises in tenantable repair.
6.10.3 Subject to clause . . . to keep all other electrical and mechanical appliances
        (including door bells) on the Property serviceable and to replace any that
        are lost or damaged irreparably or at the option of the Landlord to pay to
        the Landlord the cost of replacement.
6.10.4 The Tenant's obligations under clause . . . shall not extend to making good
        any damage or deterioration which is solely due to fair wear and tear unless
        it falls within clause . . . .

6.11   *Septic tank*[1]
        To empty the septic tank serving the Property without delay whenever
        needed [but not less often than once every twelve months] and in any event
        during the last month of the tenancy.★ (*delete as appropriate*)

6.12   *Internal decoration*
6.12.1 To keep the inside of the Property adequately decorated but not to change
        the colour scheme without the Landlord's written consent except that the
        Tenant is not obliged to make good any damage to such decoration caused
        by a risk against which the Landord is insured at the relevant time unless the
        insurance moneys are withheld because of any act or omission of the
        Tenant or anyone on the Property with the Tenant's consent.
6.12.2 Not to drill holes in or drive nails into or attach or suspend any fitment or
        item to or from any wall or ceiling other than any attached or suspended at
        the start of the tenancy.

6.13   *Keep clean and tidy*

To keep the Property clean and tidy any garden properly tended and any hedge properly trimmed and not to damage remove from or move within any such parts any garden furniture or ornaments or other items or any tree shrub or perennial plant.

6.14   *Notice to do repairs*

If the Landlord gives to the Tenant notice of any defect for which the Tenant is responsible to start the work within one month (or any longer period stated in the notice) or immediately in the case of an emergency and to proceed with it diligently. In case of any default the Landlord is entitled (but not obliged) to enter the Property to do it and the Tenant must pay the cost of it on demand.

6.15   *Report defects*

To inspect the Property regularly for defects and report promptly to the Landlord all defects in the Property which it is the Landlord's duty to repair.

6.16   *Copy notices*

To give the Landlord promptly a copy of any notice received concerning the Property or any nearby property.

6.17   *Not to prejudice insurance*

Not to act in a way which will or may result in the insurance of the Property being void or voidable or in the premium for it being increased.

6.18   *Not to insure*

Not to insure any part of the Property including any addition to or landlord's fixture in it.

6.19   *Entry*

To allow the Landlord on giving at least two days' notice to enter the Property whenever required to inspect it or to carry out any obligation of the Landlord or for any other reasonable purpose.

6.20   *Entry for dealings*

To allow the Landlord and any person with written authority from the Landlord or the Landlord's agent to enter the Property at any reasonable time on reasonable notice to view it as or for a prospective purchaser tenant or mortgagee.

6.21   *Access for others*
Whenever so required by the Landlord to allow anyone who reasonably needs access in order to inspect repair or clean nearby property or any sewers drains pipes wires or cables serving nearby property to enter the Property at any reasonable time. The person requiring access is to give at least two days' notice and make good any damage to the Property promptly.

6.22   *Sale notice*
To allow the Landlord to affix a notice to the outside of the Property announcing it is for sale or (in the last two months of the tenancy) to let.

6.23   *Occupation*
At all times to occupy the Property as the Tenant's only or principal home and not to use the Property or any part of it for any purpose other than as a dwellinghouse in single family occupation.

6.24   *Comply with regulations*
To comply with the Regulations and ensure that any other occupiers of the Property also do so.

6.25   *No assignment*
Not to assign sub-let mortgage charge part with possession or share occupation of the Property or any part of it and in particular not to take in lodgers or paying guests.

6.26   *No alterations*
Not to alter or add to the Property.

6.27   *Forbidden uses*
Not to use the Property or any part of it for any activity which is dangerous offensive noxious noisome illegal or immoral or which is or may become a nuisance or annoyance to the Landlord or to the owner or occupier of any nearby property.

6.28   *No auctions*
Not to hold any auction sale on the Property.

6.29   *No public access*
Not to invite the public generally or any specified section of it to come to the Property nor to use it for a purpose which attracts casual callers.

6.30   *No advertisements*
Not to display any notice or advertisement either on the outside of the Property or visible from outside it.

6.31   *No aerials*
Not without the Landlord's written consent to affix to or erect on the Property any wireless or television aerial or similar receiving or transmitting apparatus.

6.32   *Prevent rights*
To prevent any person from using any part of the Property in such a way that he may acquire an indefeasible right to continue that use and not to stop up any window on the Property.

6.33   *Termination*
On the day the tenancy ends:

6.33.1 to return the Property to the Landlord in the state in which this Agreement requires the Tenant to keep it;

6.33.2 not to leave in the Property anything which belongs to the Tenant or which he ought to remove;

6.33.3 to return all keys to the Landlord by noon.

7.   Landlord's obligations
Subject to the provisions of clause ... the Landlord's obligations are:

7.1   *No interference*
So long as the tenancy continues and the Tenant complies with its terms to allow the Tenant to occupy the Property without interference.

7.2   *Repairs*
EITHER
To do the repairs to the Property which the Landlord and Tenant Act 1985 requires a landlord to do.
OR

7.2.1   To keep in good repair the outside the foundations the roof and the structure which includes any load bearing walls within the Property and the supporting structures of the ceilings and the floors but excludes both the decorative surfaces of those walls ceilings and floors within the Property and the glass in the windows in the external walls.

7.2.2   To keep any fences and boundary walls on the Property in good repair.

7.2.3   To keep any septic tank and pipes serving the Property in good repair and condition and cause the septic tank to be emptied without delay when required and so notified by the Tenant.

7.2.4   To do any other repairs to the Property which by statute are the obligation of the Landlord.

7.3   *External decoration*
To decorate the outside of the Property whenever the Landlord considers it necessary.

6 RESIDENTIAL TENANCIES

7.4   *Repay deposit*
        When the tenancy ends to repay the Deposit to the Tenant without interest
        after deducting all sums due to the Landlord under the terms of this
        Agreement or as a result of any of its terms being broken.

8.   Agreements
        It is agreed as follows:

8.1   *Forfeiture*
        The Landlord is entitled to forfeit this Agreement by entering any part of
        the Property whenever:
8.1.1   the Tenant is fourteen days late in paying the Rent even if it was not
        formally demanded;
8.1.2   the Tenant has not complied with any of his obligations as Tenant;
8.1.3   the Tenant (or if there is more than one Tenant one of them) is adjudicated
        bankrupt or has an interim receiver appointed;
8.1.4   the court has power to make an order for possession of a dwellinghouse on
        one or more of the grounds set out in Schedule 2 to the Housing Act 1988.
        Forfeiture of this Agreement does not cancel any outstanding obligation
        which the Tenant owes the Landlord.

8.2   *Rent reduction*
        During any period when all or part of the Property cannot be put to its
        accustomed use because of damage from an insured risk the Rent is
        cancelled or reduced as appropriate except to the extent that the insurers do
        not pay under the policy because of something done or not done by the
        Tenant or any person on the Property with his consent. Any dispute about
        whether or how this clause applies is to be referred to arbitration.

8.3   *Use of deposit*
        During the tenancy and on its termination the Landlord may use the
        Deposit to pay for anything done by the Landlord to make good any
        obligation broken by the Tenant.

8.4   *Landlord's liability*
        The Landlord's obligations under this Agreement are entered into by the
        Landlord named in this Agreement for himself and subsequent owners
        successively so that each person who is the Landlord is bound only during
        his period of ownership [and in particular if he has paid the Deposit to the
        next owner he shall have no responsibility for its repayment to the Tenant]
        (*delete as appropriate*).

8.5   *Notices*
8.5.1   Notice is hereby given that the Landlord's address for service of notices
        (including notices in proceedings) is as stated in the Particulars until the
        Tenant is notified in writing of a different address in England and Wales.
8.5.2   Without prejudice to the previous sub-clause any notice to be served by or
        on the Landlord may be served by or on the Landlord's agents.

8.6   *Arbitration*

Any disputed matter referred to arbitration under this Agreement is to be decided by arbitration under the Arbitration Act 1996 by a single arbitrator appointed by the parties to this dispute. If they do not agree on the appointment then the President of the Royal Institution of Chartered Surveyors may appoint the arbitrator at the request of either party.

THE PROPERTY SCHEDULE

THE dwelling known as [*Property details*]/as shown edged [*colour*] on the attached plan TOGETHER WITH the benefit of any rights it may have which until now have been enjoyed by the occupier of the premises and are needed in order to use it for residential purposes SUBJECT to any rights or quasi-rights (of whatever nature) which have been enjoyed until now over the premises by the occupier of any nearby property.

THE REGULATIONS SCHEDULE

1.   No caravans or (except in places designated for them by the Landlord) cars motor cycles or other vehicles are to be parked on any part of the Property.

2.   No musical instrument television or radio set or sound reproduction equipment is to be played at any time so as to be audible in any nearby property.

3.   All chimneys are to be swept at least once a year.

4.   All windows are to be cleaned inside and outside at least once a month.

5.   Nothing is to be allowed to obstruct the drainage system.

6.   No electric wiring plumbing gas or telephone installation is to be altered or extended.

7.   Adequate measures are to be taken to prevent frost damage to the plumbing and heating installations including draining the hot water and heating system whenever that is required to prevent frost damage during a period when the property is unoccupied.

8.   No animal of any kind is to be kept at the Property.

THE CONTENTS SCHEDULE

1.   In this schedule 'the Contents' means the items listed in the Inventory and 'the Inventory' means the inventory which is either attached to this Agreement or has been signed by or on behalf of the parties and is identified as being the Inventory for the purposes of this Agreement.

2.   The Tenant is to keep the Contents clean and in as good condition as at the start of the tenancy and is to repair any damage to the Contents (in each case except damage caused by fair wear and tear).

3.   If any of the Contents is lost or irreparably damaged the Tenant is to replace it or at the option of the Landlord to pay to the Landlord the cost of replacement.

4.   At the end of the tenancy the Tenant is to return to the Landlord all the Contents in the position they were in at the start of the tenancy [as recorded in the Inventory] (*delete as appropriate*).

AS WITNESS the hands of the parties hereto the day and year first before written.

SIGNED by the said [*name*]
in the presence of:

}

....

....

....

....

SIGNED by the said [*name*]
in the presence of:

}

....

....

....

....

---

1   If septic tank serves more than the Property, see Occasional Clauses.

2   TENANT'S NOTICE PROPOSING CHANGE FROM ASSURED TENANCY TO ASSURED SHORTHOLD TENANCY

FORM No 8

Housing Act 1988 Schedule 2A, paragraph 7(2) as inserted by Schedule 7 to the Housing Act 1996

Tenant's notice proposing that an Assured Tenancy be replaced by an Assured Shorthold Tenancy

- Please write clearly in black ink.

- Please cross out text marked with an asterisk (★) that does not apply.

- This notice should only be used by an assured tenant. You should only use this notice to notify your landlord that you wish your assured tenancy to be replaced by an assured shorthold tenancy.

- This notice must be served by a tenant on a landlord before an assured tenancy can be replaced by an assured shorthold tenancy.

- **You should be aware that by serving this notice, you will be giving up your right to stay in the property after the first six months of the assured short-hold tenancy or, if you agree a fixed term with your landlord, after the end of the fixed term.**

- **You do not have to complete this form even if your landlord has asked you to do so. Your existing security of terms as an assured tenant will be unaffected if you do not complete it.**

- **If you are in any doubt about whether to complete this form, take it immediately to a citizen's advice bureau, housing advice centre, a law centre or a solicitor.**

- Once you are clear that you wish to issue this notice, complete the form and send it to your landlord.

---

1. To: ....

Name(s) of landlord(s)

---

2. I/We★, the tenant(s) of:

....

....

....

Address of premises

give notice that I/we★ propose that the assured tenancy to which this notice relates should be replaced by a shorthold tenancy.

---

3. I/We★ propose that the new shorthold tenancy should commence on:

………/ ………/ ………
  day   month   year

- The new shorthold tenancy cannot commence until after the date this notice is served on the landlord.

4.(a)   I/We★ understand that under my/our★ existing tenancy, I/we★ can only be required to give up possession in accordance with the grounds set out in Schedule 2 to the Housing Act 1988, whereas under the new shorthold tenancy, the landlord(s) will be able to recover possession of the premises without being required to prove a ground for possession, after the first six months of the assured shorthold tenancy, or, if there is a fixed term for longer than six months, at the end of that fixed term, subject to two months' notice.

Signed ……………………………………… Date ……………………………………

…………………………………………

…………………………………………

To be signed and dated by the tenant. If there are joint tenants each tenant must sign.

(b)   Name and address of tenant
Name(s) (*Block Capitals*): ……………………………………………………

……………………………………………………

……………………………………………………

Address:

………………………………………………………………………………

………………………………………………………………………………

……………………………………………………………………

Telephone – Daytime ……………………… Evening ………………………

3 LANDLORD'S NOTICE PROPOSING ASSURED SHORTHOLD TENANCY

FORM No 9

Housing Act 1988 Schedule 2A, paragraph 9, as inserted by Schedule 7 to the Housing Act 1996

Landlord's notice proposing an Assured Shorthold Tenancy where the tenancy meets the conditions for an Assured Agricultural Occupancy

- Please write clearly in black ink.

- Please tick boxes where appropriate.

- If the agricultural worker condition in Schedule 3 to the Housing Act 1988 is met with respect to the property to which the proposed assured tenancy relates, and the landlord wishes that tenancy to be an assured shorthold tenancy, he must serve this notice on the tenant before the tenancy is entered into.

- **This notice cannot be used where the landlord has already granted to the prospective tenant (or, in the case of joint tenants, to at least one of them) a tenancy or licence under section 24 of the Housing Act 1988 (an assured agricultural occupancy).**

- **This notice does not commit the tenant to taking the tenancy.**

---

1. To: ....

....

....

Name of the proposed tenant. If a joint tenancy is being offered, enter the names of the joint tenants.

---

2. You are proposing to take a tenancy as the following address:

....

....

....

commencing on ..../ ..../ ....
                  day   month   year

---

3. This notice is to tell you that your tenancy is to be an assured shorthold tenancy.

- Provided you keep to the terms of the tenancy, you are entitled to remain in the property for at least six months after the start of the tenancy. Depending on the terms of the tenancy, once the first six months have elapsed, the landlord may have the right to seek possession at any time, subject to two months' notice.

- As an assured shorthold tenant, you have the right to apply to a rent assessment committee for the determination of a reasonable rent for the tenancy. An application to your local rent assessment committee must be made on the form headed *Application to a Rent Assessment Committee for a determination of a rent under an Assured Shorthold Tenancy* within six months of the beginning of the tenancy. You can obtain the form from a rent assessment panel or a law stationer.

- If you need help or advice about this notice, and what you should do about it, take it immediately to a citizens' advice bureau, a housing advice centre, a law centre or a solicitor.

4. Name and address of landlord.

To be signed and dated by the landlord or his agent (someone acting for him). If there are joint landlords, each landlord or the agent must sign unless one signs on behalf of the rest with their agreement.

Signed .... Date ....

....

....

Please specify whether: landlord ☐   joint landlords ☐   agent ☐

Name(s) (*Block Capitals*): ....

....

Address:

....

....

....

Telephone – Daytime .... Evening ....

4   LANDLORD'S LETTER PROPOSING RENT INCREASE

To

[name and address of tenant(s)]

Dear *[Sir]* *[or as the case may be]*

YOUR TENANCY OF *[PROPERTY]*

It is considered that the rent of the above premises is now due for review. It is proposed that as from *[date – an appropriate date will usually be a rent day]* the rent is increased to £[...] per *[month/quarter/annum]*★.

If the proposal is acceptable please sign, date and return to us the enclosed copy of this letter to signify your agreement. If you pay rent by standing order, please instruct your bank to make the necessry adjustment, letting us have a copy of the instruction.

If you do not respond to this letter within [...] days we shall serve on you a notice under section 13(2) of the Housing Act 1988 (Landlord's Notice Proposing a new Rent under an Assured Periodic Tenancy or Agricultural Occupancy).

Your faithfully,

Agents for the Landlord *[name of Landlord]*

[To be typed on copy]

I/We agree that the rent on the above premises is increased to £[...] per *[month/quarter/annum]*★ as from *[date]*.

Signed ....   Dated ....
                 Tenant(s)

★*delete as appropriate.*

5 NOTICE PROPOSING DIFFERENT TERMS FOR STATUTORY PERIODIC TENANCY

SCHEDULE

FORMS PRESCRIBED FOR THE PURPOSES OF PART 1 OF THE HOUSING ACT 1988

FORM No 1

Housing Act 1988 section 6(2)

Notice proposing different terms for a Statutory Periodic Tenancy

- Please write clearly in black ink.

- Please tick boxes where appropriate and cross out text marked with an asterisk (★) that does not apply.

- This form can be used by either a landlord or a tenant to propose changes to the terms of a statutory periodic tenancy, which arises when a fixed term of an assured tenancy, an assured shorthold tenancy or an assured agricultural occupancy ends.

- This notice must be served on the landlord or tenant no later than the first anniversary of the day on which the former fixed term tenancy or occupancy ended.

- Do not use this notice if you are a landlord proposing only an increase in rent. Instead, you should use the form headed *Landlord's Notice proposing a new rent under an Assured Periodic Tenancy or Agricultural Occupancy*, which is available from a rent assessment panel or law stationers.

---

1. To: ....

Name(s) of landlord(s)/tenant(s)★

Address of premises to which the tenancy relates:

....

....

....

---

2. This is to give notice that I/we★ propose different terms for the statutory periodic tenancy from those of the fixed term assured tenancy which has now ended and that they should take effect from:

....

Insert date which must be at least three months after the date on which this notice is served.

---

3. Changes to the terms

(a) The existing provisions of the tenancy to be changed are:

....

....

....

Please attach relevant sections of the tenancy agreement if available.

(b) The proposed changes are:

....

....

....

Continue on another sheet if necessary.

4. Changes to the rent (if applicable). Go to section 5 if this does not apply.

●   You should not propose a change on this form unless it is to take account of the proposed new terms at section 3. A change may be made if either the landlord or the tenant considers it appropriate.

(a)   The existing rent is: £.....................per...............
                                                   (eg week, month, year)

(b)   Does the rent include council tax?   Yes ☐   No ☐
(c)   If yes, the amount that is included for
      council tax is: £.....................per...............
                                                   (eg week, month, year)

(d)   Does the rent include water charges?   Yes ☐   No ☐
(e)   If yes, the amount that is included for water
      charges is: £.....................per...............
                                                   (eg week, month, year)

(f)   The new rent which takes into account the
      proposed changes in the terms of the tenancy
      will be: £.....................per...............
                                                   (eg week, month, year)

(g)   Will the new rent include council tax?   Yes ☐   No ☐

(h)   If yes, the amount that will be included for
      council tax is: £.....................per...............
                                                   (eg week, month, year)

(i)   Will the new rent include water charges?   Yes ☐   No ☐

(j)   If yes, the amount that will be included for
       water charges is: £..........................per ....
                                                                 (eg week, month, year)

---

5. Name and address of landlord or tenant proposing the changes

*To be signed and dated by the landlord or his agent (someone acting for him) or the tenant or his
agent. If there are joint landlords or joint tenants each landlord/tenant or the agent must sign
unless one signs on behalf of the rest with their agreement.*

Signed .... Date ....

             ....

             ....

Please specify whether: landlord ☐ landlord's agent ☐ tenant ☐ tenant's agents ☐

Name(s) (*Block Capitals*)

....

....

....

Address:

....

....

....

Telephone – Daytime .... Evening ....

What to do if this notice is served on you

- If you agree with the new terms and rent proposed, do nothing. They will
  become the terms of the tenancy agreement on the date specified in section 2.

- If you don't agree with the proposed terms and any adjustment of the rent (see
  section 4), and you are unable to reach agreement with your landlord/tenant,
  or you do not wish to discuss it with him, you may refer the matter directly to
  your local rent assessment committee, before the date specified in section 2,
  using the form headed *Application referring a Notice proposing different terms for a
  Statutory Periodic Tenancy to a Rent Assessment Committee* which you can obtain
  from a rent assessment panel or a law stationer.

- The rent assessment committee will decide what, if any, changes should be
  made to the terms of the tenancy and, if applicable, the amount of the new rent.

- If you need help or advice about this notice and what you should do about it,
  take it immediately to a citizens advice bureau, a housing advice centre, a law
  centre or a solicitor.

6 APPLICATION REFERRING A NOTICE PROPOSING DIFFERENT TERMS FOR STATUTORY PERIODIC TENANCY TO RENT ASSESSMENT COMMITTEE

FORM No 2

Housing Act 1988 section 6(3)

Application referring a Notice proposing different terms for a Statutory Periodic Tenancy to a Rent Assessment Committee

- Please write clearly in black ink.

- Please tick boxes where appropriate and cross out text marked with an asterisk (★) that does not apply.

- This form should be used by a landlord or a tenant who has been served with a notice under section 6(2) of the Housing Act 1988, varying the terms of a statutory periodic tenancy which arises when a fixed term of an assured tenancy, an assured shorthold tenancy or an assured agricultural occupancy ends.

- When you have completed the form, please send it to your local rent assessment panel with a copy of the notice served on you proposing the new terms of the statutory periodic tenancy.

---

1. Name(s) of tenant(s):

....

....

....

2. Address of premises to which the tenancy relates:

....

....

....

3. Name(s) of landlord(s)/agent★:

....

....

....

Address of landlord(s)/agent★:

....

....

....

4. Details of premises.

(a) What type of accommodation is rented?
Room(s) ☐   Flat ☐   Terraced House ☐
Semi-Detached House ☐   Fully Detached House ☐   Other ☐
(*Please specify*) ....

(b) If it is a flat or room(s), what floor(s) is it on?
Ground ☐   First ☐   Second ☐   Other ☐ (*Please specify*) ....

(c) Give the number and type of rooms, eg living room, bathroom etc

....

....

(d) Does the tenancy include any other facilities, eg garden, garage or other separate
building or land?
       Yes ☐   No ☐

(e) If yes, please give details:

....

....

....

(f) Is any of the accommodation shared with:

    (i) the landlord?   Yes ☐   No ☐
    (ii) another tenant or tenants?   Yes ☐   No ☐

(g) If yes, please give details:

....

....

....

5. When did the statutory periodic tenancy begin?

....

6. Services.

(a) Are any services provided under the tenancy (eg cleaning, lighting, heating, hot
water or gardening etc.)?

       Yes ☐   No ☐

(b) If yes, please give details:

....

....

....

(c) Is a separate charge made for services, maintenance, repairs, landlords' costs of management or any other item?

Yes ☐   No ☐

(d) If yes, what charge is payable?   £ ....   per ....

(eg week, month, year)

(e) Does the charge vary according to the relevant costs?

Yes ☐   No ☐

(f) If yes, please give details:

....

....

....

7. (a) Is any furniture provided under the tenancy?

Yes ☐   No ☐

(b) If yes, please give details. Continue on a separate sheet if necessary or provide a copy of the inventory.

....

....

....

8. What repairs are the responsibility of:

(a) the landlord? Continue on a separate sheet if necessary.

....

....

....

(b) the tenant? Continue on a separate sheet if necessary.

....

....

....

6 RESIDENTIAL TENANCIES

9. Give details (if known) of the other terms of the tenancy, eg can you assign the tenancy (pass it on to someone else) and if so is a pemium (a payment which is in addition to rent and equivalent to more than two months' rent) payable on an assignment? Continue on a separate sheet if necessary.

....

....

....

10.(a)   Is there a written tenancy agreement?   Yes ☐   No ☐

(b)   If yes, please attach the tenancy agreement (with a note of any variations). It will be returned to you as soon as possible.

11.(a)   I/We* attach a copy of the notice proposing changes to the statutory periodic tenancy and, if applicable, an adjustment of the amount of rent and apply for it to be considered by the rent assessment committee.

Signed   ....   Date   ....

....

....

To be signed and dated by the landlord or his agent (someone acting for him) or the tenant or his agent. If there are joint landlords or joint tenants, each landlord/tenant or the agent must sign unless one signs on behalf of the rest with their agreement.

Please specify whether: landlord ☐   landlord's agent ☐   tenant ☐   tenant's agent ☐

(b)   Name and address of landlord or tenant referring to the rent assessment committee.

Name(s) (*Block Capitals*):   ....

....

....

Address:

....

....

....

Telephone – Daytime   ....   Evening   ....

7   NOTICE SEEKING POSSESSION OF PROPERTY LET ON ASSURED TENANCY/ASSURED AGRICULTURAL OCCUPANCY

FORM No 3

Housing Act 1988 section 8 as amended by section 151 of the Housing Act 1996

Notice seeking possession of a property let on an Assured Tenancy or an Assured Agricultural Occupancy

- Please write clearly in black ink.

- Please tick boxes where appropriate and cross out text marked with an asterisk (★) that does not apply.

- This form should be used where possession of accommodation let under an assured tenancy, an assured agricultural occupancy or an assured shorthold tenancy is sought on one of the grounds in Schedule 2 to the Housing Act 1988.

- Do not use this form if possession is sought on the 'shorthold' ground under section 21 of the Housing Act 1988 from an assured shorthold tenant where the fixed term has come to an end or, for assured shorthold tenancies with no fixed term which started on or after 28 February 1997, after six months has elapsed. There is no prescribed form for these cases, but you must give notice in writing.

---

1. To: ....
Name(s) of tenant(s)/licensee(s)★

2. Your landlord/licensor★ intends to apply to the court for an order requiring you to give up possession of:

....

....

....

Address of premises

3. Your landlord/licensor★ intends to seek possession on ground(s) .... in Schedule 2 to the Housing Act 1988, as amended by the Housing Act 1996, which read(s):

....

....

....

Give the full text (as set out in the Housing Act 1988 as amended by the Housing Act 1996) of each ground which is being relied on. Continue on a separate sheet if necessary.

4. Give a full explanation of why each ground is being relied on:

....

....

....

Continue on a separate sheet if necessary.

Notes on the grounds for possession

●   If the court is satisfied that any of grounds 1 to 8 is established, it must make an order (but see below in respect of fixed term tenancies).

●   Before the court will grant an order on any grounds of 9 to 17, it must be satisfied that it is reasonable to require you to leave. This means that, if one of these grounds is set out in section 3, you will be able to suggest to the court that it is not reasonable that you should have to leave, even if you accept that the ground applies.

●   The court will not make an order under grounds 1, 3 to 7, 9 or 16, to take effect during the fixed term of the tenancy (if there is one) and it will only make an order during the fixed term on grounds 2, 8, 10 to 15 or 17 if the terms of the tenancy make provision for it to be brought to an end on any of these grounds.

●   Where the court makes an order for possession solely on ground 6 or 9, the landlord must pay your reasonable removal expenses.

5. The court proceedings will not begin until after:

....

Give the earliest date on which court proceedings can be brought.

●   Where the landlord is seeking possession on grounds 1, 2, 5 to 7, 9 or 16, court proceedings cannot begin earlier than 2 months from the date this notice is served on you (even where one of grounds 3, 4, 8, 10 to 13, 14A, 15 or 17 is specified) and not before the date on which the tenancy (had it not been assured) could have been brought to an end by a notice to quit served at the same time as this notice.

●   Where the landlord is seeking possession on grounds 3, 4, 8, 10 to 13, 14A, 15 or 17, court proceedings cannot begin earlier than 2 weeks from the date this notice is served (unless one of 1, 2, 5 to 7, 9 or 16 grounds is also specified in which case they cannot begin earlier than two months from the date this notice is served).

●   Where the landlord is seeking possession on ground 14 (with or without other grounds), court proceedings cannot begin before the date this notice is served.

- Where the landlord is seeking possession on ground 14A, court proceedings cannot begin unless the landlord has served, or has taken all reasonable steps to serve, a copy of this notice on the partner who has left the property.

- After the date shown in section 5, court proceedings may be begun at once but not later than 12 months from the date on which this notice is served. After this time the notice will lapse and a new notice must be served before possession can be sought.

---

6. Name and address of landlord/licensor★.

To be signed and dated by the landlord or licensor or his agent (someone acting for him). If there are joint landlords, each landlord or the agent must sign unless one signs on behalf of the rest with their agreement.

Signed ....   Date ....

....

Please specify whether: landlord ☐ licensor ☐ joint landlords ☐ landlord's agent ☐

Name(s) (*Block Capitals*): ....

....

....

Address:

....

....

....

Telephone – Daytime ....   Evening ....

What to do if this notice is served on you

- This notice is the first step requiring you to give up possession of your home. You should read it very carefully.

- Your landlord cannot make you leave your home without an order for possession issued by a court. By issuing this notice your landlord is informing you that he intends to seek such an order. If you are willing to give up possession without a court order, you should tell the person who signed this notice as soon as possible and say when you are prepared to leave.

- Whichever grounds are set out in section 3 of this form, the court may allow any of the other grounds to be added at a later date. If this is done, you will be told about it so you can discuss the additional grounds at the court hearing as well as the grounds set out in section 3.

- If you need advice about this notice, and what you should do about it, take it immediately to a citizens' advice bureau, a housing advice centre, a law centre or a solicitor.

---

8   LANDLORD'S NOTICE PROPOSING NEW RENT UNDER ASSURED PERIODIC TENANCY OR AGRICULTURAL OCCUPANCY

FORM No 4

Housing Act 1988 section 13(2)

Landlord's Notice proposing a new rent under an Assured Periodic Tenancy or Agricultural Occupancy

- Please write clearly in black ink.

- Please tick boxes where appropriate.

- This form should be used to propose a new rent under an assured periodic tenancy, including an assured shorthold periodic tenancy.

- This form may also be used to propose a new rent or licence fee for an assured periodic agricultural occupancy. In such cases reference to 'landlord'/'tenant' can be read as references to 'licensor'/'licensee' etc.

- Do not use this form if there is a current rent fixing mechanism in the tenancy.

- Do not use this form to propose a rent adjustment for a statutory periodic tenancy solely because of a proposed change of terms under section 6(2) of the Housing Act 1988. You should instead use the form headed *Notice proposing different terms for a Statutory Periodic Tenancy* which you can obtain from a rent assessment panel or a law stationer.

---

1. To: ....

Name(s) of tenant(s)

---

2. Address of premises to which the tenancy relates:

....

....

....

---

3. This is to give notice that as from: .... your landlord proposes to charge a new rent.

● The new rent must take effect at the beginning of a new period of the tenancy and not earlier than any of the following:

(a) the minimum period after this notice was served.

(The minimum period is:

— in the case of a yearly tenancy, six months;

— in the case of a tenancy where the period is less than a month, one month;

— in any other case, a period equal to the period of the tenancy;)

(b) the first anniversary of the start of the first period of the tenancy except in the case of:

— a statutory periodic tenancy, which arises when a fixed term assured tenancy ends; or

— an assured tenancy which arose on the death of a tenant under a regulated tenancy;

(c) If the rent under the tenancy has previously been increased by a notice under section 13 or a determination under section 14 of the Housing Act 1988, the first anniversary of the date on which the increased rent took effect.

6 RESIDENTIAL TENANCIES

4.(a) The existing rent is: £..................per............
                                                            (eg week, month, year)

(b) Does the rent include council tax?   Yes ☐   No ☐
(c) If yes, the amount that is included for
    council tax is: £..................per............
                                                            (eg week, month, year)

(d) Does the rent include water charges?   Yes ☐   No ☐
(e) If yes, the amount that is included for water
    charges is: £..................per............
                                                            (eg week, month, year)

5.(a) The proposed new rent will be: £..................per............
                                                            (eg week, month, year)

(b) Will the new rent include council tax?   Yes ☐   No ☐

(c) If yes, the amount that will be included for
    council tax is: £..................per............
                                                            (eg week, month, year)

(d) Will the new rent include water charges?   Yes ☐   No ☐

(e) If yes, the amount that will be included for
    water charges will be: £..................per............
                                                            (eg week, month, year)

6. Name and address of landlord.

To be signed and dated by the landlord or his agent (someone acting for him). If there are joint landlords each landlord or the agent must sign unless one signs on behalf of the rest with their agreement.

Signed .... Date ....

....

....

Please specify whether: landlord ☐ joint landlords ☐ landlord's agent ☐

Name(s) (*Block Capitals*):

....

....

....

Address:

....

....

....

Telephone – Daytime .... Evening ....

What to do if this notice is served on you

You should read this notice carefully. Your landlord is proposing a new rent.

- If you agree with the new rent proposed, do nothing. If you do not agree and you are unable to reach agreement with your landlord or do not want to discuss it directly with him, you may refer this notice to your local rent assessment committee prior to the date specified in section 3, using the form headed *Application referring a Notice proposing a new rent under an Assured Periodic Tenancy or Agricultural Occupancy to a Rent Assessment Committee.* You can obtain this form from a rent assessment panel or a law stationer.

- The rent assessment committee will consider your application and will decide what the rent for the premises will be. The committee may set a rent that is higher, lower or the same as the landlord has proposed in section 5.

- If you are required to include payments for council tax and water charges in your rent, the rent the committee determines will be inclusive of council tax and water charges.

- If you need help or advice please take this notice immediately to a citizens advice bureau, a housing advice centre, a law centre or a solicitor.

CHAPTER 7: BUSINESS TENANCIES

INDEX

7 BUSINESS TENANCIES

CHAPTER 7: BUSINESS TENANCIES

INTRODUCTION

It is important to be on the lookout for letting arrangements in the countryside which, in effect, are not farm business tenancies but business tenancies under the Landlord and Tenant Act 1954, Part II. The distinction can sometimes be difficult to make. For example, use as a stud farm constitutes a business use rather than an agricultural use. On the other hand, a letting for grazing purposes will be an agricultural letting rather than a business letting. Unless it is quite clear which is the predominant user, the cautious practitioner will endeavour to prepare an agreement which meets his purposes so far as possible under both statutory regimes. Most importantly in the context of security of tenure and compensation, this may need to include an application to the court to contract out of the security of tenure provisions of the Landlord and Tenant Act 1954, s 38.

A precedent is included for letting farm buildings which are no longer required in the agricultural business. This is an ordinary warehouse letting under the business tenancy regime and as such agreements go, relatively short. If the letting is long term, further clauses may be thought necessary. The landlord must bear in mind that such a letting carries with it various fiscal implications:

- *Inheritance tax*. The building will no longer be eligible for agricultural relief for inheritance tax purposes because it is no longer occupied jointly with farmland. It may perhaps be eligible for business relief but only if the requirements set out in *Farmer v IRC* (1999) STC (SCD) 321 can be met.

- *Capital gains tax*. On a similar basis, there may be a risk of losing business taper relief and rollover relief.

- *Rating*. The business will be liable to rates, although one would anticipate that these would be passed on to the tenant.

It might be more appropriate if, instead of letting the building for storage purposes, the landlord was prepared to run a business storing goods on behalf of a third party. Clearly this would incur work and liability for the property owner, but he might take the view that the fiscal advantages are worth it. However, this would not assist with the rating question.

Woodlands are another grey area. For inheritance tax purposes, if occupied as ancillary to agricultural land, they will attract agricultural relief. There is separate relief available for woodlands but that is not entirely satisfactory since it defers the tax charge until the timber is realised. If woodlands are being managed with a view to profit, business relief may be available. Any lettings of the woods on their own are unlikely to be agricultural.

7 BUSINESS TENANCIES

There is a separate tax code relating to royalties for minerals. If any minerals are to be disposed of, it is clearly important to consider carefully the tax implications of the disposal and whether an attempt should be made to secure a capital disposal rather than royalty treatment. The arrangements regarding the minerals will depend on the deal negotiated between the parties.

PRECEDENTS

1   LEASE OF FARM BUILDINGS

THIS LEASE is made the [*date*]

BETWEEN:

'The Landlord': [*name*] of [*address*]
'The Tenant': [*name*] of [*address*]

1.   In this Lease the following terms have the meanings hereunder assigned to them:

1.1   *'the Demised Premises'*:
        The building shown coloured . . . on the annexed plan;

1.2   *'the Term'*:
        The period of . . . year[s] commencing on and including the . . . [*date*][1] and thereafter until determined by either party giving to the other not less than three months' notice in writing expiring at any time

1.3.   *'the Rent Days'*:
        [*dates*] in each year;

1.4.   *'the Permitted Use'*:
        Use for [*specify use*];

1.5.   *'the Bank'*:
        . . . Bank Plc or the Bank which is the successor to the business of that Bank or if any such Bank ceases to trade in such circumstances that no one Bank succeeds to that business such member of the Committee of London Clearing Bankers as the Landlord nominates.

2.   In the interpretation of this Lease where the context so admits:

2.1   'the Landlord' includes the person for the time being entitled to the reversion immediately expectant on the termination of the Term;

2.2   'the Tenant' includes the persons in whom for the time being the Demised Premises are vested for the Term;

2.3   whenever any party hereto consists of more than one person every covenant on the part of such party herein contained shall be deemed to be made jointly and severally by those persons;

2.4   in any case where the Tenant covenants not to do any act or thing such covenant shall include a covenant not to permit such act or thing to be done;

2.5   a reference to a statute includes any amendment or re-enactment thereof (whether made before or after the date hereof) and any secondary legislation made under that statute;

7 BUSINESS TENANCIES

2.6   'the Planning Acts' means the Town and Country Planning Act 1990, the
        Planning (Listed Buildings and Conservation Areas) Act 1990, the
        Planning (Hazardous Substances) Act 1990, the Planning (Consequential
        Provisions) Act 1990 and the Planning and Compensation Act 1991;

2.7   'Base Rate' means the published Base Rate from time to time of the Bank
        but if no such rate is published then a rate of two per centum above the rate
        paid by the Bank from time to time on deposits of the minimum sum
        accepted at interest for repayment on seven days' notice;

2.8   'interest' is at the annual rate of four per centum above the Base Rate from
        time to time compounded with rests on each Rent Day;

2.9   any covenant to pay interest is a covenant to pay interest both before and
        after any judgment or arbitration award;

2.10   'insured risks' means fire lightning explosion earthquake landslip subsid-
        ence riot civil commotion aircraft aerial devices storm flood impact and
        damage by malicious persons and vandals together with such other risks
        against which the Landlord from time to time reasonably deems it prudent
        to insure;

2.11   'service media' means any pipes wires sewers drains ducts cables conduits or
        other channels through which water sewage gas electricity and other
        services are conveyed;

2.12   any reference to a clause is to that clause of this Lease.

3.   The Landlord hereby demises unto the Tenant ALL THOSE the Demised
        Premises TOGETHER WITH[2] the benefit of such rights set out in the
        Schedule hereto as have hitherto been enjoyed by the Demised Premises
        and the occupier thereof over neighbouring property or need to be so
        enjoyed for the reasonable use of the Demised Premises for the Permitted
        Use BUT EXCEPTING AND RESERVING[3] unto the Landlord such of
        the rights set out in the Schedule as have hitherto been enjoyed over the
        Demised Premises by neighbouring property and the occupier thereof TO
        HOLD the same unto the Tenant for the Term YIELDING AND
        PAYING therefor the yearly rent of £. . . by equal quarterly instalments in
        advance on the Rent Days (the first payment being made on the date hereof
        and the last payment being (if appropriate) of a proportionate sum) AND
        YIELDING AND PAYING as further rent sums equal to the premiums
        from time to time expended by the Landlord in effecting and maintaining
        insurance of the Demised Premises in accordance with the Landlord's
        obligations herein contained such sums to be paid on the Rent Day next
        following the demand therefor.

4.   The Tenant covenants with the Landlord as follows:

4.1   To pay the rent hereby reserved on the days and in the manner aforesaid
        without any deductions whatsoever and without exercising any right of
        set-off.

4.2   To pay interest from the due date until payment on all or any part of any
        instalment of rent hereby reserved and on all other sums covenanted to be
        paid by the Tenant to the Landlord which are not paid within fourteen days
        after the same become due.

4.3   To bear and pay to the appropriate authorities respectively responsible for collecting the same all taxes and outgoings in respect of the Demised Premises including any imposed or becoming payable after the date hereof whether or not of a novel nature but not:

4.3.1   any tax assessed upon the aggregate or any proportion of the income or the value of the assets of the Landlord; or

4.3.2   any tax assessed or payable by reason of the act of the Landlord in granting this Lease.

4.4   To keep the whole of the Demised Premises in good repair and decorative order (damage by any insured risk excepted unless and to the extent that any act or omission of the Tenant renders the insurance money irrecoverable) and to yield up the same and all fixtures annexed thereto in good repair and decorative order to the Landlord on the termination of the Term howsoever determined.[4]

4.5.1   To permit the Landlord or any person authorised by him to enter the Demised Premises at any reasonable time upon at least seven days' notice (or without notice in an emergency) to inspect the state of repair and decoration thereof and on the Landlord giving notice of any want of repair or decoration by reason of a failure to perform the obligations of the Tenant hereunder within three months thereafter (or forthwith in an emergency) to start and diligently to proceed to make good the same.

4.5.2   Upon any failure to comply with a notice under this sub-clause to permit the Landlord to enter the Demised Premises with workmen and others to execute the works required to comply with such notice and to pay to the Landlord on demand the costs thereof notwithstanding that the carrying out of such works in a reasonable and proper manner may cause temporary obstruction annoyance or inconvenience to the Tenant or anyone else.

4.6   Without prejudice to the generality of any other covenant by the Tenant to contribute a fair proportion according to use of the cost of repairing maintaining cleansing and renewing all party walls party structures yards forecourts ways and service media used by the occupier of the Demised Premises in common with the occupier of any other property such fair proportion to be conclusively determined by the Landlord's surveyor.

4.7   To permit the Landlord or any person authorised by him with workmen and others to enter the Demised Premises at any reasonable time on at least seven days' notice (or without notice in an emergency) to repair maintain cleanse or renew the Demised Premises or any adjoining or neighbouring property or any service media serving the same.

4.8   Not to make any alterations or additions to the Demised Premises.

4.9   Not to effect any policy of insurance covering the Demised Premises or any part thereof or addition or fixture thereto.

4.10.1 To the extent that any insurance premium payable in respect of any adjoining or neighbouring property of the Landlord is increased by reason of the use to which the Tenant puts all or any part of the Demised Premises to pay to the Landlord on demand the amount of such increase.

4.10.2 Not to do anything that will or may render void or voidable any policy of insurance covering the Demised Premises or increase the premium payable thereon.

7 BUSINESS TENANCIES

4.11   Not to use the Demised Premises or any part thereof otherwise than for the Permitted Use.

4.12   Not to use the Demised Premises or any part thereof for any dangerous offensive noxious noisome illegal or immoral activity or in a manner which in the opinion of the Landlord (which the Tenant agrees to accept without dispute) is or may become a nuisance annoyance or disturbance to the Landlord or to the owner or occupier of any neighbouring premises and in particular (without prejudice to the generality of the foregoing):

4.12.1 not to bring into or near the Demised Premises anything of an explosive or inflammable nature or to endanger the structure of the buildings erected on the Demised Premises or the floors thereof by overloading;

4.12.2 not to use in or bring into the Demised Premises any form of non-electric portable heater or any form of heater using liquid fuel or gas cylinders;

4.12.3 not to obstruct the area coloured … on the annexed plan or leave any articles thereon or use the same for parking vehicles or for any purpose other than as a means of access to the Demised Premises.

4.13.1 At all times and at the Tenant's expense to comply with the requirements of the Planning Acts insofar as they affect the Demised Premises and (without prejudice to the statutory indemnity in that behalf) to indemnify and keep indemnified the Landlord against all actions proceedings costs expenses claims objections representations or appeals in respect thereof as the Landlord may require.

4.13.2 Not to apply for permission to carry out on the Demised Premises any development requiring permission under the Planning Acts.

4.13.3 Forthwith upon receipt of any notice relating to the development of the Demised Premises or any neighbouring property to deliver a copy thereof to the Landlord and if so required by the Landlord to join with the Landlord at the expense of the Tenant in making representations concerning the same.

4.13.4 Whenever required to permit the Landlord to enter upon the Demised Premises to comply with any requirement lawfully made of him under the Planning Acts by any competent authority notwithstanding that any action reasonably necessary for compliance interferes with the Tenant's enjoyment of the Demised Premises.

4.14.1 At all times to observe and comply with the provisions of or imposed under any statute licence or registration regulating or permitting the use of the Demised Premises for the purpose for which they are for the time being used and the requirements of any competent authority in that connection and at the expense of the Tenant to do all that is necessary to obtain maintain and renew all licences and registrations required by law for the use of the Demised Premises for that purpose.

4.14.2 To comply promptly and at the cost of the Tenant with all orders notices regulations or requirements of any competent authority pursuant to any statute requiring any alteration addition modification or other work on or to the Demised Premises and forthwith to notify the Landlord of the receipt by the Tenant of any such notice regulation or requirement and to deliver to him a copy thereof.

4.15   Not to display any notices or advertisements on the exterior of the Demised Premises or within the Demised Premises but visible from the outside except any to which the Landlord has given prior written consent.

4.16   Not to assign sub-let mortgage charge part with the possession of or share the occupation of the Demised Premises or any part thereof.

4.17.1   In connection with any prospective dealing with the Landlord's interest in the Demised Premises or after notice terminating the Term has been given any prospective letting of the Demised Premises to permit any person on presenting a written authority from the Landlord or the Landlord's agents to inspect the Demised Premises on reasonable prior notice.

4.17.2   To permit the Landlord or any person authorised by him to erect and display on the Demised Premises a board announcing that the same are for sale or (during the last six months of the Term) to let PROVIDED THAT such board does not impede the reasonable conduct of the business of the Tenant on the Demised Premises.

4.18.1   To pay all costs (including solicitor's costs and surveyor's fees) incurred by the Landlord of and incidental to the preparation and service of:

4.18.1.1   a notice under section 146 of the Law of Property Act 1925 notwithstanding that forfeiture is avoided otherwise than by order of the court;

4.18.1.2   a schedule of dilapidations recording breaches of the Tenant's covenant to yield up the Demised Premises in repair at the termination of the Term.

4.18.2   To pay the costs and disbursements of the Landlord's solicitors incurred in the preparation and completion of this Lease (including stamp duty on the counterpart thereof).

4.18.3   To pay all costs (including the expenses and commission of a certificated bailiff) incurred by the Landlord of and incidental to distraining for rent arrears.

4.18.4   To pay all costs and expenses (including solicitor's costs and surveyor's fees) incurred by the Landlord in connection with and incidental to any application made by the Tenant for the consent of the Landlord whether the same be granted refused or proffered subject to any lawful qualifications or conditions or whether the application be withdrawn.

5.   The Landlord covenants with the Tenant as follows:

5.1   That so long as the Tenant is not in breach of any of his obligations hereunder he shall be entitled peaceably and quietly to hold and enjoy the Demised Premises without any lawful interruption by the Landlord or any person claiming under or in trust for the Landlord.

5.2.1   At all times to keep the Demised Premises and all additions thereto of which the Tenant has notified the Landlord insured to the full cost of reinstatement under a policy complying with the terms of this clause.

5.2.2   An insurance policy complies with the terms of this clause if:

5.2.2.1   it provides cover against loss or damage by any of the insured risks to the extent that such cover is for the time being available for buildings of the type on the Demised Premises;

5.2.2.2   it insures an appropriate percentage of the rebuilding costs for professional fees incurred in rebuilding or reinstating any building destroyed or damaged by an insured risk;

5.2.2.3 it is effected in some insurance office of repute or at Lloyds.

6. PROVIDED ALWAYS AND IT IS HEREBY AGREED AND DECLARED as follows:

6.1 If at any time the rent hereby reserved or any part thereof is twenty-one days in arrear (whether formally demanded or not) or if the Tenant has failed to observe or perform any of the lessee's covenants herein contained or if the Tenant or any guarantor of this Lease (or in either case if more than one any of them) being an individual is adjudicated bankrupt or an interim receiver is appointed of the property of the Tenant or being a company goes into liquidation otherwise than for the purposes of amalgamation or reconstruction without insolvency or an administrative receiver of it is appointed or an administration order is made in respect of it or if the Demised Premises are left vacant or unoccupied for a period exceeding thirty days then and in any such case the Landlord may at any time thereafter re-enter upon the Demised Premises or any part thereof in the name of the whole and thereupon the Term shall absolutely determine but without prejudice to any claim by the Landlord against the Tenant for any antecedent breach of any of the covenants herein contained.

6.2 Nothing herein contained shall confer on the Tenant any right to the benefit of or to enforce any covenant or agreement contained in any lease or other instrument relating to any other premises belonging to the Landlord.

6.3 The Landlord gives no warranty express or implied that the use of the Demised Premises for the purposes hereby permitted is in accordance with the provisions of the Planning Acts so far as they relate to the Demised Premises.

6.4 The Landlord named herein shall not be under any liability in respect of the Landlord's obligations hereunder after he has ceased to hold any interest in the Demised Premises.

6.5 The Tenant hereby acknowledges that the Landlord shall be under no liability in respect of injury to any person in the Demised Premises during the Term and undertakes to keep the Landlord indemnified in respect thereof.

6.6 The Tenant shall not be or become entitled to any compensation under the provisions of section 37 of the Landlord and Tenant Act 1954 unless the conditions set forth in sub-section (2) of section 38 of that Act are satisfied in relation to the Tenant claiming compensation.

6.7 This Lease shall not confer or be deemed to include (by implication or otherwise) in favour of the Tenant any rights or privileges not expressly herein set out and the Landlord shall have the power at all times without obtaining any consent from or making any compensation to the Tenant (a) to deal as the Landlord may think fit with any building or buildings or any of the land and property which is now or at any time hereafter held by the Landlord adjoining opposite or near to the Demised Premises and to erect or suffer to be erected thereon any structures whatsoever whether such structures do or do not affect or diminish the light or air which now or at any time or times during the Term is enjoyed by the Tenant or otherwise constitute a nuisance or inconvenience or derogate from the grant hereby made and/or (b) alter the route of any road or service media over or through which any right hereby granted is exercised provided that there are at all times adequate access and provision of services to the Demised Premises (any period during which necessary works are being carried out excepted).

6.8 Any sums payable hereunder by the Tenant shall be deemed to be exclusive of Value Added Tax and the amount of any such tax payable thereon (whether by the Tenant or by the Landlord) shall be paid by the Tenant to the Landlord.

6.9 Section 196 of the Law of Property Act 1925 shall apply to any notice required or authorised by this Lease.

6.10 In distraining for arrears of rent any rent not quantified on the date for payment and any interest on arrears of rent shall be deemed to be payable on the date for payment of rent immediately preceding the date that distress is levied.

6.11 If the Demised Premises are damaged by an insured risk so as to be unfit for occupation or use the Landlord may at any time within three months from the occurrence of such damage give to the Tenant written notice to determine the Term and thereupon the same and everything herein contained shall cease and be void as from the date of the giving of such notice but without prejudice to any right of action or remedy of the Landlord in respect of any antecedent breach of any of the covenants conditions or agreements on the part of the Tenant herein contained.

7. Having been authorised to do so by order of [*name*] County Court on [*date*] under the provision of sub-section (4) of section 38 of the Landlord and Tenant Act 1954 sections 24–28 of that Act shall not apply to this Lease.[5]

8. It is hereby certified that there is no agreement for Lease to which this Lease gives effect.

IN WITNESS whereof this Deed has been executed by the parties hereto the day and year first before written.

SCHEDULE

All rights of way water air drainage passage of gas and electricity and support TOGETHER WITH the right to use and maintain the service media therefor.

7 BUSINESS TENANCIES

SIGNED and delivered as a Deed by
the said [*name*] in the presence of: }

....

....

....

....

SIGNED and delivered as a Deed by
the said [*name*] in the presence of: }

....

....

....

....

Note. Stamp duty based on rent and term.

1   If a court order is to be obtained, the lease must be for a fixed term, although a break clause could
    be included.
2   It may be necessary to be more specific about the rights.
3   It may be necessary to be more specific about the rights.
4   This may be unfair to the Tenant depending on the circumstances.
5   Any agreement relating to a tenancy to which Part II of the 1954 Act applies (unless the Court
    sanctions it) is void under the Landlord and Tenant Act 1954, section 38(1) insofar as it precludes
    the Tenant from making an application or request for a new tenancy. This is so whether the
    contracting out agreement is contained in the lease itself or some other document. This
    prohibition is absolute and applies to every tenancy which comes within Part II of the 1954 Act.
    However, the Court may sanction such agreement to exclude the statutory right to the renewal of
    a tenancy provided that the application for the Court's approval is requested jointly by the
    Landlord and the Tenant before the Agreement is entered into. For the contracting out provisions
    to be effective even with the Court's approval, it must be contained in or endorsed on the
    instrument containing the tenancy.

CHAPTER 8: GRAZING AGREEMENTS

INDEX

8 GRAZING AGREEMENTS

CHAPTER 8: GRAZING AGREEMENTS

INTRODUCTION

There are three precedents in this section:

- A profit à prendre agreement;
- A licence;
- A tenancy agreement.

The detailed terms of each agreement will depend on the outcome of negotiations between the parties. However, the type of agreement to be used also depends to a great extent on tax considerations, particularly if there is to be only one occupier for grazing purposes of the grassland.

The issue is likely to be important principally for capital taxation reasons. Business taper relief and roll-over relief for capital gains tax will be available only if the landowner is occupying the property. Similarly, agricultural relief for inheritance tax purposes (on the basis of occupation) will be available if the agreement is appropriately structured and the landowner is prepared to do sufficient work to prove that he is indeed in occupation. This may be particularly important if the grassland is ancillary to a farmhouse and it is hoped to obtain inheritance tax relief on the house itself. A tenancy will not give any of these tax advantages.

There are various cases establishing that a licence will suffice to give the landowner occupation provided that he is effectively managing the property. See, for example, *CIR v Forsyth-Grant* 1943 SC 528, 25 TC 369.

The safest document is, however, likely to be the profit à prendre agreement which the Country Land and Business Association has encouraged. Accordingly, drafts of both the profit à prendre agreement and the grazing licence appear in this section.

The licence is exclusive but a non-exclusive licence may be safer. The draft can easily be amended to provide for this but must not be a sham.

PRECEDENTS

1   DEED OF PROFIT À PRENDRE

THIS DEED of Profit à Prendre is made the [*date*]

BETWEEN:

(1)   THE OWNER [*name*] of [*address*]

(2)   THE GRAZIER [*name*] of [*address*]

NOW THIS DEED WITNESSES as follows:

1.   IN consideration of the payment of £ . . . (the receipt whereof the Owner hereby acknowledges) the Owner grants to the Grazier the [sole] right of herbage [together with others entitled to a like right] on all those pieces or parcels of land ('the land') and situate at . . . in the County of . . . being OS Numbers . . . on the OS Map for the district . . . Edition . . . TO HOLD unto the Grazier from [*date*] to [*date*].

2.   THE Owner hereby covenants:
2.1   To mow or spray spear thistle, creeping or field thistle, curled dock, broad leaved dock and ragwort.
2.2   To keep fertilised the land every spring and where and when necessary reseed and crop the grass.
2.3   To keep gates fences and ditches in good order other than damage caused by the Grazier his servants or stock.

3.   THE Grazier hereby covenants:
3.1   Not to permit any trespass on the land.
3.2   To use the land for the purpose of grazing [*number and type of animals*] only and not to cut or mow the grass.
3.3   Not to allow any animals other than his own to graze the land.
3.4   Not to allow horses, diseased or quarantined stock or confirmed fence breakers on the land.
3.5   Not to allow more than [. . .] persons on the land.
3.6   To ensure that he his servants or agents and any person attending or for the time being in charge of the livestock present on the land will comply with the Welfare of Farmed Animals (England) Regulations 2000 or any statutory modification or re-enactment of such Regulations for the time being in force.
3.7   To indemnify the Owner in respect of all liabilities and payments including legal costs and expenses incurred by the Owner as a result of proceedings brought in respect of the welfare of livestock under the Agriculture (Miscellaneous Provisions) Act 1968 and the Welfare of Farmed Animals (England) Regulations 2000 or any statutory modification or re-enactment of such Regulations for the time being in force.

3.8   To indemnify the Owner against any claims made by third parties resulting from any activities or negligence by the Grazier on the land.

3.9   Not to assign underlet or part with possession of the grazing right granted by this Deed.

4.   IT IS HEREBY AGREED that the Owner shall have lien upon all the Grazier's animals for the time being pastured on the land for any sum owing or expense incurred for which under this Agreement the Grazier is liable and this lien may be enforced by the sale of any animal or animals belonging to the Grazier for the time being pastured upon the land.

IN WITNESS whereof this Deed has been executed by the parties hereto the day and year first before written.

SIGNED and delivered as a Deed by
the said [*name*] in the presence of: } ....

....

....

....

SIGNED and delivered as a Deed by
the said [*name*] in the presence of: } ....

....

....

....

2   GRAZING AGREEMENT

THIS AGREEMENT is made the [*date*]

1.	**Particulars**	
1.1	the Owner	[*name*] of [*address*]
1.2	the Grazier	[*name*] of [*address*]
1.3	the Plan	ALL THOSE plots of land situate at [*detailed address*] for the purpose of identification only edged red on the Plan and more particularly described in the Schedule to this Agreement
1.5	the Period of Occupation	a period beginning on the [*date*] and ending on the [*date*]
1.6	the Grazing Fee	the sum of £ ... (... pounds)
1.7	the Payment Date	the [*date*]

2.   Interpretation

2.1   Unless the context otherwise requires:

2.1.1   words importing one gender shall be construed as importing any other gender;

2.1.2   words importing the singular shall include the plural and vice versa;

2.1.3   words importing persons shall include corporations;

2.1.4   where there are two or more persons included in the expressions the Owner and/or the Grazier the obligations of such persons under this Agreement shall be deemed to be joint and several.

2.2   The clause headings in this Agreement shall not affect the construction of this Agreement.

2.3   Any reference in this Agreement to a statutory provision shall be deemed to include any later provision substituted for or amending the same.

3.   Right to graze

The Grazier shall have the right to occupy the Land for grazing purposes only during the Period of Occupation.

4.   Grazier's covenants

The Grazier shall:

4.1   Pay to the Owner the Grazing Fee on or before the Payment Date.

4.2   Use the Land for the purpose of grazing by [...] only and for no other purpose.

4.3   Graze and use the Land in a good and husbandlike manner.

4.4 Not allow the Land to be entered upon or in any way used by [. . .] or any vicious or diseased animal. In the event of the Grazier admitting any animal on the Land in contravention of this sub-clause the Owner may treat the animal as a trespasser and impound it at the expense of the Grazier who shall be liable for all loss or damage caused by such animal either by straying or in any other way.

4.5 Not allow the Land to become poached by treading during wet weather conditions and if the Owner or his agent shall certify that any damage is being caused then the Grazier shall upon demand immediately remove his animals.

4.6 Not permit any trespass on the Land but shall not obstruct any rights of way used or enjoyed over the Land prior to the granting of this Agreement.

4.7 Keep all fences ditches and watercourses in proper stockproof condition so as to prevent his animals straying or being injured and indemnify the Owner against all costs claims and demands made by the owners or occupiers of adjoining land or any other person for damages or other money arising from the escape from the Land of all or any of the animals placed by the Grazier upon the Land.

4.8 Preserve all trees or bushes on the Land from injury by animals or otherwise.

4.9 Not sub-let the grazing rights granted by this Agreement nor place upon the Land any agisted animals.

4.10 Not erect any building or structure, nor place any advertisement on the Land.

5. Owner's lien

The Owner shall have a lien upon all the Grazier's animals for the time being depastured on the Land for any sum owing or expense incurred for which under this Agreement the Grazier is liable and this lien may be enforced by the sale of any such animal or animals.

6. Owner's right of entry

The Owner and any person he authorises shall have the right to enter the Land at any time for any reasonable purposes other than for grazing animals there.

[7. Exclusion of milk quota

No milk quota is intended to be transferred by the Owner to the Grazier or vice versa by reason of any change of occupation of the Land in consequence of this Agreement and both parties shall co-operate the one with the other in signing and lodging all appropriate and necessary documents including any required by the Intervention Board the Ministry of Agriculture or other statutory authority or otherwise to ensure so far as is lawfully possible that no such transfer is brought about by reason of this transaction.[1]

8 GRAZING AGREEMENTS

[8.   **Consideration for milk quota**

If notwithstanding the provisions of the preceding clause any milk quota is transferred from either party to the other pursuant to the decision of an arbitrator appointed under the Dairy Produce Quotas Regulations 1997, SI 1997/733 or otherwise the transferee shall forthwith effect at his sole expense the re-transfer to the transferor of the milk quota so transferred or if for reasons beyond his control such re-transfer cannot be effected pay to the transferor all lawfully recoverable losses thereby sustained to include (*inter alia*) all costs incurred in the acquisition of milk quota of comparable butterfat base and usage to replace such milk quota.][1]

9.   **Termination of agreement**

If the Owner requires the whole or any part of the Land for any purpose whatsoever other than for grazing animals on it he shall have the right to determine this Agreement in relation to either the whole or any part of the Land upon giving one month's written notice to the Grazier whereupon the Owner shall refund to the Grazier a proportionate part of the Grazing Fee.

10.   **Owner's right to written notice**

The Owner is entitled by written notice to determine this Agreement forthwith upon the death of the Grazier or upon any breach by the Grazier of any of his obligations under this Agreement.

11.   **No undertaking for new agreement**

It is expressly agreed between the parties and hereby acknowledged by the Grazier that the Owner does not undertake to repeat this Grazing Agreement for another period.

AS WITNESS the hands of the parties hereto the day and year first before written.

SCHEDULE

PARTICULARS OF LAND

OS No.   ACREAGE

SIGNED by the OWNER
in the presence of:

....

....

....

....

SIGNED by the GRAZIER
in the presence of:

}

....

....

....

....

....

---

1   If the term is for more than 10 months and if the land is or has been, within the last 5 years, used
    for milk production, or the grazier uses the land for grazing by dairy cows these clauses should be
    included out of an abundance of caution, in case the agreement could be construed as a tenancy.

---

3   HORSE AND PONY GRAZING AGREEMENT[1]

PARTICULARS

(a)   Date: [*date*]

(b)   The Landlord: [*name*] of [*address*]

(c)   The Tenant: [*name*] of [*address*]

(d)   The Holding: The property described in Schedule 1

(e)   The Term: [*length of term*]

(f)   The Rent: The amount specified in Schedule 5 of this
                               Agreement

(g)   Rent instalments: Equal instalments payable in advance on the Rent
                               Days

(h)   Rent days: [*date*] and [*date*] in each [*period*]

(i)   Permitted purpose: The right to graze for the Tenant's own use and
                               enjoyment no more than [*number*] of the Tenant's
                               horses or ponies on the Holding [and to use the
                               buildings on the Holding only for [stabling and
                               for] purposes ancillary to the exercise of such
                               right] and to the exclusion of any business use

(j)   The Expert   [*name*] of [*address*] and if the Expert shall die or be
                               unwilling to act then such other expert as may be
                               appointed on the application of either party by the
                               President of the Royal Institution of Chartered
                               Surveyors

8 GRAZING AGREEMENTS

THIS AGREEMENT is made on the Date set out in the Particulars
BETWEEN:

(1)   The Landlord named in the Particulars ('the Landlord')
(2)   The Tenant named in the Particulars ('the Tenant')

IT IS AGREED as follows:

1.   Definitions and interpretations
In this Agreement words and phrases used have the meaning assigned to them in schedule 4.

2.   Letting
The Landlord lets the Holding to the Tenant at the Rent for the Term [TOGETHER WITH the rights set out in schedule 2] SUBJECT TO existing rights and other matters affecting the Holding during the Term [and EXCEPTING AND RESERVING to the Landlord the rights set out in schedule 3].

3.   Tenant's agreements
The Tenant agrees with the Landlord:

3.1   *Rent*
To pay the Rent on the days and in the manner required by this Agreement.

3.2   *Outgoings*
To pay all rates, taxes and outgoings whatever relating to the Holding during the Term.

3.3   *Maintenance*
3.3.1   To keep the buildings and fixed equipment on the Holding in their current state of repair and condition [as evidenced by the attached [photographic] schedule of condition].
3.3.2   To keep all fences, hedges and gates in proper stockproof condition so as to prevent his horses or ponies from straying or being injured and so indemnify the Landlord against all costs claims or demands made by the owners or occupiers of any adjoining land or any other persons for damages or other money arising from the escape from the Holding of all or any of the horses or ponies placed upon the Holding by the Tenant.
3.3.3   Not to remove or alter any fence hedge or other boundary on the Holding nor to destroy or damage any trees hedges or fences on the Holding and to ensure that no such damage is caused by the Tenant's horses or ponies.
3.3.4   To keep all ditches and drains clean and free from obstructions.

3.4   *Use and management of the Holding*
3.4.1   Not to use or farm the Holding or any part of it for the purposes of a trade or business.

3.4.2   Not at any time during the Term to use the Holding other than for the Permitted Purpose set out in the Particulars.

3.4.3   Not to do or suffer to be done on the Holding anything which may be or become a nuisance or annoyance to the Landlord or the owners or occupiers of any adjoining land and to indemnify the Landlord against any claim caused by or arising from the Tenant's occupation of the Holding.

3.4.4   Not to sell off or remove from the Holding any hay or straw and not to mow the permanent pasture.

3.4.5   To permit the Landlord to enter the Holding or any part of it on giving to the Tenant reasonable notice (save in the event of an emergency).

3.4.6   To comply with any other restrictions which the Landlord may reasonably require.

3.4.7   Not to allow the Holding to become poached by treading and if the Landlord gives the Tenant written notice that any such damage is in the Landlord's opinion being caused immediately to remove his horses or ponies from the Holding.

3.4.8   Not to bring cause or permit to be done or brought any object or matter or thing upon the Holding by which any policy of insurance of the Landlord might be prejudiced.

3.4.9   Not to bring any diseased animal onto the Holding and to compensate the Landlord for all losses incurred as a result of any diseased animal being on the Holding.

3.4.10   On entering the Holding to give all necessary notices and make all necessary applications and payments to preserve any existing licence granted in respect of the Holding under the Water Resources Act 1991 or any similar enactment and subsequently to continue the licence in force during the Tenancy and not at any time by any act or omission to jeopardise the licence nor to surrender it without the consent in writing of the Landlord.

3.4.11   On the termination of the Tenancy to make such application for the continuance or renewal of the licence as may be requisite for the time being under regulations then in force to preserve the licence for the benefit of the Landlord or his nominee without payment.

3.4.12   Not to enter into any agreement or licence for the supply of water from any spring or well pond stream watercourse or underground water supply on the Holding to any adjoining or neighbouring premises and to reimburse to the Landlord on demand all charges costs and expenses reasonably incurred by the Landlord in connection with the provision or the improved provision of water to the Holding.

3.5   *Alienation*

Not to assign sublet part with or share possession or occupation of the Holding or any part of it.

3.6   *Alteration of buildings*

Not to alter remove or make additions to any building or other item of fixed equipment or erect any new buildings or other item of fixed equipment or make any other improvements to the Holding.

8 GRAZING AGREEMENTS

3.7 *Legislation*

3.7.1 At all times immediately upon receipt of any notice order direction or other matter whatever affecting or likely to affect the Holding to produce the same for the Landlord's inspection and to permit the Landlord to take a copy.

3.7.2 To comply immediately with and give sufficient effect to every notice direction or other matter whatever affecting or likely to affect the Holding served or made by any Authority.

3.7.3 Fully to comply with all legal obligations relating to the Holding and to keep the Landlord effectively indemnified against all actions proceedings costs expenses claims and demands in respect of any matter contravening any Legal Obligation.

3.8 *Yield up*
On termination of this Agreement to yield up the Holding to the Landlord with vacant possession in a state of repair and condition which is consistent with the proper performance of the Tenant's agreements and obligations in this Agreement.

4. Landlord's agreement
The Landlord agrees with the Tenant that if the Tenant observes and performs the Tenant's agreements and obligations in this Agreement the Tenant may peaceably hold and enjoy the Holding during the Term without any lawful interruption or disturbance from or by the Landlord or any person claiming through under or in trust for the Landlord.

5. Mutual agreements

5.1 *Forfeiture*
Without prejudice to any other rights of the Landlord if:

5.1.1 the whole or part of the Rent remains unpaid 21 days after becoming due (whether demanded or not); or

5.1.2 any of the Tenant's agreements in this Agreement are not performed or observed; or

5.1.3 the Tenant:

5.1.3.1 proposes or enters into any composition or arrangement with his creditors generally or any class of his creditors; or

5.1.3.2 is the subject of any judgment or order made against him which is not complied with within 7 days or is the subject of any execution distress sequestration or other process levied upon or enforced against any part of his undertaking property assets or revenue; or

5.1.3.3 being a company:

5.1.3.3.1 is the subject of a petition presented or an order made or a resolution passed or analogous proceedings taken for appointing an administrator of or winding up such company; or

5.1.3.3.2 an incumbrancer takes possession or exercises or attempts to exercise any power of sale or a receiver or administrative receiver is appointed of the whole or any part of the undertaking property assets or revenues of such company; or

5.1.3.3.3 stops payment or agrees to declare a moratorium or becomes or is deemed to be insolvent or unable to pay its debts within the meaning of the Insolvency Act 1986, section 123; or

5.1.3.4 being an individual:

5.1.3.4.1 is the subject of a bankruptcy petition or bankruptcy order; or

5.1.3.4.2 is the subject of an application or order or appointment under the Insolvency Act 1986, section 253 or section 273 or section 286; or

5.1.3.4.3 is unable to pay or has no reasonable prospect of being able to pay his debts within the meaning of the Insolvency Act 1986, sections 267 and 268; or

5.1.4 any event occurs or proceedings are taken with respect to the Tenant in any jurisdiction to which it is subject which has an effect equivalent or similar to any of the events mentioned in clause 5.1.3,

then and in any such cases the Landlord may at any time (and notwithstanding the waiver of any previous right of re-entry) upon giving the tenant two months' prior notice in writing re-enter the Holding whereupon the tenancy granted by this Agreement will absolutely determine but without prejudice to any right of action of the Landlord in respect of any previous breach by the Tenant of this Agreement.

5.2 *Break clause*

5.2.1 Either party to this Agreement will be entitled on the death of the other or (in the case of more than one landlord or tenant) on the death of [any or the last] of them to terminate this Agreement by serving on the relevant deceased party's personal representatives not less than [two months' or six months' or one year's] prior written notice of his intention to do so [such notice to expire at the end of a period of the tenancy].

5.2.2 If the Landlord wishes to determine this Agreement at any time during the Term and shall give to the Tenant not less than one year's notice in writing then upon the expiration of such notice the Term shall immediately cease and determine but without prejudice to the respective rights of either party in respect of any antecedent claim or breach of covenant.

5.3 *Dispute resolution*

5.3.1 In the event of any dispute arising under this Agreement between the parties the same will be determined by the Expert named in the Particulars who is to act as independent expert and not as an arbitrator and who is to be appointed on the written application of either party.

5.3.2 The appointment of the Expert is to specify that his decision will be made following representations in writing by the parties and the costs of the Expert will be borne as directed by the Expert and his decision will be final and binding on all parties.

8 GRAZING AGREEMENTS

5.4   *Whole agreement*
        This Agreement contains the whole agreement between the Landlord and
        the Tenant concerning the Holding.

6.   Agreement for tenancy (stamp duty certificate)
        It is certified that there is no prior agreement for tenancy to which this
        Agreement gives effect.

IN WITNESS whereof this Deed has been executed by the parties hereto the day
and year first before written.

SCHEDULE 1

THE HOLDING

ALL THAT land which for the purposes of identification only is edged red on the
plan annexed hereto.

SCHEDULE 2

RIGHTS GRANTED TO THE TENANT

A right of way for the Tenant his agents and authorised persons at all times with or
without vehicles plant machinery or animals over the track [shown for the purpose
of identification only] coloured [brown] on the attached plan].

SCHEDULE 3

RESERVATIONS TO THE LANDLORD

1.   All mines minerals quarries stones sand brick earth clay gravel turf
        petroleum and its relative hydrocarbons and all other gases and substances
        in or under the Holding of kind ordinarily worked or removed by
        underground or surface working with power to the Landlord and all
        persons authorised by him to enter on the Holding to search for win dress
        and make merchantable and carry them away from the Holding and to
        execute all incidental works including the right to let down the surface of
        the land the Tenant being paid reasonable compensation for all damage
        caused to him by the exercise of such power.

2.   The right to grant any wayleave contract easement or licence to any public or local authority or public utility company or other company or persons with a right to authorise servants and agents of such parties with or without vehicles machinery and plant to enter upon the Holding and carry out their works (subject to the payment of reasonable compensation for damage provided a claim in writing is made by the Tenant to the Landlord within a reasonable time from the occurrence of the damage) together with the benefit of all present or future such contracts agreements for easements or licenses and all rents and other money payable under them and the power to carry out on the Holding at the Landlord's cost anything required to be done under them by the Landlord.

3.   All timber and other trees saplings pollards and underwood with liberty for the Landlord and all persons authorised by him to enter upon the Holding in order to mark fell cut and carry them away and to replant them and to cart them from the Holding without making any payment to the Tenant for the use but making reasonable compensation to the Tenant for any damage done in the exercise of the rights reserved providing a claim in writing is made by the Tenant to the Landlord within a reasonable time.

4.

4.1   All the game wildfowl woodcock snipe and other wild birds listed in the Second Schedule to the Wildlife and Countryside Act 1981 their nests and eggs together with the exclusive right for the Landlord and all persons authorised by him to go upon the Holding with such equipment and persons as the Landlord authorises for the purposes of shooting fishing hawking sporting taking preserving and rearing such wildlife and also the right to hunt or permit hunting on foot or with horses and hounds.

4.2   Subject to the Ground Game Acts 1880 (as amended by s 12 of the Wildlife and Countryside Act 1981) and 1906, the right for the Landlord and all persons authorised by him to kill shoot and take away rabbits hares pigeons or any other pests.

5.   The right for the Landlord and all persons authorised by him with or without vehicles horses machinery and plant to enter on any part of the Holding at all reasonable times for all the above and all reasonable purposes and in particular but without prejudice to the generality of the above the right to run pipes drains conduits cables wires or other works (either already existing or any new ones) for the benefit of any other part of the Landlord's estate and the right to carry out works for the benefit of any other part of the same estate the Tenant being paid reasonable compensation for damage caused to them by the exercise of the right for the benefit of any other part of the same estate.

8 GRAZING AGREEMENTS

SCHEDULE 4

DEFINITIONS AND INTERPRETATION

1. **Definitions**

1.1 'Authority' means any statutory public local or other authority or any court of law or any government department or any of their duly authorised officers.

1.2 'Enactment' means

1.2.1 any Act of Parliament or

1.2.2 any European Community Legislation or decrees having effect of law in the United Kingdom.

1.3 'Holding' means the land (including all buildings and fixed equipment on the land) set out in the Particulars as more fully described in schedule 1.

1.4 'Legal Obligations' means any obligation from time to time created by any Enactment or Authority which relates to the Holding or its use.

1.5 'Particulars' means the Particulars page set out at the beginning of this Agreement.

1.6 'Rent' means the sums of rent set out in the Particulars payable by the instalments set out in the Particulars.

1.7 'Term' means the term of the tenancy set out in the Particulars.

2. **Interpretation**

In this Agreement unless the context otherwise requires:

2.1 words importing any gender include every gender;

2.2 words importing the singular number include the plural number and vice versa;

2.3 words importing persons include firms companies and corporations and vice versa;

2.4 references to a numbered clause or schedule are references to the relevant clause in or schedule to this Agreement;

2.5 references in any schedule to this Agreement to numbered paragraphs relate to the numbered paragraphs of that schedule;

2.6 where any obligation is undertaken by two or more persons jointly they are to be jointly and severally liable in respect of that obligation;

2.7 any obligation on any party not to do or omit to do anything is to include an obligation not to allow that thing to be done or omitted to be done;

2.8 any party who agrees to do something will be deemed to fulfil that obligation if that party procures that it is done;

2.9 the headings to the clauses schedules and paragraphs of this Agreement will not affect the interpretation;

2.10 any sum payable by one party to the other is to be exclusive of Value Added Tax which will where it is chargeable be paid in addition to the sum in question at the time when the sum in question is due to be paid;

2.11 any reference to an Enactment includes the reference to that Enactment as amended or replaced from time to time and to any subordinate legislation or bye-law made under that Enactment.

SCHEDULE 5

RENT

In this Schedule:

1. 'the Index' means the Index of retail prices published by HM Government;

2. 'the Relevant Percentage' means such percentage as is equal to the percentage increase (if any) in the figure at which the Index stands at the relevant date over the figure for the Index last published prior to the date hereof PROVIDED THAT in the event of any change after the date hereof in the reference base used to compile the Index the figure taken to be shown in the Index after such change shall be the figure which would have been shown in the Index had the reference base current at the date hereof been retained or in the event of it becoming impossible or impracticable by reason of any change after the date hereof in the methods used to compile the Index or for any other reason whatsoever to calculate the said percentage increase under the foregoing provision then such percentage increase shall be that calculated to give the same purchasing power at the relevant date as at the date hereof the amount of such percentage to be agreed between the parties hereto or in default of agreement to be determined at their joint expense by such independent person as they shall agree or in default as shall be appointed by the President of the Institute of Chartered Accountants in England and Wales such determination to be made as an expert and to be final and binding on all persons concerned;

3. during the Term the rent in every year commencing on the date hereof and subsequent anniversaries thereof (and proportionately for that part of a year) shall be £ ... together with the Relevant Percentage of such sum calculated at the commencement of each such year.

SIGNED and delivered as a Deed by
the said [*name*] in the presence of:

....

....

....

....

SIGNED and delivered as a Deed by
the said [*name*] in the presence of:

....

....

....

SIGNED and delivered as a Deed by
the said [*name*] in the presence of:

....

....

....

---

1   Stamp duty based on rent.

CHAPTER 9: SPORTING RIGHTS

INDEX

CHAPTER 9: SPORTING RIGHTS

INTRODUCTION

Farmers need to maximise their assets and, accordingly, in appropriate cases, shooting may be let off. This may not be possible if the farmer is a tenant and the rights are reserved to the landlord, or if a freeholder and the rights are reserved out of the conveyance or transfer to the farmer. The tenancy agreement/deeds should be checked carefully before such an agreement is entered into. The agreement in this chapter refers to land primarily destined for shooting purposes. If it is ancillary to farmland, the landowner might wish to impose more restrictions on the lessee.

Again, to protect his interests under inheritance tax legislation, it will be desirable for the landowner to remain in occupation for agricultural purposes. However, if the land is principally a shooting property, both income and sale proceeds, if it is sold, are likely to be chargeable to VAT; there is also likely to be a rates issue.

PRECEDENTS

1   SPORTING RIGHTS: LONG-TERM AGREEMENT

THIS DEED is made the [*date*]

1.	**Particulars**	
1.1	the Grantor	[*name*] of [*address*]
		(which expression shall where the context admits include his successors in title)
1.2	the Grantee	[*name*] of [*address*]
		(which expression shall where the context admits include his successors in title)
1.3	the Plan	the plan annexed hereto
1.4	the Land	the Land of the Grantor described in the First Schedule hereto
1.5	the Rights of Access	the rights of access referred to in the First Schedule hereto
1.6	the Buildings	the Buildings (if any) coloured ... on the Plan
1.7	the Sporting Rights	the exclusive right to shoot sport kill and carry away game (other than by coursing) from the Land
1.8	Game	the game specified in the Second Schedule
1.9	Ground Game	the Ground Game as defined in the Ground Game Act 1880 and the Ground Game (Amendment) Act 1906
1.10	the Term	... years from the [*date*]
1.11	the Fee	the sum of £ ... together with VAT yearly in advance (subject to the provision for review hereinafter contained) the first payment to be made on the signing hereof and subsequent payments to be made on the [*date*] in each year
1.12	the Return Date	the [*date*] in each year of the Term

| 1.13 | Estate Management | the right of the Grantor to carry out on the Land all normal acts (including the creation and demolition of buildings construction of roads and paths and the laying of pipes and cables) which a prudent landowner would do to ensure the good management of the Land |
| 1.14 | the Rate of Interest | ...% above the base lending rate from time to time of [*name*] Bank plc |

2. Interpretation

Unless the context otherwise requires:

2.1 words importing one gender shall be construed as importing any other gender;

2.1.1 words importing the singular shall include the plural and vice versa;

2.1.2 words importing persons shall include corporations;

2.1.3 where there are two or more persons included in the expressions the Grantor and/or the Grantee the obligations of such persons under this Agreement shall be deemed to be joint and several.

2.2 The clause headings in this Agreement shall not affect the construction of this Agreement.

2.3 Any reference in this Agreement to a statutory provision shall be deemed to include any later provision substituted for or amending the same.

3. Grant exceptions and reservations

In consideration of the Grantee's covenants hereinafter set out and of the Fee the Grantor grants to the Grantee the Sporting Rights over and upon the Land and the right to kill and take Ground Game and to shoot and trap all vermin and demises to the Grantee the Buildings TOGETHER WITH the Rights of Access and the right to enter on and pass over the Land for the exercise of the Sporting Rights and for the purpose of preserving and rearing the Game SUBJECT TO the provisions of the Fourth Schedule but RESERVING to the Grantor the rights of good Estate Management and the rights of all persons in occupation of any parts of the Land as tenants of the Grantor whether such rights arise under a tenancy or by general law TO HOLD the same unto the Grantee for the Term paying throughout the Term (subject as hereinafter provided) the Fee PROVIDED THAT on the expiry of the ... year of the term hereby granted and the expiry of each succeeding ... year the Grantor may increase the rent hereby reserved provided that he gives the Grantee not less than three months' notice of his intention so to do such notice to specify the rent payable from its expiry.

4. Covenants by the grantee

The Grantee covenants with the Grantor to comply with the conditions set out in the Third Schedule hereto.

5. **Covenants by the grantor**

The Grantor covenants with the Grantee that he will comply with the conditions set out in the Fourth Schedule hereto subject to the Grantee complying with the conditions set out in the Third Schedule hereto.

6. **Provisos**

It is agreed that the provisions of the Fifth Schedule hereto shall apply to this Deed.

IN WITNESS whereof this Deed has been executed by the parties hereto the day and year first before written.

FIRST SCHEDULE

THE LAND

ALL THAT [*description of land*]

TOGETHER WITH a right of access to and egress from the Land over and along the roads marked ... on the Plan with or without vehicles AND ALSO a right to park not more than ... vehicles on the area marked ... on the Plan.

SECOND SCHEDULE

THE GAME

Such of the following (and no other) as are for the time being lawful to kill or take: [*insert appropriate game*];

all vermin rabbits hares grey squirrels stoats and weasels.

THIRD SCHEDULE

GRANTEE'S OBLIGATIONS

1. To pay the Fee and VAT thereon in the manner specified

2. To indemnify the Grantor against:

2.1 all rates taxes assessments duties impositions and outgoings charged assessed or imposed on the Land or the owner or occupier thereof in respect of the Buildings or Sporting Rights;

2.2 VAT chargeable in respect of any payment made by the Grantee under this deed or in respect of any payment made by the Grantor on behalf of the Grantee.

3. To protect preserve and keep a reasonable stock of Game on the Land and to preserve nests eggs and young of the Game from destruction and interference and in the last year of the Term to introduce on to the Land a reasonable stock of Game for breeding purposes the number thereof to be agreed between the Grantor and the Grantee.

4.

4.1 To keep down the Ground Game and control the vermin on the Land to prevent them causing injury or damage to the Land crops woods and valuations of the Grantor or his tenants.

4.2 Not to use any spring trap or snares except in accordance with the Pests Act 1954.

4.3 Not to cause any damage to the Land woods banks fences hedged crops access roads footpaths or other property of the Grantor or his tenants and to pay full compensation to the Grantor or his tenants for any damage so caused.

5. To exercise the Sporting Rights by legal methods only and during the proper seasons and not without the written consent of the Grantor to use any guns other than single- or double-barrelled shotguns not exceeding twelve bore in calibre.

6. To employ a gamekeeper to supervise the Land to protect the Game and to prevent poaching and trespassing.

7. To give notice to the Grantor of any claims made by a third party in respect of the Sporting rights and to permit the Grantor to take proceedings in the name of the Grantee (but at the expense of the Grantor) against any such claims.

8. Not to assign underlet or transfer the Sporting Rights or any part of them without the written consent of the Grantor (such consent not to be unreasonably withheld).

9. To comply with the provisions of the Wildlife and Countryside Act 1981 and ensure that the natural flora and fauna are protected and preserved.

10. To indemnify the Grantor against all proceedings costs claims and expenses arising from the grant of Sporting Rights and the demise (except to the intent that the same shall have been caused by the negligence of the Grantor his servant or agent) PROVIDED THAT the Grantor may not settle or compromise any such claim or proceedings without the written consent of the Grantee (such consent not to be unreasonably withheld).

11. To effect with a reputable insurance company or underwriter proper insurance against all liability arising out of the exercise of the Sporting Rights in such sum as the Grantor shall approve (but in any event not less than £ ...) and to produce to the Grantor the policy and the receipt for the last premium due.

12. On or before the Return Date in each year of the Term to produce to the Grantor a return of all Game (including Ground Game) killed in the preceding twelve months.

13.

13.1 To use the Buildings only for the occupation of a person employed as a gamekeeper in accordance with paragraph 6 of this Schedule.

13.2 To ensure at all times that the occupation of the Buildings is not granted under a tenancy but granted only to a person occupying the Buildings under the terms only of his employment.

13.3 To insure at all times the Buildings in the joint names of the Grantor and Grantee with a reputable insurance company or underwriter against all normal risks covered by a normal comprehensive policy and such special rent as the Grantor might require for such sum as the Grantor shall from time to time require and to produce to the Grantor on demand the policy and the receipt for the last premium due.

13.4 To maintain the Buildings in good and tenantable repair and condition both internally and externally.

13.5 On the determination of the Term hereby granted to yield up the Buildings with vacant possession.

14. To pay interest on all monies due under this deed which are not paid within seven days of the date upon which they fall due (whether formally demanded or not) at the Rate of Interest.

15. At the end or sooner determination of the Term hereby granted peaceably to yield up the Sporting Rights and the Buildings to the Grantor.

FOURTH SCHEDULE

GRANTOR'S OBLIGATIONS

1. The Grantee may peaceably enjoy the Sporting Rights and the demise without interference from the Grantor or any person claiming under him.

2. Subject to the right of good Estate Management herein reserved the Grantor will not without the written consent of the Grantee (such consent not to be unreasonably withheld):

2.1 cut fell or trim woodlands or coverts on the Land;

2.2 destroy hedges banks and undergrowth on the Land;

2.3 use any pesticides chemicals or other noxious substances which cause or may cause harm to the Game (except such substances properly used for the control of vermin).

3. To ensure that the method of Estate Management of the Land is conducted in such a way as to prevent harm to the Game.

FIFTH SCHEDULE

PROVISOS

1. The Grantor will be liable to the Grantee (notwithstanding Paragraph 10 of the Third Schedule) whether to person or property due to anything on the Land causing a danger but only if the Grantor has received written notice of the danger and has failed to remove repair or make safe the same within ninety days of receipt of such notice.

2. The Grantor may determine the grant of the Sporting Rights and the demise by twenty-one days' notice in writing to the Grantee (but without prejudice to any antecedent rights of action by either party) in any one of the following events:

2.1 if the rent is twenty-one days or more in arrear;

2.2 if the Grantee becomes bankrupt or a receiver is appointed to manage his affairs;

2.3 if the Grantee executes any assignment for the benefit of or makes any arrangement with his creditors;

2.4 if the Grantee being a company goes into liquidation (except for voluntary liquidation for the purpose of reconstruction or amalgamation) or has a receiver or administrative receiver appointed;

2.5 if there is any breach of the Grantee's obligations as set out in the Third Schedule hereto.

3. Either party may determine the grant of Sporting Rights at the end of the . . . year and any succeeding year by giving six months' notice in writing to the other (but without prejudice to any antecedent rights of action by either party).

4. The Law of Property Act 1925 as amended by the Recorded Delivery Act 1962 applies to any notice served under this Deed.

5.

5.1 Any dispute between the parties in relation to this Deed is to be referred to arbitration for determination by a single arbitrator under the Arbitration Act 1996.

5.2 The arbitrator is to be agreed in writing by the parties or failing such agreement within one month is to be nominated by the President of the Country Land and Business Association.

SIGNED and delivered as a Deed by
the said [*name*] in the presence of:

....

....

....

....

SIGNED and delivered as a Deed by
the said [*name*] in the presence of: }

....

....

....

....

CHAPTER 10: MILK QUOTA

INDEX

10 MILK QUOTA

CHAPTER 10: MILK QUOTA

INTRODUCTION

In view of their economic importance, it is felt that milk quotas deserve a chapter of their own. It is extremely important to consider the quota implications on any dealing with a dairy farm, or farmland which has been used for milk production purposes in the broadest sense (see *Puncknowle Farms v Kane* [1985] 3 All ER 790; (1985) 275 EG 1283) during the period of five years before the transaction giving rise to a change of occupation.

Milk quota will be registered in the name of the producer.

Milk quota can be sold with or without land. Regulation 11 of the Dairy Produce Quotas Regulations 1997 ('the Regulations') makes provision for the sale without land. In this event the Intervention Board must give its prior consent and there are restrictions on the acquisition of further quota by the transferor and the disposal of quota by the transferee during the current and following quota year. These restrictions mean that the disposal of milk quota without land is relatively uncommon.

Quota transfer documentation should be obtained from the Intervention Board and is updated in each milk quota year which commences on 1 April in each year.

Most permanent transfers of milk quota take place on the basis of a short-term letting (using a short form FBT agreement) of land for more than 10 months (the minimum period stipulated in the Regulations) – usually 11 months. This is because under Regulation 7(5) a letting for less than 10 months is disregarded. The Ministry of Agriculture has indicated that it will not accept that more than 20,000 litres per hectare can be a reasonable apportionment of milk quota. If it does exceed this litreage the transfer will automatically be referred to the Intervention Board for checking. This is in addition to the 'spot checks' carried out by the Board from time to time. This is not stated in any of the Regulations. It is a Ministry guideline. The apportionment of milk quota should be in proportion to areas used for milk production during the five years preceding the quota transfer.

Milk quota should be transferred with occupation of the land when the tenancy is granted. At the conclusion of the tenancy the quota remains with the transferee, the land returning to the transferor free of quota.

There is often a contracting agreement whereby the occupier of an adjoining farm (preferably not the vendor of the quota) carries out works on behalf of the tenant quota transferee. A package of relevant documents appears in this chapter. In addition to these documents the Intervention Board Form MQ1 will need to be completed and a crop sale agreement may sometimes be required, to complete the package (not included here because of the wide variety).

In connection with the disposal of all or part of a dairy farm, or land which has been used for milk production during the last five years, the quota implications must be borne in mind. Reference may be made to the contract provisions in Chapter 3 for a clause preventing quota transferring. The practitioner must bear in mind the apportionment of quota rules considered in *Puncknowle Farms v Kane* [1985] 3 All ER 790 and *Posthumus v Oosterwoud* [1992] 2 CMLR 336. See also the Partition Deed included in Chapter 3.

Moving from one holding to another is also fraught with difficulty. See *Holdcroft v Staffordshire County Council* (1994) 28 EG 131 for a horror story. Arrangements can be made to transfer quota based on the usual form of transfers with land which will involve the creation of a tenancy in a different name. The land can be sold with quota and fresh land acquired with quota. Most commonly, there is a period of time when both farms are occupied and the registration is moved. However, this cannot be regarded as free from risk and appropriate indemnities and warnings must be given and taken.

Reference is made to milk quota in the relevant tenancy agreements in Chapters 4 and 5. Tenancies created before 2 April 1984, and renewals of or succession to those tenancies, are covered by the provisions of s 13 of and Schedule 1 to the Agriculture Act 1986. These provide for quota compensation to be paid to a tenant subject to a claim being made within the appropriate time-scale. The rules are extremely complicated. A questionnaire for calculating this compensation is included in this chapter for reference.

Practitioners must note that this does not affect AHA 1986 tenancies created on or after 6 April 1984 (other than certain succession tenancies) or farm business tenancies. Compensation will depend in the case of AHA 1986 tenancies on the terms agreed, and in the case of farm business tenancies on the terms agreed, subject perhaps to the implications of the provisions relating to compensation for improvements, where appropriate.

It is important to consider to whom the quota belongs as mentioned in the introduction to Chapter 1.

Milk quota is also considered in the surrender agreement and surrender (precedents 7 and 8) in Chapter 4.

For a useful guide, the Intervention Board publishes some guidance notes which can be obtained, free of charge, by telephoning its helpline number in Reading. Currently, that number is 0118 968 7888.

PRECEDENTS

1 MILK QUOTA TRANSFERS – ENQUIRIES BEFORE CONTRACT

As to the Quota	
1. Please provide a copy of the Vendor's Quota Notification letter for the current producer year	
2. Please provide a copy of the Vendor's latest Milk Statement	
3. Is the Quota registered solely in the name of the Vendor? If not: (a) in whose name is it registered; (b) please confirm that all the registered holders will sign the appropriate documents; (c) if any registered holder will not be signing personally please state what alternative arrangements are proposed and supply a copy of any written authority	
4. (a) Is the Vendor still producing milk? (b) If so, what is the expected date for cessation of production?	
5. Please specify: (a) the extent to which the Quota to be transferred has been used to date; (b) the expected user to the operative date of transfer	
6. Please state the butterfat base applicable to the Quota to be transferred	
7. (a) Is this transfer of part only or the entirety of the Quota being sold by the Vendor? (b) If of part only, please list the parties and quantities involved with the relevant areas of land to which the Quota attaches	
8. Please confirm that the Quota has been apportioned to the land based upon the areas of land used for milk production during the last five years	

10 MILK QUOTA

As to the Quota	
9. What is the proposed date of transfer of the Quota?	
As to the land	
10. Please confirm that the land comprising part of the Vendor's Holding which is being used for Quota transfer purposes ('the Transfer Land'): (a) has been used for milk production throughout the last five years; (b) has not previously been used for the purpose of effecting any transfer of Milk Quota	
11. (a) Is the Transfer Land vested in the sole name(s) of the Vendors(s)? (b) If not, who is/are the owners(s)?	
12. Please identify precisely the parts of the Transfer Land which in relation to the Vendor are: (a) freehold; (b) held under a tenancy	
13. In relation to any land occupied under a tenancy, please supply a copy of any relevant document	
14. (a) Is there any existing Mortgage or Legal Charge on the Transfer Land? (b) If so, please: (i) give the full name and address of the Lender; (ii) produce a copy of the Lender's consent to the Transfer and also confirm that the Lender has agreed to sign the relevant section of the Intervention Board Transfer	
15. (a) Do any other parties have an interest in the Transfer Land (Landlord, mortgagee etc)? (b) If so, please confirm that all those with an interest will sign the appropriate documents. (c) If any such person will not be signing personally, state what alternative arrangements are proposed and supply a copy of any written authority	

As to the land

16 (a) Is the Vendor selling the Transfer Land to which the Quota is attached? (b) If so, please supply a copy of (or certified extract from) the Contract for Sale to show that the Quota is excluded from passing with the Transfer Land	
17. (a) Is the Vendor intending to sell the Transfer Land during the period of the Purchaser's tenancy? (b) If so, please confirm that the purchaser of the land has been advised of this Quota sale and produce evidence of confirmation on the part of the purchaser that no claim will be made in respect of the Quota	

Generally

18. Please confirm that the Vendor is not aware of any past present or potential court or arbitration proceedings which affects or may affect the Transfer Land or the Quota being sold.	

Dated this [*date*]

Signed: ....

10 MILK QUOTA

2   MILK QUOTA SALE AGREEMENT (WITH LAND)

Table of Contents

Particulars

Date of agreement:	....
The Seller:	....
The Buyer:	....

Quota: ....[wholesale/direct sales slom] litres of milk
                                quota
                           complying with the Quota Specification

Quota specification
   board ref: ....
   butterfat base: .... per cent
   unused: .... litres
   used: .... litres

Compensation rate: .... pence per litre

Contract date: The date of this Agreement

Completion: The date on which the Board issues written confirmation of
                      the registration of the Quota in the Buyer's name

THIS AGREEMENT is made on the Date set out in the Particulars
BETWEEN:
(1)   the Seller and
(2)   the Buyer

IT IS HEREBY AGREED that:

1.   Defined terms

In this Agreement the terms defined in the Particulars and the Schedule
bear the meanings there set out.

2.   Quota transfer

2.1   Pursuant to the Tenancy Agreement in respect of land forming part of the
Seller's Holding and in accordance with the Regulations the Seller shall
transfer to the Buyer the Quota for the Price on the terms of this
Agreement to the intent that upon registration by the Board the Quota will
be amalgamated with and form part of the milk quota now registered in the
Buyer's name (if any) and will be available from the Contract Date for the
continuing use of the Buyer or for his benefit.

2.2   This Agreement and the Tenancy Agreement together form a single
transaction for the sale of the Quota and both have been completed
simultaneously.

3.   Seller's warranties and undertakings

3.1   The Seller warrants:

3.1.1   that the Quota is correctly registered in his name and that he is authorised
on behalf of himself and all those for whose benefit the Quota is held to sell
the same to the Buyer;

3.1.2   that he has complied with the requirements of the Board as set out in the
Transfer Form and the explanatory notes thereto;

3.1.3   that all parties with an Interest in the Seller's Holding have signed the
relevant section of the Transfer Form;

3.1.4   that he has correctly determined his butterfat adjusted deliveries made up to
the Contract Date and that his said deliveries ('the Seller's Deliveries')
permit the transfer of the Quota to the Buyer with the Quota Specification;

3.1.5   that the apportionment of the Quota to the land comprised in the Tenancy
Agreement complies with the Regulations and that he is not prohibited by
contract or otherwise from entering into the Tenancy Agreement in
respect of that land;

3.1.6   that in the twelve month period preceding the Current Quota Year he
either produced against or leased out some of the milk quota registered in
his name and that so far as he is aware no action is being taken by the Board
to confiscate or otherwise amend the milk quota registered in his name;

3.1.7   that he has not converted the Quota from wholesale to direct sales or vice
versa in the Current Quota Year and that he is not restricted by contract or
in any other way from transferring the Quota to the Buyer;

3.1.8   that he has not acquired milk quota without land under Regulation 11 of
the Regulations in the period commencing twelve months before the
Current Quota Year and ending on the Contract Date;

10 MILK QUOTA

3.1.9   that he has not sold or contracted to sell the Quota or applied for the transfer of the Quota to any third party.

3.2   The Seller undertakes to inform his Purchaser within seven days of the Contract Date of the change in the milk quota registered in his name as a result of the transfer of the Quota under this Agreement.

4.   Buyer's warranties and undertaking

4.1   The Buyer warrants:

4.1.1   that he is a Producer registered with a Purchaser and engaged in milk production and supplying milk or milk products to the Purchaser;

4.1.2   that he has not transferred milk quota without land from his Holding under Regulation 11 of the Regulations in the period commencing twelve months before the Current Quota Year and ending on the Contract Date;

4.1.3   that he has complied with the requirements of the Board as set out in the Transfer Form and the explanatory notes thereto.

4.2   The Buyer undertakes that he will inform his Purchaser within seven days of the Contract Date of the change in the milk quota registered in his name as a result of the transfer of the Quota under this Agreement.

5.   Contract

5.1   On the Contract Date the Buyer shall pay the Price (in cleared funds) to the Seller's Agents to be held by them on the terms of this Agreement and shall hand a completed Transfer Form to the Seller's Agents.

5.2   On the Contract Date the Seller shall send the completed Transfer Form to the Board.

6.   Completion

6.1   The Seller's Agents shall hold the Price together with any rent or other sum payable under the Tenancy Agreement in a stakeholder account ('the Stakeholder Account') until Completion whereupon the Seller's Agents shall immediately release to the Seller the above-mentioned sums (together with any interest earned) subject to deduction of any commission due to the Seller's Agents.

6.2   On receipt of the said sums the Seller shall send a value added tax ('VAT') invoice (if appropriate) to the Buyer.

7.   Co-operation with the Board

7.1   The Seller and the Buyer agree that they shall co-operate with the Board in disclosing any documentation signing any further documentation and/or taking any further steps to give effect to the transfer of the Quota in accordance with this Agreement.

7.2   The Seller and the Buyer shall take all necessary steps to ensure that any milk quota not transferred or not intended to be transferred by this Agreement remains registered in their respective names or for their benefit and will be available for their continued use and benefit AND if milk quota is transferred between the parties contrary to the terms of this Agreement the transferee of such milk quota shall compensate the transferor to the extent of all lawfully recoverable losses including the cost to the transferor at the time of such transfer of replacing the milk quota and all associated costs.

7.3 If quantification of the loss suffered as described in the above clause is or may be impossible whether by reason of milk quota having no separate value or otherwise the recoverable loss shall be determined by reference to the reduction in value (if any) of the transferor's Holding from which milk quota has been transferred otherwise than on the terms of this Agreement.

8.   Transfer refused or delayed

8.1 If the Board refuses or fails to effect the transfer of the Quota within four months of the Contract Date for any reason outside the control of the Seller or the Buyer then (subject to clause 8.3 hereof) either party may terminate this Agreement by serving on the other a Notice of Termination.

8.2 On service of a Notice of Termination:

8.2.1 the party serving the Notice of Termination shall immediately inform the other party and the Board that the parties no longer wish the transfer of the Quota to proceed; and

8.2.2 upon receipt by either party of written confirmation from the Board that the transfer will not be processed the Price and rent paid pursuant to the Tenancy Agreement shall be released to the Buyer from the Stakeholder Account PROVIDED THAT a proportion of the said rent shall be deducted and released to the Seller the proportion to be calculated pro rata on a daily basis in accordance with the proportion of the term granted by the Tenancy Agreement which has elapsed at the date of such receipt.

8.2.3 Upon receipt of the said written confirmation from the Board the parties shall immediately enter into a deed of surrender in respect of the tenancy granted by the Tenancy Agreement and shall bear the cost of drawing up such deed in equal shares.

8.3 This clause shall not apply if the reason for not effecting the transfer of the Quota within four months of the Contract Date is that the Board has selected the transfer hereby intended to be effected for verification and such verification results in the transfer being thereafter processed by the Board PROVIDED THAT either party may serve a Notice of Termination if the Board has not provided written confirmation of the transfer of the Quota to the Purchaser before the expiry of six months after the Contract Date.

9.   Adjustments to the price

9.1 If after the Contract Date a national reduction in milk quota is imposed the Buyer shall not be entitled to any refund of the Price PROVIDED THAT if the reduction is retrospective to a date before the Contract Date the Seller shall on Completion pay to the Buyer a sum bearing the same proportion to the Price as the reduction in the amount of milk quota actually transferred to the Purchaser bears to the Quota.

10 MILK QUOTA

9.2   If on account of the amount of the Seller's Deliveries the Quota is transferred to the Buyer with a greater number of litres of milk quota having been used than is specified in the Quota Specification the Seller shall immediately pay to the Buyer a sum equal to the additional number of used litres of milk quota transferred to the Buyer multiplied by the Compensation Rate together with the VAT (if any) attributable to the additional used litres but the Seller shall not be otherwise liable to the Buyer.

10. Agreement to bind grantees and successors

10.1   The Seller and the Buyer shall take all such steps as are necessary to ensure that the provisions of this Agreement are binding on the grantees of any interest in part or all of their respective Holdings to which milk quota registered in their respective names or for their respective benefit attaches for the period of 5 years from the Contract Date.

10.2   The provisions of this Agreement shall bind the Seller and the Buyer, their successors in title, assignees, personal representatives and any insolvency practitioner appointed in respect of the affairs of either of them.

11. VAT

11.1   All sums payable under this Agreement are exclusive of any VAT chargeable in respect of the supply of goods or services for which the payment is or is deemed to be consideration.

11.2   In the case of any such payment which attracts VAT or in respect of which the relevant authority demands VAT to be paid the Buyer shall pay to the Seller such VAT on receipt from the Seller of a written demand for the same together with an appropriate VAT invoice.

12. Arbitration

12.1   Any dispute arising out of the terms of this Agreement may be referred by either party for determination by an arbitrator who (in default of agreement) shall be appointed by the President of the Royal Institution of Chartered Surveyors.

AS WITNESS the hands of the parties hereto the day and year first before written.

SCHEDULE
(DEFINED TERMS)

'Board': The Intervention Board or such other Government agency or department as is responsible for administering milk quotas in the United Kingdom.

'Current Quota Year': The period of 12 months ending on 31 March following the Contract Date.

'Holding': a 'holding' as defined in the Regulations.

'Interest': an 'interest' as defined in the Regulations and interpreted by the Board.

'Notice of Termination': a written notice to terminate this Agreement served in accordance with the terms of this Agreement.

'Particulars': the Particulars page set out at the beginning of this Agreement.

'Producer': a 'producer' as defined in the Regulations.

'Purchaser': a 'purchaser' as defined in the Regulations.

'Regulations': the Dairy Produce Quotas Regulations 1997 or any amending or substituted legislation regarding milk quotas.

'Tenancy Agreement': the tenancy agreement completed on the Contract Date between (1) the Seller (landlord) and (2) the Buyer (tenant).

'Transfer Form': Form MQ/1 or such other form as the Board shall prescribe for the transfer of milk quota with land by which the Quota is to be transferred to the buyer.

In this Agreement unless the context otherwise requires:

1. Words importing any gender include every gender.
2. Words importing the singular number include the plural number and vice versa.
3. Words importing persons include firms, companies and corporations and vice versa.
4. Where any obligation is undertaken by two or more persons jointly they shall be jointly and severally liable in respect of that obligation.
5. References to clauses or schedules refer to clauses in and schedules to this Agreement.

SIGNED by the SELLER in the
in the presence of:

}

....

....

....

....

SIGNED by the BUYER in the
presence of:

}

....

....

....

....

MILK QUOTA 10

3   AGREEMENT FOR THE SUPPLY OF CONTRACT SERVICES

Table of contents

Particulars

Date of agreement: ....

Contractor: .... of ....

Owner: .... of ....

The land: ....

Appointment date: The date of this agreement

Term of contract: From the appointment date to ....

The contract charge: .... plus VAT @ 17.5% (if applicable)

THIS AGREEMENT is made on the Date of Agreement

BETWEEN:

(1)   the Contractor
(2)   the Owner

1.   Definitions
1.1   The Particulars shall form part of this Agreement and the detail contained in the left-hand column of the same shall unless the context otherwise requires have the same meaning (as set out in the right-hand column) throughout this Agreement.
1.2   In this Agreement unless the context otherwise requires:
1.2.1   words importing the masculine only shall include the feminine and neuter;
1.2.2   words importing persons shall include firms, companies and corporations and vice versa;
1.2.3   where there are two or more persons included in the expression the Contractor and/or the Owner the obligations and liabilities of such persons under this Agreement shall be joint and several;

1.3   the clause headings are not part of this Agreement and shall not affect its construction;

1.4   any reference in this Agreement to a statutory provision shall be deemed to include any later provisions substituted for or amending the same.

2.   Agreement

The Owner hereby appoints the Contractor as contractor for the purpose of discharging the obligations set out below during the Term of Contract.

3.   Obligations of the contractor

The obligations of the Contractor are as follows:

3.1   To undertake all such acts of husbandry as are required of him by the Owner including but without prejudice to the generality of the foregoing the [. . .] and to comply with the Owner's instructions from time to time in connection with the [. . .].

3.2   To advise the Owner as soon as is reasonably practicable of any event or occurrence that:

3.2.1   may or may be about to affect [. . .]; or

3.2.2   may or may be about to give rise to any matter detrimental to [. . .]; or

3.2.3   may require any other acts of husbandry of him from time to time.

3.3   Not to do anything which may prejudice [. . .].

3.4   To indemnify the Owner against any claim against the Owner by any third party of whatever nature arising out of the performance by the Contractor of his obligations hereunder and to maintain Third Party insurance cover in the sum of not less than five million pounds (£5m) throughout the period of this Agreement and to produce a copy of the policy to the Owner on request.

4.   Contractor's remuneration

The Owner shall pay to the Contractor the Contract Charge on presentation of his invoice by the Contractor.

5.   Termination provisions

5.1   This Agreement may be terminated by the Owner giving not less than [. . .] days' notice in writing to the Contractor in any of the following events:

5.1.1   if there shall be any persistent breach by the Contractor of the terms of this Agreement;

5.1.2   if the Contractor shall after proper warning fail to comply with any lawful directions given by the Owner in writing in accordance with the provisions of this Agreement;

5.1.3   if the Contractor shall through illness, accident or any other cause be incapacitated or prevented from carrying on his duties under this Agreement for a continuous period of not less than 28 days;

10 MILK QUOTA

5.1.4   if the Contractor shall commit any act of bankruptcy or become bankrupt or make any composition or voluntary arrangement with his creditors or have any distress levied or any process by way of execution ordered against his property which shall not have been discharged within fourteen (14) days.

5.2   This Agreement may be terminated forthwith by the Owner in the event of the death of the Contractor.

5.3   This Agreement may in the event of the death of the Owner be terminated by his personal representatives giving to the Contractor not less than 28 days' notice in writing.

6.   General

Nothing in this Agreement, and nothing done in pursuance of this Agreement shall be deemed to create or constitute a partnership, share farming arrangement, relationship of Principal and Agent or contract of employment between the parties.

7.   Arbitration provision

Any dispute arising out of the terms of this Agreement shall be referred to the arbitration of a single Arbitrator to be agreed upon between the parties and in default of such agreement appointed by the President for the time being of the Royal Institution of Chartered Surveyors.

AS WITNESS the hands of the parties hereto the day and year first before written.

[On Original]

SIGNED by the CONTRACTOR
in the presence of:

....

....

....

[On Counterpart]

SIGNED by the OWNER in the
presence of:

}

....

....

....

....

---

4   CONTRACT SERVICES AGREEMENT

Table of Contents

Particulars

Date of agreement: ....

Employer: ....

Contractor   ....

The land: ....

Appointment date: The date of agreement

Term of contract: .... months from the appointment date

The contract charge: £....................

THIS AGREEMENT is made on the Date of Agreement

BETWEEN:

(1)   the Contractor
(2)   the Employer

1. Definitions

In this Agreement:

1.1 The attached Particulars are incorporated and unless the context otherwise requires expressions set out in the left-hand column of the Particulars have the respective meanings shown opposite them in those Particulars.

1.2 Words importing one gender only include the other genders.

1.3 Words importing the singular include the plural number and vice versa.

1.4 Words importing persons include corporations and vice versa.

1.5 Where there are two or more persons included in the expression 'the Contractor' or 'the Employer' the obligations of such persons under this Agreement are joint and several.

1.6 The clause headings shall not affect its construction.

1.7 Any reference to a statutory provision includes any later provision substituted for or amending it.

2. Agreement

The Employer hereby appoints the Contractor as contractor for the purpose of discharging the obligations set out below during the Term of Contract.

3. Obligations of the contractor

The obligations of the Contractor are:

3.1 To undertake all such acts of husbandry as are required under the terms of a tenancy agreement of the land dated .... and made between .... (1) and the Employer (2) so far as it relates to the Land and in particular to cultivate, fertilise, spray and mow the grass on the Land in accordance with the Employer's instructions from time to time.

3.2 To indemnify the Employer against any claim against the Employer by any third party arising out of the performance by the Contractor of his obligations hereunder.

4. Contractor's remuneration

As remuneration for his services the Contractor shall be entitled to the Contract Charge payable against the appropriate VAT invoice on the date hereof.

5. General

5.1 Notwithstanding the provisions of this Agreement the Employer shall at all times retain occupation and control of the Land and the Contractor's right of entry onto the Land shall only be for the purpose of carrying out his obligations under the terms of this Agreement.

5.2 This Agreement shall not constitute a partnership or share farming arrangement and neither party shall hold himself out as being in partnership or a share farming arrangement with the other.

5.3 If the Employer sub-lets all or any part of the Land the sub-tenant shall take the place of the Employer in relation to this Agreement in respect of the Land or the part sub-let (as the case may be) any necessary apportionments being made pro rata to acreage.

6.   Arbitration provision

Any dispute arising out of the terms of this Agreement shall be referred to the arbitration under the Arbitration Act 1996 of a single arbitrator to be agreed upon between the parties or in default of such agreement appointed by the President for the time being of the Royal Institution of Chartered Surveyors.

AS WITNESS the hands of the parties hereto the day and year first before written.

[On Original]

SIGNED by the EMPLOYER
in the presence of: }

....

....

....

....

[On Counterpart]

SIGNED by the CONTRACTOR
in the presence of: }

....

....

....

....

_____

10 MILK QUOTA

5   FARM BUSINESS TENANCY

Table of contents

Particulars

Date of agreement: ....

The landlord: .... of ....

The tenant: .... of ....

Commencement date: ....

Term: The period of .... months from and including
                          the Commencement Date

Rent: £.....................

Rent instalments: Equal instalments payable in advance on the rent days

Rent days: .... and ....

Permitted use: Use in the trade or business of agriculture ....

THIS FARM BUSINESS TENANCY AGREEMENT is made on the Date of
Agreement

BETWEEN:

(1)   The Landlord
(2)   the Tenant

1.   Particulars and definitions

1.1   The attached Particulars are incorporated in this Agreement and to the
         extent allowed by the context the expressions in the left-hand column of
         the Particulars have the respective meanings shown opposite them.

1.2   In this Agreement to the extent allowed by the context the following
         phrases have the respective meanings set under them:

1.2.1	'the Fixed Equipment' means the buildings, structures, fixtures and fittings (if any) affixed to any works constructed on, in or over the Holding from time to time except any which are to be regarded as belonging to the Tenant;[1]
1.2.2	'the Holding' means the property described in the Holding Description Schedule;
1.2.3	'Insured Risks' means such risks in relation to the insurance concerned as the Landlord may from time to time reasonably require;
1.2.4	'the Tenancy' means the tenancy hereby created;
1.2.5	'the 1995 Act' means the Agricultural Tenancies Act 1995.

2.   Interpretation

In this Agreement to the extent allowed by the context:

2.1	'the Holding' includes any part of the Holding;
2.2	'the Landlord' includes whoever for the time being owns the interest in the Holding which gives the right to possession of it at the end of the Tenancy;
2.3	'the Tenant' includes any substituted or additional tax of a similar nature;
2.4	'Value Added Tax' includes any substituted or additional tax of a similar nature;
2.5	unless stated otherwise any reference to a sum of money is to that sum exclusive of Value Added Tax and any Value Added Tax charged on it is payable in addition;
2.6	a right given to the Landlord to enter the Holding extends to anyone the Landlord authorises to enter and includes the rights to bring workmen and appliances onto the Holding for the stated purpose;
2.7	authority given to a person to enter the Holding after giving less notice than specified for without giving notice;
2.8	any obligation not to do any act or thing includes an obligation not to cause or allow anyone else to do that act or thing;
2.9	whenever any party in relation to the Tenancy comprises two or more persons the obligations of that party may be enforced against any one of those persons alone or against all or some of them jointly;
2.10	the act or default of any person on the Holding with the express or implied consent of the Tenant shall be deemed the act or default of the Tenant;
2.11	words importing the singular number include the plural and vice versa; words importing persons include corporations and vice versa; words importing only one gender include the other genders;
2.12	any reference to this Agreement includes its schedules;
2.13	any reference to a page clause or schedule is to that page clause or schedule in this Agreement;
2.14	the clause and paragraph headings are for convenient reference only and shall not affect its construction;
2.15	any reference to a statute Regulation Order or Code of Practice includes any later provision substituted for or amending the same and any subsidiary provision made under powers thereby conferred.

3.   Tenant's covenants

The Tenant covenants with the Landlord:

3.1   *Rent*
        To pay the Rent by the Rent Instalments on the Rent Days.

3.2   *Outgoings*
        To pay all existing and future rates taxes assessments and outgoings of any
        kind charged or imposed upon the Holding or upon the owner or occupier
        thereof.

3.3   *Value added tax*
        To pay all Value Added Tax which may be payable on any taxable supply
        made to the Tenant in relation to the Tenancy or on any payment by the
        Landlord which the Tenant is required to reimburse to the Landlord.

3.4   *Repair*
3.4.1   At all times to maintain and keep in good condition and (where
        appropriate) neat and tidy the Holding and all fixtures and fittings (whether
        belonging to the Landlord or the Tenant) on it or on any other property
        but serving the Holding.[1]
3.4.2   To keep clear and free from obstruction all land drains and ditches on the
        Holding.
3.4.3   To keep all boundary features on the Holding in such state as is adequate for
        their purpose and (in the case of hedges) reasonably cut back.
3.4.4   To pay to the Landlord on demand an appropriate proportion of the costs
        from time to time incurred by the Landlord in the maintenance and repair
        of any items used in common with any adjoining or neighbouring
        property.

3.5   *Good husbandry*
        To farm in accordance with the requirement of good husbandry so as to
        keep the Holding at all times in good heart and condition.

3.6   *Permitted use*
        To use the Holding for the Permitted Use only and in particular not to use
        any part of the Holding as a market garden.

3.7   *Alteration*
        The Tenant shall not on the Holding:
3.7.1   commit waste of any kind;
3.7.2   plant any trees, coppice, saplings, pollards or underwood;
3.7.3   make any alteration, any addition or any tenant's improvement falling
        within the provision of Part III of the 1995 Act other than by any routine
        improvements as defined in section 19(10) of the 1995 Act.

3.8   *Statutory obligations*
        At the Tenant's own expense to do everything in relation to the Holding or
        its use which is required to comply with any statutory or other obligation
        (whether such obligation is imposed on the owner or the occupier) and in
        particular those relating to:

3.8.1   the health safety and welfare of the persons using or employed on or about or visiting the Holding;

3.8.2   waste effluent manure or other matter or thing of a noxious, dangerous or offensive nature.

3.9   *Not to obstruct roadway*
        Not to obstruct any roadway or track by which access to and from the Holding or any neighbouring property is gained.

3.10   *No nuisance*
        Not to do or allow to remain upon the Holding anything which may be or become or cause a nuisance, disturbance, inconvenience, injury or damage to the Landlord or the owner or occupier of any neighbouring property.

3.11   *Adverse rights*
        To take all reasonable steps to prevent any right over the Holding being acquired and to prevent trespassers on the Holding.

3.12   *Indemnity – loss*

3.12.1 Not to do or omit to do on or near the Holding any act or thing which may render the Landlord liable to pay any penalty, damages, compensation, costs, charges or expenses or to carry out any work of whatever nature.

3.12.2 At all times to keep the Landlord fully indemnified against all losses, claims, actions and liabilities arising (whether directly or indirectly) as a result of any act or default of the Tenant

3.13   *Dilapidations notice*
        To pay to the Landlord on an indemnity basis all expenses incurred by the Landlord in the preparation and service of a notice under section 146 of the Law of Property Act 1925 or in relation to proceedings under section 146 or 147 of the Act notwithstanding that forfeiture is avoided otherwise than by relief granted by the Court.

3.14   *Alienation*
        Not without the consent of the Landlord to assign underlet charge or part with possession of the whole or any part of the Holding or permit anyone else to occupy the whole or any part of the Holding.

3.15   *Notices*
        To give full particulars to the Landlord of any notice, direction, order or proposal relating to the Holding made given or issued to the Tenant within seven days of receipt and to take all necessary steps to comply with it.

3.16   *Yield up*
        On the determination of the Tenancy to yield up the Holding in such repair and so cultivated as to be in accordance with the terms of this Agreement and with vacant possession.

4.   Landlord's agreement
        The Landlord agrees with the Tenant to permit the Tenant on paying the Rent and performing and observing the several obligations of the Tenant in relation to the Tenancy peaceably and quietly to hold and enjoy the Holding during the Tenancy without any interruption or disturbance from or by the Landlord or any person claiming under or in trust for the Landlord.

10 MILK QUOTA

5.   **Re-entry**

At any time after the happening of any of the events specified in the following paragraphs of this clause it shall be lawful for the Landlord after giving two months' notice to the Tenant of his intention to do so to re-enter the Holding or any part thereof in the name of the whole and thereupon the Tenancy shall absolutely determine but without prejudice to any right of action or remedy of the Landlord in respect of any antecedent breach by the Tenant of any of his obligations in relation to the Tenancy.

5.1   If the Tenant:

5.1.1   is unable to pay a debt or has no reasonable prospect of being able to pay a debt within the meaning of section 268 of the Insolvency Act 1986;

5.1.2   makes an application to the court for an interim order under section 253 of the Insolvency Act 1986;

5.1.3   makes any assignment for the benefit of or enters into any arrangement with his creditors either by composition or otherwise;

5.1.4   does anything which would entitle a petition for a bankruptcy order to be made against him.

6.   **Custom**

The rights of the parties under this agreement or otherwise in respect of the Tenancy shall not depend upon or be affected by any custom of the country.

7.   **Certificate**

It is hereby certified that there is no agreement for lease to which this document gives effect.

IN WITNESS whereof this Deed has been executed by the parties hereto the day and year first before written.

THE HOLDING DESCRIPTION SCHEDULE

ALL THAT shortly described as .... and more particularly described below by reference to the Ordnance Survey Plan (..................... Edition) of the district TOGETHER with the benefit of any rights which are appurtenant to the Holding or which are reasonably needed for its proper enjoyment by the Tenant and capable of grant by the Landlord.

SUBJECT TO any rights which are expressly excepted or reserved out of the Holding and any rights or quasi-rights which have been enjoyed until now over the Holding by any occupier of any neighbouring property or the Landlord SUBJECT ALSO TO any subsisting obligations under any covenants affecting the Holding but with any subsisting obligations under any covenants.

OS Number   *Area Acres*

....

SIGNED and delivered as a Deed by ⎫
the said [*name*] in the presence of: ⎭ ....

....

....

....

SIGNED and delivered as a Deed by ⎫
the said [*name*] in the presence of: ⎭ ....

....

....

....

---

1   It is highly unlikely that the farm business tenancy will include any buildings. If it does not, these
    provisions can be deleted.

6 QUESTIONNAIRE FOR CALCULATION OF TENANT'S COMPENSATION ON TERMINATION OF TENANCY UNDER SECTION 13 OF THE AGRICULTURE ACT 1986

MILK QUOTA
CALCULATION OF TENANT'S COMPENSATION ON THE TERMINATION OF THE TENANCY

LANDLORD: ESTATE:

TENANT: REGISTERED MILK PRODUCER:

Address: Address:

                                             Intervention Board No:
Telephone No: MAFF Holding No:

What was the BASE Year used for your Milk Quota Assessment?

PART ONE: SUMMARY of LAND OWNERSHIP and OPERATION as at the Base Year: 1983

RENTS PAID as at December 1983 – £

FARM or FARMLAND	OWNED	TENANTED	LICENCE	TOTAL	TOTAL per acre	LANDLORD
Farm 1						
Farm 2						
Farm 3						
Land 1						
Land 2						
Land 3						
Land 4						
Land 5						

Total Area
Farmed

PART TWO: DETAILS OF MILK PRODUCTION

Production Period (litres)	Jan to Mar	Apr to Jun	Jul to Sep	Oct to Dec	TOTAL YEAR	Average Cow Nos	Average Yield/Cow
1983							
2000/2001							
1999/2000							
1998/99							
1997/98							
1998/97							

PART THREE: MILK QUOTA ALLOCATION and SUBSEQUENT TRANSFERS

MILK QUOTA ALLOCATION	Primary	Secondary	Total
Wholesale Quota:			
Direct Sales Quota:	_____	_____	_____
Total Allocated Quota:	_____	_____	_____

MILK QUOTA TRANSFERRED

Quota Year: 1984/85 to 2000/01 (details for each transfer please) of litres and cost

paid for by Tenant

paid for by Landlord

paid for Jointly

_____ _____ _____ _____ _____ _____ _____

Total transferred
quota:
Temporary transfers
(leased) Quota:

_____ _____ _____ _____ _____ _____ _____

Total transferred/
Leased Quota:

_____ _____ _____ _____ _____ _____ _____

TOTAL MILK QUOTA
AVAILABLE for
PRODUCTION after
statutory
deductions (litres)

_____

PART FOUR: DETAILS OF STOCKING AND CROPPING

A. STOCKING GLU Total LIVESTOCK Factor GLUs	Base Year 1983	Previous Five Years From[1]					Five Year Average
	0	−1	−2	−3	−4	−5	
NUMBERS							
Dairy Bulls							
Dairy Cows							
Heifers 24 mths +							
Heifers 12–24 mths							
Heifers 0–12 mths							
Total Dairy LIVESTOCK							
IC Heifers Into Herd							
OTHER GRAZING LIVESTOCK							
Beef Cows/Bulls							
Beef 12–24 mths							
Beef 0–12 mths							
Ewes and Rams							
Lambs							
Others 1							
Others 2							
Others 3							
Non-Dairy Livestock							

B. CROPPING SUMMARY	Base Year 1983	Previous Five Years From[1]					Five Year Average
	0	−1	−2	−3	−4	−5	
Cereals for Sale							
Cereals for Home Feeding							
Other Cash Crops							
Arable Silage/Forage							
Grass for Silage							
Grass for Hay							
Grass for Grazing							
Total Cropping (Acres)							

C. HOME GROWN FEED CONSUMPTION (Tonnes)	0	−1	−2	−3	−4	−5
Home Grown Cereals Fed to: Dairy Cows						
Dairy Replacements						
Other stock						
Silage Fed to: Dairy Cows						
Dairy Replacements						
Other Stock						
Hay Fed to: Dairy Cows						
Dairy Replacements						
Other stock						

10 MILK QUOTA

PART FIVE: AREAS USED FOR MILK PRODUCTION

a) TENANTED LAND

	ON THIS TENANCY							ON OTHER TENANCIES						
	Base Year 1983	Previous 5 yrs from[1]						Base Year 1983	Previous 5 yrs from[1]					
		−1	−2	−3	−4	−5			−1	−2	−3	−4	−5	
LIVESTOCK NUMBERS														
Dairy Cows														
Dairy Replacements														
Other Dairy Livestock														
Beef Cattle														
Sheep														
FORAGE/FEED AREA (Acres)														
Grass – Dairy Cows														
Grass – Replacement														
Grass – Others														
Forage Crops														
Dairy Cows														
Replacements														
Others														
Forage Area (Acres)														
Cereals for Home Feed														
Cereals for Sale														
Other Crops														
Fallow														

Total Farmed area:

Area of Buildings used
for Milk Production:

	Base Year 1983	−1	Previous 5 yrs from[1] −2	−3	−4	−5
b)	_____	_____	_____	_____	_____	_____

LIVESTOCK
NUMBERS

Dairy Cows
Dairy Replacements
Other Dairy Livestock
Beef Cattle
Sheep

FORAGE/FEED AREA
(Acres)

Grass – Dairy Cows
Grass – Replacement
Grass – Others
Forage Crops
　Dairy Cows
　Replacements
　Others

Total Forage Area

Cereals
– for Home Feed
– for Sale
Other Crops
Fallow

Total Farmed area:

Area of Buildings
used for Milk Production:

10 MILK QUOTA

SCHEDULE OF TENANT'S IMPROVEMENTS

TENANT'S NAME

Item No	Description	Dairy/Other	Date of Improvement	Gross Cost	Nett Cost	Landlord Consent and terms of lease	Landlord Contribution	Rental Value

TOTAL COST of TENANT'S IMPROVEMENTS

367

SCHEDULE OF LANDLORD'S IMPROVEMENTS

TENANT'S NAME

Item No	Description	Tenant's Item No	Dairy/Other	Date of Improvement	Gross Cost	Nett Cost	Rental Value

TOTAL COST OF LANDLORD'S IMPROVEMENTS

10 MILK QUOTA

SCHEDULE OF FIELD CROPPING ON TENANTED LAND UNDER THIS TENANCY

TENANT'S NAME:

ESTATE:
LANDLORD'S NAME:

O.S. NUMBER	FIELD NAME	AREA * 1983 [1]

* (Please state whether using acres or hectares)

TOTAL AREA

SCHEDULE OF FIELD CROPPING ON TENANTED LAND UNDER OTHER TENANCIES (Please show separately)

TENANT'S NAME:

ESTATE:

LANDLORD'S NAME:

O.S. NUMBER	FIELD NAME	AREA *	1983	

★ (Please state whether using acres or hectares)

TOTAL AREA

10 MILK QUOTA

Milk Quota

SCHEDULE OF FIELD CROPPING ON OWNER-OCCUPIED LAND

O.S. NUMBER	FIELD NAME	AREA *	1983	1

TOTAL AREA

* (Please state whether using acres or hectares)

7 SUPPLEMENTAL DEED APPORTIONING MILK QUOTA BETWEEN TENANTED HOLDINGS AND OWNED LAND[1]

THIS DEED is made the [*date*]

BETWEEN

[*name*] and [*name*]

(hereinafter together called 'the Tenant') of the first part

[*name*]

(hereinafter called 'the First Landlord') of the second part and

[*name*]

(hereinafter called 'the Second Landlord') of the third part.

WHEREAS

1. This Deed is supplemental to:
1.1 an Agreement for Tenancy dated [*date*] and made between [*name*] and [*name*] (hereinafter called 'the First Tenancy Agreement') in respect of [*address of holding*];
1.2 an Agreement for Tenancy dated [*date*] and made between [*name*] and [*name*] (hereinafter called 'the Second Tenancy Agreement') in respect of [*address of holding/other tenancy agreement*];
1.3 Subject to the provisions of this Deed the parties hereto have agreed to the apportionment throughout the Holding being the property occupied in the First Tenancy Agreement and the property occupied in the Second Tenancy Agreement and land belonging to the Tenant of the Relevant Quota being the Milk Quota registered in the name of the Tenant as hereinafter appearing.

NOW THIS DEED WITNESSES as follows:

1. The Relevant Quota is apportioned to the various parts of the Holding in accordance with the Dairy Produce Quotas Regulations 1997 (the Regulations) and as agreed between the parties the details of such agreed apportionment being set out in the Schedule hereto.

2. The First Landlord and the Second Landlord respectively acknowledge the Tenant's right to compensation in full in respect of such parts of the Relevant Quota as attach to those parts of the Holding held of them by the Tenant in accordance with the provisions of the Agriculture Act 1986 on the termination of the respective tenancy agreements and that nothing in this Deed shall affect those rights.

3. The Tenant covenants with the First Landlord:

3.1   not to transfer charge lease or otherwise remove from the land comprised in the First Tenancy Agreement the whole or any part of that part of the Relevant Quota which presently attaches thereto without the previous consent in writing of the First Landlord;

3.2   to take all such steps as are necessary to ensure that that part of the Relevant Quota which presently attaches thereto continues to attach to the land comprised in the First Tenancy Agreement (and to no other property) throughout the duration of the First Tenancy Agreement to the intent that the same will be transferable to the First Landlord or to an incoming tenant on the termination of the First Tenancy Agreement;

3.3   not to do or omit anything the doing or omission of which would cause a loss forfeiture or reduction in that part of the Relevant Quota which attaches to the land comprised in the First Tenancy Agreement;

3.4   to carry out during the continuance of the First Tenancy Agreement any obligation imposed upon the Tenant as occupier or producer with regard to notices compliance with directions payment of levies maintenance of records or otherwise in connection with milk quota under the Regulations and/or the Agriculture Act 1986;

3.5   to supply the First Landlord with copies of any notices served on the Tenant which affect or may affect that part of the Relevant Quota which attaches to the land comprised in the First Tenancy Agreement;

3.6   to co-operate with the First Landlord on the termination of the First Tenancy Agreement to ensure that the First Landlord or a person nominated by him will be registered by the Intervention Board in respect of that part of the Relevant Quota which attaches to the land comprised in the First Tenancy Agreement.

4.   The Tenant covenants with the Second Landlord:

4.1   not to transfer charge lease or otherwise remove from the land comprised in the Second Tenancy Agreement the whole or any part of that part of the Relevant Quota which presently attaches thereto without the previous consent in writing of the Second Landlord;

4.2   to take all such steps as are necessary to ensure that that part of the Relevant Quota which presently attaches thereto continues to attach to the land comprised in the Second Tenancy Agreement (and to no other property) throughout the duration of the Second Tenancy Agreement to the intent that the same will be transferable to the Second Landlord or to an incoming tenant on the termination of the Second Tenancy Agreement;

4.3   not to do or omit anything the doing or omission of which would cause a loss forfeiture or reduction in that part of the Relevant Quota which attaches to the land comprised in the Second Tenancy Agreement;

4.4   to carry out during the continuance of the Second Tenancy Agreement any obligation imposed upon the Tenant as occupier or producer with regard to notices compliance with directions payment of levies maintenance of records or otherwise in connection with milk quota under the Regulations and/or the Agriculture Act 1986;

4.5   to supply the Second Landlord with copies of any notices served on the Tenant which affect or may affect that part of the Relevant Quota which attaches to the land comprised in the Second Tenancy Agreement;

4.6   to co-operate with the Second Landlord on the termination of the Second Tenancy Agreement to ensure that the Second Landlord or a person nominated by him will be registered by the Intervention Board in respect of that part of the Relevant Quota which attaches to the land comprised in the Second Tenancy Agreement.

[5.   If at any time any of the Relevant Quota shall have been charged to any person firm or company to secure any form of indebtedness and the First Landlord or the Second Landlord (as the case may be) shall pursuant to such charge pay compensation in respect of that quota to the chargee such payment shall be deemed to satisfy *pro tanto* any claim for compensation which might otherwise be due to the Tenant in respect of the same quota litreage.]

6.   So far as that part of the Relevant Quota not attaching either to the land comprised in the First Tenancy Agreement or that comprised in the Second Tenancy Agreement is concerned the First Landlord and the Second Landlord respectively covenant with the Tenant that the First Landlord and/or the Second Landlord (as the case may be) will sign all necessary forms and do all necessary things to enable the Tenant to transfer that part of the Relevant Quota attaching to the Tenant's Land to one or more third parties in the event of the Tenant wishing to transfer the same.

7.   The parties covenant each with the other not to make any further representation to the Intervention Board the Ministry of Agriculture or other statutory authority nor to make any further claims either personally or through any third party or parties in respect of the Relevant Quota.

8.   If notwithstanding the terms of this Deed any claims are made outside the provisions of this Deed in respect of the Relevant Quota or any part or parts thereof consequent upon the termination of the First Tenancy Agreement the Second Tenancy Agreement or either of them or otherwise resulting in an apportionment of the same in favour of the First Landlord or the Second Landlord or the Tenant pursuant to a decision of an Arbitrator appointed under the Regulations or otherwise the First Landlord the Second Landlord or the Tenant (as the case may be) will pay to the other party or parties all lawfully recoverable losses thereby incurred by the other party or parties including all costs incurred by the other party in the acquisition of milk quota of comparable butterfat base and usage to replace such quota.

9.   To the extent that quantification of the losses referred to in clause 8 hereof is or may be impossible whether by reason of milk quota having no independent value or otherwise the recoverable losses shall be determined by reference to any reduced value of the Holding (or any part of it) consequent upon the loss of the milk quota therefrom.

10 MILK QUOTA

10. In the event of there being an additional allocation of or reduction in milk quota imposed by the Ministry of Agriculture Fisheries and Food as Agent for the EU or otherwise howsoever such additional allocation or reduction (as the case may be) shall be borne rateably by all parts of the Relevant Quota.

11. The provisions of this Deed shall benefit and bind the successors in title of the parties hereto their assigns and any insolvency practitioner appointed in respect of the affairs of any of them.

12. References herein to the Agriculture Act 1986 and to the Dairy Produce Quotas Regulations 1997 shall apply to:

12.1 such legislation and/or subordinate legislation as amended;

12.2 any substituted legislation and/or subordinate legislation.

13. In the event of any dispute arising in relation to this Deed the same shall be determined by an Arbitrator to be appointed on the application of any party to the Deed to the President for the time being of The Royal Institution of Chartered Surveyors.

14. In this Deed where the context so admits words importing the singular number only shall include the plural and vice versa and words importing the masculine gender only shall include the feminine and vice versa and where two or more persons are included in the words 'the Tenant' 'the First Landlord' or 'the Second Landlord' any agreements or obligations entered into by them shall be deemed to be entered into jointly and severally.

IN WITNESS whereof this Deed has been executed by the parties hereto the day and year first before written.

SCHEDULE

SIGNED and delivered as a Deed by
the TENANT in the presence of:

....

....

....

SIGNED and delivered as a Deed by the
FIRST LANDLORD in the presence of:

....

....

....

SIGNED and delivered as a Deed by
the SECOND LANDLORD in the
presence of:

....

....

....

} ·

....

---

1   No stamp duty.

---

8   DEED REGULATING OWNERSHIP OF QUOTA BETWEEN LANDLORD, TENANT AND PRODUCER

THIS DEED is made the [*date*]

BETWEEN [*name*] whose registered office is at [*address*] ('the Landlord') of the first part [*name*] of [*address*] ('the Tenant') of the second part and [*name*] LIMITED trading as [*name*] whose registered office is at [*address*] ('the Producer') of the third part.

SUPPLEMENTAL to a lease ('the Lease') made the [*date*] between the Landlord of the one part and the Tenant of the other part as subsequently amended relating to [*holding details*] ('the Holding').[1]

WHEREAS:

1.   The Landlord is the landlord and the Tenant is the tenant of the Holding under the Lease.

2.   The Producer is registered with the Intervention Board under Producer Number [*no*] as a producer of milk on the Holding the Producer's registered quota prior to entering into this Deed being . . . litres (a copy of the Wholesale Producer Register being attached hereto).

3.   The Producer wishes to purchase further milk quota to be added to the milk quota registered in its name.

NOW THIS DEED WITNESSES as follows:

1.   If the Producer purchases milk quota after the date hereof it shall notify the Landlord of such milk quota purchased ('the Purchased Quota').

2.   It is hereby agreed and declared that the Purchased Quota shall be deemed to be and for all purposes shall be treated as Transferred Quota within the meaning of paragraph 2(2) Schedule 1 to the Agriculture Act 1986 and that in respect of Purchased Quota the Producer shall be deemed to be and shall be treated as the tenant for the purposes of section 13 of the said Act but not further or otherwise.

10 MILK QUOTA

3. If the Producer wishes to dispose of all or any part of the Purchased Quota during the subsistence of the tenancy created by the Lease the Landlord will facilitate such disposal by giving all necessary consents (including permitting the Tenant to grant a short-term farm business tenancy notwithstanding the terms of the Lease) and/or taking any other action required by the Intervention Board the Ministry of Agriculture Fisheries and Food or any other statutory authority to facilitate such disposal.

4. The entirety of the proceeds of sale of Purchased Quota will be payable to and belong to and retained by the Producer.

5. The provisions hereof are without prejudice to the rights of the parties hereto in respect of the milk quota now registered in the name of the Producer in respect of the Holding on the termination of the tenancy created by the Lease and shall bind the respective successors in title of the parties hereto and the expressions the Landlord the Tenant and the Producer shall be construed appropriately.

6. The Landlord and the Producer shall co-operate with each other in the signing and lodging of all necessary documents including any required by the Intervention Board the Ministry of Agriculture Fisheries and Food or other statutory authority so as to ensure so far as possible that there shall be no transfer of Purchased Quota from the Producer to the Landlord.

7. If notwithstanding the terms hereof the whole or any part of the Purchased Quota is transferred to or becomes vested in the Landlord howsoever or if the Landlord shall receive all or any part of the proceeds of sale of the Purchased Quota the Landlord shall pay to or reimburse the Producer the full value thereof.

IN WITNESS whereof this Deed has been executed by the parties hereto the day and year first before written.

SIGNED and delivered as a Deed by
the said [*name*] in the presence of: } ....

....

....

....

SIGNED and delivered as a Deed by
the said [*name*] in the presence of: } ....

....

....

....

SIGNED and delivered as a Deed by
the said [*name*] in the presence of: }   ....

....

....

....

SIGNED and delivered as a Deed by
the said [*name*] in the presence of: }   ....

....

....

....

Note. Stamp duty £5.
1   This assumes the Producer is not the tenant and also assumes the Producer farms no other land.

9   DECLARATION OF TRUST

THIS DEED is made the [*date*]
BETWEEN
[*name*] of [*address*] ('the Tenant') of the one part and [*name*] whose registered office is at [*address*] aforesaid ('the Producer') of the other part.[1]

WHEREAS:

1   The Tenant is the tenant of certain land known as the [*holding*] ('the Holding') which is farmed by the Producer.

2   The Producer is registered with [*name*] under Producer Number [   ] as a producer of milk on the Holding.

3   The Producer's registered quota at the date hereof is . . . litres of . . . milk quota with butterfat of . . . % ('the Registered Quota').

4   Having regard to the cuts which have been imposed the milk quota originally allocated to the Producer ('the Allocated Quota') is . . . litres of . . .% butterfat and the milk quota subsequently purchased by the Producer ('the Purchased Quota') is . . . litres.

5   No change has been made to the butterfat level of the Registered Quota to date.

6   It has been agreed that the Purchased Quota which was paid for by the Producer belongs beneficially to the Producer absolutely [and a deed was completed on the [*date*] with the landlord of the Holding at that time protecting the Producer's position in respect thereof] (if applicable).

NOW THIS DEED WITNESSES as follows:

1   It is hereby agreed and declared that the Producer is beneficially entitled to the Purchased Quota.

2   If the Producer wishes to dispose of all or any part of the Purchased Quota the Tenant will do everything in his power to achieve the same including obtaining the Landlord's consent to a sub-letting and to sign any relevant forms.

3   The entirety of the proceeds of sale of Purchased Quota will be payable to and belong to and be retained by the Producer.

4   The parties agree that the Allocated Quota belongs to the Tenant and the Producer agrees to sign all relevant forms to facilitate any dealing therewith at the Tenant's request or the payment of compensation in respect thereof to the Tenant.

5   The entirety of the proceeds of sale of the Allocated Quota or compensation received in respect thereof will be payable to and belong to and be retained by the Tenant.

6   The provisions hereof shall bind the respective successors in title of the parties hereto.

7   If notwithstanding the terms hereof the Allocated Quota or any sale proceeds or compensation payable in respect thereof are transferred or paid to the Producer the Producer shall compensate the Tenant to the extent that the Producer has been enriched thereby.

8   To the extent that the Purchased Quota the proceeds thereof or compensation payable in respect thereof are received by the Tenant the Tenant shall compensate the Producer to the extent that the Tenant has been enriched thereby.

IN WITNESS whereof this Deed has been executed by the parties hereto the day and year first before written.

SIGNED and delivered as a Deed by
the said [*name*] in the presence of:
....

....

....

....

SIGNED and delivered as a Deed by
the said [*name*] in the presence of:
....

....

....

....

SIGNED and delivered as a Deed by
the said [*name*] in the presence of:

....

....

....

-----

1   This assumes the tenant and producer are not the same persons.

10 MILK QUOTA

CHAPTER 11: OTHER USES OF LAND

INDEX

CHAPTER 11: OTHER USES OF LAND

INTRODUCTION

This chapter contains a selection of items which may be of interest to the rural practitioner. There is almost no limit to the variables and therefore, of necessity, this can only be a selection based on the authors' experience.

11 OTHER USES OF LAND

PRECEDENTS

1 DEED OF GRANT OF RECIPROCAL EASEMENTS[1]

THIS DEED OF GRANT OF EASEMENT is made the [*date*]

BETWEEN

1. THE FIRST OWNER: [*name*] of [*address*]

2. THE SECOND OWNER: [*name*] of [*address*]

3. [*First Owner's lender*]: [*name*] of [*address*]

4. [*Second Owner's lender*]: [*name*] of [*address*]

NOW THIS DEED WITNESSES as follows:

1.   Interpretation

1.1   'the First Property' means the property more particularly described in the First Schedule and belonging to the First Owner;

1.2   'the Second Property' means the property more particularly described in the Second Schedule and belonging to the Second Owner;

1.3   'the First Charge' means a legal charge/mortgage dated [*date*] and made between [*name*] (1) and [*name*] (2) and affecting the first property;

1.4   'the Second Charge' means a legal charge/mortgage dated [*date*] and made between [*name*] (1) and [*name*] (2) and affecting the Second Property.

2.   The grant

2.1   **EITHER** IN consideration of £ ... (... pounds) (the receipt of which the First Owner acknowledges)

OR IN consideration of the grant made below by the Second Owner the First Owner with full title guarantee (and with the consent of [*name*]) GRANTS to the Second Owner and its successors in title for the benefit of the Second Property and each and every part thereof the rights mentioned in the Third Schedule in fee simple.

2.2   IN consideration of the grant made above by the First Owner the Second Owner with full title guarantee (with the consent of [*name*]) grants to the First Owner and its successors in title for the benefit of the First Property and each and every part thereof the rights mentioned in the Fourth Schedule in fee simple.

3.   Covenants

3.1   THE First Owner for itself and its successors the owners and occupiers for the time being of the First Property and each and every part (jointly and severally) covenants with the Second Owner and its successors in title the owners and occupiers for the time being of the Second Property and each and every part [*set out the covenants*].

11 OTHER USES OF LAND

3.2   THE Second Owner for itself and its successors the owners and occupiers for the time being of the Second Property and each and every part (jointly and severally) covenants with the First Owner and its successors in title the owners and occupiers for the time being of the First Property and each and every part [*set out the covenants*].

4.   Acknowledgement for production

4.1   THE First Owner acknowledges the right of the Second Owner to the production of the documents listed in the Fifth Schedule and to delivery of copies of them.

OR

THE First Owner covenants with the Second Owner that as and when any of the documents listed in the Fifth Schedule shall come into its or its successors in title's possession it or they will when requested and at the cost of the Second Owner or its successors in title execute a statutory undertaking for the safe custody of such documents and that in the meantime every person having possession of the documents will keep them safe unless prevented from doing so by fire or other inevitable accident. [*First Owner's lender*] acknowledges the right of the Second Owner to the production and delivery of the documents listed in the Fifth Schedule.

4.2   THE Second Owner acknowledges the right of the First Owner to the production of the documents listed in the Sixth Schedule and to delivery of copies of them.

OR

THE Second Owner covenants with the First Owner that as and when any of the documents listed in the Sixth Schedule shall come into its or its successors in title's possession it or they will when requested and at the cost of the First Owner or its successors in title execute a statutory undertaking for the safe custody of such documents and that in the meantime every person having possession of the documents will keep them safe unless prevented from doing so by fire or other inevitable accident. [*Second Owner's lender*] acknowledges the right of the First Owner to production and delivery of copies of the documents listed in the Sixth Schedule.

IN WITNESS whereof this Deed has been executed by the parties hereto the day and year first before written.

[4.3   (Certificate of value – stamp duty.)[2]]

FIRST SCHEDULE

DESCRIPTION OF FIRST OWNER'S PROPERTY

SECOND SCHEDULE

DESCRIPTION OF SECOND OWNER'S PROPERTY

THIRD SCHEDULE

RIGHTS GRANTED BY FIRST OWNER TO SECOND OWNER

FOURTH SCHEDULE

RIGHTS GRANTED BY SECOND OWNER TO FIRST OWNER

FIFTH SCHEDULE

DOCUMENTS ACKNOWLEDGED BY FIRST OWNER (OR ITS LENDER)

Date   Document   Parties

SIXTH SCHEDULE

DOCUMENTS ACKNOWLEDGED BY SECOND OWNER (OR ITS LENDER)

Date   Document   Parties

SIGNED and delivered as a Deed by
the said [*name*] in the presence of: } ....

....

....

....

SIGNED and delivered as a Deed by
the said [*name*] in the presence of: } ....

....

....

....

11 OTHER USES OF LAND

SIGNED and delivered as a Deed by
the said [*name*] in the presence of: } ....

....

....

....

SIGNED and delivered as a Deed by
the said [*name*] in the presence of: } ....

....

....

....

---

1   No stamp duty if suitable certificate of value can be inserted.
2   Insert suitable certificate of value.

---

2   LICENCE FOR STORAGE

THIS LICENCE is made the [*date*]

BETWEEN

1.   [*Name of Owner*] of [*Address of Owner*] ('the Owner')

2.   [*Name of Licensee*] of [*Address of Licensee*] ('the Licensee')

NOW IT IS AGREED as follows :

1.   Definitions and interpretation
        In this Licence the following expressions have the meanings given in this
        clause.

1.1   *The Premises*
        The 'Premises' mean the land and buildings shown for identification
        purposes only edged purple on the plan annexed to this Licence.

1.2 *The Accessways*

The 'Accessways' mean the roads and paths of the Premises the use of which is necessary to obtain access to and egress from the Designated Space and Designated Parking Space or those of them that afford reasonable access and egress thereto and therefrom and that the Owner from time to time in his absolute discretion designates.

1.3 *The Building*

The 'Building' means part of the Premises shown for identification purposes only edged blue on the plan annexed to this Licence.

1.4 *The Car Park*

The 'Car Park' means the part of the Premises shown for identification purposes only edged green on the plan annexed to this Licence.

1.5 *The Designated Hours*

The 'Designated Hours' means [*specify hours*] on [*specify days*] or such other hours as the Owner from time to time in his absolute discretion determines.

1.6 *The Designated Parking Space*

The 'Designated Parking Space' means the space shown for identification purposes only edged brown on the plan annexed to this Licence or such other space within the Car Park, being suitable and of sufficient size for the parking of [*number*] cars as the Owner in his absolute discretion designates.

1.7 *The Designated Space*

The 'Designated Space' means the area shown for identification purposes only edged red on the plan attached to this Licence or such other storage space, comprising a single area of not less than [*number*] square metres within the Building as the Owner may from time to time in his absolute discretion designate.

1.8 *Headings*

The clause and sub-clause headings do not form part of this Licence and must not be taken into account in the construction or interpretation.

1.9 *The Licence Fee*

The 'Licence Fee' means £... a month.

1.10 *The Licence Period*

The 'Licence Period' means the period from the date of this Licence until the date on which the Licensee's rights under clause 2 are determined in accordance with clause 4.

1.11 *Reference to Clauses*

Any reference in this Licence to a clause or sub-clause without further designation is to be construed as a reference to the clause or sub-clause of this Licence so numbered.

1.12 *VAT*

'VAT' means value added tax or any other tax of a similar nature.

11 OTHER USES OF LAND

2.   The licence

Subject to clauses 3 and 4, the Owner gives the Licensee the right, for the Licence Period and during the Designated Hours, in common with the Owner and all others authorised by the Owner so far as is not inconsistent with the rights given, to use the Designated Space for [*specify purpose*] to use the Designated Parking Space for parking [*number*] car(s) and to use the Accessways for access to and egress from the Designated Space and the Designated Parking Space.

3.   Licensee's undertaking

The Licensee agrees and undertakes as set out in this clause 3.

3.1   *Licence fee and outgoings*

The Licensee must pay the Licence Fee, together with any VAT, in advance on the first day of each month by standing order to the Owner's Bank Account [*specify account number*] at [*specify Bank*], the first payment, or a due proportion of it apportioned on a day-to-day basis to be made on the date of this Licence.

3.2   *Interest*

The Licensee must pay interest at the rate of 4% over the base rate of [*insert Bank*] on any Licence fee and outgoings that are outstanding more than 14 days after they fall due.

3.3   *Deposit*

The Licensee must deposit £... with the Owner as security for the performance and observance of the undertakings contained in this clause 3, to be repayable to the Licensee – less any amount due to the Owner in respect of any non-performance or non-observance by the Licensee – within 14 days of the determination of the Licence Period or such longer period as may be necessary to ascertain any amount due to the Owner.

3.4   *Condition of property*

The Licensee must keep the Designated Space and the Designated Parking Space clean and tidy and clear of rubbish and leave them in a clean and tidy condition and free of the Licensee's equipment, goods and chattels at the end of the Licence Period. Any such items not removed by the end of the Licence Period may be disposed of or sold by the Owner who may recoup his costs of disposal or sale.

3.5   *Accessways*

The Licensee must not obstruct the Accessways or make them dirty or untidy, or leave any rubbish on them.

3.6   *Nuisance*

The Licensee must not use the Designated Space, the Designated Parking Space or the Accessways in such a way as to cause any nuisance, damage, disturbance, annoyance, inconvenience or interference to the Premises or adjoining or neighbouring property or to the owners, occupiers or users of any adjoining or neighbouring property.

3.7   *Dangerous substances*

The Licensee must not without the prior written consent of the Owner bring onto, or permit on, the Premises any dangerous or noxious substance or thing, inflammable material or high temperature equipment.

3.8   *Statutory requirements and insurance*
        The Licensee must not do anything that will or might constitute a breach of
        any statutory requirement affecting the Premises or that will or might
        wholly or partly vitiate any insurance effected in respect of the Premises
        from time to time.

3.9   *Indemnity*
        The Licensee must indemnify the Owner, and keep the Owner indemni-
        fied, against all losses, claims, demands, actions, proceedings, damages,
        costs or expenses or other liability arising in any way from this Licence, any
        breach of any of the Licensee's undertakings contained in this clause, or the
        exercise or purported exercise of any of the rights given in clause 2.

3.10   *Insurance*
        The Licensee must take out his own insurance in respect of all items stored
        and against third party liability for a minimum cover of £5,000,000 (five
        million pounds).

3.11   *Owner's rights*
        The Licensee must not in any way impede the Owner, or his servants or
        agents, in the exercise of his rights of possession and control of the Premises
        and every part of the Premises.

4.   General

4.1   *Determination*
        The rights granted in clause 2 are to determine (without prejudice to the
        Owner's rights in respect of any breach of the undertakings contained in
        clause 3):

4.1.1   immediately on notice given by the Owner at any time following any
        breach by the Licensee of his undertakings contained in clause 3; and

4.1.2   on not less than 28 days' notice given by the Owner or the Licensee to the
        other party to expire on the last day of a month.

4.2   *Assignment prohibited*
        The benefit of this Licence is personal to the Licensee and not assignable,
        and the rights given in clause 2 may only be exercisable by the Licensee and
        his employees.

4.3   *Warranty excluded*
        The Owner gives no warranty that the Premises are legally or physically fit
        for the purposes specified in clause 2.

4.4   *Liability excluded*
        The Owner is not to be liable for damage to any property of the Licensee
        (or employees) or for any losses, claims, demands, actions, proceedings,
        damages, costs or expenses or other liability incurred by them in the
        exercise or purported exercise of the rights granted by clause 2.

SIGNED by the parties hereto the day and year first before written.

SIGNED by the OWNER ....

SIGNED by the LICENSEE ....

---

3 METAL DETECTING LICENCE

LICENCE dated [*date*]

BETWEEN:

1. THE OWNERS: [*name(s)*] and anyone who becomes entitled to the Owners' interest in the Property

2. THE LICENSEE: [*name*]

   IT IS HEREBY AGREED AS FOLLOWS:

1.1 The Owners agree that the Licensee may use the property described below ('the Property') for the purposes described below only for [*period*] starting on [*date*].

1.2 The Property is [*description*] as more particularly identified on the plan annexed hereto.

1.3 The Licensee is entitled to obtain access to the Property over the accessway coloured brown on the said plan but by no other route.

1.4 While this Licence continues the Licensee is entitled:

1.4.1 to search for, examine and dig for items of buried metal or other material, whether antique or modern, or any other item or objects including those specified as follows:

   ....;

1.4.2 to use equipment agreed by the Owners for searching or digging;

1.4.3 to enter the Property with the agreed mechanical/electronic devices for searching and/or digging on the Property but for no other purposes whatsoever.

1.5 Either party can end this Licence at any time by giving the other at least one month's notice taking effect at the end of a month.

1.6 Notwithstanding the grant of this Licence, the Owners are entitled to possession of the Property and have a right of access to it at all times and for all purposes.

1.7 This Licence is personal to the Licensee and cannot be transferred. The Licensee is not allowed to allow any other person to use the Property.

2. THE Licensee agrees with the Owners:

2.1 To pay the sum of £ ... on the signing of this Agreement.

2.2 To pay a payment of . . .% of the net sale proceeds or Treasure award or agreed valuation.

2.3 To indemnify the Owners and to produce evidence of existing insurance or where there is none or it is for inadequate cover to insure on terms agreed by the Owners against all injuries damage claims and demands arising from the activities authorised by this Licence.

2.4 To fill any holes, replacing soil and grass carefully, repair or restore any fences, buildings or enclosures dismantled, opened or altered as a result of the activities of the Licensee.

2.5 To protect any livestock upon the Property and prevent their escape.

2.6 To protect the wildlife whether plant or animal upon the Property.

2.7 To protect any archaeological deposits below plough soil depth.

2.8 To prevent fire.

2.9 To bear full responsibility for any damage to the Property including the livestock wildlife plant and animals thereon and including any injuries suffered by the Licensee or any other person as a result of the Licensee's activities thereon.

2.10 To report immediately to the Owners and to the Coroner:

2.10.1 any objects containing gold or silver or any alloy containing gold or silver;

2.10.2 coins containing either gold or silver or being at least three hundred years old;

2.10.3 any objects found in association with 2.10.1 and 2.10.2;
with a view to an Inquest being held to determine whether the object(s) is/are treasure.

2.11 To inform immediately the owner of the Property of any finds of whatsoever nature.

2.12 To report any archaeological object to the Owners and where the Owners so agree to the County Sites and Monuments Record.

2.13 To report any bombs or live ammunition to the Police having marked the spot.

2.14 To respect the country code as issued by the Countryside Agency or the Countryside Council for Wales.

2.15 Not to use the Property, or any part of it, for any of the following nor allow any one else to do so:

2.15.1 activities which are dangerous, offensive, noxious, noisome, illegal or immoral, or which are or may become a nuisance or annoyance to the Owners or occupier or to the owner or occupier of any adjoining property.

2.16 To carry and produce on request an identification card [*membership card of the National Council for Metal Detecting and a Certificate of Public Liability Insurance*].

3. THE parties agree:

3.1 That all objects found other than treasure are the property of the Owners and will be recorded or disposed of according to the Owners' wishes.

11 OTHER USES OF LAND

3.2   The value of any objects will be determined by agreement between the Owners and the Licensee or by sale for the highest available price or by appraisal by at least two independent persons jointly selected. Thereafter payment of any monies due to either party to this Licence must be made upon the sale or within ... days of any valuation or sale.

3.3   If there shall be any breach or non-observance by the Licensee of any of the terms and conditions of this Licence the Owners may revoke this Licence and thereupon the Licence and all the rights hereby granted shall cease and be determined with or without notice by the Owners and immediately on being requested to do so the Licensee will vacate the Property.

4.   IT IS FURTHER AGREED:

4.1   That where the excavation is not limited to the disturbance of plough-soil the Licensee will discuss with the Owners the need to consult the appropriate County Sites and Monuments Records and should the Owners so direct the Licensee will undertake such consultations.

4.2   That the Licensee will not search for or dig for items on areas of permanent pasture.

4.3   That where the landowner agrees the Licensee will submit all finds to the County Sites and Monuments Records for identification and recording by archaeologists.

AS WITNESS the hands of the parties hereto the day and year first before written.

SIGNED by the OWNERS in the
in the presence of:

....

....

....

....

SIGNED by the LICENSEE
in the presence of:

}

....

....

....

....

4　FILM CONTRACT

AGREEMENT dated [*date*]

BETWEEN

1.　THE OWNERS: [*name*]

2.　THE COMPANY: [*name*]

IT IS HEREBY AGREED AS FOLLOWS:

1.　　　The Owners agree that the Company may use the areas of the property ('the permitted areas') described in the First Schedule for the purposes specified in the Second Schedule on the following dates [*dates*] between the hours of [*times*].

2.　　　The Company agrees with the Owners:

2.1　　To pay the fees calculated in accordance with the formula set out in the Third Schedule.

2.2　　To pay for all electricity, telephone calls and other expenses incurred during the period covered by this Agreement.

2.3　　To supply in advance a list of all persons authorised ('authorised persons') by the Company to enter the permitted areas.

2.4　　To ensure that the authorised persons carry and produce on request an identification card.

2.5　　To comply at all times with the Lighting Specification in the Fourth Schedule.

2.6　　Not to use the property, or any part of it nor allow anyone else to do so for:

2.6.1　　activities which are dangerous, offensive, noxious, noisome, illegal or immoral, or which are or may become a nuisance or annoyance to the owner or occupier or to the owner or occupier of the adjoining property, so that this clause shall not preclude the exercise by the Company of the rights granted in the Second Schedule.

11　OTHER USES OF LAND

2.7   Not to smoke in any of the permitted areas.

2.8   Not to do any damage to the permitted areas or the contents thereof.

2.9   To compensate the Owners for any damage to property or contents, the value of the loss to be determined by an expert appointed by agreement between the parties or in default of agreement by the President of the Royal Institution of Chartered Surveyors.

2.10   To ensure that no food or drink is consumed except in the designated parts of the permitted areas.

2.11   To use only [*specify area*] for relaxation and not other parts of the permitted areas.

2.12   To indemnify the Owners against all injuries damage claims and demands arising from the activities authorised by this Agreement.

2.13   To remove all equipment and leave the premises in a clean and tidy condition on the last of the dates specified in clause 1 above.

3.   IT IS FURTHER AGREED:

3.1   The wording of the credit for the use of the permitted areas shall be ...

3.2   The copyright of the photographs/films will be vested in ...

3.3   The photographs/films shall be used for ... but not for any other purpose whatsoever.

3.4   If there shall be any breach or non-observance by the parties of the terms and conditions of this Agreement the party not in breach may revoke the Agreement forthwith but without prejudice to any of the rights and liabilities of either party accruing before such breach.

SIGNED by the parties hereto the day and year first before written.

FIRST SCHEDULE

PERMITTED AREAS AND ADDRESS OF THE PROPERTY

SECOND SCHEDULE

RIGHTS GRANTED

(eg including parking and catering facilities in designated areas)

THIRD SCHEDULE

CALCULATION OF FEES

FOURTH SCHEDULE

LIGHTING SPECIFICATION

SIGNED by the OWNERS ....

SIGNED by the COMPANY ....

5   PERMISSIVE PATH AGREEMENT BETWEEN LANDOWNER AND LOCAL AUTHORITY

Particulars

The Date	:	[*date*]
The Landowner	:	[*name*] of [*address*]
The Tenant	:	[*name*] of [*address*]
The District Council	:	[*name*]
The Permissive Path	:	[*description*]
Width	:	[*metres*]
The Whole Path	:	[*description*]
Permitted Purposes	:	[*description*]
Limitations on Use	:	[*description*]
The Term	:	[*length/dates*]
Payment	:	£ ...

THIS AGREEMENT is made on the date set out in the Particulars

BETWEEN:

1.   THE GRANTOR: the Landowner [and Tenant]

2.   THE COUNCIL: the District Council

IT IS AGREED as follows:

The Particulars
1.   The details in the Particulars apply to and are part of this Agreement.

11 OTHER USES OF LAND

The grant

2.   In consideration of £ ... and the covenants given by the Council in clause 8 below the Grantor grants to the Council and its servants and agents the following rights:

2.1   To use and allow the public to use the permissive path for the permitted purposes [subject to the limitations on use].

2.2   To enter on the permissive path and the land on either side for a distance of [*one*] metre for the purposes of clearing undergrowth and maintaining the permissive path.

2.3   To execute the works described in the Schedule hereto.

2.4   To enter on the permissive path and do work which is necessary to comply with clause 7.2 below where the Grantor has failed to do so.

Duration

3.   The rights will subsist throughout the Term beginning on ... unless this Agreement is terminated in accordance with clause [*4.2 or*] 4.3 below.

Termination

4.1   The Agreement will terminate automatically on the expiration of the Term.

[4.2   The Grantor may terminate this Agreement at any time on or after the completion of the [*fifth*] [*tenth*] year of the term by giving three months' prior notice in writing and at the expiration of a valid notice this Agreement shall absolutely determine without prejudice to the rights and liabilities of either party against the other for any antecedent breach of covenant].

4.3   The Agreement will terminate where there is a breach of covenant by the Grantor or the Council which is not remedied within twenty-one days after the service by one party of written notice on the other specifying the breach and the steps which are necessary to remedy the same but without prejudice to the rights and liabilities of either party against the other for any antecedent breach of covenant.

Diversion

5.1   Either the Council or the Grantor may request that the permissive path be diverted.

5.2   Where the request is granted any costs incurred in making the diverted path suitable for use for the public and any costs incurred in order to publicise to the public the change in the path should be borne by the person making the request.

Temporary closure

6.   The Grantor may close all or part of the path on a temporary basis for agricultural or other land management operations or sporting events or where it is reasonable to do so for security reasons provided that the conditions set out below are observed:

6.1   Save in an emergency prior written notice of at least two weeks is given to the Council.

6.2 Signs giving Notice of the intended closure and reasons for it and the date of the re-opening of the path are posted at each end of the path where it is to be closed.

6.3 Such signs are removed when the path is re-opened in accordance with the date given in the Notices referred to in clause 6.2 above.

6.4 The path is not closed for more than [*ten*] days in any year.

Covenants by the grantor

7. The Grantor covenants:

7.1 Not to dispose of the land or part of the land over which the permissive path runs without using his best endeavours to ensure that the new landowner or tenant enters into a similar agreement with the Council.

7.2 To keep the permissive path clear of growing crops and other obstructions and in a reasonably tidy state.

7.3 To reimburse the Council the costs of any work undertaken by the Council where the Grantor has failed to comply with clause 7.2 above, reasonable notice having been given to him to do so.

[7.4 Not to keep bulls more than ten months old or any animals known to be dangerous or unpredictable in any field through which the path runs].

7.5 Not to do or permit to be done anything whereby the Public Liability Insurance maintained by the Council in accordance with clause 8.15 may become void or voidable or whereby the insurer may refuse payment of any claim in whole or in part or whereby the rate of premium may be increased.

7.6 To notify the Council forthwith of any notice circumstances or events which may affect the said insurance policy or give rise to a claim thereunder.

7.7 To repay to the Council on demand all expenses incurred as a result of a breach of the covenants in clauses 7.5 and 7.6 above.

Covenants by the council

8. The Council hereby covenants:

8.1 Forthwith to execute the works described in the Schedule hereto and thereafter to maintain such works in good repair and condition.

8.2 On the termination of the Agreement or permanent closure of the permissive path to remove all signs and other works which have been executed by the Council.

8.3 To keep the surface of the permissive path free from all natural vegetation and to trim back vegetation growing from the sides or above the permissive path as may be required to keep the path in a suitable condition for the permitted purposes.

8.4 To keep the permissive path free from litter and rubbish.

8.5 To erect and maintain any gates stiles footbridges and other furniture relating to the permissive path in an appropriate condition.

8.6 Not to cut down or maim or injure any tree or sapling other than as provided for in clause 8.3 above without the previous consent in writing of the Grantor.

11 OTHER USES OF LAND

8.7   To put up and maintain coloured waymarks of the size and colour and in such a position as may be agreed in writing with the Grantor.

8.8   To erect Notices at either end of the Whole Path stating that the path is available for use by the public on a permissive basis only and stating the permitted purposes and any limitations on use which must be observed.

8.9   To erect Notices warning users of the permissive path of any dangers on or near the path.

8.10   To take all reasonable steps to ensure that dogs are kept on a lead where this is specified in the Particulars as a limitation on use.

8.11   Not to assign or part with possession or control of any of the rights hereby granted.

8.12   Not to do anything in connection with the rights hereby granted which may be or become a nuisance or annoyance or cause damage to the Grantor or to the Tenants or occupiers of the property or to the owners tenants or occupiers of any adjoining or neighbouring property.

8.13   To indemnify and keep indemnified the Grantor from and against all costs charges expenses claims and demands and damages of any description in any way arising or connected with any act or default on the part of the Council or their duly authorised officers servants agents or other persons authorised or impliedly authorised in relation to the rights hereby granted.

8.14   To ensure that the Council's Public Liability Policy covers the use by the public of the Permitted Path and to maintain such cover throughout the Term unless the policy shall be vitiated by any act of the Grantor or by anyone acting with the express or implied authority of the Grantor.

8.15   To pay all the proper costs and expenses incurred by the Grantor in connection with the preparation of this Agreement.

Disputes

9.   If there shall be a dispute between the parties concerning their rights and obligations under the terms of this Agreement the parties may refer the dispute for determination by an independent expert appointed in accordance with the sub-clauses set out below.

9.1   After such a dispute has arisen the parties may agree in writing to refer the dispute to an independent expert appointed by them both whose decision shall be final and binding upon them.

9.2   The procedure to be adopted by the independent expert shall be determined by him but shall provide an opportunity for the parties to state their case orally or in writing as the independent expert may direct.

9.3   The independent expert shall have the discretion to award the costs of the appointment failing which the costs shall be borne equally by the parties.

9.4   In the event of the parties failing to agree to refer the dispute to an independent expert or on the person to be appointed within one month of the dispute arising either party may apply to the President of the Royal Institution of Chartered Surveyors for the appointment of an expert to determine the dispute.

No deemed dedication

10.   For the avoidance of doubt it is hereby declared that nothing herein contained shall amount to or be construed as a permanent grant demise or dedication of or agreement for a public right of way.

AS WITNESS the hands of the parties hereto the day and year first before written.

SCHEDULE

WORKS WHICH THE COUNCIL HAVE AGREED TO UNDERTAKE

SIGNED by the GRANTOR in the
presence of: }   ....

....

....

....

SIGNED by the COUNCIL in the
presence of: }   ....

....

....

....

11   OTHER USES OF LAND

6   STATEMENT AND DECLARATION FOR PURPOSES OF SECTION 31(6) OF THE HIGHWAYS ACT 1980, AS AMENDED BY THE COUNTRYSIDE AND RIGHTS OF WAY ACT 2000

Deposit of Statement and Map
Section 31(6) of the Highways Act 1980

To [*name*] Council

1.   I am the owner within the meaning of the above section of the land known as [*name of farm, etc.*] more particularly delineated on the map accompanying this statement and thereon edged red.

*2.   The ways coloured brown on the said map have been dedicated as highways with vehicular status.

*3.   The ways coloured green on the said map have been dedicated as bridleways.

*4.   The ways coloured purple on the said map have been dedicated as footpaths.

*5.   No [other] ways over the land have been dedicated as highways and I have no intention of dedicating further highways.

* *Delete as applicable.*

Signed (landowner)   ....

Name (of landowner)   ....

Address   ....

                              ....

                              ....

Date   ....

Signed (witness)   ....

Name (of witness)   ....

Address   ....

                              ....

Occupation   ....

STATUTORY DECLARATION

SECTION 31(6) OF THE HIGHWAYS ACT 1980

I [*landowner*] DO SOLEMNLY AND SINCERELY DECLARE as follows:

1.   I am the owner of the land known as [*name of farm, etc*] more particularly delineated on the map accompanying this declaration and thereon edged red.

2.   On the [*date*] I [*or my predecessor in title (name)*] made a statement which was deposited with [*name*] Council, being the appropriate Council, a statement accompanied by a map delineating my property by red edging which stated that [the ways coloured brown on the said map and on the map accompanying this declaration had been dedicated as highways with vehicular status] [the ways coloured green on the said map and on the map accompanying this declaration had been dedicated as bridleways] [the ways coloured purple on the said map and on the map accompanying this declaration had been dedicated as footpaths] [no [other] ways had been dedicated as highways over my property].

★3.   On the [*date*] I [*or my predecessor in title (name)*] deposited with [*name*] Council, being the appropriate Council, a statutory declaration dated [*date*], stating that no additional ways [other than those marked in the appropriate colour on the map accompanying this declaration] had been dedicated as [highways with vehicular status] [bridleways] [footpaths] since the deposit of the Statement referred to in clause 2 above.

4.   No additional ways have been dedicated over the land edged red on the map accompanying this declaration since the statement dated [*date*] referred to in clause 2 above [since the date of the statutory declaration referred to in clause 3 above] [other than those (highways with vehicular status) (bridleways) (footpaths) marked in the appropriate colour on the map accompanying this declaration] and at the present time I have no intention of dedicating any more public rights of way over my property.

★ *Delete if not applicable*

AND I MAKE this solemn declaration on the [*date*] conscientiously believing it to be true and by virtue of the Statutory Declarations Act 1835.

Declared at [*address*] .... (signature of landowner) ....

....
Before me

....
[Commissioner for Oaths or a
Justice of the Peace or Solicitor]

7   AGREEMENT FOR DEPOSIT OF ARCHIVES WITH COUNTY RECORDS OFFICE

THIS AGREEMENT is made the [*date*]

BETWEEN

1.   THE BAILOR: [*owner of the Documents*]

2.   THE BAILEE: [*Record Office*]

WHEREAS IT IS AGREED as follows:

1.   THE Bailor agrees to deposit the documents ('the documents') listed in the Schedule on the terms and conditions set out in this Agreement.

2.   THE Bailor shall at all times retain title to the documents.

3.   THE Bailment shall continue until either the Bailor or the Bailee terminates this Agreement in accordance with clause 6.2 or 6.3 below.

4.   Obligations of bailee

4.1   THE Bailee agrees to provide the Bailor with a receipt and description of the documents received from the Bailor.

4.2   To provide the Bailor free of charge with copies of any lists of the documents made by the Bailee in accordance with its current practice.

4.3   To store the documents taking no less care than it does in the storage of its own documents and to take reasonable precautions againt damp, fire, vermin and illegal access.

4.4   To maintain its Public Liability Insurance Policy in respect of damage to its archive collections arising from the negligence of the Bailee or its employees and to ensure that the documents are covered by such a policy.

4.5   Not without the Bailor's written consent:

4.5.1   to allow the documents or extracts from them to be published;

4.5.2   to remove the documents from the Record Office for exhibitions, lecture or for any other purpose whatsoever;

4.5.3   to produce the documents for any official or legal purpose.

5.   Rights of bailee

5.1   THE Bailee may photograph or microfilm the documents or any of them for purposes of security or where the documents are to be returned under clause 6.1 and 6.2 below for record purposes and the copyright and ownership of such photographs or microfilms shall remain vested in the Bailee but subject to clauses 4.5.1 and 4.5.2 above.

5.2   The Bailee may mark the documents with a finding reference for safety and identification purposes.

5.3   With the consent of the Bailor the Bailee may undertake any necessary conservation work on the documents.

5.4   The Bailee shall be entitled to publish the lists referred to in clause 4.2 above and the copyright of such lists shall be vested absolutely in the Bailee.

5.5   The Bailee may make any documents more than thirty years old and with the consent of the Bailor documents of less than thirty years old available to the public for inspection free of charge under supervision during advertised opening hours and in accordance with search room regulations but not otherwise.

5.6   Subject to the requirements of the Copyright Acts 1911–1988 the Bailee may provide on request by a member of the public, photographic copies of the documents for the purposes of private study and research only, provided that the originals would not be damaged by such photocopying and any further reproduction of such photocopies is prohibited.

6.   Withdrawal and termination

6.1   ON the giving of prior written notice of at least five working days the Bailor may withdraw the documents for any reason for a period not exceeding three months or longer with the consent of the Bailee.

6.2   On the giving of prior written notice of at least one calendar month the Bailor may terminate the Agreement and withdraw the documents provided that if the Bailee has with the consent of the Bailor expended labour and materials on the documents while in the custody of the Bailee the Bailor shall repay to the Bailee a sum equivalent to the cost of the labour and materials so expended.

6.3   On the giving of prior written notice of at least one calendar month the Bailee may return the documents to the Bailor.

SIGNED by the parties hereto the day and year first before written.

SCHEDULE

SIGNED by BAILOR [*name*]   ....

SIGNED for and on behalf of
RECORDS OFFICE [*name*]   ....

---

8   DRAFT AGREEMENT TO FORM A COMMON LAND MANAGEMENT ASSOCIATION

THIS AGREEMENT IS MADE ON [*date*]

BETWEEN the persons whose respective names and addresses are set out in the first and second columns of the Schedule ('the Members').

WHEREBY it is agreed as follows:

1.   The members by signing this memorandum of agreement agree to form an Association ('the Association') to be known as the Common Land Management Association and to become its first members.

2.   The rules of the Association shall be in the form annexed to this agreement and initialled for identification by the members.

3.   The first Officers and members of the Committee shall be such of the members against whose respective names and addresses in the schedule appears in the third column the office or rank to which they are respectively appointed.

AS WITNESS the hands of the parties hereto the day and year first before written.

THE SCHEDULE

Name	Address	Office	Signature

9   DRAFT CONSTITUTION AND RULES OF A COMMON LAND MANAGEMENT ASSOCIATION

1.   **Name**
       The name of the Association is [*name*] ('the Association').

2.   **Objects**
2.1   It shall be the object of the Association to take such steps as appear to it to be necessary and practicable, for continuing the exercise of the commoners' and owners' rights; the maintenance of the common and the protection of proper livestock husbandry thereon; and in discharging the duty the Association shall promote the conservation and enhancement of the natural beauty of the common and access to it by persons for the purpose of open air recreation. Nothing in the duty shall imply that the rights of its members have been transferred to the Association.
2.2   In particular this Association shall have the following powers:
       (i)   to organise the co-operative efforts of its members in putting into effect an approved management scheme;
       (ii)   to regulate the turning out of animals on the common;
       (iii) to appoint and remunerate officials and agents to carry out the activities and responsibilities of the Association and to remove them when appropriate;
       (iv)   to raise revenue by means of licence fees and levies on owners and commoners in order to defray the administrative costs of the Association and the costs of activities otherwise consonant with the purposes of the Association; and
       (v)   to act so as to secure compliance with the byelaws regulating the conduct of the public on the common.

3.   Membership

3.1   Every person who is an owner, lessee of sporting and mineral rights for a term exceeding one year, or who has registered rights in the common and representatives of the county or district authorities shall be entitled to attend and vote at the initial meeting of the Association and become members. The names and addresses of the members must be lodged with the Secretary of the Association and shall be available for inspection by any member of the Association.

3.2   A member shall cease to be a member:

(i)   if he gives to the Clerk written notice of the resignation of his membership;

(ii)   if the member having committed some act or been guilty of some behaviour inconsistent with membership of the Association the Executive Committee resolves by a majority of three-quarters to remove him from membership;

(iii) if he ceases to have an interest as specified in clause 3.1 above.

4.   Officers and committees

4.1   The Association has a Chairman [see Rule 7.4] and a Clerk [see Rule 5.5].

4.2   The Association has two Committees, the Executive Committee [see Rule 5] and the Commoners' Committee [see Rule 6].

5.   Executive committee

5.1   The Executive Committee shall be composed of [X] members being the owners of the soil or the owners of minerals if held apart from the ownership [Y] members being commoners appointed by the Committee of Commoners and [Z] members being the nominees of local authorities.

5.2   The first Executive Committee shall be elected at the initial general meeting. Executive Committee members so elected will remain in office until the next Annual General Meeting.

5.3   Vacancies occurring during the year may be filled by the Committee, so as to ensure a continuation of the balanced representation. The Committee shall have power to co-opt members with special knowledge.

5.4   A person ceases to be a member of the Committee if:

(i)   he ceases to be a member of the Association; or

(ii)   he suffers from mental disorder and is admitted to hospital for treatment under the Mental Health Act 1983 or any subsequent mental health legislation, or a court having jurisdiction in matters concerning mental disorders orders his detention or the appointment of a receiver of his property or affairs or an enduring power of attorney by him is registered; or

(iii) he resigns his office by notice to the Association; or

(iv)   he fails to attend three consecutive meetings of the Executive Committee without giving a reason acceptable to it.

5.5   The Committee shall appoint a Clerk who will act as Clerk to the Association.

5.6   The Committee is responsible for managing the Association and subject only to a resolution of a general meeting is to perform all the duties and exercise all the powers of the Association for that purpose. In particular the Committee shall have the duty to see that proper books of account are kept and that annual accounts are prepared and audited by a qualified person. Such audited accounts shall be presented by the Committee to the Annual General Meeting. In addition the Committee shall have power to rule that any stint holder who does not pay a levy properly authorised at a general meeting shall lose his voting and grazing rights until such time as his share of the levy has been paid.

5.7   The Committee may delegate any of its powers to any one or more of its members or to any agent of the Association. The Committee has no power to delegate irrevocably.

5.8   The quorum at a Committee meeting is [. . .].

5.9   The Committee decides questions by a majority vote. In the case of an equality of votes the Chairman has a second casting vote.

5.10   The Clerk is to take minutes of all Committee meetings and record them in a minute book.

5.11   A resolution in writing, signed by all Committee members and recorded in the minute book, takes effect as if it had been passed at a meeting of the committee.

5.12   The Association must pay Committee members all reasonable expenses properly incurred in carrying out their duties.

6.   Committee of commoners

6.1   The Committee of Commoners shall be elected by and from those members having rights of common.

6.2   The Committee shall have as many members as is necessary to provide adequate representation of all commoners' rights, namely [*insert list of different rights*].

6.3   The first Commoners' Committee shall be elected at the initial general meeting. Commoners' Committee members so elected will remain in office to the next Annual General Meeting.

6.4   A person ceases to be a member of the Committee:
(i)   if he ceases to have rights of common; or
(ii)   if he suffers from mental disorder and is admitted to hospital for treatment under the Mental Health Act 1983 or any subsequent mental health legislation, or a court having jurisdiction in matters concerning mental disorders orders his detention or the appointment of a receiver of his property or affairs or an enduring power of attorney granted by him is registered; or
(iii)   he resigns his office by notice to the Association; or
(iv)   if he fails to attend three consecutive meetings of the Commoners' Committee without giving a reason acceptable to it.

6.5   The Committee shall appoint a Secretary to act as Secretary to the Commoners' Committee and a Chairman.

6.6 The Committee is responsible for regulating the turning out of animals on the common and the maintenance of proper standards of husbandry. If rights other than those of grazing of pasture are registered, the Committee of Commoners shall be responsible for seeing that they are exercised in a fair and equitable manner.

6.7 The quorum at a Committee Meeting is [...].

6.8 A Committee member is not entitled to appoint an alternative or proxy to act as a Committee member on his behalf.

6.9 The Committee decides questions by majority vote. In the case of equality of votes the Chairman has a second casting vote.

6.10 The Secretary is to take minutes of all Committee meetings and record them in a minute book.

6.11 The Committee of Commoners shall report to the Executive Committee. It shall choose [...] members to serve on the Executive Committee.

7. General meetings

7.1 All members are entitled to attend and vote at general meetings.

7.2 A general meeting is called by the Clerk (or if there is no Clerk by those requiring the meeting) giving at least twenty-one days' notice to all those entitled to attend. The notice must state the time and place of the meeting, the text of any resolution to be proposed and the general nature of the business to be transacted. It must also state that a member has a right to appoint a proxy who need not be a member, to attend and vote at the meeting on his behalf.

7.3 In cases of emergency a meeting may be called on less than twenty-one days' notice.

7.4 The initial general meeting will by resolution set the policy of the Association, elect the Chairman of the Association, Executive Committee and the Commoners' Committee. It will also by resolution determine how the revenue of the Association is to be raised and appoint auditors for the Association.

7.5 An Annual General Meeting is to be held every year after the first Annual General Meeting and within fifteen months of the previous one.

7.6 Notice of an Annual General Meeting must name it as such, and be accompanied by a copy of the audited accounts.

7.7 At the Annual General Meeting the accounts are to be approved and auditors appointed for the following year. The methods of raising revenue are to be reviewed and changed by resolution if necessary.

7.8 Other general meetings are to be called whenever required either by the Committee or by at least two members who are together entitled to at least 10% of the total votes.

8. Procedure at general meetings

8.1 No business is to be transacted at any meeting unless a quorum is present. [X] members, or their proxies, are a quorum.

8.2 If no quorum is present within [...] minutes of the time stated in the notice for the start of the meeting, it is to be abandoned.

11 OTHER USES OF LAND

8.3   A general meeting is chaired by:
        (i)   the Chairman if he is present;
        (ii) in his absence, a member of the Executive Committee selected by the
              members present;
        (iii) if there is none, a member selected by the members present.

8.4   No business may be transacted at any general meeting unless it was
        specified in the notice of the meeting or is of a trivial nature and the
        Chairman of the meeting agrees.

8.5   The Chairman of any meeting may, with the consent of the meeting,
        adjourn it from time to time and place to place. If any adjournment is for
        longer than fourteen days at least seven days' notice of the time and place at
        which it is to be resumed must be given to all those entitled to notice of the
        meeting.

8.6   The Clerk is to take minutes of all general meetings and record them in a
        minute book.

9.   Votes

9.1   Voting at a general meeting shall be by show of hands or a recorded vote if
        demanded by three or more members.

9.2   Where votes are taken on financial resolutions which would apply to all or
        some stint holders, voting shall be by value of interest if so demanded by
        any member.

9.3   In the case of equality of votes, the Chairman of the meeting has a second
        casting vote.

9.4   A member may appoint a proxy, who need not be a member, to attend a
        general meeting, to speak and vote on his behalf.

9.5   A proxy must be appointed in writing. The appointment may be in the
        following form, or in some other usual or similar form.

Common Land Management Association

I, [*name*] of [*address*], a member of the Association, hereby appoint [*name*] of
[*address*], or failing him, [*name*] of [*address*] as my proxy to vote in my name
and on my behalf at the general meeting of the Association to be held on
[*date*] and at any adjournment thereof.

[The proxy is to vote for/against resolution[s] number[s] ... in the notice
calling the meeting].

Signed ....

Dated ....

10.   Minutes

10.1   Minutes are to be taken at all general and Committee meetings of the
        Association.

10.2   The minutes are to be approved and signed by the Clerk or Secretary at the
        following general or Committee meeting.

10.3   A member is entitled to inspect the minutes of general meetings and of Committee meetings and the accounting records, correspondence and other documents belonging to the Association. Such documents shall be available for inspection at general meetings and on notice.

11.   Notice

11.   Notice given under these rules:
  (i)   to the Association, is to be sent by post or delivered to the Chairman at his address recorded in the minutes of the last general meeting;
  (ii)   to a member, is to be handed to him personally, sent by post or delivered to an address in the United Kingdom notified by the member of the Association;
  (iii) to any other person, is to be sent by post or delivered to the last address known to the Association.

12.   Indemnity

12.   The members of the Executive and Commoners' Committee shall not be liable for any loss suffered by the Association as a result of the discharge of their duties on its behalf except such loss as arises from their respective wilful default, and they shall be entitled to an indemnity out of the assets of the Association for all expenses and other liabilities incurred by them in the discharge of their respective duties.

11 OTHER USES OF LAND

INDEX

References are to page numbers.